NEW DIRECTIONS IN THE
WORLD ECONOMY

NEW DIRECTIONS IN THE WORLD ECONOMY

Bela Balassa

Professor of Political Economy
The Johns Hopkins University
and
Consultant, The World Bank

NEW YORK UNIVERSITY PRESS
Washington Square, New York

Manufactured in Hong Kong

First published in the U.S.A. in 1989 by
NEW YORK UNIVERSITY PRESS
Washington Square
New York, N.Y. 10003

Library of Congress Cataloging-in-Publication Data
Balassa. Bela A.
New directions in the world economy / Bela Balassa.
p.   cm.
Includes index.
ISBN 0–8147–1128–6
1. Developing countries—Economic policy.   2. Exports—Developing
countries.   3. Agriculture—Economic aspects—Developing countries.
4. Economic history—1971–   I. Title.
HC58.7.B2885   1989
338.9′009172′4—dc′9   89–30385
                                                           CIP

To Carol, Mara, and Gabor

Contents

PART VI ECONOMIC POLICIES IN FRANCE

List of Tables

Preface

Policy makers in developing countries face important challenges during the rest of the century and beyond. The choice of development strategies will largely determine the direction in which these economies will be moving in the future. In making this choice, the governments of the developing countries can learn from the experience of other countries in the developing world as well as from the experience of developed and socialist countries. The essays of this volume aim to assist in the making of policy choices.

The essays of Part I examine the effects of alternative development strategies in the developing countries. They are followed by the essays of Part II that raise the question if external constraints would limit choices among these strategies. The essays of Part III focus on a long-neglected sector, agriculture, which should play an important role in the growth process in most developing countries. In turn, the essays of Parts IV to VI analyze issues of privatization and the experience of Mexico; evaluate the reform efforts of two socialist countries, Hungary and China; and examine recent policy changes in a developed country, France. Finally, the essays of Part VII review issues relating to trade and trade negotiations between developed and developing countries.

The essays have been prepared as policy advisory reports for individual governments, presented at international conferences and seminars, or written for the World Bank. All the essays have been published, or are scheduled to be published, in professional journals and collective volumes. Permission for publication to all concerned is acknowledged in the Reader's Guide to the volume. Apart from the essays of Part VI and Essay 21, all the essays have been prepared in the framework of a consultant arrangement with the World Bank.

I am indebted to Shigeru Akiyama for excellent research assistance. Special thanks are due to Norma Campbell who performed the task of typing the manuscript, including its many revisions, with devotion and at a high level of professional competence.

I wish to express my appreciation to government officials, businessmen, and economists in the individual countries for helpful discussions. However, I am alone responsible for the opinions expressed in these essays that should not be interpreted to reflect the views of particular governments or the World Bank.

Washington, DC   BELA BALASSA

A Reader's Guide

The volume begins with a discussion of the importance of international trade for the developing countries. Essay 1 further examines the impact of trade orientation on economic performance in these countries, drawing on evidence in the periods preceding and following the quadrupling of oil prices. The existence of a positive relationship between exports and economic growth is also established in the essay.[1]

Essay 2 provides additional evidence on the impact of trade orientation on economic performance. The essay analyzes the external shocks developing countries suffered in the 1974–8 and 1979–83 periods and examines their policy responses to these shocks. It further indicates the superior performance of outward-oriented as compared to inward-oriented countries.[2]

Inward orientation introduces distortions in product markets. Such distortions will affect factor markets and vice versa. Essay 3 examines distortions in labor and capital markets in the developing countries and their interaction with distortions in product markets under alternative development strategies. Information is also provided on the adverse effects of factor market distortions on the efficiency of resource allocation and employment in the developing countries.[3]

The three essays of Part I on development strategies and their economic effects are followed by the essays of Part II that raise the question as to whether external constraints limit policy choices for the developing countries. The essays show that concerns with external constraints have been much exaggerated.

The adherents of the Cambridge Group have claimed that economic growth in the developed countries is unlikely to be sufficiently rapid to generate the desired rates of industrial expansion in the developing countries through exports. Essay 4 documents the unfavorable effects of the resulting policy prescriptions for industrialization behind high protection in Mexico and Tanzania. The essay also disproves some pessimistic views as to future export prospects for the developing countries.[4]

Essay 5 provides a critical appraisal of the tenets of the dependency school. According to this school, international trade leads to unequal exchange between developed and developing countries to the detriment of the latter. The essay shows that, rather than stunting their economic growth, international trade has contributed to favorable economic performance in the developing countries.[5]

Essay 6 provides a detailed examination of the view, according to which the widespread application of outward-oriented policies would encounter market constraints in the developed countries. The essay provides evidence on the predominance of domestic supply over foreign demand factors in the expansion of developing country exports. It also concludes that continued rapid growth of the manufactured exports of these countries would not cause serious adjustment problems in the developed countries while permitting the emergence of new exporters in the developing world.[6]

The essays of Part III deal with a long-neglected sector, agriculture, which should play an important role in the growth process in most developing countries. Essay 7 shows that exports in general, and agricultural exports in particular, strongly respond to price incentives. It further indicates that outward-oriented countries had a far better export performance in regard to agricultural exports, just as for merchandise exports, than inward-oriented countries.[7]

The methodology employed in Essay 7 is applied to sub-Saharan Africa in Essay 8. While the popular view has been that the exports of sub-Saharan African countries respond less to price incentives than those of countries at higher levels of development, the opposite conclusion is obtained. This conclusion applies to exports in general and to agricultural exports in particular, when the latter appear more responsive to price incentives than the former. Evidence is further provided that in sub-Saharan Africa market-oriented countries gained, and interventionist countries lost, export market shares that, in turn, affected their economic growth.[8]

Agriculture is considered in a world-wide context in Essay 9. The essay shows the desirability of lowering agricultural protection across-the-board. It recommends that this be done in the framework of the Uruguay Round of multilateral trade negotiations and suggests particular procedures for the negotiations on agriculture.[9]

Part IV begins with Essay 10 on the experiences of developing countries with privatization. It notes that while at one time developing countries considered public enterprise as the mainstay of economic development, there has been an increasing disillusionment with public enterprise in recent years and proposals have been made for privatization in various areas. However, for privatization to succeed, certain policy conditions need to be met, including a shift towards outward orientation and increased competition.[10]

These policies are of particular relevance to Mexico where privatization is an important issue. Essay 11 indicates that the policies applied in the period 1973–82 had unfavorable effects in Mexico and examines policy reforms that can reverse these unfavorable changes. Apart from privatization, these reforms relate to exchange rate policy, trade policy, and foreign direct investment.[11]

Essay 12 focuses on short-term economic issues in Mexico. It reviews the policy conditions of the July 1986 agreement on the rescheduling of the Mexican debt, with particular attention given to the tax system, public service prices, and current public expenditures. The essay further returns to the question of public enterprise and discusses the need for monetary reform in Mexico.[12]

Part V is devoted to the reform experiences of two socialist countries: Hungary and China. These experiences assume considerable interest in view of the Soviet reform efforts proposed under Gorbachev. But they also have an interest for developing countries, several of which have followed policies that resemble those applied in socialist countries.

Essay 13 notes that the exigencies of reducing Hungary's external debt and the requirements of the reform effort repeatedly came into conflict after 1978 and, more often than not, this conflict was resolved in favor of the former objective. This involved limiting the firms' freedom of action, both through binding regulations and through case-by-case interventions, with adverse effects on Hungary's economic performance.[13]

Essay 13 makes recommendations for renewing the Hungarian reform effort. Essay 14 extends these recommendations to improving the operation of labor and capital markets. The essay further suggests the need for reducing consumption and increasing investment, with the reallocation of investment from energy and heavy industry to light industry and engineering.[14]

Essay 15 reviews the economic reforms introduced in China after 1978 and analyzes the performance of agriculture and industry following the reforms. It further makes recommendations for extending the reform effort while establishing macroeconomic equilibrium in China. The essay places the Chinese reform in a comparative perspective, with particular attention given to the Hungarian experience that predates the reform in China by a decade.[15]

The French experience, described in the essays of Part VI, offers an interest to developed countries and developing countries alike. The developed countries may learn that expansionary policies in a single country cannot be sustained. The developing countries may learn about the adverse consequences of a socialist experiment in a market economy.

Essay 16 provides an evaluation of five years of socialist economic policy in France. It is shown that while the socialist government abandoned its excessively expansionary policies, the competitiveness of industry continued to deteriorate and productive investments in 1985 were below the 1980 level. Yet, new investments would have been necessary for structural change as French industry was losing export market shares.[16]

Essay 17 focuses on the industrial policies of the French socialist government. In accordance with its expansionary stance after May 1981, the government set high targets for the coal and steel industries that soon proved to be unrealistic. At the same time, providing for the increased financial needs of declining sectors limited the availability of funds for the expansion of high-technology activities. Nor did the nationalized firms become the vanguard of modern technology as had been assumed.[17]

The program of privatization adopted by the new majority in France not only reversed the nationalizations of 1981 but also a part of the nationalizations of 1945. Essay 18 explains that the new government further accelerated the process of price and foreign exchange liberalization and introduced greater flexibility in labor regulations. However, in the absence of a devaluation of sufficient magnitude, the competitiveness of French industry did not improve, resulting in continued losses in export market shares. The essay make recommendations for policy changes that would reverse these tendencies and contribute to the acceleration of economic growth in France.[18]

Part VII of the volume returns to the question of trade policies. Essay 19 provides evidence on the cost of protection in developed and in developing countries. It is shown that this cost burdened primarily the countries imposing the protective measures themselves and that, protection in the developed countries notwithstanding, developing country exports to these countries increased to a considerable extent.[19]

Essay 20 suggests that trade between developed and developing countries should be an important focus of the Uruguay Round of multilateral negotiations. The essay considers the scope, content, and modalities of negotiations between the two groups of countries, with special attention given to the need for reciprocity on the part of the newly-industrializing countries that have seen their exports rising at a rapid rate.[20]

Essay 21 considers a special case, that of Japan. The essay shows that Japan fell increasingly behind other developed countries in providing markets for developing country exports. This is explained by informal measures of import protection applied in Japan. The essay presents evidence of Japanese protection on imports from newly-industrializing countries, drawing on information provided by the governments of these countries.[21]

NOTES

1. This essay was presented as an invited paper at the Conference on the Role and Interests of the Developing Countries in Multilateral Trade Negotiations, held in Bangkok, Thailand in October–November, 1986, under the auspices of the World Bank and the Thailand Development Research Institute. It was published in *Banca Nazionale del Lavoro Quarterly Review*, XL (1987) pp. 437–70.
2. Essay 2 was presented as an invited paper at the December 1985 Meetings of the American Economic Association. It was published in the *American Economic Review, Papers and Proceedings*, LXXVI (1986) pp. 75–8.
3. Essay 3 was prepared as a Background Paper for the 1987 *World Development Report*. It was published in *World Development*, a publication of Pergamon Press Ltd, XVI (1988) pp. 449–63.

4. This essay was first published in *The World Economy*, the quarterly journal of the Trade Policy Research Centre, London, VIII (1985) pp. 201–18.
5. Essay 5 was published in *The World Economy*, IX (1986) pp. 259–74.
6. Essay 6 was prepared as a Background Paper for the 1988 *World Development Report*. It is scheduled for publication in *Banca Nazionale del Lavoro Quarterly Review*.
7. Essay 7 was presented as an invited paper at the Eighth Congress of the International Economic Association, held in New Delhi, India in December 1986. It will be published in the Proceedings of the Congress.
8. This essay was prepared as a Background Paper for the 1986 *World Development Report*. It is scheduled for publication in *World Development*.
9. This essay was presented as an invited paper at the Vth European Congress of Agricultural Economics held in Belatonszéplak, Hungary in August–September 1987. It was published in the *Journal of Policy Modeling*, a publication of Elsevier Science Publishing Co., X (1988) pp. 249–64.
10. Essay 10 was presented as the Böhm-Bawerk Memorial Lecture in Innsbruck, Austria in June 1987 and at the 43rd Congress of the International Institute of Public Finance, held in Paris in August 1987. It will be published in the Proceedings of the Congress. German translation in *Wirtschaftspolitische Blätter* 5 (1987) pp. 699–713.
11. This essay was presented as an invited paper at the Conference on Industrial Organization, Trade and Investment in North America held in Mérida, Mexico in December 1985. It will be published in the Proceedings of the Congress. Spanish translation in *Medio Siglo de Financiamento y Promoción del Comercio Extérior de Mexico. II Essayes Commemorativos* (Mexico, DF: Banco Nacional de Comercio Exterior – El Colegio de Mexico, 1987) pp. 185–204.
12. This essay was presented as an invited paper at the International Congress of the North American Economics and Finance Association, held in Montréal, Canada in July 1986. It was published in the Proceedings of the Congress, Rodrigue Tremblay (ed.), *Issues in North American Trade and Finance* (Montréal: North American Economics and Finance Association, 1986) pp. 11–30.
13. Essay 13 was presented as an invited paper at the 9th U.S.–Hungarian Roundtable held in Berkeley, California in June 1985. It was published in *Banca Nazionale del Lavoro Quarterly Review*, XXXXVIII (1985) pp. 347–72 and in the Proceedings of the Roundtable, J. C. Brada and J. Dobozi (eds), *The Hungarian Economy in the 1980s: Reforming the System and Adjusting to External Shocks* (Greenwich, Connecticut: JAI Press, 1988), pp. 3–32.
14. This essay was presented as an invited paper at the 10th U.S.–Hungarian Roundtable, held in Budapest, Hungary in December 1986. It will be published in the Proceedings of the Roundtable.
15. Essay 15 was presented at an invited paper at a Conference on Chinese Economic Reform held in Alden House, New York in September 1986. It was published in the Proceedings of the Conference in the *Journal of Comparative Economics*, XI (1987) pp. 410–26.
16. Essay 16 was published in *The Tocqueville Review*, VIII (1985/1986) pp. 269–84 and, in French translation, in *Commentaire*, IX (1986) pp. 62–71.
17. This essay was presented as an invited paper at the December 1984 Meetings of the American Economic Association. It was published in the *American Economic Review, Papers and Proceedings*, LXXV (1985) pp. 315–19 and, in French translation, in *Commentaire*, VIII (1985) pp. 579–88.

18. Essay 18 was published in *The Tocqueville Review*, IX (1986/1987) pp. 311–24 and, in French translation, in *Commentaire*, X (1987) pp. 377–415.
19. This essay, written jointly with Constantine Michalopoulos, was published in the *Journal of World Trade Law*, XX (1986) pp. 3–28.
20. Essay 20, written jointly with Constantine Michalopoulos, was published in Dominick Salvatore (ed.), *The New Protectionist Threat to World Welfare* (Amsterdam: North-Holland, 1987) pp. 482–504.
21. This essay was presented as an invited paper at the Second United States – Asia Conference, held in New York, NY in September–October 1985. It was published in the *Journal of International and Economic Integration* I (1986) pp. 1–19 and in the Proceedings of the Conference, M. Dutta (ed.), *Asia-Pacific Economics: Promises and Challenges* (Greenwich, Connecticut: JAI Press, 1987) pp. 49–68.

Part I
Development Strategies and International Trade in Developing Countries

Essay 1 The Importance of Trade for Developing Countries

INTRODUCTION

Participation in international trade provides a variety of benefits to the developing countries. They may obtain gains through resource allocation according to comparative advantage; the exploitation of economies of scale and increased capacity utilization; improvements in technology; increases in domestic savings and foreign direct investment; and increased employment.

At early stages of development, countries will generally benefit from specializing in natural resource products. In the process of industrialization, it will be advantageous to concentrate first on products utilizing mainly unskilled labor, with subsequent upgrading in the product composition of exports as the country accumulates physical and human capital. International specialization according to the changing pattern of comparative advantage will bring important gains to developing countries; conversely, limiting participation in the international division of labor through high import protection can entail considerable losses.

The domestic markets of even the largest developing countries are relatively small. In regard to manufactured goods, where economies of scale can be obtained, India's market is smaller than that of Belgium, a country extensively engaged in international trade, and Brazil's is only one-sixth of that of Germany, for which trade has been of considerable importance.

International trade makes it possible for developing countries to overcome the limitations of their domestic markets in exploiting economies of scale and ensuring full capacity utilization, thereby avoiding the dilemma of building ahead of demand and operating with a low degree of capacity utilization *or* constructing less than optimal size plants.

But, even in cases when a developing country's market can provide for the exploitation of economies of scale and full capacity utilization, it may not permit domestic competition, thus leading to the establishment of monopolies and oligopolies. It has often been observed that such firms prefer 'quiet life' to innovative activity, which entails risk and uncertainty. In turn, the carrot and the stick of competition provides inducements for

3

technological change. Exporting firms, in particular, try to keep up with modern technology in order to maintain or improve their market position.

In generating higher incomes, participation in international trade will also lead to higher domestic savings, which will increase further to the extent that a higher than average share of incomes generated by exports is saved. Also, as export expansion improves the balance of payments, a country may become more attractive to foreign investments.

As long as labor is not fully employed, increases in output resulting from participation in international trade will benefit employment, when additional gains are obtained to the extent that exports are more labor intensive than import substitution. Higher employment, in turn, will contribute to increases in wages that tend to improve the distribution of incomes.

Having briefly indicated the benefits developing countries may obtain through international trade, this essay will provide an empirical and policy analysis of the principal issues involved. It will review past trends in developing country exports; present evidence on exports and on economic growth in developing economies following alternative development strategies; evaluate the effects of trade orientation on economic performance; and indicate the implications of the findings for trade liberalization in the framework of multilateral negotiations.

Section I of the essay will provide information on trends in international trade in major product groups in the 1963–84 period; analyze the relationship between trade and economic growth during this period; and examine the export performance of groups of developing economies. Section II will report on the growth of exports and GDP in developing economies applying outward-oriented and inward-oriented policies, with separate consideration given to the pre-1973 and the post-1973 periods. In Section III, the relationship of exports and economic performance will be analyzed, using GDP growth, employment, and income distribution as performance indicators.

I CHANGES IN TRADE FLOWS DURING THE POSTWAR PERIOD

The expansion of trade in major commodity groups

Table 1.1 provides information on the geographical and commodity composition of the exports of developed and developing countries in the years 1963, 1973 and 1984, expressed in 1975 prices.[1] In the entire 1963–84 period, the total exports of the developed countries increased nearly fourfold whereas the developing countries experienced a less than two-and-a-half fold rise. Closer inspection reveals, however, that these differences are in large part explained by differences in the commodity composition of exports.

Rapidly growing manufactured exports accounted for only one-fifteenth of the total exports of the developing countries in the base year, 1963, while manufactured products had a nearly two-thirds share in the exports of the developed countries. From this low base, developing country manufactured exports rose fourteen-fold between 1963 and 1984, reaching four-tenths of their total exports; in the same period, the developed countries increased these exports four-and-a-half times, approaching three-fourths of the total.

The growth of the developing countries' manufactured exports and the increase in their share in the exports of these commodities by the developed and the developing countries combined from one-twentieth in 1963 to nearly one-seventh in 1984 was the most important change in trade flows during the postwar period. It shows the extent of transformation in the export structure of the developing countries and the availability of markets in the developed countries for their manufactured exports.

At the same time, the developing countries lost market shares in the exports of nonfuel primary products. Thus, the near doubling of these exports between 1963 and 1984 compares with a more than two-and-a-half fold increase for the developed countries. The results reflect the unfavorable commodity composition of developing country exports: they have had a much larger share in industrial materials, which experienced slow increases in world exports, than in foods and beverages, for which increases exceeded the average for nonfuel primary products.

Finally, whereas the fuel exports of the developing countries rose by less than one-third between 1963 and 1984, the developed countries increased these exports two-and-a-half times. Within this period, 1973 represents a turning point. While world fuel exports more than doubled between 1963 and 1973, they decreased by one-fourth between 1973 and 1984, due largely to the energy saving measures taken in response to the rapid increases in petroleum prices. The decline was even greater in the developing countries whose 1984 fuel exports did not reach three-fifths of the 1973 level, compared with an increase by one-half in the developed countries. Petroleum and gas discoveries in the United Kingdom, Norway, and the Netherlands and the substitution of coal for oil importantly contributed to these results.

Excluding fuels, differences in the growth of exports in developed and in developing countries are much reduced and, in the 1973–84 period, reversed. For the 1963–84 period, taken as a whole, nonfuel exports quadrupled in the developed countries and increased three-and-a-half times in the developing countries. But, while these exports rose two-and-a-half times in the developed countries and by only four-tenths in the developing

TABLE 1.1 *The geographical and commodity composition of exports, 1963, 1973 and 1984* ($ billion, 1975 prices)

Origin/Destination	Fuels			Nonfuel primary products			Manufactured goods			Nonfuel products			Total		
	DC	LDC	World	DC	LDC	World	DC	LDC	World	DC	LDC	World	DC	LDC	World
Absolute values															
1963															
Developed countries	16.5	2.1	19.6	52.5	10.2	66.2	99.7	36.1	144.5	152.2	46.3	210.7	168.7	48.4	230.3
Developing countries	44.7	16.0	62.7	30.1	6.1	39.6	4.1	3.0	7.4	34.2	9.1	47.1	79.0	25.1	109.3
Market economies	61.2	18.1	82.4	82.6	16.3	105.8	103.8	39.2	151.9	186.4	55.5	257.8	247.6	73.5	340.2
1973															
Developed countries	28.8	1.9	32.7	82.8	14.7	104.9	299.9	78.5	397.9	382.7	93.1	502.9	411.5	95.0	535.5
Developing countries	108.9	28.6	142.4	34.3	8.3	47.7	19.2	8.5	28.9	53.5	16.8	76.6	162.4	45.4	219.0
Market economies	137.8	30.4	175.1	117.0	23.0	152.6	319.2	86.9	426.8	436.2	109.9	579.4	574.0	140.4	754.5
1984															
Developed countries	44.6	3.7	50.5	126.2	37.7	178.2	476.3	154.0	661.8	602.5	191.7	840.0	647.1	195.4	890.5
Developing countries	55.2	23.0	80.0	44.7	18.6	73.5	66.5	31.1	103.8	111.2	49.7	177.3	166.4	72.8	258.0
Market economies	99.7	26.7	131.2	171.0	56.3	251.7	542.8	185.2	765.6	713.7	241.5	1017.3	813.5	268.2	1148.5

Percentage change

1963–73														
Developed countries	75	67	58	44	58	201	117	175	151	101	139	144	96	132
Developing countries	143	127	14	37	20	367	179	288	56	84	63	106	81	99
Market economies	125	113	42	41	44	208	122	181	134	98	125	132	91	122
1973–84														
Developed countries	55	54	53	157	70	59	96	66	57	106	67	57	106	66
Developing countries	−49	−43	31	123	54	245	268	259	108	196	131	2	60	18
Market economies	−28	−25	46	145	65	70	113	79	64	120	76	42	91	52
1963–84														
Developed countries	171	157.	140	270	169	378	326	358	296	314	299	284	303	287
Developing countries	23	29	48	205	86	1514	925	1294	225	445	277	111	190	135
Market economies	63	59	107	246	138	423	373	404	283	335	295	228	265	238

NOTES: The data have been expressed in constant prices by the use of deflators derived from price indices published in the United Nations, *Monthly Bulletin of Statistics* which is also the source of the current price trade data. For primary products, the price indices for individual commodities and commodity groups have been weighted by the commodity composition of exports for developing and for developed countries, respectively; for manufactured goods, use has been made of import price indices for the two groups of countries published in the above source.

The data pertain to the exports of fuels (SITC class 3); nonfuel primary products, including foods and beverages (SITC classes 0 and 1); industrial materials (SITC classes 2 and 4) and nonferrous metals (SITC category 68); manufactured goods (SITC categories 5 to 8 less nonferrous metals); nonfuel products (SITC classes 0 to 2 and 4 to 8), and total exports (SITC classes 0 to 8). They do not include SITC Class 9, commodities and transactions not classified according to kind, which rarely exceeds 2 percent of the total.

Under the UN classification scheme used in the table, developed countries are identified with the member countries of the OECD. Developing countries comprise the countries of Latin America, Africa (other than South Africa), and nonsocialist Asia (other than Israel and Japan); the rest of the world includes the socialist countries, Israel, and South Africa.

SOURCE: United Nations, *Monthly Bulletin of Statistics*, various issues.

countries between 1963 and 1973, a two-thirds increase in the former group of countries was accompanied by a two-and-a-half fold rise in the latter between 1973 and 1984.

As increases in primary nonfuel exports were somewhat larger in the developed than in the developing countries during the second period, even though considerably reduced compared to the first, the observed results reflect differential rates of export expansion in manufactured goods. The developing countries increased these exports three-and-a-half times between 1973 and 1984 while the developed countries experienced only a two-thirds rise.

With the bulk of the developing country exports of manufactured goods destined to developed country markets, access to these markets was the major factor in the observed result. In fact, the share of the developed countries as markets for the exports of the developing countries rose during the 1963–84 period, and it exceeded two-thirds by 1984. However, developing country exports of fuels and of nonfuel primary products increased more rapidly to developing country, than to developed country, markets. All in all, the total exports of the developing countries to other developing countries nearly tripled between 1963 and 1984 while their exports to the developed countries slightly more than doubled, indicating the growing importance of interdeveloping country trade.

The relationship between trade and economic growth

The acceleration in the growth of the developing countries' nonfuel exports after 1973 is even more remarkable if account is taken of the slowdown of economic growth in the developed countries, where an average rate of GDP growth of 4.7 percent between 1963 and 1973 gave place to a growth rate of 2.5 percent between 1973 and 1984. The nonfuel exports of developing countries to the developed countries grew at average annual rates of 5.3 and 8.3 percent in the two periods, respectively. The corresponding growth rates are 2.5 and 4.6 percent for nonfuel primary products[2] and 14.2 and 12.4 percent for manufactured goods (In the case of manufactured goods, the very low base year figure raised the growth rate in the first period.)

The relationship between economic growth in the developed countries and their imports from the developing countries has been analyzed by the use of regression analysis, with the addition of price variables.[3] The estimates are reported in Table 1.2 for the entire 1963–84 period; the shortness of the time series limited the statistical significance of the estimates for the two subperiods.

The results show that a 1 percent increase in the gross domestic product of the developed countries was associated with a 1.5 percent rise in their total imports from the developing countries in the 1963–84 period. The

TABLE 1.2 *The effects of developed country GDP and relative prices on their imports from developing countries, 1963–84*
(t-values in parentheses)

Exports	Constant	Gross domestic product	Relative prices	$\bar{R}^2$	D.W.
Total exports	5.35	1.47	−0.29	0.897	0.49
	(8.06)**	(9.88)**	(−3.52)**		
Nonfuel primary exports	8.42	0.48	−0.43	0.909	1.27
	(56.61)**	(14.02)**	(−6.80)**		
Foods and beverages	7.17	0.61	−0.53	0.834	0.96
	(26.83)**	(10.07)**	(−6.02)**		
Industrial materials	8.33	0.27	−0.29	0.626	1.60
	(39.73)**	(5.66)**	(−2.97)**		
Nonferrous metals	5.06	0.71	−0.17	0.767	1.23
	(10.01)**	(6.38)**	(−1.49)		
Fuels	2.84	1.88	−0.41	0.437	0.36
	(1.42)	(4.21)**	(−3.36)**		
Manufactured exports	−7.10	3.84	−0.63	0.984	0.54
	(−14.95)**	(35.40)**	(−0.98)		

NOTES: All variables have been expressed in logarithmic terms. Relative prices have been defined as the ratio of the export prices of the particular product groups in the developing countries to the export prices of manufactured goods in the developed countries (For explanation, see text.)

The symbol ** indicates that the results are statistically significant at the 1 percent level.

SOURCES: Export values and prices – United Nations, *Monthly Bulletin of Statistics* and *Yearbook of International Trade Statistics*, various issues.
Gross domestic product – International Monetary Fund, *International Financial Statistics*, 1985 yearbook.

corresponding estimates are 0.5 percent for nonfuel primary products, 1.9 percent for fuels, and 3.8 percent for manufactured goods. Disaggregating nonfuel primary exports, the results are 0.6 percent for foods and beverages, 0.3 percent for industrial materials, and 0.7 percent for nonferrous metals. All the estimates are statistically significant at the 1 percent level.

The empirical results further indicate the effects of changes in relative prices on the imports of the developed countries from the developing countries. This has been done by relating price indices for developing country exports of various product groups to the price index of the developed countries' manufactured exports.

The estimates reported in Table 1.2 show that a 1 percent increase in developing country export prices, relative to the manufactured export prices of the developed countries, leads to a 0.3 percent decline in these imports. The corresponding estimates are 0.4 percent for nonfuel primary products, 0.5 for foods and beverages, 0.3 for industrial materials, and 0.4

for fuels. They are all statistically significant at the 1 percent level; however, the relative price variables are not significant for the imports of nonferrous metals and manufactured goods.[4]

It is apparent, then, that economic growth in the developed countries is associated with more than proportionate increases in their imports from the developing countries, with manufactured goods being much above and nonfuel primary products below the average. For reasons noted below, the rise in their exports, in turn, contributes to economic growth in the latter group of countries.

The latter relationship has been estimated for the 1973–84 period, with the addition of a relative price variable. The results show that a 1 percent increase in the exports of the developing countries to the developed countries raises the former's GDP growth rate by 0.73 percentage points. A 1 percent improvement in the terms of trade of the developing countries, measured as the ratio of their export prices to the manufactured export prices of the developed countries, adds another 0.47 percentage points to their GDP growth rate.[5]

Export performance for groups of developing economies

Further interest attaches to the export performance of different groups of developing economies. For this purpose, distinction has been made among newly-industrializing economies (NICs), newly-exporting countries (NECs), and less developed countries (LDCs), with a further breakdown based on geographical location. Table 1.3 provides the list of countries in the first two groups and reports the results obtained for the years 1963, 1973, and 1980.[6]

In an earlier study by the author, newly-industrializing countries were defined as countries having a share of manufactured value added of 20 percent or higher in the gross domestic product in 1977 and per capita incomes of at least $1100 in 1978.[7] The same list of countries is obtained by applying the 20 percent benchmark to 1984 and using a per capita income figure of $1700 for the year.[8]

The newly-exporting countries have been defined by the joint requirement that the share of manufacturing value added in GDP was at least 15 percent or manufactured goods accounted for at least 30 percent of total exports in 1984 *and* manufactured export reached $250 million, i.e. 0.03 percent of world manufactured exports, and 0.2 percent of manufactured exports by the developing countries, in 1984.[9]

Limiting attention to nonfuel products, the results show that the market share of the Far Eastern NICs (Hong Kong, Korea, Singapore and Taiwan, China) in the combined exports of the developing countries rose from 9.1 percent in 1963 to 22.9 percent in 1973, and, again, to 32.3 percent in 1980. All other groups lost export market shares during this period. The losses were particularly pronounced in the South Asian NECs (Bangladesh, India, Pakistan, and Sri Lanka), the market share of which decreased from 10.7 percent in 1963 to 5.6 percent in 1980, followed by the North African and Middle Eastern NECs (Egypt, Jordan, Morocco, and Tunisia) where the decline was from 4.5 to 2.4 percent.

Among major product groups, changes in export market shares were the largest for manufactured goods. Although the Far Eastern NICs had a relatively high export share of 32.2 percent in these products already in 1963, they increased this share to 55.8 percent by 1980. In the same period, the market share of the South Asian NECs fell from 23.0 to 6.4 percent, with a decline from 3.6 to 1.9 percent observed in the North Africa–Middle East group.

In turn, the Latin American NICs (Argentina, Brazil, Chile, Mexico, and Uruguay) and, in particular, the Far Eastern NECs (Indonesia, Malaysia, Philippines, and Thailand) were gainers, with increases in manu- factured export market shares from 8.6 percent in 1963 to 12.0 percent in 1980 in the first case and from 2.8 to 5.8 percent in the second. But while in the Latin American NICs the 1980 result represented a deterioration following the progress made between 1963 and 1973, the growth of the exports of the Far Eastern NECs accelerated after 1973. Finally, increases between 1963 and 1973 were undone afterwards in the Latin American NECs (Colombia, Costa Rica, Guatemala, Peru, and Venezuela).

The Far Eastern NICs also made the largest gains in nonfuel primary products, with their export market share rising from 4.8 percent in 1963 to 7.8 percent in 1984. The South Asian NECs again experienced the largest losses in market shares, from 8.5 to 4.8 percent, followed by the North African and Middle Eastern NECs, where the decline was from 4.6 to 2.9 percent. Smaller changes occurred in the other country groups.

These developments are closely linked to the policies applied by the various countries. The Far Eastern NICs began a policy of outward orien- tation[10] in the early 1960s and continued with this policy afterwards. The South Asian NICs, however, persisted with highly protectionist inward- oriented policies. In the North Africa–Middle East area, the unfavorable results were dominated by Egypt that failed to productively utilize the bonanza provided by increased oil earnings, toll receipts from the Suez Canal, and workers' remittances from the Middle East.

During the period under consideration, the increased outward orienta- tion of the Far Eastern NICs accounts for the acceleration of the growth of their manufactured exports while changes in the policies applied explain the reversal in manufactured export market shares in Latin America. These countries reformed their economic policies after the mid-1960s, involving a (partial) shift from inward to outward orientation but again turned inward after 1973, with Brazil providing a partial exception.

The preceding discussion concerned six developing country groups,

TABLE 1.3 *Exports by groups of developing economies, 1963, 1973, and 1980*
($ billion, 1975 prices, percent)

	Fuels		Nonfuel primary products		Manufactured goods		Nonfuel products		Total	
	$bn	%	$bn	%	$bn	%	$bn	%	$bn	%
1963										
(1) NIC Latin America	0.39	0.6	8.63	21.8	0.64	8.6	9.27	19.7	9.66	8.8
(2) Far East	1.30	2.1	1.91	4.8	2.38	32.2	4.29	9.1	5.59	5.1
(3) NEC Latin America	16.72	26.7	3.11	7.9	0.21	2.8	3.33	7.1	20.04	18.3
(4) North Africa–Middle East	0.33	0.5	1.83	4.6	0.27	3.6	2.10	4.5	2.43	2.2
(5) South Asia	0.11	0.2	3.35	8.5	1.70	23.0	5.05	10.7	5.16	4.7
(6) Far East	2.08	3.3	5.19	13.1	0.21	2.8	5.40	11.5	5.48	5.0
(7) Less developed countries	41.77	66.6	15.58	39.3	1.99	26.9	17.57	37.4	61.44	55.9
	62.70	100.0	99.60	100.0	7.40	100.0	47.00	100.0	109.80	100.0
1973										
(1) NIC Latin America	0.39	0.3	11.66	24.4	3.96	13.7	15.62	20.4	16.01	7.3
(2) Far East	2.53	1.8	2.90	6.0	14.61	50.5	17.51	22.9	20.04	9.2
(3) NEC Latin America	14.91	10.5	3.21	6.7	0.98	3.4	4.19	5.4	21.10	9.6

(4) North Africa–Middle East	0.80	0.6	1.92	4.0	0.64	2.2	2.56	3.3	3.36	1.5
(5) South Asia	0.19	0.1	2.40	5.0	2.76	9.5	5.16	6.7	5.35	2.4
(6) Far East	5.97	4.2	7.47	15.7	1.10	3.9	8.57	11.2	14.54	6.6
(7) Less developed countries	117.61	82.6	18.14	38.0	4.85	16.8	22.99	30.0	138.60	63.3
	142.40	100.0	47.70	100.0	28.90	100.0	76.60	100.0	219.00	100.0

1980

(1) NIC Latin America	3.75	3.2	14.62	23.7	7.70	12.0	22.32	17.7	26.07	10.7
(2) Far East	1.78	1.5	4.85	7.8	35.44	55.8	40.59	32.3	42.37	17.3
(3) NEC Latin America	6.46	5.4	4.58	7.4	1.88	2.9	6.46	5.1	12.92	5.3
(4) North Africa–Middle East	1.11	0.9	1.77	2.9	1.19	1.9	2.96	2.4	4.07	1.7
(5) South Asia	0.13	0.1	2.98	4.8	4.11	6.4	7.09	5.6	7.22	3.0
(6) Far East	6.47	5.4	5.41	8.8	3.72	5.8	9.13	7.3	15.60	6.4
(7) Less developed countries	98.90	83.4	27.59	44.6	9.68	15.1	37.25	29.6	136.15	55.7
	118.60	100.0	61.80	100.0	64.00	100.0	125.80	100.0	244.40	100.0

NOTE: (1) Argentina, Brazil, Chile, Mexico, Uruguay; (2) Hong Kong, Korea, Singapore, Taiwan China; (3) Colombia, Costa Rica, Guatemala, Jamaica, Peru, Venezuela; (4) Egypt, Jordan, Morocco, Tunisia; (5) Bangladesh, India, Pakistan, Sri Lanka; (6) Indonesia, Malaysia, Philippines, Thailand.
(7) The difference between the total exports of the developing countries shown in Table 1, and the sum of exports of country groupings (1) to (6).

SOURCES: Table 1.1 and World Bank data-base.

defined according to their level of economic development and geographical location. While the remaining group of less developed countries is too heterogeneous to derive any firm conclusions, it may be observed that increases in their market shares in nonfuel primary products were more than offset by declines in manufactured export shares.

The next section will consider individual country experiences with economic policies and the effects of these policies on exports and economic growth during the postwar period. As an introduction to the discussion, the concepts of outward and inward orientation will be defined.

II TRADE ORIENTATION AND ECONOMIC GROWTH

Defining inward and outward orientation

In examining the postwar experience of developing economies with alternative policies, distinction may be made between inward-oriented and outward-oriented development strategies. Inward-oriented developing countries have protected their domestic industries by the use of tariffs and quantitative import restrictions without providing commensurate export subsidies. The application of these measures has biased the system of incentives in favor of import substitution and against exports. By contrast, under outward orientation, similar incentives have been granted to import substitution and exports, with export subsidies offsetting, on the average, the effects of import protection.

Outward-oriented developing countries have also maintained realistic exchange rates, and avoided variations in real exchange rates (nominal exchange rates, adjusted for changes in relative prices at home and abroad) over time, so as to encourage exports. Conversely, exchange rates have often been overvalued in developing countries pursuing inward oriented policies, with the degree of overvaluation varying over time, as intermittent devaluations periodically caught up with domestic inflation, thereby creating uncertainty for exporters.

In addition to fluctuations in the extent of overvaluation leading to changes in incentives over time, there has been considerable variation in incentives among manufacturing industries in inward-oriented developing countries that has not generally been the case under outward orientation. Also, inward-oriented, but not outward-oriented, developing countries have generally discriminated against agriculture.

The described characteristics of outward-oriented and inward-oriented development strategies are exemplified by the experience of the last quarter of a century. In the 1960–73 period of rapid growth in the world economy, a contrast may be drawn among three groups of developing countries: those pursuing outward-oriented policies, inward-oriented developing countries undertaking policy reforms, and developing countries characterized by continued inward orientation. The choice between outward and inward orientation has further relevance in the period of external shocks, owing to increases in oil prices and recessionary conditions in the world economy after 1973. The following discussion concentrates on nine developing economies that established basic industries and may be considered representative of alternative policy regimes.

The period of rapid world economic growth (1960–73)[11]

Among the nine developing countries under consideration, Korea, Singapore and Taiwan adopted outward-oriented policies in the early 1960s. In turn, India, Chile, and Uruguay continued with inward-oriented policies throughout the 1960–73 period. An intermediate position was taken by Brazil, and to a lesser extent, by Argentina and Mexico, which had followed inward-oriented policies but undertook policy reforms in the mid-1960s, reducing the extent of discrimination against agriculture and, in particular, against manufactured exports.

At the same time, there were several important differences between the policies applied by the three Far Eastern and the three Latin American developing countries. These differences largely reflected the fact that the latter group of countries endeavored to maintain the high-cost industries, which had earlier been established, following the policy reforms.

In the three Far Eastern developing countries, exporters were free to choose between domestic and imported inputs; they were exempted from indirect taxes on their output and inputs; and they paid no duty on imported inputs. The same privileges were extended to the producers of domestic inputs used in export production, thus providing essentially free trade treatment to the export sectors. With additional subsidies and low import protection, exports in the manufacturing sector received, on the average, similar incentives as import substitution in these countries. At the same time, there was little discrimination against primary exports, and against primary activities in general, and the system of incentives was quite uniform.

In reforming their system of incentives, the three large Latin American developing countries reduced the extent of import protection. They did not provide, however, exporters with a free choice between domestic and imported inputs. Rather, in order to safeguard existing industries, exporters were required to use domestic inputs produced under protection. To compensate exporters for the resulting excess cost, the three Latin American countries granted export subsidies, but these did not suffice to provide producers with export incentives comparable to the protection of domestic markets. Thus, there continued to be a bias in favor of import substitution and against exports, in particular traditional primary exports, albeit to a lesser extent than had been previously the case.

Among developing countries that continued with a policy of inward-orientation, Chile traditionally had the highest level of import protection in Latin America and, after brief experimentation with import liberalization, reimposed quantitative restrictions in the early 1970s. Protection levels also remained high in Uruguay and little effort was made to promote exports. Finally, the introduction of selected export subsidies in the mid-sixties was far overshadowed by the continued use of import prohibitions and investment controls in India.

The system of incentives applied importantly affected export performance in the three groups of developing countries. The share of exports in manufactured output rose from 1 percent in 1960 to 14 percent in 1966 and to 41 percent in 1973 in Korea, from 11 percent to 20 percent and to 43 percent in Singapore, and from 9 percent to 19 percent and to 50 percent in Taiwan.

After slow increases in the 1960–66 period, the growth of manufactured exports accelerated between 1966 and 1973 in the three Latin American economies that reformed their system of incentives during this period. In particular, the share of exports in manufactured output rose from 1 percent in 1966 to 4 percent in 1973 in both Argentina and Brazil, with smaller increases occurring from a higher initial level – explained by its common border with the United States – in Mexico.

Chile, Uruguay, and India, which continued with an inward-oriented development strategy, experienced a decline in the share of exports in manufacturing output. India lost ground in textiles, its traditional exports, and was slow in developing new manufactured exports. As a result, its share in the combined exports of manufactured goods of the nine countries under consideration declined from 57 percent in 1963 to 13 percent in 1973. In the same period, Chile's share fell from 2 percent to below one-half of 1 percent, while Uruguay's share declined to the same level from 1 percent in 1963.

In turn, the three Far Eastern developing countries increased their combined market share in the manufactured exports of the nine developing countries under consideration, from 17 to 60 percent, and the combined share of the three Latin American countries rose slightly, from 23 to 24 percent between 1963 and 1973. The Far Eastern developing countries also gained market shares in nonfuel primary exports; gains in Brazil were approximately offset by losses in Argentina and Mexico; and India, Chile, and Uruguay all experienced losses in nonfuel primary exports (Table 1.4).[12]

The experience of the nine developing countries further provides evidence of the favorable effects of outward orientation of economic growth during the period preceding the 1973 oil crisis. The three Far Eastern countries had by far the highest GNP growth rates throughout the period;

the three Latin American developing countries that undertook policy reforms improved their growth performance to a considerable extent after the reforms were instituted; and Chile, Uruguay, and India remained at the bottom on the growth league. For the 1960–73 period, taken as a whole, per capita incomes rose at rates ranging between 6 and 8 percent in the first group, between 3 and 4 percent in the second, and between 1 and 2 percent in the third.

The period of external shocks (1973–85)[13]

Developing countries experienced substantial external shocks between 1973 and 1983. In the first half of the period, the quadrupling of oil prices was accompanied by a world recession and followed by a slow recovery; in the second half, oil prices increased three times, the developed countries again experienced a recession, and interest rates increased considerably. At the same time, policy responses to these shocks in the individual countries varied greatly.

The three Far Eastern developing countries continued with their outward-oriented development strategy and were joined by Chile and Uruguay which, however, again introduced price distortions after mid-1979 when their exchange rates became seriously overvalued. In turn, after earlier efforts made to reduce the bias of the incentive system against exports, Argentina and Mexico, and to a lesser extent Brazil, increased the degree of inward orientation while India continued with its inward-oriented stance.

Outward-oriented developing countries maintained realistic exchange rates, with little variation over time whereas exchange rates were generally overvalued in inward-oriented countries, with the degree of overvaluation varying during the period. This explains that outward-oriented countries continued to gain export market shares in nonfuel exports while inward-oriented countries experienced losses in foreign markets (As shown in Table 1.4, in the case of Brazil losses in nonfuel primary exports offset gains in manufactured goods.)

We also find that more import substitution occurred in outward-oriented, than in inward-oriented, developing countries during the 1973–83 period. Various considerations may explain this, prima facie surprising, result. To begin with, the former but not the latter group of developing economies maintained realistic exchange rates that contribute to export expansion as well as to import substitution. Also, the exploitation of economies of scale in the export industries of outward-oriented developing countries permits replacing imports by domestic production in these industries while import replacement becomes increasingly costly, and net import savings decline, under continued inward orientation. Finally, virtual lack of discrimination in the system of incentives against agriculture in outward-

Strategies and Trade in Developing Countries

TABLE 1.4 *Exports by selected developing economies*
(\$ million, 1975 prices)

	Fuels	(%)	Nonfuel primary products	(%)	Manufactured goods	(%)	Nonfuel products	(%)	Total	(%)
1963										
Korea	17	1.0	97	0.9	84	3.3	181	1.4	198	1.3
Singapore	1 207	69.2	78	0.7	73	2.9	151	1.1	1 358	9.1
Taiwan	21	1.2	584	5.5	272	10.8	856	6.5	877	5.9
Argentina	74	4.2	2 641	24.9	169	6.7	2 810	21.4	2 884	19.4
Brazil	62	3.6	2 941	27.7	90	3.6	3 031	23.1	3 094	20.8
Mexico	256	14.7	1 461	13.7	316	12.6	1 777	13.5	2 033	13.7
India	107	6.1	1 562	14.7	1 445	57.5	3 007	22.9	3 114	20.9
Chile	0	0.0	998	9.4	45	1.8	1 044	8.0	1 044	7.0
Uruguay	1	0.1	264	2.5	17	0.7	275	2.1	277	1.9
Total	1 745	100.0	10 626	100.0	2 511	100.0	13 132	100.0	14 879	100.0
1973										
Korea	117	4.0	541	3.8	3 180	22.4	3 721	13.2	3 838	12.3
Singapore	2 269	76.9	121	0.9	1 176	8.3	1 297	4.6	3 567	11.4
Taiwan	46	1.6	899	6.4	4 321	30.4	5 220	18.4	5 266	16.9
Argentina	19	0.6	2 587	18.4	860	6.0	3 447	12.2	3 465	11.1
Brazil	276	9.3	5 499	39.1	1 433	10.1	6 932	24.5	7 208	23.1
Mexico	82	2.8	1 653	11.7	1 299	9.1	2 952	10.4	3 035	9.7
India	131	4.4	1 586	11.3	1 838	12.9	3 424	12.1	3 555	11.4
Chile	9	0.3	970	6.9	54	0.4	1 025	3.6	1 033	3.3
Uruguay	3	0.1	217	1.5	61	0.4	278	1.0	281	0.9
Total	2 952	100.0	14 073	100.0	14 222	100.0	28 296	100.0	31 248	100.0
1980										
Korea	11	0.2	1 036	5.3	9 844	28.8	10 879	20.3	10 891	18.4
Singapore	1 596	29.2	338	1.7	3 045	8.9	3 383	6.3	4 979	8.4
Taiwan	97	1.8	1 280	6.5	10 982	32.2	12 262	22.8	12 359	20.9
Argentina	95	1.7	3 722	19.0	1 170	3.4	4 892	9.1	4 987	8.4
Brazil	122	2.2	6 691	34.2	4 721	13.8	11 412	21.2	11 534	19.5
Mexico	3 510	64.3	1 865	9.5	1 084	3.2	2 949	5.5	6 459	10.9
India	11	0.2	1 845	9.4	2 775	8.1	4 621	8.6	4 632	7.8
Chile	20	0.4	2 389	12.2	263	0.8	2 652	4.9	2 672	4.5
Uruguay	0	0.0	404	2.1	253	0.7	657	1.2	657	1.1
Total	5 462	100.0	19 570	100.0	34 137	100.0	53 707	100.0	59 170	100.0

SOURCE: See Table 1.1.

oriented countries allows import substitution to occur in this sector that is not the case under inward orientation.

Outward-oriented developing countries thus undertook domestic adjustment through output-increasing policies of export expansion and efficient import substitution that was not the case under inward orientation. At the same time, the former group generally eschewed highly capital-intensive projects that were undertaken by the public sector and by the greatly protected private sector in inward-oriented developing countries.

While, owing to their greater exposure to foreign markets, external shocks were considerably larger in outward-oriented than in inward-oriented developing countries, these differences were offset several times by differences in economic growth rates. Notwithstanding the external shocks they suffered, average per capita GDP growth rates remained at 5 percent a year between 1963–73 and 1973–79 in outward-oriented developing countries while declining from 5 to 3 percent in inward-oriented economies (Apart from the developing economies referred to above, the latter group includes Israel, Portugal, Turkey, and Yugoslavia.)

These results obtained despite the fact that inward-oriented developing countries borrowed heavily abroad, since the borrowed funds were generally not utilized efficiently. In particular, slow increases in exports led to a substantial rise in the debt–export ratios of inward-oriented countries while this ratio remained approximately unchanged in outward-oriented countries.

Correspondingly, increases in world interest rates bore greatly on inward-oriented developing countries, necessitating the application of deflationary policies that led to stagnation in their per capita incomes in the 1979–82 period. And while outward-oriented developing countries also applied deflationary measures on a temporary basis, with their per capita GDP growth rates declining to 2 percent in 1979–82, they rebounded again in subsequent years. Between 1982 and 1985, per capita GDP growth rates averaged 4 percent in outward-oriented countries as compared to a slight decrease in inward-oriented countries that had to pay the price for their excessive indebtedness.

The overall conclusions reached in regard to the two groups of developing countries neglect the variety found within each. Among Latin American countries, particular interest attaches to Chile, where two important policy shifts were undertaken within a short period. Note may further be taken of the experience of Turkey where the adjustment policies applied permitted moving from virtual bankruptcy to creditworthiness for commercial bank lending within a few years.

The September 1973 military takeover found Chile with a 500 percent rate of inflation and economic stagnation in a highly regimented economy. The situation was further aggravated as the quadrupling of oil prices was accompanied by a substantial fall in the price of copper. The Pinochet government applied strong deflationary measures to cope with the situation, which led to a large decline in national income. It subsequently undertook a far-reaching policy reform, representing a shift from inward to outward orientation.[14]

Following the turn towards outward orientation, Chile reached one of the highest per capita GNP growth rates, 7 percent, among developing economies in the 1976–9 period, although this result represented in part a reversal after the earlier decline. Rapid economic growth was supported by export expansion as the policies applied led to considerable increases in nontraditional exports.

A policy change occurred in mid-1979, however, when Chile fixed its exchange rate in terms of the US dollar, supposedly forever, and simultaneously reinforced the indexation of wages. Between June 1979 and October 1981, average wages doubled as a result while the exchange rate remained unchanged, compromising the competitive position of Chilean export and import-substituting activities in agriculture as well as in manufacturing. At the same time, under the virtual exchange rate guarantee, a large inflow of foreign capital ensued as domestic inflation rates exceeded foreign interest rates by a considerable margin, and the resulting negative real interest rates provided inducements for borrowing abroad. Since the production of goods entering into international trade became increasingly unprofitable, the borrowed funds were used to increase consumption and to invest in luxury housing and the stock market.

The resulting artificial boom came to an end in early 1982 as it became apparent that Chile could no longer continue financing its growing balance-of-payments deficit. Several devaluations were undertaken in succession, but the large burden of the foreign debt and the greatly weakened condition of domestic financial institutions will make it difficult for Chile to return to the growth path of the years 1976–79 for some time to come.

The moral of the story is summarized in a recent article on 'Policy Experiments in Chile, 1973–83' by the author. The article concludes that 'liberalization in Chile was perverted by increasing price distortions after 1979,' adding that 'it will be inappropriate, however, to declare the experience of the entire decade a failure, when it is a policy reversal that led to the predicament in which Chile now finds itself.'[15]

Turkey was practically bankrupt in 1979 and, with increasing foreign exchange stringency, it experienced considerable shortages of energy, raw materials, and spare parts. Industrial output declined and inflation accelerated as a result. This was the consequence of excessive borrowing and the use of borrowed funds in inefficient projects in the public sector as well as in the highly-protected private sector.

The January 1980 policy reforms aimed at redressing the situation and changing the inward-oriented development strategy Turkey had followed in the previous decades.[16] While the reform measures had to be carried out in a deflationary environment, exports rose rapidly, leading to the resumption of economic growth.[17] Rapid export expansion, in turn, provided a boost to economic growth in Turkey, with per capita GNP rising at an average annual rate of 2 percent between 1980 and 1985. In addition, inflation rates declined from 140 to 40 percent, although further decreases are desirable.

Turkey provides an example of successful adjustment through export expansion. Apart from the resumption of economic growth, Turkey again became creditworthy for borrowing from commercial banks. This is the more remarkable since Turkey was one of the most inward-oriented countries in the developing world, with an export-GNP share of only 3 percent in 1979. The turn towards outward orientation meant that this share reached 15 percent in 1985.

III EXPORT EXPANSION AND ECONOMIC PERFORMANCE

Exports and economic growth

The experiences of developing countries discussed in the previous section of the essay indicate the favorable effects of exports on economic growth. This conclusion has been confirmed by a statistical analysis of the results obtained for these countries. The estimates, made in an intercountry framework, show a high correlation between the growth of exports and that of production in agriculture, in manufacturing, as well as in the national economy taken as a whole.[18] In the latter case, it has also been shown that the growth of exports is highly correlated with the growth of GNP less exports, indicating the indirect effects of exports on the rest of the economy.[19]

Estimates made by Anne Krueger[20] for a partially overlapping group of developing economies[21] confirm these results. She has found that, in the 1954–71 period, Brazil's 25 percent rate of growth of exports increased its GNP growth rate by 2.75 percentage points while Korea's 40 percent rate of growth of exports raised its GNP growth rate by 4.4 percentage points. In turn, for a group of 31 semi-industrial economies Feder (1983) has estimated that shifting resources from nonexport to export industries was responsible for a 1.8 percentage point difference in GNP growth rates in the 1964–73 period.[22]

Explaining GNP growth in terms of export growth omits the effects of other economic variables. Michalopoulos and Jay have endeavored to remedy this deficiency by introducing data on labor and capital, in addition to exports, to explain intercountry differences in GNP growth rates. Using data for 39 developing economies, these authors have found that intercountry differences in the growth of labor and in domestic and foreign investment explain 53 percent of intercountry variations in GNP growth rate, while adding export growth increases this ratio to 71 percent.[23] Similar results have been reached by applying this procedure to the combined 1960–66 and 1966–73 data for the developing economies referred to above.[24]

The cited estimates refer to the period of rapid growth in the world economy. Further interest attaches to the question as to how these results hold up in the subsequent period of external shocks. Applying the same procedure to the 1973–8 period, the earlier findings on the importance of exports for economic growth have again been reconfirmed.[25]

Data available for 43 developing economies have further permitted analyzing the implications for economic growth of trade orientation at the beginning of the period of external shocks and of policy responses to external shocks in the 1973–8 period. The extent of trade orientation in the initial year has been defined in terms of deviations of actual from hypothetical per capita exports, the latter having been estimated by reference to per capita incomes, population, and the ratio of mineral exports to GNP. In turn, alternative policy responses have been defined as export promotion, import substitution, and additional net external financing.[26]

The impact of trade orientation on economic growth is indicated by the existence of a difference of 1 percentage point in GNP growth rates between developing countries in the upper quartile and the lower quartile of the distribution in terms of trade orientation, corresponding to the median among outward-oriented and inward-oriented countries, respectively. Furthermore, a difference of 1.2 percentage points in GNP growth is obtained in comparing the upper and the lower quartiles of the distribution as regards reliance on export promotion, as against import substitution and additional external financing.

The results are cumulative, indicating that both initial export orientation and reliance on exports in response to external shocks importantly contributed to economic growth in developing economies during the period under consideration. These factors explain a large proportion of intercountry differences in GNP growth rates in the 1973–8 period, with a difference of 3.2 percentage points between the upper quartile and the lower quartile of the distribution in the 43 developing economies.

Factors affecting economic growth

The results show that export expansion favorably affects economic growth in developing economies. As noted in the introduction to this Essay this may be explained by reference to gains from resource allocation according to comparative advantage; the exploitation of economies of scale and increased capacity utilization; improvements in technology; and increases in domestic savings and foreign direct investment under an outward-oriented development strategy. There may be further gains through increased employment if labor is not fully employed.

The obverse of gains from specialization is *the cost of protection* incurred under inward orientation. For the first half of the 1960s, this cost, including monopoly profits, has been estimated at 9.5 percent of GNP in Brazil, 6.2 percent in Chile, 6.2 percent in Pakistan, and 3.7 percent for the Philippines; the estimated cost was 2.5 percent of GNP for Mexico, which had relatively low levels of protection in 1960, the year of the estimate.[27] Furthermore, Krueger has concluded that the reallocation of resources from import-substitution to export industries under free trade would lead to a doubling of the world market value of manufacturing production in Turkey; with manufacturing industries accounting for one-seventh of GNP, this is equivalent to a cost of protection of 7 percent of Turkey's GNP.[28]

These estimates do not take account of the effects of protection on the prices of the factors of production, capital and labor. To do so, general equilibrium estimates are needed. Such estimates have first been made for Colombia, which had protection levels comparable to Mexico, for the year 1970. The cost of protection has been estimated at 3.8 percent of GNP under full employment assumptions and 5.8 percent if labor is available at a constant real wage.[29]

There are several more recent estimates derived in a general equilibrium framework. Grais, de Melo, and Urata have estimated the cost of protection for Turkey in 1978 (i.e. prior to the 1980 reforms) at 5.5 percent of GDP, by taking account of the implications of quantitative import restrictions.[30] And while, according to Kayser tariff reductions would hardly affect GDP in Bangladesh, his results are vitiated by neglecting quantitative import restrictions that are pervasive in Bangladesh and by excluding changes in production structure in response to tariff reductions – truly, Hamlet without the Prince.[31]

None of these estimates consider the gains obtainable through the exploitation of *economies of scale* under outward orientation that permits overcoming the limitations of small national markets. These have been incorporated in a general equilibrium model estimated by Harris. The results show a 3.6 percent increase in GNP associated with the unilateral elimination of Canada's relatively low tariffs, with the bulk of the gain attributed to economies of scale.[32]

Gains from economies of scale under increased outward orientation can be expected to be greater in developing economies. With the exception of Brazil, these economies have smaller domestic markets for manufactured goods, where economies of scale are important, than does Canada and their protection levels are considerably higher.

Exporting also permits increased *capacity utilization*. In fact, in the small domestic markets of the developing countries, the choice often is between building ahead of demand and operating with involving a low degree of capacity utilization or constructing less than optimal size plants. This dilemma arises under traditional economies of scale, which entail reductions in production costs with increases in plant size in industries producing standardized products, such as steel, copper and newsprint.

Other forms of economies of scale include cost reductions obtainable through horizontal specialization (involving reductions in product variety as in the case of machine tools) and vertical specialization (involving the manufacture of parts, components, and accessories in separate establishments as in the case of automobiles) in differentiated products.

At the same time, according to the time-honored infant industry argument, incurring the cost of protection will be warranted as long as subsequent *improvements in productivity* offset this cost. But high protection may have the opposite effect by limiting competition in the small domestic markets of the developing countries as the resulting monopolies and oligopolies will often prefer 'quiet life' to innovative activity, which entails risk and uncertainty. In turn, the carrot and the stick of competition will provide inducements for technological change under outward orientation. Exporting firms, in particular, try to keep up with modern technology in order to maintain or improve their market position.

These conclusions are supported by empirical evidence. Thus, export expansion has been shown to be positively, and import substitution negatively, correlated with changes in total factor productivity (i.e. the productivity of the factors of production combined) in 13 Korean, Turkish, and Yugoslav industries during the period preceding the quadrupling of oil prices in 1973.[33]

The results obtained for Turkey confirm the conclusions reached earlier by Krueger and Tuncer for this country.[34] Also, India, which had a particularly pronounced inward-orientation during the postwar period, experienced a decline in total factor productivity between 1959–60 and 1979–80.[35] The same result has been obtained in an unpublished World Bank study for Mexico for the 1970–82 period, when the economy became increasingly outward-oriented.

The advantages of outward-orientation are also apparent from comparisons of estimates of total factor productivity for 20 developing economies covering the postwar period. Thus, Chenery[36] reports that total factor productivity increased at annual rates of over 3 percent in outward-oriented economies[37] while increases were 1 percent or less in countries with especially pronounced inward orientation.[38]

In generating higher incomes, outward orientation would raise *domestic savings*. Assume, for example, that the incremental capital–output ratio (the relationship between an increment in the capital stock to that of output) is 4, the average domestic savings ratio is 16 percent, and the marginal savings ratio is 33 percent. Eliminating protection, taking to represent a loss of 6 percent of GNP, would now raise the rate of economic growth from 4.0 to 4.5 percent by increasing the amount saved.

This conclusion is supported by estimates of Mercenier and Waelbroeck who also include the rise in investment owing to the increased imports of capital goods in the event of trade liberalization.[39] According to their results, a unilateral tariff cut by 50 percent would increase GNP by 0.9 percent in the low-income, and 1.9 percent in the middle-income, oil-importing developing economies excluding, and 2.1 and 4.3 percent including, savings and investment effects.[40]

Domestic savings would increase further if a higher than average share of incomes generated by exports were saved. This proposition has received support from a cross-section study of fourteen developing economies by Weisskopf, who has found a positive correlation between exports and domestic savings.[41] Weisskopf's results have been confirmed by Papanek in a cross-sectional analysis of 34 developing economies for the 1950s, and 51 developing countries for the 1960s.[42]

A positive correlation between exports and domestic savings has also been found in a time-series analysis of four developed and eight developing economies by Maizels (1968, ch. 4) for the early post-World War II period extending to 1962.[43] Maizels' sample includes India; for the same country Bhagwati and Srinivasan have obtained inconclusive results in a comparative study of ten industries for the 1950s and 1960s.[44] Given India's orientation toward import substitution during the entire period, however, the lack of clear-cut results in an interindustry framework may not modify the cross-sectional and time-series results obtained for the developing economies cited above.[45]

As export expansion improves the balance of payments, a country may become more attractive to *foreign investors*. While Weisskopf and Papanek have found a negative correlation between domestic and foreign savings, Grinols and Bhagwati have brought into question the validity of these results.[46] Furthermore, on the basis of the experience of the developing economies included in the NBER project, Bhagwati has concluded in regard to the application of an export promotion (EP) strategy that a 'substantial inflow of foreign capital seems to attend such a strategy [and that] this inflow is *not* exogenous to the EP strategy, as is sometimes assumed, but can be seriously argued to be a result in large part of the EP strategy itself.'[47]

Trade orientation, employment, wages, and income distribution

As long as labor is not fully employed, the rapid growth of output under an outward-oriented strategy benefits *employment*, and additional gains are obtained to the extent that exports are more labor intensive than import substitution. However, these gains are reduced in the event that outward orientation leads to more rapid increases in labor productivity than would otherwise be the case.

Banerji and Riedel have analyzed the effects of these factors on industrial employment in Taiwan, China and in India. Their results indicate that the favorable effects of rapid output growth on employment were enhanced by the shift towards labor-intensive export activities in the first case while output rose at a slower rate and a shift occurred towards relatively capital-intensive import-substituting activities in the second. With higher productivity growth, industrial employment grew at a average annual rate of 8 percent between 1954 and 1971 in the former, and 2 percent a year between 1950 and 1969 in the latter case.[48]

Furthermore, in a comparative study of eight inward-oriented developing economies, Anne Krueger has found that considerable employment gains may be obtained through a shift from import-substitution to export orientation.[49] These gains, calculated by the use of labor input coefficients for individual sectors, varied between 21 and 107 percent, with results for Indonesia and Thailand exceeding 100 percent.[50]

Fields has examined the employment effects of outward orientation in the Far East. He found that, between the early 1960s and the early 1970s, unemployment rates declined from 8 to 4 percent in Korea, and from 6 to 2 percent in Taiwan, China; little change occurred in these rates in subsequent years of outward orientation.[51] Also, Carvalho and Haddad have shown that greater outward-orientation in Brazil after mid-1960 led to 27 percent increase in the labor-intensity of exports relative to import substitution in Brazil.[52]

Apart from its impact on economic growth and on the interindustry allocation of the factors of production, trade orientation will affect employment through changes in factor prices. Under inward orientation capital goods are underpriced, both because the exchange rate is overvalued and because tariffs on capital goods tend to be low or nonexistent.

Among countries for which estimates have been made, the elimination of protection would involve reducing capital costs by 30 to 40 percent in Chile, Pakistan, and Turkey and by 8 percent in Argentina.[53] As a 1 percent change in the relative prices of capital and labor has been shown to be associated with a 1 percent change in the use of labor relative to capital,[54] eliminating this distortion would lead to increases in employment commensurate with the rise in the relative cost of capital.

With the growth of employment, *real wages* increased considerably in outward-oriented economies where exports expanded rapidly. This increase reflects the fact that the rate of growth of the demand for labor on the part of the manufacturing sector exceeded the rate of growth of the supply of labor to this sector. As a result, between 1966 and 1973, real wages in manufacturing doubled in Korea and increased by nearly three-fifths in Taiwan. Also, real wages in manufacturing rose by three-tenths in Brazil after its shift towards increased outward orientation. In turn, real wages decline by one-tenth in India between 1966 and 1973, which continued with inward-oriented policies during this period.[55]

The described tendencies continued during the period of external shocks. Between 1973 and 1983, real wages more than doubled in Korea and nearly doubled in Taiwan, China while Argentina and Mexico experienced a decline and in no major Latin American developing economies did real wages increase by as much as one-half.[56]

Rapid increases in wages, together with the growth of agricultural incomes contributed to the rise of incomes of the poor. In fact, in the two cases where export promotion began earliest and was the most far-reaching, income inequalities were reduced. Thus, the Gini coefficient, measuring the extent of *income inequality*, declined from 0.37 in 1964 to 0.35 in 1970 in Korea, and from 0.33 in 1964 to 0.31 in 1973 in Taiwan, China. Also, in Korea, between 1964 and 1972, the incomes of the poorest 60 percent of the population grew 40 percent faster than the national average.[57]

Myint has further compared the experiences of Korea and Sri Lanka that may be considered as archetypes of outward- and inward-oriented countries. Based on work carried out by Surjit Bhalla, Myint reports that the decline of exports was associated with a one-fifth percent fall in per capita incomes in terms of purchasing power parities between 1960 and 1977 in Sri Lanka, where the number of people living below the poverty line actually increased. In the same period, per capita incomes more than tripled in Korea, leading to a substantial fall in the number of people living below the poverty line.[58]

Improvements have occurred in Sri Lanka following the policy reforms undertaken in 1977, which have involved a move towards outward orientation. Between 1977 and 1984, per capita incomes rose by more than one-fourth, employment increased to a considerable extent, and food and other expenditures by the poor surpassed the levels reached in 1973.[59]

CONCLUSIONS

This essay has examined the importance of international trade for the developing countries. Following an analysis of change in traded flows in the postwar period, it has been shown that outward-oriented countries experienced gains and inward-oriented countries losses in their world market shares. The essay has further examined the experience of individual countries in the period of rapid world economic growth (1960–73) and of external shock (1973–85).

The conclusion is reached that outward-oriented countries succeeded in rapidly expanding their exports and reaching higher growth rates than inward-oriented countries in both periods. This conclusion is supported by a statistical analysis of exports and economic growth.

The favorable effects of exports on economic growth are explained by reference to gains from resource allocation according to comparative advantage; the exploitation of economies of scale and increased capacity utilization; improvements in technology; and increases in domestic savings and foreign direct investment under an outward-oriented development strategy. Such a strategy also brings larger gains in employment, wages, and income distribution than a strategy of inward orientation.

NOTES

1. 1963 has been chosen as the initial year because the United Nations statistics do not provide trade data in the necessary commodity and geographical breakdown for earlier years. On data sources, the classification scheme utilized, and the method used in expressing data in 1975 prices see the notes to Table 1.1.
2. The estimates are 2.1 and 5.9 percent for foods and beverages, 2.9 and 2.8 percent for industrial materials, and 3.5 and 3.9 percent for nonferrous metals for the 1963–73 and the 1973–84 periods, respectively. They have been calculated by regressing exports on time.
3. The statistical formulation assumes that the causation goes from economic growth in the developed countries to their imports from the developing countries. In view of the small share of trade with the developing countries in developed country GDP (2 percent in 1984), we may neglect the possibility of a reverse causation.
4. In the former case fixed input coefficients in the short run, in the latter case the intercorrelation between the prices of developed and developing country manufactured exports may account for the observed results.
5. Both regression coefficients are statistically significant at the 1 percent level; the adjusted R^2 is 0.95.
6. Data for most recent years are not available for several developing countries included in these groups.
7. B. Balassa, 'The Newly-Industrializing Developing Countries after the Oil Crisis,' *Weltwirtschaftliches Archiv*, CXVII (1981) pp. 142–94 and Essay 2 in Bela Balassa, *The Newly Industrializing Countries in the World Economy* (New York: Pergamon Press, 1981) pp. 29–81.
8. This is the lower limit for the upper middle-income countries in World Bank, *World Development Report 1986* (Washington, DC, 1986) Table 1.
9. Alternative definitions of the newly-exporting countries are provided in O. Havrylyshyn and I. Alikhani, 'Is There Cause for Export Optimism? An Inquiry into the Existence of a Second Generation of Successful Exporters,' *Weltwirtschaftliches Archiv*, CXVIII (1982) pp. 651–63, and G. H. Hughes and D. M. G. Newbery, 'Protection and Developing Countries' Exports of Manufacturers,' *Economic Policy*, I (1986) pp. 409–41. The former include countries with manufactured export growth rates in excess of average growth rates by the NICs during the 1970s; the latter include countries with populations in excess of 10 million and per capita incomes of at least $750 in 1983. Both of these definitions have the disadvantage of excluding India, whose manufactured exports exceed that of any newly-exporting country under the two definitions, and Pakistan that also surpassed the majority of the NECs.
10. For definitions, see the next section.
11. This section draws on B. Balassa and Associates, *Development Strategies in Semi-Industrial Countries* (Baltimore, Md.: The Johns Hopkins University Press, 1982).
12. As in Table 1.3, the data refer to 1963, 1973, and 1980.
13. This section utilizes in part the results reported in Essay 2.
14. Quantitative import restrictions were abolished and tariffs reduced to 10 percent over a five-year period, the only exception being the automobile industry. These measures were part of a package of economic reforms that included a large devaluation in real terms, the abolition of price control, the establishment of realistic prices for public utilities, the elimination of budget

deficits, the establishment of positive interest rates, and the liberalization of financial markets.

15. B. Balassa, 'Policy Experiments in Chile, 1973–83', in G. M. Walton (ed.), *The National Economic Policies of Chile* (Greenwich, Conn.: JAI Press, 1985) pp. 203–38, and Essay 8 in B. Balassa, *Change and Challenge in the World Economy* (London: Macmillan, 1985) pp. 157–84.

16. The policy changes comprised stabilization measures, with the twin objectives of reducing the rate of inflation and improving the balance of payments, as well as reform measures, with a view to turning the Turkish economy in an outward direction and giving an increased role to market forces. Stabilization objectives were pursued by lowering the rate of money creation and reducing the public sector deficit. Both stabilization and reform objectives were served by a large devaluation. Furthermore, the bias against exports was substantially reduced through export subsidization and import liberalization. Finally, industrial prices and interest rates were freed.

17. Between 1980 and 1985, the dollar value of exports increased threefold. Increases were the largest for exports to the Middle East, but Turkey also gained export market shares in the OECD countries. Thus, the dollar value of Turkish exports to these countries more than doubled between 1980 and 1985, although total OECD imports hardly changed during this period.

18. In the investigation, use has been made of data for the 1960–66 and 1966–73 periods for the countries in question, with the addition of Israel and Yugoslavia; however, the calculations omit Uruguay. Balassa and Associates, *Development Strategies in Semi-Industrial Countries*, Ch. 3.

19. The latter procedure also avoids the statistical problem of intercorrelation due to the inclusion of exports in production.

20. A. O. Krueger, *Foreign Trade Regimes & Economic Development: Liberalization Attempts and Consequences* (Cambridge, Mass.: Ballinger, 1978), p. 282.

21. Brazil, Chile, Colombia, Egypt, Ghana, India, Israel, Korea, Philippines, and Turkey.

22. G. Feder, 'On Exports and Economic Growth,' *Journal of Development Economics* XII (1983) pp. 59–73.

23. C. Michalopoulos, and K. Jay, 'Growth of Exports and Income in the Developing World: A Neoclassical View,' *Discussion Paper No. 28*, (Washington, DC: Agency for International Development, 1973).

24. B. Balassa and Associates, *Development Strategies in Semi-Industrial Countries*, Ch. 7.

25. B. Balassa, 'Exports, Policy Choices, and Economic Growth in Developing Countries after the 1973 Oil Shock,' *Journal of Development Economics*, XVIII (1985) pp. 23–35.

26. External shocks refer to the effects of the slowdown in the growth of world exports and changes in the terms of trade. Among policy responses to these shocks, export promotion is represented by changes in export market shares; import substitution refers to decreases in the income elasticity of import demand; and additional net external financing has been derived by extrapolating past trends in such financing.

27. B. Balassa and Associates, *The Structure of Protection in Developing Countries* (Baltimore, Md.: The Johns Hopkins Press, 1971) p. 82.

28. A. O. Krueger, 'Some Economic Costs of Exchange Control: The Turkish Case,' *Journal of Political Economy*, LXXIV (1966) pp. 466–80.

29. J. de Melo, 'Estimating the Cost of Protection: A General Equilibrium Approach,' *Quarterly Journal of Economics*, XCII (1978) p. 217. The results

are 11.0 percent and 15.8 percent, respectively, postulating an optimal export tax for coffee, which is subject to an international agreement.

30. W. Grais, J. de Melo, and S. Urata, 'A General Equilibrium Estimation of the Effects of Reductions in Tariffs and Quantitative Restrictions in Turkey in 1978,' in T. N. Srinivasan and J. Whalley (eds), *General Equilibrium Trade Policy Modeling* (Cambridge, Mass.: MIT Press, 1986) p. 77.

31. M. A. Kayser, 'Short-Run Impact of Trade Liberalization Measures in the Economy of Bangladesh: Exercises in Comparative Statics for the Year 1977,' in Srinivasan and Whalley (eds), *General Equilibrium Trade Policy Modeling*, p. 273.

32. R. G. Harris with D. Cox, *Trade, Industrial Policy, and Canadian Manufacturing* (Toronto, Economic Council, 1983).

33. M. Nishimizu, and S. Robinson, 'Trade Policies and Productivity Change in Semi-Industrialized Countries,' *Journal of Development Economics*, XVI (1984), Table 5.

34. A. O. Krueger, and B. Tuncer, 'An Empirical Test of the Infant Industry Argument,' *American Economic Review*, LXXII (1982) pp. 1142–52.

35. I. J. Ahluwalia, *Industrial Growth in India* (Delhi: Oxford University Press, 1985).

36. H. B. Chenery, 'Structural Chance,' in H. B. Chenery, S. Robinson, and M. Syrquin (eds), *Industrialization and Growth: A Comparative Study* (Oxford: Oxford University Press, 1986) Table 2.2.

37. Hong Kong, Korea, Taiwan, China and, in earlier periods, Israel and Spain. An exception is provided, however, by Singapore.

38. Argentina, Chile (prior to 1974), India, and Venezuela.

39. J. Mercenier, and J. Waelbroeck, 'Effects of a 50% Tariff Cut in the Varuna Model,' in Srinivasan and Whalley (eds), *General Equilibrium Trade Policy Modeling* pp. 301–3.

40. These estimates do not include the gains obtainable through the elimination of quantitative restrictions.

41. T. E. Weisskopf, 'The Impact of Foreign Capital Inflow on Domestic Savings in Underdeveloped Countries,' *Journal of International Economics*, II (1972) pp. 25–38.

42. G. Papanek, 'Aid, Foreign Private Investment, Savings, and Growth in Less Developed Countries,' *Journal of Political Economy*, LXXXI (1973) pp. 120–30.

43. A. Maizels, *Exports and Economic Growth in Developing Countries* (Cambridge, England: Cambridge University Press, 1968) Ch. 4.

44. J. N. Bhagwati, and T. N. Srinivasan, *Foreign Trade Regimes and Economic Development: India* (New York: Columbia University Press, 1975).

45. At the same time, one may agree with Bhagwati that 'while there is much empirical evidence in support of a statistical association between exports and saving, there is little evidence so far for some of the hypotheses that could provide a *rationale* for such an association implying a causal relationship running from exports to savings.' J. N. Bhagwati, *Foreign Trade Regimes and Economic Development: Anatomy and Consequences of Exchange Control Regimes* (Cambridge, Mass.: Ballinger, 1978) p. 147.

46. E. Grinols, and J. N. Bhagwati, 'Foreign Capital Savings and Dependence,' *Review of Economics and Statistics*, LVIII (1976) pp. 416–24.

47. Bhagwati, p. 211. Bhagwati's definition of an export-promoting strategy (p. 207) is practically equivalent to the above definition of outward orientation.

48. R. Banerji, and J. Riedel, 'Industrial Employment Expansion under Alternative Trade Strategies: Case of India and Taiwan, 1950–1970,' *Journal of Development Economics*, VII (1980) pp. 567–77.
49. A. O. Krueger, *Trade and Employment in Developing Countries. 3 Synthesis and Conclusions* (Chicago: University of Chicago Press, 1983) Table 6.2.
50. An apparent exception is Chile but this was due to the capital-intensity of its intra-Latin American exports under the policies applied; the labor-intensity of exports in trade with developed countries much exceeded that for import substitution.
51. G. S. Fields, 'Employment, Income Distribution, and Economic Growth in Small Open Economies,' *Economic Journal*,' XCIV (1984) pp. 74–83.
52. J. L. Carvalho, and C. L. S. Haddad, 'Foreign Trade Strategies and Employment in Brazil,' in A. O. Krueger, M. B. Lary, T. Monson, and N. Akrasanee (eds), *Trade and Employment in Developing Countries 1. Individual Studies* (Chicago: University of Chicago Press, 1981) Table 2.15.
53. Krueger, *Trade and Employment in Developing Countries. 3 Synthesis and Conclusions*, Table 7.1.
54. J. B. Behrman, 'Country and Sectoral Variations in Manufacturing Elasticities of Substitution between Capital and Labor,' in A. O. Krueger, (ed.), *Trade and Employment in Developing Countries 2. Factor supply and Substitution* (Chicago: University of Chicago Press, 1982) p. 186.
55. Fields further made comparisons with three small developing countries (Barbados, Jamaica, and Trinidad and Tobago) he considered as open economies albeit, given their high level of protection, they may better be classified as inward-oriented. And, while he attributed the high level of unemployment in these countries to the application of a 'lenient' wage policy, compared to the 'strict' wage policies allegedly followed by the Far Eastern countries, this assertion conflicts with the fact that real wages rose more rapidly in the Far East than in the Caribbean countries, with an absolute decline observed in Jamaica.
56. B. Balassa, G. Bueno, P. P. Kuczynski, and M. H. Simonsen, *Toward Renewed Economic Growth in Latin America*, Mexico, D. F.: El Colegio de Mexico, Rio de Janeiro: Funadação Getulio Vargas, Washington, DC: Institute for International Economics, 1986) Table 1.6. Data for India are not available.
57. Balassa and Associates, *Development Strategies in Semi-Industrial Countries*, p. 58.
58. H. Myint, 'Growth Policies and Income Distribution,' Discussion Paper, Development Policy Issues Series, Report No. VPERS1 (Washington, DC: World Bank, 1985).
59. S. S. Bhalla, and P. Glewwe, 'Growth and Equity in Developing Countries: A Reinterpretation of the Sri Lankan Experience,' *World Bank Economic Review*, I (1986) p. 61.

Essay 2 Policy Responses to Exogenous Shocks in Developing Countries

INTRODUCTION

This essay will report on the results of research on the policy responses of developing countries to exogenous (external) shocks in the 1973–8 and 1978–83 periods. It will further examine the economic performance of outward-oriented and inward-oriented developing countries in the light of the policies applied.

Section I of the essay will describe the definition of external shocks, the forms of policy responses, and the classification of countries. Section II will present estimates on the balance-of-payments effects of external shocks and of policy responses to these shocks. Section III will provide additional information on the policy measures applied and indicate their economic effects.

I THE CLASSIFICATION SCHEME APPLIED

External shocks in the 1973–8 and 1978–83 periods included terms of trade effects, associated largely with increases in oil prices; export volume effects, resulting from the recession-induced slowdown of world trade; and, in the second period, interest rate effects, due to increases in interest rates in world financial markets. Policy responses to external shocks took the form of additional net external financing, represented by increased borrowing compared with past trends; export promotion, reflected by increases in export market shares; import substitution, expressed by decreases in the income elasticity of import demand; and deflationary macroeconomic policies, entailing a decline in the growth of demand for imports.[1]

Table 2.1 provides summary data on the balance-of-payments effects of external shocks and of policy responses to these shocks in the two periods. Developing countries were classified as outward-oriented and inward-oriented, depending on whether they provided similar incentives to exports and to import substitution or discriminated in favor of import substitution

32

TABLE 2.1 *Balance-of-payments effects on external shocks and of policy responses to these shocks*[a]

	Outward-oriented countries		Inward-oriented countries	
	1974–8	*1979–83*	*1974–8*	*1979–83*
External shocks (as percent of GNP)				
Terms of trade effects	6.3	8.4	3.6	2.8
Export volume effects	2.4	4.9	0.9	0.4
Interest rate effects	—	1.7	—	1.6
Total	8.8	15.0	4.5	5.0
Policy responses (as percent of external shocks)				
Additional net external financing	−26.4	−11.5	89.0	37.6
Export promotion	48.6	29.0	−14.9	11.5[b]
Import substitution	58.5	24.5	15.4	9.8
Effects of deflationary policy	19.4	58.0	10.5	41.1

NOTE: (*a*) For definitions, see text.
     (*b*) −2.3 excluding fuel exports.

SOURCE: World Bank data-base.

and against exports. Both groups include newly-industrializing countries (NICs) and less developed countries (LDCs) although, to save space, only their combined results are reported in the table.

Among the NICs, Korea, Singapore, and Taiwan adopted an outward-oriented development strategy in the early 1960s and continued with this strategy after 1973. In the mid-1970s, they were joined by Chile and Uruguay, which had previously applied inward-oriented policies but turned outward in response to the external shocks. Conversely, Argentina, Brazil, Israel, Mexico, Portugal, Turkey and Yugoslavia maintained, or reinforced, their inward-oriented stance. Among the LDCs, Kenya, Mauritius, Thailand, and Tunisia were classified as having followed outward-oriented, and Egypt, India, Jamaica, Morocco, Peru, Philippines, Tanzania, and Zambia as having pursued inward-oriented, policies.

The classification scheme was established for the first period of external shocks; for reasons of comparability, it was retained for the second period, even though policy changes were made in several countries. In particular, Turkey undertook a far-reaching policy reform in January 1980 while Chile and Uruguay distorted the system of incentives by failing to adjust their exchange rates *pari passu* with domestic inflation.

II EXTERNAL SHOCKS AND POLICY RESPONSES TO THESE SHOCKS IN 1973–8 AND 1978–83

The results show that outward-oriented countries (for short OOCs) suffered substantially larger terms of trade losses and adverse export volume effects than inward-oriented countries (IOCs) during both periods of external shocks (Table 2.1). This is explained by the larger share of foreign trade in their gross national product (28 percent in the OOCs, on the average, in 1973 compared with 10 percent for the IOCs) that was only partially compensated by the favorable commodity composition of their exports.

One also observes considerable differences in policy responses to external shocks in the two groups of countries, when the sequencing of these responses is of further interest. In the first period of external shocks, the IOCs offset nearly the entire adverse balance-of-payments impact of external shocks by additional net external financing. This was done with a view to maintain past economic growth rates, notwithstanding the deterioration of the external environment. They did not succeed in this effort, however, and the rate of growth of GNP declined during the period (Table 2.2).

The lack of output-increasing (expenditure-switching) policies importantly contributed to the deceleration of the rate of economic growth in the IOCs. Losses in export market shares practically offset import substitution in these countries, with their combined impact on the balance of payments and on domestic output being virtually nil. At the same time, losses in export market shares accentuated the effects of external borrowing on debt-service ratios, defined as the ratio of net interest payments and amortization to merchandise exports. This ratio nearly doubled in the space of five years, rising from 22 percent in 1973 to 43 percent in 1978, on the average.

TABLE 2.2 *GNP growth rates*
(percent)

	Outward-oriented countries	*Inward-oriented countries*
1963–73	6.6	5.8
1973–76	5.5	5.3
1976–79	8.1	4.6
1973–79	6.8	5.0
1979–82	2.4	2.6
1982–84	5.3	1.7
1979–84	3.5	2.2

NOTE: Due to the shortness of the time series, calculated between end-points.

SOURCE: World Bank data-base.

The OOCs initially applied deflationary policies to limit reliance on external finance so that their debt service ratio remained at slightly below 12 percent. The resulting decline in economic growth rates remained temporary, however, as the OOCs adopted output-increasing policies of export promotion and import substitution that fully compensated for the adverse balance-of-payments effects of external shocks and led to the acceleration of economic growth.

The second period of external shocks thus found the IOCs (but not the OOCs) with considerable foreign indebtedness. Additional borrowing was possible for a while, except for Turkey that was practically bankrupt in 1979 and Yugoslavia that encountered borrowing limitations in 1980. However, with further increases in their debt service ratios, the other IOCs also approached fiduciary limits and, following the August 1982 Mexican debt crisis, they ceased to be creditworthy for commercial bank loans.

Correspondingly, the IOCs made less use of additional net external financing in the second period of external shocks than in the first. They applied deflationary policies instead, leading to a decline in their economic growth rates. This result reflects the fact that the IOCs largely eschewed output-increasing policies of export promotion and import substitution.

In fact, the extent of import substitution in the IOCs declined during the second period of external shocks and discoveries of oil deposits in Mexico and Peru fully account for the observed increases in average export market shares. Thus, adjusting for the rise in petroleum exports, the IOCs again experienced losses in foreign markets. And although the losses were smaller than in the first period of external shocks, this was due to the improved performance of a few countries. The January 1980 policy reform, representing increased outward orientation, led to a near-doubling of Turkish exports between 1980 and 1983 while export subsidies contributed to the expansion of exports in Brazil. All other IOCs lost export market shares.

The OOCs also applied deflationary policies in response to the external shocks they suffered after 1978. But the resulting decline in GNP growth rates again remained temporary and the countries in question subsequently resumed higher rates of economic growth. This occured as the OOCs continued to apply output-increasing policies, leading to increases in export market shares and import substitution, even though they had to rely to a greater extent on deflationary policies than during the first period, when the balance-of-payments effects of external shocks were much smaller.

At the same time, the OOCs continued to limit reliance on external finance, so that their average debt service ratio remained below 14 percent notwithstanding increases in world interest rates. By contrast, debt-service ratios continued to rise in the IOCs, albeit at a slower rate than beforehand, reaching 53 percent in 1983.

III THE POLICY MEASURES APPLIED AND THEIR ECONOMIC EFFECTS

In both periods, then, the OOCs made considerable gains in export market shares. In turn, the IOCs experienced losses in market shares, even though these losses were attenuated in the second period of external shocks by the export-promoting measures applied in a few countries. Providing similar incentives to exports and to import substitution in the OOCs, compared with the continued bias of the incentive system against exports in the IOCs, importantly contributed to the observed differences in export performance.

Another contributing factor was exchange rate policy, with the adoption of realistic exchange rates in the OOCs and appreciation in real (inflation-adjusted) terms in most of the IOCs. Increased overvaluation in the IOCs was associated with to foreign borrowing that obstructed adjustment in the exchange rate as the external financing of the balance-of-payments deficit permitted maintaining an overvalued currency. In turn, the OOCs did not use foreign borrowing to suppport the exchange rate.

The OOCs also experienced import substitution to a greater extent than the IOCs. This result may appear surprising since the bias against exports favored the replacement of imports by domestic production in the latter group of countries. Various factors contributed to this outcome.

To begin with, the adoption of realistic exchange rates contributed to import substitution parallel with export expansion in the OOCs, which was not the case in the IOCs. Export expansion in the OOCs also permitted simultaneous import substitution as the exploitation of economies of scale led to lower costs. Such efficient import substitution contrasted with inefficient import replacement in many of the IOCs, where net foreign exchange savings tended to decline as shifts occured towards industries where the countries in question had a comparative disadvantage and increasingly encountered domestic market limitations.

Furthermore, the OOCs experienced import substitution in the primary sector as they provided similar incentives to primary and to manufacturing activities while primary production suffered considerable discrimination in the IOCs. Finally, the former, but not the latter, group of countries encouraged energy savings, representing import substitution in fuels under the conventions adopted in this investigation, by increasing energy prices parallel with the rise in world market prices.

The lack of discrimination against exports and against primary activities raised the level of investment efficiency in the IOCs, thereby contributing to their economic growth. The liberalization of prices and the application of economic considerations in public investment projects also had a favorable impact on the efficiency of investment in these countries. Export expansion, too, had beneficial effects by permitting higher capacity utilization and the exploitation of economies of scale.

In turn, the bias of the incentive system against exports and against primary activities, together with the widespread application of price control, reduced the efficiency of investment in the IOCs. The situation was aggravated by the lack of sufficient attention given to economic considerations in the large public investment programs of these countries.

These considerations explain the observed differences in incremental capital-output ratios (ICOR), taken to represent the level of investment efficiency notwithstanding the well-known limitations of these ratios. In the 1973–9 period, the ICORs averaged 4.1 in the OOCs and 4.9 in the IOCs; the corresponding figures were 7.4 and 8.6 in the 1979–84 period, when the deflationary policies applied raised the ICORs in both groups of countries.

The OOCs also exhibited higher domestic savings ratios than the IOCs. Between 1973 and 1979, these ratios averaged 25.6 percent in the former group of countries and 21.0 percent in the latter. The differences were maintained in the 1979–84 period, the average ratios being 25.7 percent in the OOCs and 20.9 percent in the IOCs.

These differences pertain equally to public and to private savings. While the IOCs practiced public dissaving as they incurred large budget deficits, the OOCs limited the size of these deficits. Also, real interest rates tended to be negative in the IOCs and positive in the OOCs, with corresponding effects on private savings.

Higher investment efficiency and higher domestic savings ratios in the OOCs were only partially offset by greater foreign borrowing in the IOCs. Correspondingly, rates of economic growth were considerably higher in the former than in the latter group of countries, with the differences increasing over time (Table 2.2).

CONCLUSIONS

This essay has reviewed the adjustment experience of developing countries applying different policies in response to the external shocks of the 1973–8 and 1978–83 periods. Although outward-oriented countries suffered considerably larger external shocks than inward-oriented countries, these differences were offset several times as a result of the policies followed. Thus, while the OOCs accepted a temporary decline in GNP growth rates in both periods in order to limit reliance to foreign borrowing, their economic growth accelerated subsequently, owing to the output-increasing policies applied.

The IOCs relied practically exclusively on foreign borrowing in response to the external shocks of the first period. But, the bias of the incentive system against exports and primary activities, the widespread application of price control, and the frequent choice of high-cost public investment projects did not provide for the efficient use of these funds, and of investible funds in general, leading to lower economic growth rates and compromising their creditworthiness.

In eschewing output-increasing policies, limitations on external finance in the second period of external shocks led to the application of deflationary policies in the IOCs, further increasing differences in the growth performance of the two groups of countries. Between 1982 and 1984, GNP growth rates averaged 5.3 percent in the OOCs and 1.7 percent in the IOCs.

NOTE

1. For a description of the methodology applied and results for earlier periods, see B. Balassa, 'Adjustment Policies in Developing Countries: A Reassessment,' *World Development*, IX (1984) pp. 955–72. Reprinted as Essay 5 in Bela Balassa, *Change and Challenge in the World Economy* (London: Macmillan, 1984) pp. 89–101.

Essay 3   The Interaction of Factor and Product Market Distortions in Developing Countries

INTRODUCTION

This essay will examine distortions in product and factor markets in developing countries, and the interaction of these distortions in respect to the development strategies applied. The analysis will concentrate on policy-imposed distortions, where departures from efficient resource allocation result from policy actions; these contrast with distortions resulting from market imperfections.[1]

The principal forms of product market distortions are trade policies in the form of import protection and export subsidies (taxes), exchange rate policies, and price control, all of which affect relative product prices. In turn, factor market distortions may result from social policies, financial policies, and tax policies, which affect the relative prices of capital and labor.

But, distortions in product markets will also have an impact on factor markets and vice versa. Product market distortions will give rise to distortions in factor markets through their effects on factor prices while factor market distortions will cause distortions in product markets through their effects on the cost of production.

Experience suggests that interventions in product and in factor markets are interrelated, and this fact has a bearing on the choice of development strategies. Thus, governments will be less inclined to intervene in factor markets if product markets are relatively undistorted, as is the case under an outward-oriented development strategy, lest export prospects be jeopardized. In turn, there will be less resistance to measures that distort factor prices if protection insulates the domestic economy from foreign influences under an inward-oriented development strategy.

At the same time, the existence of policy-imposed factor market distortions will affect the choice of the policies applied in regard to product markets. Distortions in factor markets will tend to discourage the adoption of an outward-oriented development strategy, whose success depends on

the operation of these markets. In particular, the impact of trade liberalization on exports will depend on the ability of capital markets to provide
funds for export-oriented investments.

The experiences of Latin American and Far Eastern countries provide
support for these propositions. While in Latin America inward-orientation
has been accompanied by considerable distortions in labor and capital
markets, in the Far East outward orientation has been associated with free
labor markets and the increased freedom of capital markets.[2]

In the mid-1960s, reforms of trade and exchange rate policies in the Far
Eastern countries were carried out simultaneously with reforms of capital
markets. Also, in the early 1980s, Turkey linked trade and exchange rate
reforms with reforms of labor and capital markets. Finally, an IMF study
has concluded that 'interest rate repression often coexists with highly
protectionist trade policies and overvaluation of the domestic currency'[3] in
developing countries.

Section I of this essay will consider the effects of product market
distortions on factor markets in the developing countries. In turn, Sections
II to III will analyze policy-imposed distortions in the labor and the capital
markets of these countries. Section IV will summarize the effects of the
policies in question on factor markets and indicate the possible impact of
factor market distortions on product markets. In each section of the essay,
the available empirical evidence will also be cited.

I EFFECTS OF PRODUCT MARKET DISTORTIONS ON FACTOR MARKETS

Developing countries tend to protect capital-intensive industries. The
resulting distortions in product markets engender a flow of resources from
labor-intensive to capital-intensive industries, thereby favoring capital at
the expense of labor.

Ceteris paribus, the protection of capital-intensive industries will raise
the price of capital relative to the price of labor. But protection will also
reduce demand for imports and cause the exchange rate to appreciate (a
unit of domestic currency will buy more foreign exchange). This, together
with relatively low tariffs on capital goods, and the use of tariff exemptions
on these products, will mean lower prices for imported capital goods in
terms of local currency.

Take the case, for example, when the exchange rate is 100 pesos to the
dollar under free trade and an average tariff of 50 percent necessitates a 20
percent appreciation of the currency in order to ensure balance-of-
payments equilibrium. Now, under an exchange rate of 80 pesos to the
dollar, tariff exemptions on capital goods will mean that capital goods cost
20 percent less under protection than under free trade. And, the net effect

will be a decline in capital goods prices as long as tariffs on these products are less than 25 percent.

NBER studies carried out under the direction of Anne Krueger indicate the combined effects of the overvaluation of the exchange rate, low import tariffs on capital goods, and tariff exemptions on these goods. The measures applied are shown to have led to reductions in capital costs ranging between 30 and 40 percent in Chile, Pakistan, and Tunisia during the period between the early 1960s and the early 1970s. Similar results have been obtained in regard to imported capital goods in Argentina. But, in Argentina the protection of the domestic capital-goods sector reduced the average cost differential for capital goods to 8 percent (Table 3.1, Column 2). At the same time, import licensing favored capital-intensive import-substituting industries over relatively labor-intensive small- and medium-size industries in Argentina and Pakistan whereas the importation of capital goods was fairly freely permitted in Chile and in Tunisia.[4]

Distortions in the prices of capital goods were associated with the application of an inward-oriented development strategy in the countries under consideration. In contrast, the effects of trade policies on the cost of capital goods were approximately nil in outward-oriented countries, such as Hong Kong and Korea. This was also the case in the Ivory Coast, and after the policy reforms of the mid-1960s, in Brazil (Table 3.1).

Reductions in the cost of capital under an inward-oriented development strategy discourage the use of labor. And while the protection of capital-intensive industries tends to raise the price of capital, it also reduces employment through the shift of resources from labor-intensive to capital-intensive industries. These effects are aggravated in cases where relatively capital-intensive industries are favored within both the import-substituting and the export sectors.

Column (4) of Table 3.2 shows the employment effects of differences in rates of import protection and of export subsidies among import-substituting and among export industries for nine developing countries. In the calculation, the average labor coefficient in import substituting industries has been taken as the benchmark for each country. The estimates pertain to the late 1960s and the early 1970s.[5]

The results reported in Table 3.2 further show differences in average labor coefficients between import-competing and export industries. It is apparent that, with two exceptions, the labor intensity of exports much exceeds that of import substitution, indicating that import-competing industries are, on the whole, more capital-intensive than export industries. The exceptions are Korea, which provided similar incentives to exports and import substitution under an outward-oriented development strategy, and Chile where the incentives applied in the 1960s distorted trade patterns to the extent that exports became more labor intensive than import substitutes.[6]

TABLE 3.1 *Percentage distortions in labor and capital costs from various sources*

Country	Period	Percentage Increase in labor costs	Percentage reduction in capital costs owing to factor market distortions					Percentage Increase in wage-rental ratio, due to	
			Trade regime	Credit allocation	Tax preferences	Together	Total	Factor market distortions	Factor and product market distortions
		(1)	(2)	(3)	(4)	(5)	(6)	(7)	(8)
Argentina	1973	15	8	9	n.a.	9	17	26	38
Brazil	1968	27	0	4	n.a.	4	431	31	n.a.
Chile	1966–8	n.a.	37	n.a.	n.a.	n.a.	n.a.	n.a.	n.a.
Hong Kong	1973	0	0	0	0	0	0	0	0
Ivory Coast	1971	23	0	3	12	15	15	45	45
Pakistan	1961–4	0	38	53	10	58	76	238	316
Korea	1969	0	0	8	2	10	10	11	11
Tunisia	1972	20	30	6	n.a.	6	36	28	87

SOURCE: Anne O. Krueger, *Trade and Employment in Developing Countries 3. Synthesis and Conclusions* (Chicago: The University of Chicago Press, 1983) Table 7.1.

TABLE 3.2 *Sources of potential increase in labor coefficients*

Country	Period	Observed direct labor coefficient (1)	Increase (percentage) with			Potential coeffi- cient (5)
			No domestic factor market intervention (2)	No trade strategy distortion (3)	No within- strategy inefficiency (4)	
		Import-competing industries				
Argentina	1973	100	16	−6	0	110
Brazil	1970	100	15	n.a.	n.a.	115
Chile	1966–8	100	n.a.	7	n.a.	107
Colombia	1970	100	n.a.	n.a.	10	110
Indonesia	1971	100	n.a.	n.a.	66	166
Ivory Coast	1972	100	25	0	12	140
Pakistan	1969–70	100	271	0	n.a.	371
Korea	1968	100	8	0	0	108
Tunisia	1972	100	17	38	51	243
		Exportable industries				
Argentina	1973	130	25	−6	0	149
Brazil	1970	207	15	n.a.	n.a.	238
Chile	1966–8	80	n.a.	7	68	144
Colombia	1970	170	n.a.	n.a.	24	210
Indonesia	1971	209	n.a.	n.a.	0	209
Ivory Coast	1972	135	25	0	0	169
Pakistan	1969–70	142	271	0	n.a.	384
Korea	1968	100	8	0	0	108
Tunisia	1972	128	17	38	0	198

NOTES: The table shows potential increases in direct labor coefficients in the event of the elimination of (a) factor market distortions; (b) the factor price effects of protection; and (c) product market distortions within import-substitution and export industries.

SOURCE: Anne Krueger, *Trade and Employment in Developing Countries 3. Synthesis and Conclusions* (Chicago: The University of Chicago Press, 1983) Table 1.

The estimates assume that labor and capital would be reallocated among industries in response to a move towards free trade. For such a reallocation to occur, the freedom of factor markets would need to be assured. Calculations by T. Paul Schultz, indicating the joint effects of product market and factor market distortions on the distribution of incomes in Colombia, provide some relevant information. Schultz concludes that

the close relationship found here between levels of effective protection and unexplained variation in labor incomes provides a prima facie case that development and trade policies have played a role in generating or at least maintaining intersectoral differences in factor incomes that look like quasi rent.[7]

He adds that 'protection may have increased the returns to both labor and capital in the more protected sectors, but the proportionate gains for employers exceed those received by employees . . .'[8] At the same time, the resulting quasi-rents have stimulated rent-seeking activity that involves a cost to the national economy.[9]

Employment will further be affected as economic growth tends to be more rapid under an outward-oriented, than under an inward-oriented, development strategy.[10] However, employment will be reduced to the extent that labor productivity is rising more rapidly under the first, than under the second, alternative. These effects, then, will modify the impact on employment of the sectoral composition of output.

Banerji and Riedel analyzed the effects of the above factors on industrial employment in India and in Taiwan, which can be taken to be representative of outward- and inward-oriented development strategies, respectively. The results indicate that the favorable effects on employment of a shift towards labor-intensive export industries in Taiwan were reinforced by rapid output growth while a shift occurred towards capital-intensive industries in India where output also grew at a slower rate. With higher productivity growth in Taiwan than in India, industrial employment rose at an average annual rate of 8 percent during the 1954–71 period in the first case and at 2 percent a year during the 1950–69 period in the second.[11]

II LABOR MARKET DISTORTIONS

A variety of policy-induced distortions are observed in the labor markets of the developing countries. They include regulations aimed at ensuring job security, social security schemes, minimum wage legislation, taxation of labor income, and wage employment policies in the public sector.

Regulations concerning job security

Developing countries have often applied measures aimed at ensuring job security. In Argentina, for example, labor laws bestow job security on employees after only one year and severance payments increase with the length of employment. The situation is similar in Venezuela.[12] In Panama, labor legislation is estimated to have raised labor costs by 30 percent, in addition to the cost of social security charges and fringe benefits, to a total of 59 percent of basic wages.[13]

Apart from reducing mobility, labor regulations aimed at limiting reductions in employment tend to have the opposite of the desired effect by increasing the cost of labor. As noted by David Laidler,

– They discourage workers from quitting voluntarily to search for other employment.

- They make it expensive for an otherwise viable firm to close down a particularly loss-making operation . . .
- Moreover, they inhibit employers from taking on new workers because of the propective cost of declaring them redundant at some time in the future. Such schemes inhibit resource mobility, slow down the pace of economic change, and increase unemployment. They do not serve simply to redistribute wealth, but to reduce the total amount of wealth available for redistribution.[14]

Social security schemes

According to data collected by the US Department of Health and Human Services, Social Security Administration, social charges exceed 20 percent of wages in India and range between 15 and 45 percent in most Latin American countries.[15] It has further been reported that employer and employee contributions, taken together, were in the 55–65 percent range for blue- and white-collar workers in industry and commerce in 1969 in Uruguay, and the ratio reached 46 percent for blue-collar workers and 65 percent for white-collar workers in 1968 in Chile. But, Chile subsequently privatized its social security system.[16]

The effects of social security schemes on the cost of labor and on employment will depend on the elasticity of supply of labor. If the labor supply was infinitely elastic in terms of the real wages, social charges would increase the cost of labor by their full amount, irrespective of whether they are paid by employers or by employees, with adverse effects on employment.

While such an extreme case is unlikely to be found in reality, in the domestic economy the supply of unskilled labor may be assumed to be more elastic than that of skilled, technical, and managerial labor, so that social security schemes will affect the cost and the employment of the former to a greater extent than of the latter. Also, the elasticity of the supply of unskilled labor is said to be higher in South Asia than in other developing areas.[17]

At the same time, according to Carmelo Mesa-Lago, 'accumulated evidence in Latin America . . . indicates that social security systems financed by contributions upon wages have a negative effect on employment.'[18] Furthermore, it has been estimated that, under realistic assumptions made about the elasticity of labor supply, average social security charges of 27 percent have reduced employment in Brazilian manufacturing by about 8 percent.[19]

These effects on labor costs of social security charges create a wedge between the demand price and the supply price of labor. In South Asia, the compulsory provision of various services, including housing, education and training, have similar effects.[20]

Minimum wage legislation[21]

Labor costs may also be raised by the statutory determination of minimum wages. In this connection, one needs to consider the extent to which raising minimum wages leads to increases in the entire wage structure as well as the effects of the resulting wage increases on employment.

The classic study of the effects of minimum wage legislation on wages and employment is *Wages, Productivity, and Industrialization in Puerto Rico* by Lloyd Reynolds and Peter Gregory. They note that

> the closeness of actual hourly earnings in most industries to the legal minimum, the parallelism in the timing of upward movements, and the tendency for the minimum to encroach gradually on the actual earnings level all suggest that it is minimum wage awards which have been forcing the pace of wage advance in Puerto Rico since 1950.[22]

On the basis of an econometric estimate, the authors conclude that 'a change in the wage could be expected to be associated with an approximately equal proportionate change in employment in the reverse direction, with the wage bill remaining roughly constant.'[23]

It has been suggested that Puerto Rico is a special case because of its close association with the United States and its superior administrative machinery,[24] as well as because of its relatively high per capita income, its small labor force, and the high share of the labor force engaged in non-agricultural occupations in the mid-fifties.[25] But it is doubtful whether Puerto Rico's association with the United States and the superior skills of its administration are relevant to the issue in question. Moreover, there were a number of developing countries with urban incomes which exceeded incomes in Puerto Rico in the early fifties, when minimum wage legislation was introduced there, and more countries have since surpassed this level.

According to an ILO report,

> the evidence . . . suggests that conditions in which increases in minimum wages exert a substantial influence on wages actually paid are widely encountered. This influence is particularly strong where minimum rates are the going rates for large numbers of workers, which seems to be the case in most African and in many other (but not all) developing countries.[26]

And, while the evidence provided on this point in a subsequent ILO report is inconclusive,[27] it should be recognized that minimum wage legislation may have adverse economic effects even if it does not lead to proportionate increases in the wage structure.

The narrowing of wage differences will discourage socially profitable investments in human capital by reducing the incentives for such investment. Also, distortions will be introduced in the choice between labor and physical capital, between unskilled labor and skilled labor, as well as between labor in the formal sector and the informal sector, where minimum wage regulations are rarely applied.

There is evidence on the effects of minimum wage legislation in several countries. In Argentina, minimum wage legislation is reported to have increased unskilled wages by 25 percent.[28] In the Ivory Coast, a 20 percent increase in the wages of unskilled labor through minimum wage legislation is said to have occurred.[29] While comparable estimates for developing countries are not available, in Canada the rate of unemployment is shown to have increased in the same proportion as the minimum wage.[30]

This is not to say that minimum wage legislation would have had a pervasive influence in the developing countries. In some countries, such as Brazil, its effects have been largely eroded by inflation.[31] At the same time, minimum wages are particularly high in socialist-oriented developing countries.[32] *The Economist*[33] reports in regard to Tanzania that 'in the towns minimum wages in some industries were set three times as high as India's, whose labor productivity was three times higher.'

According to the recent ILO report,

the problem [of setting minimum wages] is essentially viewed as one of striking a balance between the social gains to be made, in the form of improvement in the relative wage position of the lowest paid, and any costs these might entail in the form of reduced employment, slower growth and increased inflation[34]

At the same time, with minimum wage legislation generally benefiting a privileged urban labor group, the social gains themselves may be open to question.[35]

As expressed by one observer, 'this is directly contrary to the initial objective of minimum wage legislation, i.e. the protection of unorganized workers whose wages are exceptionally low.'[36] Yet, as noted in an ILO report, 'for Latin America it has been estimated that 80 percent of the urban workers receiving incomes below the legal minimum wage belong to the informal sector' and 'the enforcement of minimum wages in developing countries encounters its most serious obstacles in traditional agriculture outside the larger plantations and modernized farms.'[37] Minimum wages are also said to have contributed to the sizable differences between formal and informal sector wages in Africa and in the Middle East.[38]

Taxation of labor incomes

Tax rates on labor incomes tend to be high in developing countries with rapid inflation. Apart from Brazil where tax rates were indexed prior to the February 1986 monetary reform, income recipients are shifted to higher tax brackets as inflation proceeds. While this can be undone through periodical revisions of the tax schedule, such revisions tends to be delayed.

In Turkey, for example, minimum wage income became subject to a tax of 28 percent in 1980 as a result of inflation during the 1970s. Under the new tax schedule introduced on 1 January 1981, the minimum wage is not subject to tax but the marginal tax rate is 40 percent on incomes immediately above this level.[39]

Tax progressivity means that income tax rates are higher for skilled technical, and managerial labor than for unskilled labor. In Morocco, for example, the marginal tax rate, including the National Security Contribution and the supplementary tax, rose from 13 percent at an annual income of 6000 dirhams to 50 percent at 100 000 dirhams, and 75 percent at 750 000 dirhams in 1982, when the exchange rate was 6 dirhams to the US dollar.[40] In turn, the top marginal tax rates were 65 percent in Thailand, 55 percent in Korea, 49 percent in Colombia, and 42 percent in Mexico in the early 1980s.[41]

High marginal tax rates and the progressivity of the tax system create distortions in labor markets by providing incentives to reduce the work effort and to shift from payment in money to payment in kind. Also, schooling and training, as well as the movement of labor from lower to higher productivity sectors, are discouraged as differences in after-tax incomes are reduced.

At the same time, the elasticity of supply of such labor will be increased through international migration. And, in Morocco, tax-induced increases in the cost of foreign technicians and managers are said to be a factor discouraging the subsidiaries of foreign enterprises from establishing in the country.[42] This is because the firms in question have to assure particular levels of real income for their technicians and managers, and the high income taxes raise their salary costs.

Wage and employment policies in the public sector[43]

Governments may also affect the wage structure through public sector employment and wage policies. Heller and Tait have found that in 38 developing countries, on the average, public jobs account for 44 percent of nonagricultural employment. This ratio is inversely correlated with per capita incomes. In the sample countries, regional averages are 59 percent in Africa, 36 percent in Asia, 27 percent in Latin America, compared with 24 percent in the developed countries. Also, the ratio tends to be higher in the countries that, at one time or another, adopted a socialist orientation; it is 87 percent in Benin, 81 percent in Zambia, 78 percent in Tanzania, 72 percent in India and 74 percent in Ghana.[44]

As the authors suggest, 'the clear message from these statistics is the significant impact that government policy on wages and salaries is likely to have on the overall remuneration of employees in the nonagricultural sector in developing countries.'[45] At the same time, the ratio of the avarage central government wage to GDP per capita tends to be inversely correlated with per capita incomes; it is 6.05 in Africa, 2.90 in Asia, 2.94 in Latin America, and 1.74 in the developed countries.[46]

According to the same authors, 'this situation is not necessarily surprising, as, in poorer countries, the educational requirements of public sector employment are often much higher than that of private sector employment.'[47] But differences in educational requirements provide only a partial explanation for such public-private wage differentials. Thus, in 1971, average wages were 16 percent higher in the government and 23 percent higher in parastatals than in the private sector in Tanzania, if adjustment is made for differences in occupational composition. Moreover, the scope of fringe benefits was considerably greater in the government and in parastatals than in the private sector.[48]

Wages in the public sector exceed wages in the private sector at lower, although not at higher, levels of education in Brazil, Colombia, Greece, Malaysia, and Portugal.[49] In contributing to higher wages for the less-educated worker, public sector wage policies tend to compress the wage distribution, thereby aggravating distortions in labor markets. Also, in some African developing countries (e.g. Mali and Tanzania) the government or the parastatals are residual employers for high school and/or university graduates, thereby introducing distortions as between private and social returns to education.

It has further been reported that in Pakistan increases in public sector wages spilled over to the private sector. Taking account of the effects of minimum wage legislation, the wage policies applied in the 1970s were said to be responsible for the major part of the increase in real wages during this period.[50]

All in all, regulations aimed at ensuring job security, social security schemes, minimum wage legislation, taxation of labor incomes, and wage and employment policies in the public sector tend to raise wages in developing countries, thereby contributing to losses in efficiency and in employment. Also, the progressive taxation of wages and public policies tend to reduce differences in remuneration between highly-skilled and unskilled occupations in the formal sector. Finally, distortions are created through differences in labor costs between the formal and the informal sectors, owing to the fact that labor legislation is rarely applied, or is evaded, in the informal sector.

Estimates on the effects of social security schemes and minimum wage legislation in the formal sector have been made in the NBER studies referred to above. The estimates show the resulting increases of labor costs to have been 27 percent in Brazil, 23 percent in the Ivory Coast, 20 percent in Tunisia, and 16 percent in Argentina in the late 1960s and early 1970s (Table 3.1).

III CAPITAL MARKET DISTORTIONS

Policy-imposed distortions of capital markets may originate in financial policies or in tax policies. In all instances, the measures applied affect the rate of return on alternative investments in physical and financial assets, including money.

Financial policies

High and unstable rates of inflation discriminate against the holding of financial assets unless they are fully indexed. In the absence of indexing, nominal interest rates on financial obligations would need to be raised in order to compensate for inflation. With variations in the rate of inflation, however, real rates of interest corresponding to a particular nominal rate vary and will be subject to uncertainty.

Also, the lack of indexing of demand deposits in the face of inflation represents a tax on non-interest bearing money holdings. This implicit tax, and the uncertainty relating to the real rate of interest on financial assets, tend to induce people to reduce their holdings of such assets. Reductions in the demand for financial assets, in turn, weaken the capacity of the banking system to fulfil its function of channelling funds to efficient production and investment.

Variations in real interest rates may occur even when financial assets are indexed. Thus, while Brazil applied indexing, real interest rates varied to a considerable extent as a result of changes in macroeconomic policies. Following negative real interest rates in earlier years, these rates turned slightly positive in the mid-1960s. Real interest rates again became negative in 1980 while a year later contractionary macroeconomic policies led to very high real rates. In 1985, Treasury bills were yielding 15 percent and certificates of deposit 20 percent in real terms, with bank lending rates exceeding 30 percent. Little change occurred in these rates following the monetary reform undertaken in February 1986.

The policies applied after 1979 led to high real interest rates in the countries of the Southern Cone. Real interest rates increased further as a result of the stabilization efforts undertaken by these countries in response to the debt crisis. In Argentina, lending rates were set at 6 percent a month following the application of the Austral Plan, when the rate of inflation was about 4 percent a month. Real interest rates are also high in Mexico, with monthly lending rates of 7 percent and prices rising 5 percent a month.[51]

Excessively high real interest rates have adverse effects on existing firms and may discourage investments that are socially profitable. They also engender demands for preferential treatment on the part of would-be borrowers. Interest preferences, in turn, introduce distortions in the allocation of savings among alternative investments.

While real interest rates have been high in recent years in several developing countries, traditionally they have been low and even negative.[52] The following discussion concentrates on the effects of this policy on savings, international capital flows, financial intermediation, and the allocation of savings among alternative investments.

The effect of interest rates on savings has been subject to much controversy. *Ceteris paribus*, low interest rates will favor present consumption over future consumption (savings). However, to the extent that people have definite savings objectives, for retirement or bequest, low interest rates may give rise to higher savings.

Estimates for Asian countries by Fry[53] showed a positive correlation between real interest rates and domestic savings in a cross-country–time-series framework. But, for the same countries, Giovannini[54] found that the real interest rate loses its statistical significance if the years 1967 and 1968 for Korea are excluded from the equation and if data for longer time periods and multi-year averages are used for the individual countries. Also, estimates of the intertemporal substitutability of consumption indicated that the expected path of consumption responded to changes in the real rate of interest in five out of 18 countries while the results were inconclusive for the rest.

In interpreting these estimates, one should note the possibilities of error involved in measuring consumption and savings in developing countries and in choosing appropriate rate of interest for the calculations.[55] In the savings equations, an additional problem is the inclusion of income growth among the independent variables. The impact of real interest rates on savings will be underestimated if real interest rates positively affect the rate of economic growth.

The existence of such a relationship has been shown in an IMF study, whose conclusion deserves full quotation:

> Repression of interest rates produces lower rates of saving, of investment, and, hence, of economic growth than would result from equilibrium interest rates, chiefly because domestic financial savings are discouraged in favor of either the accumulation of goods or of foreign assets. The experience of a number of countries confirms the dependence of domestic financial saving on interest rates. Subequilibrium

interest rates also encourage businesses to undertake investments with low rates of social return, such as the accumulation of inventories, rather than using their resources to build new plant and equipment. Various selective credit arrangements that accompany subequilibrium interest rates are not likely to improve the overall quality and productivity of investment.[56]

In fact, the econometric results obtained in intercountry relationships show that high real interest rates significantly increase the rate of growth of financial assets (the broadly defined money supply) as well as that of GDP. The relationships are confirmed if the part of the rate of growth of GDP (financial assets) uncorrelated with interest rate policy is introduced in the estimating equation.[57]

The results support McKinnon[58] and Shaw[59] who have emphasized the adverse effects of below-equilibrium, in particular negative, real interest rates on the development of financial markets. But, the growth of formal financial intermediaries might take place at the expense of unorganized money markets. If reserve requirements were higher in formal than in informal markets, the availability of credit might be reduced rather than increased.[60]

The McKinnon and Shaw conclusions, however, will obtain if the shift into financial assets in the formal market comes from physical assets, such as consumer durables and gold. McKinnon and Shaw suggest that total savings will rise in response to a financial reform that increases real interest rates. This conclusion is confirmed by the experience of the financial reforms of the 1970s in Uruguay.[61]

Also, informal credit markets may be less efficient than formal ones because of market segmentation, and may require substantial reserves, because of greater risks. Finally, below-equilibrium and, in particular, negative real interest rates in formal credit markets will adversely affect the allocation of savings among alternative investments.

In such a situation, self-investment at low, and even negative, real rates of return is encouraged, thus diverting funds from higher-yielding investments in the national economy. At the same time, with low and negative real interest rates creating an excess demand for funds, there will be credit rationing that introduces arbitrariness in the decision-making process, irrespective of whether rationing is done by the banks or by the governments.

The IMF report cited earlier supports the conclusion that inward orientation tends to be accompanied by repressed interest rates. But import substituting industries will receive priority in credit allocation both by the banks, because of the low risk involved in producing for the highly-protected domestic market, and by the government, which tends to favor such activities.[62]

At the same time, since the interest rate does not equilibrate the demand for, and the supply of, investible funds, the claimants for – and the recipients of – credits will include firms whose investments are not profitable at market-clearing interest rates. Furthermore, lending at below-equilibrium interest rates will encourage the excessive use of capital in those investments which do receive financing.

Policy-imposed differences between lending and borrowing rates will introduce additional distortions by increasing the wedge between the demand price and the supply price of credit. In 1982, in Turkey, such differences were due to the existence of noninterest bearing liquidity and reserve requirements, compulsory contributions to the Differential Interest Rate Rebate Fund, and the financial transcations tax on the revenue-earning operations of the banks. These items raised the interest rates to lenders to 76 percent, compared with an interest rate of 50 percent on six-month deposits.[63]

A further consideration is that interest rates for savings which are below-equilibrium will induce private capital exports in search of higher returns. From the available evidence, it appears that low domestic interest rates have contributed to capital flight, in particular in Mexico whose financial markets are the most closely linked with US markets.[64]

Also, both above- and below-equilibrium interest rates to lenders can be expected to give rise to interventions in credit markets. When interest rates are above equilibrium, borrowers will clamor for preferential rates; when they are below, credit allocation will be necessary.

A review of the financial policies of ten developing countries in the 1970–82 period has shown the prevalence of interventions in financial markets among developing countries. Among the countries under consideration, interest rate differentials between preferential and nonpreferential credits were especially high in Peru (69 percent) and in Turkey (37 percent) in 1982. The government control of financial resources extended to one-fifth of the total in Peru and to three-fifths in Turkey; this ratio was 60–70 percent in Bangladesh and nearly 100 percent in Nigeria.[65]

Tax policies[66]

As noted above, revisions of the income tax schedule tend to lag behind inflation, thereby shifting income recipients from lower to higher brackets. Delays in the reevaluation of balance sheets may also increase tax liabilities for business enterprises as most developing countries do not use inflation accounting.

But, if investments are financed from borrowed funds, the loss in the real value of invested capital is compensated by the gain obtained through the decline in the real value of domestic debt. There is no compensation, however, if investments are financed from internally generated funds.

Correspondingly, the taxable value of profits is overstated, and reliance on loan capital is encouraged at the expense of the use of retained earnings for investment.

Further problems arise in regard to interest income since the principal loses value as a result of inflation. In Colombia, for example, nominal interest receipts are taxed at a rate of 18 percent but the effective tax rate of real (inflation-adjusted) earnings was 67.5 percent in 1983.[67]

But even if full adjustment were made for inflation, or inflation were eliminated, various features of the tax system of developing countries will give rise to distortions. To begin with, taxing the amount saved as well as the return on savings introduces a bias in favor of present and against future consumption. Yet, this is the case in most developing countries where incomes from work as well as from capital (interest income and dividends) are taxed. Only Uruguay taxes consumption rather than income.

Moreover, many developing countries follow the US practice of taxing corporate profits as well as dividends paid from these profits. At the same time, the double taxation of corporate profits discourages corporate savings, investment in shares, and hence the development of capital markets, while introducing a bias in favor of debt and against equity financing.

Taxing the earnings of capital also encourages capital flight. This conclusion applies, in particular, to the taxation of interest income, where the choice is between domestic and foreign portfolio investments. But it also applies to taxation on capital gains.

The above considerations favor the use of consumption (indirect) taxes, which may take the form of cascade-type and value added taxes. Most developing countries and all developed countries apply the so-called destination principle, under which indirect taxes are rebated on exports and imposed on imports at the same rate as on domestic products.

The application of the destination principle, however, raises problems in countries using cascade-type indirect taxes. Such taxes are levied at every stage of fabrication and their cumulative effects are difficult to gauge. Also, the burden of taxes on consumption varies according to the number of stages, thereby encouraging the vertical integration of production and discouraging the consumption of commodities that go through a greater number of stages.

To escape these difficulties, a number of developing countries, including Colombia, Korea, and Mexico, have followed the European example in adopting value added taxation, which equalizes the tax burden on all consumer goods. Also, exports are exempted from the value added tax and receive rebates for taxes paid at earlier stages of fabrication. Nevertheless, in some countries, such as Mexico, the real value of the rebate is reduced by inflation because of the passage of time between collection and reimbursement.

Further questions relate to the use of investment incentives that are widely employed in developing countries. Among the four countries covered in a World Bank study, tax credits are provided in Colombia, Korea, and Mexico, tax discounts in Colombia, and tax certificates (for paying other taxes) in Mexico. Also, tax holidays are used in Thailand and special reduced tax rates in Colombia. All four countries permit accelerated depreciation on new investment.[68]

Investment incentives tend to offset the tax disincentives for savings referred to above. They may even overcompensate for these disincentives, thereby creating a bias in the incentive system in favor of savings. At the same time, such incentives favor corporate savings over private savings.

There is a prima facie case for investment incentives to exports that are discriminated against under import protection. A case may also be made for providing tax concessions for research and development whose effects will often spread from one firm to another. Incentives favoring particular activities will, however, distort the system of incentives, unless there is evidence of external economies.

Investment incentives tend to favor large-scale over small and medium-scale enterprises in most developing countries. In Pakistan, for example, small investors faced capital costs more than twice those of large-scale firms until 1972.[69]

Also, there are considerable differences in regard to the sectoral pattern of investment incentives among the four countries covered by the World Bank study referred to earlier. Following selective promotion in the 1970s, Korea has practically ceased discrimination among sectors in the early 1980s and it limits tax concessions to export activities and to research and development expenditures. Having earlier promoted the steel and automobile industries, Colombia has also moved towards neutrality across sectors while granting tax incentives to export activities. In turn, Thailand provides limited incentives to projects that are considered desirable from the national point of view but may not be financed without tax incentives. Finally, Mexico has a complicated system of investment incentives, under which the extent of incentives depends on the sector as well as on the location of the investment.[70]

At the same time, developing countries employ a variety of instruments to provide investment incentives. The use of these instruments may entail discrimination between capital-intensive and labor-intensive projects as well as between long-lived and short-lived projects.

Tax incentives that reduce the cost of capital will discriminate in favor of capital-intensive and against labor-intensive projects. This has been shown to be the case in several of the countries in the NBER studies. Thus, it has been estimated that the tax measures applied reduced the cost of capital, on the average, by 12 percent in the Ivory Coast, by 10 percent in Pakistan, and by 2 percent in Korea (Table 3.1).

It has further been shown that initial tax allowances, tax credits on net

investment, tax credits on gross investments which are set against depreciation, as well as interest subsidies distort incentives in favor of long-lived
investment. Accelerated depreciation rates generally have similar effects.
In turn, investment allowances and tax credits on gross investment over
and above regular depreciation do not affect the choice between long-lived
and short-lived investments.[71]

IV EFFECTS OF THE POLICIES APPLIED

Combined effects of factor and product market distortions

Table 3.1 shows the effects of distortions in product, labor, and capital
markets on the prices of labor and capital in the countries of the NBER
study during the period spanning the early 1960s and the early 1970s. It is
apparent that capital market distortions (credit allocation and tax preferences) were by far the largest in Pakistan, where the effect was to reduce
the average cost of capital by 58 percent. It was followed by the Ivory
Coast (15 percent), Korea (10 percent), Argentina (9 percent), Tunisia (6
percent), and Brazil (4 percent), with no distortions observed in Hong
Kong.

The relative importance of distortions in labor and in capital markets
also varies among countries, with the former being more important in
Argentina, Brazil, the Ivory Coast, and Tunisia and the latter in Pakistan
and Korea. However, Brazil shifts into the second group if account is taken
of reductions in capital costs due to trade policy.

Further interest attaches to the relative effects of trade policies and of
factor market distortions on wage-rental ratios. Apart from Chile and
Tunisia, factor market distortions predominated during the period under
consideration, often by a large margin. This was the case also in Pakistan,
where both trade policy-induced distortions and factor market distortions
were the largest among the eight countries, but the latter was much more
important than the former.

It follows that the combined effects of distortions in product and factor
markets on the wage–rental ratio were the largest in Pakistan (316 percent). These distortions increase the wage–rental ratio in all other countries as well, the exception being Hong Kong that was free of product and
factor market distortions. The ranking was Tunisia, 87 percent; the Ivory
Coast, 45 percent; Argentina, 38 percent; Brazil, 31 percent; and Korea,
11 percent (for lack of information, estimates could not be made for
Chile).

The ranking changes if the employment effects of product and factor
market distortions are considered (Table 3.2). At the same time, comparability between the two sets of estimates is reduced by reason of the fact that

for several countries (Brazil, Ivory Coast, Pakistan, and Korea), the estimates refer to a different year. And, the effects of distortions on employment have also been estimated for Colombia and Indonesia (no estimates are provided for Hong Kong, where there are no policy-imposed product or factor market distortions).

In both import-competing and export industries the impact of factor market distortions on employment was the largest in Pakistan. It was followed by Tunisia, Indonesia, and the Ivory Coast as far as the first, and by Brazil, Colombia, and Indonesia as far as the second, group of industries is concerned. Finally, differences in labor coefficients between import-substituting and export industries were the largest in Indonesia, followed by Brazil, Colombia, and Pakistan.

The effects of factor market distortions on product markets

Following Gottfried Haberler's pathbreaking contribution (1950), a large number of articles in economic journals have dealt with the implications of factor market distortions for product markets. It has been shown that, under certain conditions, these distortions can lead to the wrong pattern of specialization, in the sense that the 'wrong' commodity, i.e. which does not correspond to the country's factor endowment, will be exported and the 'wrong' commodity imported.

As we have seen, to a greater or a lesser extent, policy-imposed factor market distortions in the developing countries will cause the wage-rental ratio to rise. At the same time, available evidence suggests that, on the average, this has not led to factor reversal in the sense that a developing country would import labor-intensive and export capital-intensive commodities.[72]

This does not mean, however, that factor reversal would not have occurred in regard to particular commodities, with the country importing some labor intensive and exporting some capital-intensive commodities as increases in wage–rental ratios raised the cost of the former and reduced the cost of the latter. Also, international trade is discouraged as a result of policy-imposed distortions in factor markets, which raise wage–rental ratios.

Another way to approach the issue is to consider the loss of exports that may occur, owing to distortions in factor markets. This possibility has been investigated by Anne Krueger who has tested for the existence of a statistical relationship between labor market distortions and exports in a comparative framework.

Krueger has taken the ratio of the UN daily per diem allowance to per capita incomes as a proxy for the realism of the real wage, on the grounds that the former reflects largely the cost of labor-intensive nontraded goods – and hence that of labor – in the country concerned. She has subsequently correlated this variable with per capita exports, taken as an indicator of a country's success or failure to exploit its export potential.

The tests for 33 countries in four benchmark years show a high degree of statistical significance for the real wage proxy while the coefficient of determination is in the 0.17–0.24 range. The elasticity is about 0.5, indicating that 1 percent increase in the real wage relative to per capita incomes would reduce exports by one-half of 1 percent.[73]

CONCLUSIONS

This essay has provided evidence on the unfavorable effects which factor market distortions have on the efficiency of resource allocation and on employment in developing countries. It has further been shown that policy-imposed distortions in product markets tend to aggravate these adverse effects in the countries concerned.

Rationing in the product, labor, and capital markets also contributes to inefficiency in resource allocation by generating rent-seeking activities. Such activities misdirect productive energies and tend to lead to excess investments in activities that stand to benefit from rationing.

Inefficiencies in resource allocation, in turn, will have adverse effects on economic growth. For one thing, less is saved and invested as the distortions lower income levels. For another thing, the efficiency of investments is reduced as capital is directed into industries that do not correspond to the country's comparative advantage.

It may be objected that there will also exist endogenous distortions (factor market imperfections) in developing countries that the policy makers may wish to remedy. Thus, it had long been argued that in a number of these countries the marginal productivity of labor is low, and even nil, because of the existence of surplus labor, and that the prevalence of informal credit markets provides evidence of imperfections in capital markets. The validity of these propositions has increasingly been brought into question, however.

To begin with, drawing on macroeconomic as well as on microeconomic evidence available by the mid-1970s, Berry and Sabot concluded that 'labor markets functions at a comparatively high level of efficiency'[74] in developing countries. Also, a subsequent review of rural labor markets has disproved the contention that the marginal product of labor in agriculture would be nil.[75] These and other pieces of evidence have led Anne Krueger to conclude that 'if earnings do not more-or-less appropriately reflect trade-offs and relative scarcity values of different types of labor, the observed distortion is more likely to be a consequence of government intervention than it is of inherent "market failure".'[76]

In fact, to the extent that wages overstate the opportunity cost of labor, as has been alleged, government interventions which raise the price of labor have aggravated these imperfections. Public interventions in labor markets thus have had the opposite of the desired effect.

Finally, it should be understood that informal credit markets in the developing countries are often the result of policy distortions that limit the scope of financial intermediation. And, in cases when this was not the case, informal credit markets should be regarded as a normal phase of the development of financial intermediation, which permits bringing together lenders and borrowers in cases when the cost of doing so through formal channels would be overly high because of lack of information, distance, and other factors.

NOTES

1. The latter have been termed 'endogenous,' as opposed to 'policy-imposed,' distortions by J. N. Bhagwati, 'The Generalized Theory of Distortions and Welfare,' in N. J. Bhagwati, R. W. Jones, R. A. Mundell, and J. Vanek (eds), *Trade, Balance of Payments and Growth*, Papers in International Economics in Honor of Charles P. Kindleberger (Amsterdam: North-Holland, 1971) pp. 69–90.
2. B. Balassa, G. Bueno, P. P. Kuczynski, and M. H. Simonsen, *Toward Renewed Economic Growth in Latin America* (Mexico, DF: El Colegio de Mexico, Rio de Janeiro: Fundação Getulio Vargas, Washington, DC: Institute for International Economics, 1986) Ch. 4.
3. A. Lanyi, and R. Saracoglu, 'Interest Rate Policies in Developing Countries,' Occasional Paper 22 (Washington DC: International Monetary Fund, 1983) p. 14.
4. A. O. Krueger, *Trade and Employment in Developing Countries 3. Synthesis and Conclusions* (Chicago: The University of Chicago Press, 1983) pp. 145–50.
5. In Pakistan, they indicate the effects of policy changes undertaken in the second half of the 1960s while the results for this country reported in Table 3.1 relate to the early 1960s.
6. This was the case in trade with Latin American countries, which dominated Chile's exports of manufactured goods, but not for Chile's trade with the developed countries.
7. T. P. Schultz, 'Effective Protection and the Distribution of Personal Income by Sector in Colombia,' in A. O. Krueger (ed.), *Trade and Employment in Developing Countries 2. Factor Supply and Substitution* (Chicago: University of Chicago Press, 1982) pp. 109–10.
8. Ibid., p. 110.
9. A. O. Krueger, 'The Political Economy of a Rent-Seeking Society,' *American Economic Review*, LXIV (1974) p. 110.
10. B. Balassa, 'Exports, Policy Choices, and Economic Growth in Developing Countries after the 1973 Oil Shock,' *Journal of Development Economics*, XVIII (1985), pp. 23–35.
11. R. Banerji, and J. Riedel, 'Industrial Employment Expansion under Alternative Trade Strategies: Case of India and Taiwan, 1950–1970,' *Journal of Development Economics*, VII (1980) Tables 1 and 2.

12. Balassa, Bueno, Kuczynski, and Simonsen, *Toward Renewed Economic Growth in Latin America*, p. 134.
13. B. Fischer, and D. Spinanger, 'Factor Market Distortions and Export Performance: An Eclectic Review of the Evidence,' Working Paper No. 259 (Kiel: Institute of World Economics, 1986) pp. 25–8.
14. D. Laidler, 'Entrepreneurship and Labour Market Mobility,' in *Growth and Entrepreneurship: Opportunities and Challenges in a Changing World* (Paris; International Chamber of Commerce, 1981) p. 81.
15. United States Department of Health and Human Services, Social Security Administration, *Social Security Programs Throughout the World 1981*, Research Report No. 58 (Washington, DC, 1984).
16. C. Mesa-Lago, *Social Security in Latin America. Pressure Groups, Stratification and Inequality* (Pittsburgh: University of Pittsburgh Press, 1978) pp. 50, 96.
17. W. A. Lewis, 'Development with Unlimited Supplies of Labour,' *Manchester School*, XXII (1954) pp. 139–62.
18. Mesa-Lago, *Social Security in Latin America*, p. 16.
19. J. L. Carvahlo, and C. L. S. Haddad, 'Foreign Trade Strategies and Employment in Brazil,' in A. O. Krueger, H. B. Lary, T. Monson, and N. Akrasanee (eds), *Trade and Employment in Developing Countries 1. Individual Studies* (Chicago: University of Chicago Press, 1981) p. 67.
20. A. O. Krueger, 'The Relationship between Trade, Employment, and Development,' paper prepared for the 25th Anniversary Symposium on The State of Development Economics: Progress and Perspectives, Economic Growth Center (New Haven, Conn.: Yale University, 1986) mimeo, p. 16.
21. This section derives from B. Balassa, 'Public Finance and Social Policy – Explanation of Trends and Developments: The Case of Developing Countries,' in *Public Finance and Social Policy* (Detroit, Michigan: Wayne State University Press, 1983) pp. 41–58.
22. L. G. Reynolds, and P. Gregory, *Wages, Productivity and Industrialization in Puerto Rico* (Homewood Ill.: Richard D. Irwin, 1965) p. 60.
23. Ibid., p. 100.
24. S. Watanabe, 'Minimum Wages in Developing Countries: Myth and Reality,' *International Labour Review*, CXIII (1976) pp. 347.
25. L. Squire, *Employment Policy in Developing Countries – A Survey of Issues and Evidence*, A World Bank Research Publication (New York: Oxford University Press, 1981) p. 111.
26. International Labour Office, *Minimum Wage Fixing and Economic Development* (Geneva, 1968) p. 19.
27. G. Starr, *Minimum Wage Fixing* (Geneva: International Labour Office, 1981) pp. 160–84.
28. Krueger, *Trade and Employment in Developing Countries 3. Synthesis and Conclusions*, p. 131.
29. T. Monson, 'Trade Strategies and Employment in the Ivory Coast,' in Krueger, Lary, Monson, and Akrasanee (eds), *Trade and Employment in Developing Countries 1. Individual Country Studies* pp. 273–4.
30. J. Schaafsma, and W. D. Walsh, 'Employment and Labor Supply Effects of the Minimum Wage: Some Pooled Time-Series Estimates from Canadian Provincial Data,' *Canadian Journal of Economics*, XLI (1983) p. 97.
31. Krueger, *Trade and Employment in Developing Countries 3. Synthesis and Conclusions*, p. 132.
32. Watanabe, 'Minimum Wages in Developing Countries,' p. 354.

33. 30 April 1983.
34. Starr, *Minimum Wage Fixing*, p. 15.
35. An attempt to measure these effects has been made in the United States. It has been found that the income distributional effects of minimum wage legislation are very weak and
    'even if the elasticity of demand for low-wage labor is as low as 0.2, the reduction in national income is as large as the entire gain to the lower half of the income distribution when marginal taxation effects are ignored, and the reduction in national income is about twice as large as the net gain to the lower half of the income distribution when they are incorporated,' W. R. Johnson and E. K. Browning, 'The Distributional and Efficiency Effects of Increasing the Minimum Wage: A Simulation,' *American Economic Review*, LXIII (1983) p. 211.
36. Watanabe, 'Minimum Wages in Developing Countries,' p. 356.
37. Starr, *Minimum Wage Fixing*, p. 140.
38. Krueger, 'The Relationship between Trade, Employment, and Development,' p. 16.
39. B. Balassa, *et al.*, *Turkey: Industrialization and Trade Strategy*. A World Bank Country Study (Washington, DC; World Bank, 1982) Ch. 4.
40. B. Balassa, *et al.*, *Morocco: Industrial Incentives and Export Promotion*, A World Bank Country Study (Washington, DC: World Bank, 1984) Table 3.3.
41. C. Leechor, 'Tax Policy and Tax Reform in Semi-Industrialized Countries,' Industry and Finance Series, Vol. 13 (Washington, DC: World Bank, 1986) p. 14.
42. Balassa, *Morocco: Industrial Incentives and Export Promotion* p. 104.
43. This section derives from Balassa, 'Public Finance and Social Policy – Explanation of Trends and Development: The Case of Developing Countries.'
44. P. S. Heller, and A. A. Tait, 'Government Employment and Pay: Some International Comparisons,' Occasional Paper 24 (Washington, DC: International Monetary Fund, 1983) pp. 7, 42–3.
45. Heller and Tait, p. 7.
46. Ibid., p. 18.
47. Ibid.
48. D. L. Lindauer, and R. H. Sabot, 'The Public/Private Wage Differential in Poor Urban Economy,' *Journal of Development Economics*, XII (1983) pp. 141–3.
49. G. Psacharopoulos, 'Education and Private versus Public Sector Pay,' *Labour and Society*, VIII (1983) pp. 123–34.
50. S. Guisinger, with the assistance of M. Irfan, 'Trade Policies and Employment: The Case of Pakistan,' in Krueger, Lary, Monson, and Akrasanee (eds), *Trade and Employment in Developing Countries 1 Individual Studies*, pp. 325–6.
51. Balassa, Bueno, Kuczynski and Simonsen, *Toward Renewed Economic Growth in Latin America*, pp. 105–6.
52. It has been estimated that the adoption of below-equilibrium interest rates reduced capital costs by 53 percent in Pakistan and between 9 and 3 percent in Argentina, Korea, Tunisia, Brazil, and the Ivory Coast in the early 1960s and the early 1970s (Table 3.1). In interpreting these estimates, it should be understood that capital costs include the cost of machinery and equipment.
53. M. J. Fry, 'Interest Rates in Asia' (Honolulu: University of Hawaii, 1981), mimeo.
54. A. Giovannini, 'Saving and the Real Interest Rates in LDC's,' *Journal of Development Economics*, XVIII (1985) pp. 197–218.

55. In view of these error possibilities, it may be surprising that statistically significant results have been obtained for five countries (also, in two additional countries, *t*-values exceed 2).
56. Lanyi and Saracoglu, 'Interest Rate Policies in Developing Countries,' p. 19.
57. Ibid., Table 4.
58. R. I. McKinnon, *Money & Capital in Economic Development* (Washington, DC: The Brookings Institution, 1973).
59. E. S. Shaw, *Financial Deepening in Economic Development* (New York: Oxford University Press, 1973).
60. S. van Wijnbergen, 'Interest Rate Management in LDC's,' *Journal of Monetary Economics*, XII (1983) pp. 433–52.
61. At the same time, a positive response of savings to interest rates was established in the pre-reform, but not in the post-reform, period. J. de Melo, and J. Tybout, 'The Effect of Financial Liberalization on Savings and Investment in Uruguay,' *Economic Development and Cultural Change*, XXXIV (1986) pp. 561–87
62. Evidence on the latter point is provided in Krueger, *Trade and Employment in Developing Countries 3. Synthesis and Conclusions*, p. 129.
63. Balassa *et al.*, *Turkey: Industrialization and Trade Strategy*, Table 3.8. While changes have been made in subsequent years, a considerable spread between lending and deposit rates remains.
64. In the case of Mexico, the domestic interest rate variable has been highly significant in explaining changes in capital flight in a time-series investigation. And while this has not been the case for other countries, it should be understood that data on capital flight are subject to considerable error. J. T. Cuddington, 'Capital Flight: Estimates, Issues, and Explanations,' CPD Discussion Paper No. 1985–51 (Washington, DC: World Bank, 1986) Table 3.
65. J. A. Hanson, and C. R. Neal, 'Interest Rate Policies in Selected Developing Countries 1970–1982,' Industry and Finance Series, Vol. 14 (Washington, DC: World Bank, 1986) pp. 37–9.
66. This section draws on Balassa, Bueno, Kuczynski, and Simonsen, *Toward Renewed Economic Growth in Latin America*, Ch. 3.
67. Leechor, 'Tax Policy and Tax Reform in Semi-Industrialized Countries,' p. 20.
68. Ibid., pp. 17–18.
69. Guisinger, 'Trade Policies and Employment,' p. 333.
70. Leechor, 'Tax Policy and Tax Reform in Semi-Industrialized Countries,' pp. 35–7.
71. R. Boadway, 'Investment incentives, Corporate Taxation, and Efficiency in the Allocation of Capital,' *Economic Journal*, LXXXVIII (1978) pp. 480.
72. In the case of Chile, preferential trade with other Latin American countries, rather than factor-market distortions, appears to have given the perverse result noted above.
73. Krueger, 'The Relationship between Trade, Employment, and Development,' pp. 36–9.
74. A. Berry, and R. M. Sabot, 'Labour Market Performance in Developing Countries: A Survey,' *World Development*, VI (1978) p. 1230.
75. H. P. Binswanger, and M. R. Rosenzweig, *Contractual Arrangements, Employment, and Wages in Rural Labor Markets in Asia* (New Haven, Conn.; Yale University Press, 1984) Ch. 1.
76. Krueger, 'The Relationship between Trade, Employment, and Development,' pp. 17–18.

Part II
Policy Choices and External Constraints
in Developing Countries

Essay 4   The Cambridge Group and the Developing Countries

INTRODUCTION

The policy prescriptions of the Cambridge Economic Policy Group (CEPG) for the United Kingdom are well known. They involve all-round protection of British industry that would allegedly permit reaching simultaneously higher output levels, lower unemployment rates, and lower inflation rates. Since first presented in February 1975, the views of the Cambridge Group have been several times and have been repeatedly subjected to criticism.[1]

The CEPG's views on developing country policies are less well known. Yet, these views should command interest, in part because they purport to provide policy prescriptions for all developing countries and in part because they have influenced the policies applied in at least two countries, Mexico and Tanzania.

Section I of this chapter will review the policy prescriptions of the Cambridge Group for developing countries and subject them to scrutiny. Section II will examine the experience of developing countries with outward and inward orientation. Section III will critically analyze pessimistic views on the prospects for developing country exports. Sections IV and V, respectively, will provide an appraisal of CEPG policy advice to Mexico and Tanzania in the light of the recent experience of these countries.

I CEPG POLICY PRESCRIPTIONS FOR DEVELOPING COUNTRIES[2]

The Cambridge Group suggests the need for rapid industrialization in the developing countries. At the same time, it claims that economic growth in the developed countries is unlikely to be sufficiently rapid to generate desired rates of industrial expansion in the developing countries through exports, and hence these countries 'will have to rely much more on their internal dynamics – on the growth of internal demand rather than on world market forces – to generate economic expansion. They will need greater import substitution, more internal technological development and more economic and technological cooperation between themselves.'[3]

It is added that 'the strategic policy perspective outlined here is rather different from that of many orthodox economists and of international organizations such as the World Bank and IMF which advocate export-led growth as an answer to the economic problems of the developing countries.'[4] In reference to the export-oriented strategy followed by four East Asian developing countries (Hong Kong, Korea, Singapore, and Taiwan), it is alleged that

> there is an obvious fallacy in the view that such a strategy can succeed for all or even the leading newly industrializing countries in a slow-growing world economy. Studies by Nayyar and Cline suggest that even on very conservative assumptions about increased growth of exports from a small member of other newly industrializing countries, and favorable assumptions about expansion of world trade, the manufactured exports of the developing countries to the advanced countries would soon exceed the latter's threshold levels of tolerance in many industries and thus invite retaliation or widespread protection.[5]

Emphasis is further given to the vulnerability of open economies, with reference made to Keynes who in the midst of the Great Depression suggested the need for greater national self-sufficiency in order to reduce the vulnerability of the British economy to foreign events. In this connection, a contrast is drawn between the experience of two large Latin American (Brazil and Mexico) and two large Asian (India and China) economies.

It is maintained that 'Brazil and Mexico are today in deep economic crisis, and unless the world economy has a spectacular revival or other arrangements between the borrowers and lenders can be negotiated, these two countries are likely to be condemned to negative or very low growth for much of the present decade.'[6] By contrast, so it is claimed, 'China and India have done relatively very well in the recent period despite the world economic crisis. The main reason for their success lies in the fact that since their independence, these countries have deliberately followed policies of self-reliance, based on import substitution, and inward looking industrial strategies.'[7] It is further alleged that 'the essential reason for the economic differences between Brazil and Mexico, on the one hand, and China and India, on the other, is that during the last 15 years the former countries chose to follow export-oriented, outward-looking industrial strategies based on multinational investment and foreign debt.'[8]

But can other developing countries follow the example of China and India? It is admitted that their larger size 'means that they are, in principle, much more capable of insulating themselves from the impulses of the world economy.'[9] In turn, 'industrialization in smaller developing countries does require much more intra-developing country trade, which is more likely to increase and to aid the development of all participating countries, if it is planned than free trade.'[10]

II EXPERIENCE WITH OUTWARD AND INWARD ORIENTATION

The proposition that slow growth in the industrial countries will not provide sufficient impetus to economic growth in the developing countries harks back to the days of Nurkse and Prebisch. The CEPG has also revived Prebisch's policy prescription for industrial protection in the developing countries. In this way, the recommendations made for the United Kingdom are extended by the Cambridge Group to all the developing countries.

In support of its pessimistic views on economic growth through trade, the paper referred to above cites Arthur Lewis' Nobel Prize lecture 'The Slowing Down of the Engine of Growth.'[11] Lewis assumes that 'LDCs want their GDP to grow at 6 percent per annum, and that this requires their imports to grow at 6 percent.'[12] He further assumes that 'industrial production in MDCs grows more slowly than it was growing before 1973, and that the imports of these countries grow only 4 percent a year, over the next twenty years'.[13] The latter proposition is derived from the relationship Lewis purports to have established between primary product imports and economic growth in the more developed countries (MDCs). According to Lewis, this relationship was quantitatively the same over a hundred years, with an income elasticity of import demand of 0.87. He concludes that economic growth in the LDCs is limited by growth in the MDCs as manufactured export expansion could not compensate for the slow growth of primary exports because of market limitations in the MDCs.

In a critique of Lewis's thesis, James Riedel suggests that 'the elasticity assumptions on which the trade engine theory is based apply best to traditional LDC exports of broadly non-competing tropical commodities. Such products, however, have been shown to constitute a relatively small and declining share of export in most developing countries'.[14] In the case of all other commodities, primary as well as manufactured, the developing countries can increase their export market shares. This, in turn, depends largely on the policies followed.

In the case of primary exports, which compete with production in the developed countries, there is evidence that the pursuit of import substitution-oriented policies by developing countries contributed to a substantial decline in their world market shares after the Second World War.[15] In turn, subsequent changes in policies have led to some spectacular successes, such as the emergence of Brazil as a major exporter of soybeans.

The pursuit of import-substitution oriented policies was also responsible for the decline in India's share in the combined manufactured exports of the eleven major NICs (Argentina, Brazil, Chile, Colombia, Mexico, Israel, Yugoslavia, Korea, Singapore, Taiwan, and India) from 65 percent in 1953 to 51 percent in 1960, 31 percent in 1966, and 10 percent in 1973, with further decreases occurring in subsequent years. In turn, outward-oriented economies not only raised their export market shares in the combined exports of the eleven countries, but increasingly established positions in industrial country markets. As a result, the share of developing country exports in the consumption of manufactured goods in the major industrial countries rose from 0.2 percent in 1963 to 0.9 percent in 1973 and, subsequently, to 2.3 percent in 1983.[16]

Also, in a time-series analysis of data for 27 developing countries in the postwar period, it has been shown that competitiveness greatly dominates external market factors in determining the rate of growth of exports.[17] Intercountry differences in competitiveness, in turn, are explained by differences in the policies applied. Whereas outward-oriented economies provided, on balance, similar incentives to exports and import substitution, and to agriculture and manufacturing, inward-oriented economies biased the system of incentives in favor of import substitution in industry and against primary and manufactured exports.

At the same time, the growth of exports and that of output are highly correlated. Nor is this correlation limited to manufactured goods. Thus, for the eleven countries cited, the Spearman rank correlation coefficient between export and output growth was 0.6 in agriculture, 0.7 in manufacturing, and 0.9 for the national economy, taken as a whole, in the 1960–73 period; the coefficients are statistically significant at the 1 percent level in all cases.[18]

The empirical results are hardly affected if export growth rates are correlated with the growth of output *net* of exports. These results indicate the favorable indirect effects of exports that operate via input–output relationships and higher incomes in the export sector. More generally, apart from the static benefits of resource allocation according to comparative advantage, export expansion contributes to economic growth through the exploitation of economies of scale, increased capacity utilization and, most importantly, technological change that is induced by the carrot and the stick of foreign competition. As a result, the technological lead of the industrial countries over outward-oriented developing economies has narrowed over time.[19]

By contrast, import substitution behind high protection involves static losses due to inefficient resource allocation as well as dynamic losses owing to domestic market limitations and insufficient inducements for technological change. Thus, while Friedrich List and his successors recommended temporary protection on infant industry grounds in the expectation that the protected industries will eventually grow up, continued protection has led to an increased technological gap in inward-oriented economies *vis-à-vis* the industrial countries.

Intercountry differences in economic performance may be indicated by incremental capital–output ratios that show the amount of investment necessary for a unit increase in output. In the 1960–73 period, these ratios ranged between 1.8 and 2.4 in the East Asian economies that followed outward-oriented policies; they were between 5.5 and 6.0 in India and Chile that pursued an inward-oriented development strategy. Thus, the latter group of countries required nearly three times the investment to achieve the same increase in output as the countries of the first group. At the same time, incremental capital–output ratios declined after 1965 in the large Latin American countries, which carried out policy reforms in the mid-sixties.

Nor were differences in incremental capital–output ratios compensated by differences in savings ratios. Rather, outward-oriented economies that adopted positive real interest rates had higher than average savings ratios. Correspondingly, average GNP growth rates in the 1960–73 period were between 9 and 10 percent in the three East Asian economies and between 5 and 7 percent in the four larger Latin American countries, but averaged only 3 percent in India and Chile.

Rapid economic expansion, in turn, contributed to employment creation in outward-oriented economies that was further enhanced by the high labor-intensity of their exports. With employment growth generating pressures for wage increases, income distribution also improved as a result. Outward orientation thus had more favorable effects on raising the incomes of the poor, thereby providing for basic needs, than inward orientation.

But how about vulnerability to external shocks under outward orientation? The adverse balance-of-payments effects of external shocks in the form of increases in oil prices and the world recession after 1973 were indeed greater in this case, owing to the higher export and import shares under outward-orientation. But, outward-oriented economies were better able to surmount the effects of external shocks, re-establishing and in some cases exceeding pre-1973 growth rates.

By contrast, countries such as Brazil and Mexico, which again turned inward in response to external shocks, experienced a decline in economic growth rates. The predicament in which these countries presently find themselves, then, may be explained by their increased inward-orientation rather than by outward-orientation as it has been alleged. At the same time, if appropriate policies are followed, Brazil and Mexico can resume their economic growth rather than stagnating for a decade as CEPG suggests.

In turn, after a long period of inward orientation, India has come to recognize the need for greater outward orientation. Correspondingly, over the last decade exports have received increased incentives and imports have been liberalized. While the process has been slow, easing the severe constraints under which the India economy operated has permitted a resurgence of economic growth.

Turkey went much further in reforming its economic policies than India. The January 1980 reform measures included a substantial devaluation, export subsidies, import liberalization, as well as the freeing of prices. After an initial slowdown associated with the application of stabilization measures, Turkey averaged GNP growth rates of 5 percent in the 1981–4 period. Rapid economic growth resulted from the expansion of exports that rose by 170 percent between 1980 and 1984 in dollar terms, representing increases in market shares in the industrial countries and, in particular, entry into new markets in the Middle East.

Thus, the post-1973 experience does not modify the conclusions reached in regard to the earlier period concerning the favorable effects of exports on economic growth. In fact, in an econometric study of 43 developing countries it has been shown that trade orientation in the initial year, as well as reliance on export promotion in response to the subsequent external shocks, explain much of intercountry differences in economic growth rates in the 1973–8 period.[20]

Nor does China represent an exception. Continued reliance on centralized physical planning and isolation from the world economy led to an increase in incremental capital–output ratios from 1.7 in 1953–7 to 3.8 in 1971–5, and even this ratio is understated because of the overestimation of the rate of economic growth due to the overpricing of industrial goods.[21] The increased inefficiency of its economic structure, in turn, led the Chinese authorities to give a greater role to market forces, first in agriculture and subsequently in industry, and to increase linkages with the world economy.

III PROSPECTS FOR DEVELOPING COUNTRY EXPORTS

The question remains if exports can be driving force for economic growth in a large number of developing countries. In support of its negative answer to the question, CEPG cites the conclusions of William Cline's paper with the provocative title 'Can the East Asian Export Model be Generalized?'[22]

Cline estimated that the manufactured exports of other developing countries would have to increase sevenfold in order to match the East Asian 'norm' in terms of the ratio of manufactured exports to GNP, with allowance made for differences in population size and per capita incomes. Reaching this ratio, in turn, would involve raising the LDC share in the manufactured imports of the seven major developed countries from 17 to 61 percent. According to Cline, these calculations indicate that it is not feasible to generalize the East Asian model of export-led development across countries.[23]

The prospects are less forbidding if one considers the prospective shares of the developing countries in the consumption of manufactured goods in the developed countries. This share was approximately 1.3 percent in 1976, the year the estimates refer to, in the industrial countries, on the average.[24] The projected increase in the manufactured exports of the developing countries would raise this ratio to 9.1 percent on the assumption that the consumption of manufactured goods in the industrial countries would remain unchanged. The introduction of lower-priced goods imported from the developing countries would, however, tend to increase manufacturing consumption.

Nor can it be assumed that countries at varying levels of development, ranging from Mali to Israel, would attain the manufactured exports norm of the four East Asian countries within a time period that has practical relevance for the problem at hand. Cline himself makes calculations for a limited group of seven countries (Argentina, Brazil, Colombia, Mexico, Indonesia, Israel, and Malaysia), he calls newly-industrializing, and obtains a fourfold increase in manufactured exports from the developing countries.

But the group includes Indonesia, which cannot be considered a newly-industrializing country and whose petroleum and other natural resources should not lead to manufacturing export ratios even remotely resembling those of East Asian economies, should it in fact reach such a status. More generally, there is no reason to assume that the adoption of outward-oriented policies would lead to identical shares of manufactured exports in all developing countries, for a given population size and per capita income, as Cline postulates. Thus, the four East Asian economies are poor in natural resources (Hong Kong and Singapore are city-states and the ratio of arable land to population is low in Korea and Taiwan) and hence one can expect them to have a much higher ratio of manufactured exports to GNP than most other developing countries. In turn, they would have a lower ratio of primary exports to GNP.

Furthermore, developing economies would use the additional foreign exchange generated through exports to increase their imports from the industrial countries, thereby creating demand for the manufactured exports of these countries. If the balance of trade in manufactured goods did not change, industrial activity in the advanced countries would not be affected *in toto* while a reallocation would occur from relatively low-skill to high-skill industries that is in the interest of these countries in question.

At the same time, such a reallocation would occur over a long period, since policy changes in the developing countries – even if carried out simultaneously and at one fell swoop – would have an impact over time. Also, experience indicates that a growing part of the expansion of trade in manufactured goods between the developed countries and the NICs involves intra-industry rather than inter-industry specialization, in which case changes occur in the product composition of the firm rather than in the industrial structure of the economy.

Rather than taking the unrealistic case when the developing countries reach identical ratios of manufactured exports to GNP, with allowance made for differences in population and per capita incomes, one should consider the import requirements of economic growth in these countries. This will be done in the following, with the exclusion of the OPEC countries.

In 1983, manufactured goods accounted for 40 percent of the exports of the non-OPEC developing countries to the developed countries. Following Lewis in assuming for these countries a 6 percent target growth rate, an income elasticity of import demand of 1.0, and a 4 percent growth rate of primary exports to industrial economies, a simple calculation will show that the import requirements of the developing countries will be met if their manufactured exports were to rise 9 percent a year. This would not exceed the rate of growth of manufactured exports from the developing to the industrial countries during the 1973–83 period that was characterized by low growth in the latter group of countries.

A 9 percent rate of export expansion would give rise to much lower market penetration ratios than implied in Cline's estimate. Assuming that the consumption of manufactured goods in the developed countries grew at an average annual rate of 4 percent over a ten-year period, the market share of the developing economies in their manufacturing consumption would increase from 2.3 percent to 3.7 percent.

If we consider that part of the expansion of exports would involve intra-industry rather than inter-industry specialization, and that the developing economies would use increments in their export earnings to buy manufactured goods from the developed countries, these estimates hardly raise the spectre of doom over the industries of these countries. But, even if the exports of manufactured goods from developing economies to the industrial countries were to rise at an average annual rate of 12 percent, their market share in the consumption of manufactured goods of these countries would not reach 5 percent after a decade.

The estimates assume that developing countries would increase their exports of manufactured goods to the other developing countries at the same rate as to the industrial countries, i.e. by 9 percent a year. But, apart from the year following the debt crisis, the exports of manufactured goods to other developing countries have been rising much more rapidly than exports to the industrial countries. This trend can be expected to continue under the assumptions made; i.e. higher economic growth rates in the developing countries will lead to more rapid increases in their demand for manufactured imports than in the developed countries. At the same time, with their increased degree of economic sophistication, the newly-industrializing countries may provide an increasing array of commodities demanded by other developing countries.

Furthermore, apart from promoting exports, an outward-oriented policy contributes to efficient import substitution. In fact, it has been shown that, during the 1973–8 period of external shocks, the outward-oriented NICs undertook more import substitution from their inward-oriented counterparts.[25] Various factors have contributed to this result.

To begin with, the adoption of realistic exchange rates was conducive to export expansion as well as to import substitution in the outward-oriented NICs. Also, these countries could replace agricultural imports through increases in domestic agricultural production that did not suffer discrimination due to high industrial protection. At the same time, the expansion of their manufactured exports allowed for efficient import substitution through the exploitation of economies of scale. By contrast, domestic market limitations in the inward-oriented NICs did not permit exploiting economies of scale in the production of a variety of intermediate goods, machinery, and transport equipment, leading to high cost manufacture and limiting net foreign exchange savings.

All in all, the advantages of outward-orientation are to be found in the establishment of an efficient production pattern that entails exporting as well as import substitution. Moreover, exposure to foreign influences contributes to the technological change, thus further improving the prospects for economic growth.

IV THE POLICY EXPERIENCE OF MEXICO

Several members of CEPG, including Terry Barker, John Eatwell, and Ajit Singh, served as policy advisors in Mexico during the Lopez Portillo administration (1976–82). Their activities were concentrated in the Ministry of National Patrimony and Industrial Development whose minister, José Andrés de Orteyza, and director-general of the Institute of Industrial Planning, Vladimir Brailovsky, were former students at Cambridge.

In a retrospective evaluation, 'Mexican Economic Policy 1978–82 and the National Industrial Development Plan,' Barker and Brailovsky distinguish three alternative policies for Mexico: protectionist, expansionist, and deflationist. The Industrial Plan prepared by CEPG for the Ministry was said to be 'perhaps the best example of the protectionist view applied to the economy' that 'advocated expansion to raise employment with control on imports to prevent balance-of-payments crises'.[26] In turn, the expansionists were said to have regarded raising oil production as the solution to

Mexico's economic problems while the advocates of the liberalization of imports, the floating of the peso, and limitations on public spending were considered deflationists by Barker and Brailovsky.

The Industrial Plan called for the application of four policy measures: (a) increases in government consumption and investment; (b) the provision of more low-cost housing; (c) increases in industrial investment; and (d) increases in the internal price of fuel. The authors note that the first three policies were carried out; in fact, investment and consumption rose more than planned. This was related to the expansion of oil production, promoted by the expansionists. In turn, imports were liberalized between 1977 and 1979, but import controls were re-established in 1981.

In the event, imports grew rapidly, surpassing 10 percent of Mexico's GNP in 1980 and 1981, compared with a ratio of 6.8 percent in 1976. According to Barker and Brailovsky, import liberalization importantly contributed to the growth of imports and was responsible for nearly one-half of the increase in the deficit in goods and factor services in 1981 compared with the Plan. This result is derived by taking the difference between actual import growth rates, adjusted for differences between actual and planned growth rates of domestic demand, and planned import growth rates.

The methodology applied attributes the residual obtained, by taking a plan projection of doubtful validity as a point of departure, to import liberalization. Other influences, in particular the appreciation of the real exchange rate, appears to have been more important.[27] The peso appreciated by 22 percent between 1976 and the fourth quarter of 1981.[28] At the same time, the extent of the appreciation of the peso was limited by the close interconnection of the US and Mexican economies that does not permit prices to get very much out of line. But, this interconnection also means that there is considerable spillover into imports as prices rise. During the period under consideration, the spillover was augmented by the high degree of capacity utilization of Mexican industry.

A more appropriate method of estimation was utilized by Jimenez and Schatán, who compared changes over time in liberalized and in controlled imports and found, on the average, little difference between the two.[29] This conclusion is hardly surprising. To begin with, trade liberalization concerned only 14 percent of the value of imports. Furthermore, tariffs were increased to compensate for the reduction in protection associated with the liberalization of import restrictions. Last but not least, import liberalization appears to have been concentrated on items where domestic producer interests were at stake to only a limited extent and the proposals of the Secretaria de Comercio for further liberalization were not acted upon.[30]

At the same time, the increased overvaluation of the exchange rate adversely affected exports. Thus, the volume of Mexican manufactured exports fell by 14 percent between 1978 and 1981, and the increase was only 13 percent in dollar terms compared to a 58 percent rise in the manufactured exports of the developing countries during this period. In fact, an absolute decline is shown in the dollar value of Mexico's manufactured exports if one excludes chemicals, based largely on petroleum, and automotive products, the exports of which were regulated under the export-import link system.

Further losses in market shares were observed in primary exports. Also, the surplus in the balance of service transactions disappeared as the appreciation of the real exchange rate adversely affected tourism, border trade, and the maquila industries in Mexico.[31]

The conclusion emerges that Mexico's unsustainable balance-of-payments deficit was due to the overheating of the economy and the maintenance of fixed exchange rates. At the same time, for the sake of maintaining fixed exchange rates, Mexico borrowed substantial amounts abroad, eventually leading to the August 1982 financial crisis.

A different view was expressed by the Cambridge Group, according to which the economy was overheated only in a very specific sense: 'Given current trade policies, the overall rate of expansion of the economy is excessive in that it leads to a rate of increase of manufactured imports which cannot be sustained in the medium term.'[32] Correspondingly, the CEPG recommendation was to restrict imports while maintaining an 8 percent rate of growth of GNP.

CEPG further objected to the devaluation of the peso on the grounds that it would lead to rapid inflation. And, the subsequent floating of the peso was said to be at the origin of Mexico's later troubles: 'The origins of the immediate crisis can be dated precisely. On 17 February 1982, the President of Mexico, instead of (or in addition to) imposing exchange controls to check as continuing capital flight, floated the peso.'[33] The devaluation was also blamed for the acceleration of capital flight and, apart from imposing import and foreign exchange controls, it was suggested that Mexico stops repaying its debt.

To begin with the last point, it has been conclusively shown that, under realistic assumptions, a default would on balance have adverse economic effects on Mexico.[34] Thus, apart from unfavorable international repercussions, stopping debt repayments would not be in Mexico's well-perceived interest.

At the same time, blaming the depreciation of the peso for Mexico's economic and financial difficulties confuses cause with effect. Thus, as noted above, these difficulties in large part find their origin in the appreciation of the real exchange rate. And, apart from its adverse effects on the balance of goods and nonfactor services, the overvaluation of the peso contributed to capital flight. There is a symmetry here that the Cambridge Group fails to recognize; i.e. undoing the adverse effects of an appreciation of the currency requires a devaluation.

Furthermore, the recommendations made for import controls fail to consider the general equilibrium effects of such measures. As shown in a recent study, increases in protection act primarily as a tax on exports.[35] The imposition of import restrictions, then, would reinforce the adverse effects of the overvaluation of the peso on exports. If one further considers the adverse dynamic effects of import protection noted earlier, the alternative proposed by the CEPG can only lead to permanently low rates of economic growth that would not make it possible to employ Mexico's growing labor force.

These conclusions are reinforced if we consider the adverse implications of CEPG's emphasis on public investments. In fact, an important factor contributing to Mexico's predicament has been the inefficiency of public investments carried out in the framework of the Industrial Plan prepared under the guidance of the Cambridge Group. With low, and even negative, rates of return on these investments in terms of world market prices, Mexico was not able to generate the foreign exchange savings or earnings necessary to service its debt.

The appropriate solution is an outward-oriented development strategy that utilizes the productive powers of the economy by promoting exports and efficient import substitution, with a greater role given to market forces. Apart from permitting Mexico to deal with its debt problem, such a strategy would provide opportunities for rapid technological change and lead to higher rates of economic growth and increased employment.

V THE POLICY EXPERIENCE OF TANZANIA

In 1979, Ajit Singh put forward the proposition that

> to meet the basic needs of the poor in the Third World in a sustainable way, it is essential to raise the rate of economic growth in these countries. This will require a more than proportional expansion of their manufacturing sector, and therefore an accelerated development of modern industry, including the establishment of appropriate capital goods industries.[36]

Singh further suggested that such a strategy was in fact applied in Tanzania, whose 'basic goal is to raise the contribution of industry to gross domestic product to 20 percent by 1995; a further objective is that by that date 60 percent of industrial output should consist of intermediate and capital goods and only 40 percent of consumer goods.'[37] At the same time, Singh expressed the view that criticisms of Tanzania's growth record are 'misconceived.' His defense of Tanzania's policy performance requires full quotation:

Although there were temporary setbacks to the economy during the mid-1970s as a consequence of serious drought and sharply adverse movements in terms of trade, over the period 1964–1974 there was significant structural change and a rapid expansion of industry (at the rate of about 10% a year). The notion of a decline in the long-term trend rate of industrial growth is not borne out by a careful examination of the evidence. In terms of the appropriate criteria for assessing economic performance in a developing economy, Tanzania's industry and economy have a creditable record. This is not to deny that there have been economic mistakes in the past or that there are economic difficulties: However, these can be best resolved within the existing policy and institutional framework.[38]

Tanzania indeed set out to apply a strategy of basic needs *and* industrialization. The process began with the Arusha Declaration of February 1967 and continued with the Basic Industries Strategy in 1975. At the same time, the implementation of the Arusha declaration took several years and the forcible settling of peasants in the Ujaama villages began in earnest only around 1970. Correspondingly, 1970 may be considered an appropriate benchmark for evaluating the policies applied. The following evaluation is based on the writings of Andrew Coulson,[39] Samuel Wangwe,[40] and Uma Lele.[41]

To begin with, the data show that, after rising by nearly one-half between 1970 and 1978, value added in manufacturing declined by nearly two-fifths between 1978 and 1981, thus falling slightly below the 1970 level. By contrast, manufacturing value added rose two-and-a-half times between 1961 and 1970.

Post-1970 developments involved a shift from consumer goods industries to heavy industry, with some of the highly capital-intensive establishments (e.g. the steel mill and the fertilizer plant) having negative value added at world market prices. At the same time, as Uma Lele notes,

the undervaluation of the foreign exchange rate and the distorted domestic prices of inputs and outputs have concealed the inappropriateness of these capital-intensive investments at this early stage of Tanzania's development. These industries have not only been uneconomic in themselves, they have also diverted local financial, manpower, and institutional resources, scarce foreign exchange, and especially domestic policy attention away from agriculture.[42]

Thus, industry's share in the government's capital expenditure rose from practically nil in the second half of the 1960s to 17 percent at the end of the 1970s while agriculture's share declined from 21 to 10 percent. Industry's share in total investment also increased, from 17 percent in 1970 to 34 percent in 1980, with commensurate declines occurring in agriculture. Furthermore, industry's foreign aid allocation increased from 10 percent in the mid-1970s to 20 percent at the beginning of the 1980s; in the same period, agriculture's share fell from 40 to 10 percent. Finally, the share of machinery, destined largely to the industrial sector, increased from 23 percent of total imports in 1971 to 31 percent in 1979 whereas agriculture's foreign exchange allocation was reduced to a considerable extent.

Agriculture also suffered the effects of the decline in investments in transportation, and the virtual lack of maintenance of the transportation network, leading to an extremely serious deterioration of the roads. Furthermore, the forcible establishment of the ujaama villages reduced agriculture's production potential.

Finally, agriculture experienced falling producer prices, with an average decline of 36.5 percent in real terms between 1971–2 and 1980–81. These declines reflected in part the government's desire to keep food prices low for the urban population and in part its intention to avoid the devaluation of the Tanzanian shilling. Uma Lele reports that, between 1970 and 1981, the trade-weighted exchange rate appreciated by 46 percent in real terms; the extent of appreciation was 78 percent against the Kenyan shilling.

Changes in marketed output tended to follow changes in producer prices. Apart from coffee, tea, and tobacco, which have a long gestation period, the marketed production of all crops fell to a considerable extent between 1970–71 and 1981–2, with declines of 45 to 60 percent for the major export crops, 47 to 49 percent for wheat and maize, and 83 percent for paddy and rice. And while official data show an increase in subsistence production, this is not consistent with the rise of the imports of grain from nil in 1970–71 to 388 million tons in 1981–2.

Manufactured exports also declined, so that in 1980 the volume of Tanzania exports hardly reached 40 percent of the 1970 level. It is this decline in exports that is largely responsible for Tanzania's balance-of-payments crisis as the terms of trade fell by less than 10 percent during the period. At the same time, Tanzania received increasing amounts of foreign capital (mostly in the form of grants) that financed over 40 percent of imports by 1980. Nevertheless, with the rapid decline in exports, the volume of imports fell by more than one-third during the 1970s.

Given the increases in the share of capital goods and food imports, the decline in imports was concentrated in intermediate products whose share in the total fell from 29 percent in 1971 to 16 percent in 1980. Apart from agriculture, industry suffered the adverse effects of decreases in these imports, leading to levels of capacity utilization of about 20 percent. Correspondingly, the population suffered shortages not only of agricultural but also of industrial products. These shortages were reinforced by the effects of price control, leading to an extensive black market, and by the inefficiencies of the parastatal enterprises that took over the distribution of products in Tanzania.

All in all, although incomes have been redistributed, the living standard of the poor deteriorated in the urban as well as in the rural areas. Urban unemployment increased by one-half between 1961 and 1975 whereas the real value of the minimum wage declined by one-half from the peak level reached in 1969 by 1978. In turn, the standard of living of rural producers fell by 27 percent during this period, representing a decrease of 45–50 percent in per capita terms. At the same time, these figures do not take account of the limited availability of the basic necessities, due to shortages.

The results indicate the failure of the Tanzanian policy experiment, which comes closest to applying the recommendations of the Cambridge Group to developing countries. The emphasis on industry and, within industry, on heavy industry, together with reliance on import restrictions as against the use of the exchange rate mechanism, the increased encroachment of the state in economic life, the extended role given to public enterprises, and the far-reaching price control, all followed the Cambridge prescriptions.

CEPG claims, however, that 'up to 1979, Tanzania's economic performance – both in terms of economic growth and meeting the basic needs of the people was highly satisfactory by comparative international standards.'[43] At the same time, the subsequent deterioration of the economy is attributed to external causes.

These claims do not stand up to scrutiny. To begin with, the cited data on the decline in living standards refer to the period up to 1978. Furthermore, the volume of exports was lower in 1979 than in 1980, and hence much lower than in 1970. Finally, while industrial output was 43 percent higher in 1979 than in 1970, the productivity of primary factors used in industry deteriorated to a considerable extent. This is apparent if we consider that industrial employment increased by 77 percent and industrial investment more than tripled in real terms during the period.

Nor can one attribute Tanzania's recent predicament to external shocks. Thus, the terms of trade declined by only 10 percent between 1979 and 1981. Also, world demand for the products Tanzania exports continued to rise, but the country experienced further losses in market shares. In fact, by 1983, Tanzania's share in the world market for its six principal export products declined, on the average, by 28 percent from its 1976–8 level.

CEPG, at the same time, suggests that 'the Tanzanian economy is in long-term structural disequilibrium, in the sense that the productive economy is unable to generate sufficient exports to pay for the required imports (i) at a socially desired rate of economic growth; (ii) at a socially acceptable exchange rate and (iii) at a normal level of current account deficit'.[44] The qualifying phrase, socially acceptable exchange rates, reflects CEPG's long-standing aversion to a devaluation.

The Cambridge Group has put forward the following argument in rationalizing its opposition to a devaluation.

> First, the IMF does not provide scientific evidence that in the present state of the Tanzanian economy *overall* agricultural production is likely to be increased by a rise in producer prices. . . . Secondly, even to the extent that there is a positive supply response for particular crops, the size of this response is far from being uniform and varies between crops. . . . Thirdly, and most importantly, if such a large increase in producer prices as suggested by the Fund is implemented, it will involve an enormous redistribution of income . . . which would inevitably cause a huge upsurge in the rate of inflation.[45]

CEPG has further expressed the view that 'the positive effects [of a devaluation] on the balance of payments in the short to medium term are small and highly uncertain' and 'suggests that the optimal government policy should be selective subsidies for particular crops . . . rather than a uniform subsidy implemented by means of a general devaluation.'[46] These conclusions again do not stand up to scrutiny.

To begin with, available information on sub-Saharan Africa countries indicates that farmers respond to incentives.[47] This is also the experience of Tanzania, where the appreciation of the real exchange rate has led to large declines in exports while the output of food crops has fallen steeply in response to the substantial fall in producer prices.

The adverse effects of the appreciation of the currency on exports would be undone through a depreciation of the exchange rate rather than through selective subsidies. Tanzania could increase its exports by 44 percent if it only regained the market shares lost between 1972 and 1978.[48] Yet, Tanzania also lost export market shares in subsequent years as the exchange rate continued to appreciate in real terms. Increased exports, in turn, would reduce foreign exchange shortages and the greater availability of imports would lessen inflationary pressures.

Higher producer prices in agriculture would also contribute to increased food production, thus further reducing inflationary pressures. In fact, in a country like Tanzania where inflation is primarily due to shortages, a devaluation associated with increases in producer prices may lower rather than increase the rate of inflation.

At the same time, infrastructural and transportation bottlenecks may be alleviated through a drastic revision of investment priorities, shifting resources from heavy industry to agriculture. This would parallel the proposed changes in the incentive system that should be linked to giving greater role to market forces. And, a re-ordering of priorities and improvements in the incentive system would eventually benefit the rural as well as the urban population, just as they both suffered the effects of misguided policies in the past.

CONCLUSIONS

This essay has provided a critical review of the policy prescriptions of the Cambridge Economic Policy Group for the developing countries. The review has indicated the disastrous effects of CEPG-type policies in Mexico and Tanzania and noted the inappropriateness of the recommendations made by the Cambridge Group to cope with the crisis that these policies have engendered.

And while the CEPG has recently come to agree with the need for increasing exports in the developing countries, it not only takes an overly pessimistic view about the prospects for the world economy but fails to recognize that import protection adversely affects exports. Continued opposition on the part of the Cambridge Group to remedying the overvaluation of the exchange rates in developing countries also reflects a lack of understanding of the need to undo the adverse effects of currency appreciation on exports.

At the same time, available evidence indicates the advantages of outward-orientation over an inward-oriented development strategy CEPG advocates. In fact, the superiority of outward orientation is apparent not only during periods of rapid world economic growth but also during periods of external shocks, even though outward-oriented countries with higher export and import shares are more exposed to such shocks than their inward-oriented counterparts.

There is further considerable evidence of the adverse effects of governmental interventions promoted by CEPG. In fact, in recent years even socialist countries such as China and Hungary have made important steps to increase the role of market forces and to open their economies to foreign influences. Thus, these countries have come to engage in trade with both developed and developing private market economies on a competitive basis, eschewing planned international exchange proposed by the Cambridge Group.

NOTES

1. The theory underlying the policy prescriptions of the Cambridge Group was explicited in F. Cripps and W. Godley, 'A Formal Analysis of the Cambridge Economic Policy Group's Model,' *Economica*, XLIII (1976). The most cogent criticism of CEPG views is provided in M. F. G. Scott, W. M. Corden, and I. M. D. Little, *The Case against General Import Restrictions*, Thames Essay No. 24 (London: Trade Policy Research Centre, 1980).

2. All citations in this section are from A. Singh, 'The Interrupted Industrial Revolution of the Third World: Prospects and Policies for Resumption,' *Industry and Development*, XII (1984) pp. 43–68, which provides a comprehensive exposition of CEPG policy prescriptions for developing countries.
3. Singh, p. 56.
4. Ibid., p. 58.
5. Ibid.
6. Ibid., pp. 59–60.
7. Ibid., p. 59.
8. Ibid., p. 60.
9. Ibid., p. 56.
10. Ibid., pp. 57–8.
11. W. A. Lewis, 'The Slowing Down of the Engine of Growth,' *American Economic Review*, LXX (1980) pp. 555–64. At the same time, it should be emphasized that Lewis, like Nurkse before him, did not recommend that the LDCs adopt protectionist policies. Lewis also counselled against preferential arrangements among LDCs.
12. Lewis, p. 559.
13. Ibid.
14. J. Riedel, 'Trade as the Engine of Growth in Developing Countries, Revisited,' *Economic Journal*, XLIV (1984) p. 65.
15. B. I. Cohen, and D. G. Sisler, 'Exports by Developing Countries in the 1960's,' *Review of Economics and Statistics*, LIII (1971) pp. 354–61 and R. C. Porter, 'Some Implications of Postwar Primary-Product Trends,' *Journal of Political Economy*, LXXVIII (1970) pp. 586–97.
16. The estimates are based on the sources cited in B. Balassa, 'Trends in International Trade in Manufactured Goods and Structural Change in the Industrial Countries,' in L. Pasinetti and P. Lloyd (eds), *Structural Change, Economic Interdependence and World Development Vol. 3 Structural Change and Adjustment in the World Economy* (London: Macmillan, 1987) pp. 123–48, and Essay 18 in Bela Balassa, *Change and Challenge in the World Economy* (London: Macmillan, 1985) pp. 403–26.
17. J. Love, 'External Market Conditions, Competitiveness, Diversification and LDC Exports,' *Journal of Development Economics*, XVI (1984) pp. 279–91.
18. B. Balassa, 'Export Incentives and Export Performance in Developing Countries: A Comparative Analysis,' *Weltwirtschaftliches Archiv*, CXI (1978) pp. 43–5. The data cited in the following also originate in this paper.
19. For a more detailed discussion, see Essay 1 in this volume.
20. B. Balassa, 'Exports, Policy Choices, and Economic Growth in Developing Countries After the 1973 Oil Shock,' *Journal of Development Economics*, XVIII (1985) pp. 23–35.
21. B. Balassa, 'Economic Reform in China,' *Banca Nazionale del Lavoro, Quarterly Review* (1982) p. 309 and Essay 14 in B. Balassa *Change and Challenge in the World Economy*, pp. 310–36.
22. W. R. Cline, 'Can the East Asian Export Model be Generalized?' *World Development*, X (1982) pp. 71–80; the work of Nayyar, published in the *Economic and Political Weekly* in Bombay, represents a less serious effort and will not be considered here.
23. Ibid., p. 85.
24. The estimate was obtained by interpolating the figures reported in Balassa, 'Trends in International Trade in Manufactured Goods and Structural Change in the Industrial Countries' for 1973 and 1978.

25. B. Balassa, 'The Newly-Industrializing Developing Countries After the Oil Crisis,' *Weltwirtschaftliches Archiv* (1981) pp. 142–94.
26. T. Barker, and V. Brailowsky, 'Mexican Economic Policy 1978–82 and the National Development Plan' (Mexico, DF, 1983) mimeo, p. 28.
27. An alternative estimate obtained in 'a more sophisticated way' by comparing projections of the Industrial Model derived on the assumptions of controlled and liberalized imports is nearly one-half lower than the plan – no plan comparison, but it is not subsequently utilized by the authors (Barker and Brailowsky, p. 25). At the same time, this estimate also suffers from the neglect of the effects of changes in the real exchange rate.
28. B. Balassa, 'Trade Policy in Mexico,' *World Development* (1983) pp. 795–812 and Essay 17 in *Change and Challenge in the World Economy*, pp. 384–99.
29. F. O. Jimenez Jaimes, and C. Schatán, 'Mexico: la nueva politica comercial y el incremento de las importaciónes de bienes manufacturados en el período 1977–80' (Mexico, DF: El Colegio de Mexico, 1982) mimeo.
30. Balassa, 'Trade Policy in Mexico,' pp. 804–5.
31. Ibid., p. 805.
32. J. Eatwell, and A. Singh, 'Se encuentra 'sobrecalentada' la económia mexicana? Un analisis de las problemas de politica económica a corto y mediano plazos' (Mexico, DF, 1981) mimeo, p. 12.
33. A. Singh, 'The Present Crisis of the Mexican Economy: From a Mexican Perspective' (Cambridge, England, 1983) mimeo, p. 1; published in an abbreviated form in 'How the Bankers' Darling Fell on Hard Times,' *South*, XXV (1982) pp. 25–7.
34. T. O. Enders, and R. P. Mattione, 'Latin America. The Crisis of Debt and Growth,' *Studies in International Economics* (Washington, DC: Brookings Institution, 1984).
35. K. W. Clements, and L. A. Sjaastad, *How Protection Taxes Exporters*, Thames Essay No. 39 (London: Trade Policy Research Centre, 1984).
36. A. Singh, 'The "Basic Needs" Approach to Development in the New International Economic Order,' *World Development*, VII (1979) pp. 600–601.
37. Ibid., p. 601.
38. Ibid.
39. A. Coulson, *Tanzania. A Political Economy* (Oxford: Clarendon Press, 1982).
40. S. M. Wangwe, 'Industrialization and Resource Allocation in a Developing Country: The Case of Recent Experiences in Tanzania,' *World Development*, XI (1983) pp. 483–92.
41. U. Lele, 'Tanzania: Phoenix or Icarus?,' in A. C. Harberger (ed.), *World Economic Growth* (San Francisco; Institute for Contemporary Studies, 1984).
42. Ibid., pp. 177–8.
43. A. Singh, 'The Continuing Crisis of the Tanzanian Economy: The Political Economy of Alternative Policy Options' (Cambridge, England, 1984) mimeo, p. 11.
44. Ibid., p. 8.
45. Ibid., pp. 19–21.
46. Ibid., p. 20.
47. See Essay 8 below.
48. B. Balassa, 'Adjustment Policies and Development Strategies in Sub-Saharan Africa, 1973–1978,' in M. Syrquin, L. Taylor, and L. E. Westphal (eds), *Economic Structure and Performance* (Orlando: Academic Press, 1984) p. 328.

Essay 5 'Dependency' and Trade Orientation

INTRODUCTION

'Dependency,' or 'Dependencia' in the Latin American literature, is a many-splendored thing. It has had a variety of interpretations and has been the subject of a vast literature over the last two decades. Rather than attempting to provide a review of these – often conflicting – writings, this essay sets out to analyze the key propositions of the dependency school that are common to most, if not all, of those under its banner.

While discussions of the dependency literature have generally concentrated on Latin America, the article will encompass in its purview major contributions in Western Europe (Arghiri Emmanuel)[1] and in Africa (Samir Amin)[2] Among Latin American authors, attention will concentrate on the views of André Gunder Frank[3] and Celso Furtado[4] whose writings are central to the development of dependency theory in the region. The so-called world economy approach, originated by Immanuel Wallerstein[5] in the United States, will not be covered in the essay.

Section I will consider the origins of the dependency theory. This will be followed by a review of the principal tenets of the dependency school (Section II). Subsequently, evidence will be presented on long-term trends in the terms of trade (Section III). Section IV will present proposals for delinking developing countries from the world economy. Section V will consider the role of foreign capital in the developing countries and Section VI will examine the effects of international trade on the domestic economy of these countries.

I THE ORIGINS OF DEPENDENCY THEORY

The principal dependency theorists profess a Marxist lineage; their views, however, contrast to a considerable extent with those of Marx.[6] According to Marx, capitalism is historically a progressive system that will inevitably spread from the advanced to the economically backward countries. In contrast, according to the dependency theorists, capitalism in the advanced countries is the principal obstacle to the economic development of the backward countries.

In the preface to the first edition of *Capital*, Marx states that 'a country which is more developed industrially only shows to the less developed the image of its future.' While the spread of capitalism to backward areas is initiated by an effort on the part of the capitalists to counteract the tendency of the falling rate of profit, the industrial development of these areas will necessarily follow. Thus, according to Marx, English capitalism will not be able to forestall the industrialization of India since, 'when you have introduced machinery into the locomotion of a country which possesses iron and coal, you are unable to withhold it from its fabrications.'[7]

But, a century later, Paul Baran contended 'that economic development in underdeveloped countries is profoundly inimical to the dominant interests in the advanced capitalist countries.'[8] He further expressed the view that these interests will prevail, thereby counteracting the tendency of the falling rate of profit. Correspondingly, 'the capitalist system, once a mighty engine of economic development, has turned into a no less formidable hurdle to economic advancement.'[9]

Rather than upholding the historical inevitability of the spread of capitalism, then, Baran claimed that the advanced capitalist countries will maintain less developed countries in a backward state.[10] This was said to involve expropriating much of the surplus value[11] they create, with the rest being squandered on luxury consumption for the traditional elite that is in cohorts with the foreign capitalists in opposing domestic industrial development. Instead of a progressive system postulated by Marx, capitalism was thus pictured as a reactionary force in the writings of Baran who may be regarded as the father of the dependency school.

II THE PRINCIPAL TENETS OF THE DEPENDENCY SCHOOL

In fact, Baran's ideas underlie propositions put forward by Arghiri Emmanuel, Samir Amin, André Gunder Frank, and Celso Furtado. According to these authors, there is a basic inequality between the advanced capitalist countries, or the center, and the less developed countries, or the periphery, which results in the transfer of the economic surplus from the latter to the former. This transfer dooms the periphery to underdevelopment and, to the extent that some industries are eatablished, they are devoted to luxury goods consumed by the domestic elite. At the same time, income inequalities tend to increase internationally as well as domestically.

There are differences, however, among these writers as to the method by which surplus value is said to be transferred from the periphery to the center. Arghiri Emmanuel has introduced the expression 'unequal exchange' to describe a situation when profits are equalized internationally while wages become increasingly unequal as productivity improvements lead to higher wages in the center but not in the periphery. Correspondingly, the fruits of the periphery's technological progress are transferred to the center through the deterioration of the terms of trade. International income inequalities will increase over time as a result, with free trade leading to immiserization in the periphery.

Essentially the same argument was made in the early postwar years by Raul Prebisch[12] and Hans Singer[13], who postulated the secular deterioration of the terms of trade in the less developed countries. Prebisch's views had considerable influence in Latin America, where several writers of the dependency school regard the secular deterioration of the terms of trade as the principal mechanism for the transfer of surplus value from the periphery to the center.[14]

In Prebisch–Singer–Emmanuel, such a result obtains in competitive product markets under free trade. These authors also assume that labor markets are competitive in the periphery but not in the center, where the bargaining power of the unions permits the worker to partake in the fruits of technological progress. In postulating the international equalization of profit rates, Emmanuel further assumes competitive capital markets and the international mobility of capital; Prebisch and Singer do not make such assumptions, permitting profit rates to differ between the center and the periphery.

The expression 'unequal exchange' is also used by Samir Amin, but he postulates a different mechanism for the transfer of surplus value. With wage differences exceeding differences in productivity, higher wages in the center than in the periphery are said to result in international differences in profit rates. The higher profits obtained in the periphery in producing goods for the center are then repatriated by the foreign capitalists to their own benefit as well as to the benefit of the unionized labor class.

Foreign ownership is also the mechanism of the transfer of surplus value according to André Gunder Frank. Amin and Frank further postulate that the profits repatriated by foreign capitalists will rise over time as wages are maintained at the subsistence level in the periphery, notwithstanding increases in productivity. In their view, this situation is the result of a political alliance between the capitalists in the center and the landowners in the periphery who are inimical to the development of capitalism in their countries.

The landowners, in turn, demand luxury goods while mass markets for consumer goods cannot develop in the periphery because of low wages. Furtado suggests that such will also be the case if domestic capitalists join the landowners as part of the elite, with domestic industry concentrating on the production of capital-intensive luxury goods (namely, consumer durables). Thus, he speaks of 'a widening gap between the consumption levels of the modernized minorities and the mass of the population in the dependent countries.'[15] Now, 'economic growth will be retarded by an increasingly unequal distribution of income coupled with the fact that the capitalist class devotes a considerable fraction of its consumption expenditure to relatively capital-intensive commodities.'[16] At the same time, according to Furtado, both the deterioration of the terms of trade and foreign ownership will act as mechanisms for transferring surplus value from the periphery to the center.

The described process is supposed to continue, perpetuating inequalities and a distorted pattern of production while limiting domestic savings and investment. This is expressed in a statement by Amin that is quoted by Ian Little:[17]

> In other words, the new division of labor would perpetuate and worsen unequal exchange. Furthermore, this unequal division of labor would perpetuate the distorted pattern of demand in the peripheries to the detriment of mass consumption, just as in the previous phases. Therefore the development of the world system would remain fundamentally unequal.[18]

With international trade and investment being the vehicle of the transfer of the surplus value from the periphery to the center and the obstacle to industrial development in the former, whatever the differences in their analysis, the policy conclusions of the dependency theorists are essentially the same. They maintain that delinking (full or selective) would offer the possibility to break out from the 'vicious circle of underdevelopment.' Or, as David Evans expressed it, 'whether implicit or explicit, there is a strong vein in the dependency tradition which sees either retreat into relative autarky for purposes of desired national development, or a temporary retreat into delinking . . . as a crucial aspect of all self-reliant development.'[19]

III THE PRESUMED DETERIORATION OF THE TERMS OF TRADE

Prebisch[20] interpreted the apparent improvement in the terms of trade of the United Kingdom in the period 1976–80 to 1946–7 as implying the deterioration of the terms of trade of the developing countries. More recently, Spraos[21] cited results obtained by Lipsey[22] as regards improvements in the US terms of trade and by Kindleberger[23] on the relative decline of the prices of primary products imported by European countries as indirect evidence on adverse changes in the developing countries' terms of trade.

This interpretation is based on the inappropriate assumption that the trading partners of the developed countries, for which the terms of trade have been estimated, are exclusively developing countries. In turn, Spraos's use of terms of trade estimates for primary products *vis-à-vis* manufactured goods to depict terms-of-trade changes for developing countries leave out of consideration the fact that developed countries export manufactured goods to other industrial countries as well and they also trade primary products among themselves.

These objections do not apply to estimates of the terms of trade between Industrial Europe and developing countries by Kravis and Lipsey[24] who found no change in the terms of trade of the developing countries during the 1872–1953 period. At the same time, as these authors note, their results – as well as those cited earlier – have the shortcoming of using a unit value index rather than a 'genuine' price index for manufactured goods. The unit value index, customarily derived as the ratio of value to weight, has an upward bias, owing to the shift from heavier to lighter materials and quality improvements over time.[25]

For the 1953–77 period, Kravis and Lipsey calculated a genuine price index for manufactured goods exported by the developed countries to the developing countries. The index shows a 127 percent increase in these prices, compared with a rise of 162 percent in the UN unit value index for manufactured exports. Deflating by the UN price index for the world exports of primary products other than petroleum, the authors have found that the terms of trade of manufactured goods exported by the developed countries to the developing countries declined by 6 percent during the period. This compares with an increase of 13 percent estimated from UN unit value indices for manufactured goods and for food and raw materials.

Replacing the UN price index for the world exports of primary commodities other than petroleum by the World Bank's (genuine) price index for 33 nonfuel primary commodities, weighted by the exports of the developing countries, results in a 10 percent decline in the terms of trade of the developed countries in their exchange of manufactured goods for nonfuel primary products imported from the developing countries (Balassa, 1984a). An even larger decline is shown if adjustment is made for quality changes. In the case of the United States, for which Kravis and Lipsey made such estimates, a 105 percent rise in the unadjusted price index for machinery and transport equipment in the 1953–77 period gives place to a 77 percent increase in the adjusted index.

Genuine price indices are not available for more recent years. And while changes in relative prices after 1977 may have offset the improvements in the terms of trade of the developing countries that occurred in the previous quarter of a century,[26] it should be remembered that 1953 was a year of high prices for primary products whereas 1985 was a year of low prices.

The comparison of the UN and the World Bank indices points to the conclusion that the prices of nonfuel primary products exported by the developing countries rose more rapidly than average world primary product prices during the period under consideration. This conclusion is confirmed by Michaely's estimates, according to which unit value indices for primary products exported by low-income countries have risen by 27 percent between 1952 and 1970, compared with an increase of 10 percent for primary products exported by high-income countries.[27] Michaely's results further show a 27 percent improvement in the terms of trade for primary products in the case of low-income countries, compared with a 23 percent deterioration for high-income countries, during this period.[28]

The unit values of manufactured goods exported by low-income countries also increased more rapidly (45 percent) than those exported by high-income countries (19 percent) between 1952 and 1970. In the same period, the terms of trade for manufactured goods improved by 14 percent in low-income countries and deteriorated by 12 percent in high-income countries.

For all merchandise trade, taken together, Michaely observed an improvement of 19 percent in the terms of trade for low-income countries, and a deterioration of 15 percent for high-income countries, during the 1952–70 period. He further established that terms of trade changes were negatively correlated with income levels in a fivefold classification scheme; the changes between 1952 and 1970 were -26, -11, -8, $+11$, and $+47$ percent as one moves from the top to the bottom quintile.

Michaely's results thus reinforced the findings of Kravis and Lipsey, indicating that the developing countries improved their terms of trade relative to the developed countries in the post-Korean war period. It is further observed that primary and manufactured commodities exported by the developing countries increased more in price than goods in the same categories exported by the developed countries and that improvements in the terms of trade were inversely correlated with the level of economic development.

IV PROPOSALS FOR DELINKING

The cited estimates effectively refute the Prebisch–Singer–Emmanuel thesis on the alleged secular deterioration of the terms of trade for the developing countries, irrespective of whether this is considered a historical proposition or as a prediction. But, observed changes in the terms of trade are affected by a number of factors, including shifts in demand and supply, and interest attaches to the question of whether the developing countries may improve their situation by limiting their participation in international trade. Such recommendations have in fact been made by dependency theorists on the grounds that reducing their primary exports would lead to welfare gains through improvements in the terms of trade of the developing countries.

The cited propositions are predicated on the assumption that developing countries have a monopolistic position in the markets for their primary export products. Apart from tropical beverages, such is not the case, however, as there are competing suppliers and/or substitutes for these products in the industrial countries. Correspondingly, limiting primary exports, whether directly through export taxes or indirectly through import protection, has led to declines in export market shares.

This has occurred in regard to temperate zone agricultural products, tropical zone products competing with those produced under a temperate climate, as well as nonfuel minerals and metals. It has been observed more recently in the case of petroleum. Thus, OPEC's share in world production declined from 68 percent in 1973 to 40 percent in 1985 as alternative supplies emerged in response to the high prices maintained by OPEC, with prices subsequently declining by nearly two-thirds from their peak of $34 per barrel in 1980. And while the application of protectionist measures encouraged high-cost import substitution in the industrial sector, countries applying such measures failed to participate in the expansion of manufactured exports.[29]

The resulting deterioration in the efficiency of resource allocation more than offset the improvement in the terms of trade attendant upon protection, thereby reducing output below its potential level. The cost of protection was estimated to have amounted to 5–10 percent of the gross national product in countries such as Brazil, Chile, and Pakistan in the mid-sixties, when protection levels were particularly high.[30]

Furthermore, highly-protected developing countries experienced a decline in the rate of growth of factor productivity. According to a summary of the findings of studies on a number of developing countries, 'the misallocation produced by conventional IS [import substituting] policies not only reduce total output below the level that it might have otherwise reached, but it also reduces the growth rate, principally through its effects on productivity growth and the flexibility of the economy.'[31]

These, 'static' and 'dynamic', costs are indicative of the fact that high protection does not permit the developing countries to exploit the possibilities offered by international trade. In turn, delinking may be considered an extreme case of protection as it essentially entails prohibitive protection with the corresponding economic costs.

In searching for actual cases of delinking, the proponents of such a policy tend to refer to China, Cambodia, Cuba, North Korea, and Tanzania. But the experience of these countries hardly supports a policy of delinking. To begin with, the high economic costs of delinking have led the Chinese government to reject this policy and to importantly increase international exchange. Also, while the consequences of delinking and of political oppression are difficult to separate in the case of Cambodia, political oppression may be a pre-condition for making delinking effective. In turn, exchanging links with capitalist countries for links with socialist countries has meant that Cuba has been unable to exploit the advantages offered by its educated labor force.

Virtual delinking from developed capitalist countries appears to have been largely responsible for North Korea increasingly losing ground in competition with South Korea. Thus, while in 1960 per capita incomes in the North were one-half higher than in the South, two decades later South Korea surpassed North Korea's income level by a considerable margin.[32]

Finally, Tanzania has practiced selective delinking through import controls, with unfavorable economic results.[33] More generally, socialist countries in sub-Saharan Africa that have, to a greater or lesser extent, practiced selective delinking had a greatly inferior performance than countries of the area that continued to participate in the international division of labor.[34]

V THE ROLE OF FOREIGN CAPITAL

According to dependency theorists, foreign capital is increasingly directed to developing countries in search of high profits, which are then repatriated, counteracting the tendency of the declining rate of profit and permitting paying high wages to labor in the developed countries. Several questions arise in this connection.

Is investment in the industrial countries increasingly oriented to developing countries? Do foreign capitalists earn higher rates of return in developing countries than elsewhere? Are profits repatriated? How important are the repatriated profits for profit and wage incomes in the industrial countries? These questions will be taken up in the following by utilizing data for the United States, the leading capitalist nation.

Contrary to the predictions of the dependency theorists, the share of the developing countries in US direct investment abroad declined continuously during the postwar period, falling by more than one-half between 1950 and 1984. The decline was especially pronounced in the nonmanufacturing sectors while it was partially reversed after 1960 in manufacturing (Table 5.1).

Latin America, where most of the *dependentistas* have labored, had a decline much in excess of the developing country average, with its share in US direct investment abroad falling from 41 percent in 1950 to 12 percent in 1984. In the same period, the share of other developing countries remained at 11 percent whereas Western Europe and the industrial countries of the Pacific area experienced substantial increases.

New investments in the developing countries have also declined in relation to domestic investment in the United States. In 1984, new investment in these countries hardly exceeded one billion dollars, with the stock of direct investment in the developing countries totalling $54 billion. By comparison, new investments of $661 billion were undertaken in the United States in 1984 alone.[35]

TABLE 5.1 US direct investment position abroad
(percent)

	World	Canada	Western Europe	Other developed	All developed	Latin America	Other developing	All developing
1950[a]								
Mining	100	30.0	1.6	3.0	34.6	58.9	6.6	65.4
Petroleum	100	12.2	12.8	1.7	26.7	43.3	30.0	73.3
Manufacturing	100	48.9	25.3	4.0	78.2	20.2	1.7	21.8
Services, others	100	27.3	10.1	4.1	41.5	56.2	2.4	58.5
Total	100	30.2	15.0	3.2	48.5	41.0	10.6	51.6
1960								
Mining	100	44.1	1.6	2.6	48.4	44.2	7.5	51.6
Petroleum	100	24.4	15.8	N.A.	N.A.	29.8	N.A.	N.A.
Manufacturing	100	43.3	34.0	6.2	83.5	14.6	1.8	16.5
Services, others	100	31.1	14.1	N.A.	N.A.	39.6	N.A.	N.A.
Total	100	34.2	20.3	4.4	58.9	28.2	8.5	36.8
1970								
Mining	100	49.1	1.2	9.3	59.6	33.2	7.2	40.4
Petroleum	100	22.1	25.2	6.6	53.9	18.0	20.4	38.4
Manufacturing	100	31.2	42.5	9.3	83.0	14.3	2.7	17.0

Services, others	100	27.5	29.0	4.6	61.1	22.9	5.4	28.3
Total	100	29.2	31.3	7.5	68.0	18.8	8.6	27.4
1980								
Mining	100	45.2	0.5	21.5	67.2	24.1	8.7	32.8
Petroleum	100	22.7	42.4	7.8	72.9	9.1	N.A.	N.A.
Manufacturing	100	21.2	50.8	8.0	80.1	16.3	3.6	19.9
Services, others	100	17.0	43.0	6.2	66.3	25.5	N.A.	N.A.
Total	100	20.9	44.8	7.8	73.5	18.0	6.7	24.7
1984								
Mining	100	29.7	0.5	29.1	59.3	31.4	9.3	40.7
Petroleum	100	18.3	39.0	6.8	64.1	9.4	19.7	29.1
Manufacturing	100	23.1	46.9	8.3	78.3	16.8	4.8	21.7
Services, others	100	21.8	50.3	8.3	80.5	6.1	11.4	17.8
Total	100	21.6	44.4	8.5	74.6	12.0	11.1	23.1

NOTE: [a] The total includes unallocated investment reported under the heading 'International.'

SOURCE: *Survey of Current Business*, various issues.

Nor is there evidence of superprofits being made in Latin America. In the years 1979–84, the after-tax profits of US manufacturing firms located in Latin America averaged 8 percent and only the 18 percent average profit rate in the other developing countries raised the overall average to 10 percent, equal to that for US manufacturing investment in the developed countries. By contrast, the after-tax profits of US firms in their domestic operations averaged 13 percent during this period. And while higher profits were obtained abroad in petroleum and mining, comparable results for US domestic operation are not available.

Data on the use of earnings from US foreign direct investment are available for 1983 and 1984. In the two years, on the average, 39 percent of earnings derived from investment in developing countries was reinvested, with the ratio being slightly higher, 41 percent, for Latin America. Distributed earnings averaged $6.6 billion in the first case and $3.3 billion in the second, compared with profits of nonfinancial corporations of $221 billion and gross national product of $38 trillion in the United States. It can hardly be said, therefore, that earnings derived from investments in developing countries would have offset 'the tendency of the declining profit rate.'

VI EFFECTS ON THE DOMESTIC ECONOMY OF DEVELOPING COUNTRIES

According to dependency theorists, trade relations with the developed countries stunt economic growth in the developing countries. Apart from the transfer of the surplus value generated in the export sector, the imitation of the consumption pattern of the industrial countries is said to orient developing economies towards the production of luxury goods, mainly consumer durables. These goods allegedly absorb the potential savings of the domestic capitalists while the large masses of the population remain at the subsistence level and do not represent effective demand for industrial products.

This presumed archetype of a developing country does not correspond to reality. To begin with, developing countries made considerable progress over the last quarter of the century, with average per capita incomes rising by altogether 120 percent. These increases exceeded the near-doubling of per capita incomes in the industrial countries, thus reducing rather than increasing international income inequalities.[36]

The rise in per capita incomes occurred as developing countries raised the share of investment in their gross domestic product from 16 percent in 1960 to 25 percent in 1982. Contrary to the views of the *dependentistas*, domestic investment was fueled largely by domestic savings that accounted for 15 percent of GDP in 1960 and 22 percent in 1982, representing a step-up in the savings effort.

In the same period, the share of manufactured goods in the gross domestic product of the developing countries rose from 14 to 19 percent. The share of consumer nondurables was 69 percent at the beginning of the period, declining to 64 percent by 1971 and to an estimated 58 percent ten years later as the industrial structure of the developing countries became more sophisticated.[37]

The process of industrialization in the developing countries thus began with the production of nondurable goods destined for general consumption. It was followed by the production of intermediate goods, machinery, and transport equipment, including consumer durables. Nor have consumer durables remained the privilege of the rich in the industrializing developing countries. Even in Chile, where economic growth rates were below the average, the share of households possessing consumer durables rose to a considerable extent within a short period. Between 1970 and 1982, the increase was from 48 to 62 percent for modern bathroom facilities, from 29 to 48 percent for refrigerators, and from 10 to 17 percent for automobiles.[38] Also, between 1960 and the late 1970s, the share of households owning cars increased from 12 to 41 percent in Argentina, from 19 to 38 percent in Venezuela, from 4 to 27 percent in Brazil, and from 7 to 21 percent in Mexico among major Latin American countries.[39]

The data on economic growth are averages that disguise considerable variations among developing countries. In particular, while the *dependentistas* assumed that participation in the international division of labor would be detrimental to developing countries, available evidence indicates the opposite. Thus, trade has contributed to economic growth in the developing countries in the postwar period.[40]

CONCLUSIONS

This essay has shown that the propositions put forward by dependency theorists do not stand up to scrutiny. There is no evidence of the transfer of surplus value generated in the periphery of developing countries to the center of industrial countries through either the secular deterioration of the terms of trade or through the repatriation of profits by foreign capitalists.

Nor has international trade stunted economic growth and industrial development in the periphery. Rather than the grim scenario of the *dependentistas*, the postwar period has seen considerable progress in the developing countries, leading to reductions in income differentials *vis-à-vis* the developed countries. At the same time, industry in the developing countries initially progressed through the manufacture of mass-produced goods rather than luxuries, with the subsequent spreading of durable consumer goods among the population.

Economic performance has been positively correlated with the extent of trade orientation in the developing countries. Available information pertaining to the 1960s indicates that outward-oriented countries were better able to increase employment, raise wages, and improve the income distribution than countries applying an inward-oriented strategy. This is because exporting permitted resource allocation according to comparative advantage, involving specialization in labor-intensive products, with demand for labor increasing further as a result of the rapid economic growth export expansion has engendered and because outward orientation has been more favorable to agriculture where much of the poor are.[41]

These conclusions were reconfirmed in the subsequent period of external shocks. Outward-oriented countries were better able to withstand the external shocks they suffered and avoided excessive reliance on foreign borrowing while regaining earlier growth rates. In turn, inward-oriented countries borrowed extensively abroad but the policies applied did not permit the efficient use of borrowed funds, leading to a large external indebtedness.[42]

NOTES

1. A. Emmanuel, *L'échange inégal* (Paris: Francois Maspero, 1969); English translation, *Unequal Exchange* (New York; Monthly Review Press, 1972).
2. S. Amin, *Le développement inégal* (Paris: Les Editions de Minuit, 1973); English translation, *Unequal Development* (New York: Monthly Review Press, 1976).
3. A. G. Frank, *Capitalism and Underdevelopment in Latin America* (New York: Monthly Review Press, 1967).
4. C. Furtado, *Formçcao Economica do Brasil (Rio de Janeiro: Editôra Fundo de Cultura, 1959); English translation, The Economic Growth of Brazil* (Berkeley, Cal.: University of California Press, 1963).
5. I. Wallerstein, *The Capitalist World Economy* (Cambridge, England: Cambridge University Press, 1979).
6. It is a different question as to whether these authors may properly be considered Marxists. In 'A Critical Assessment of Some Neo-Marxian Trade Theories,' *Journal of Development Studies*, XX (1984) pp. 202–26, H. D. Evans calls them neo-Marxists, but this is denied by Weaver and Jameson, according to whom 'neo-Marxists take as their starting point a critique of the weaknesses of dependency theory.' J. Weaver and K. Jameson, *Economic Development: Competing Paradigms* (Washington, DC: Agency for International Development, 1978) p. 91. It is not our purpose here to enter into this debate or to deal with various shades of Marxist thought on development.
7. *Future Results of British Rule in India, 1853* as cited in G. Palma, 'Dependency and Development: A Critical Overview,' in D. Seers (ed.), *Dependency Theory: A Critical Reassessment* (London: Frances Pinter, 1981) p. 26.
8. P. A. Baran, *The Political Economy of Growth* (New York: Monthly Review Press, 1957).
9. Ibid., p. 402.
10. While Baran was the first major Marxist writer to have reached such a

conclusion, in the Communist political literature the potential conflict between the capitalism of advanced countries and the interests of the less developed countries has come to be noted from the 1920s onwards. For an excellent discussion, see Palma, pp. 39–41.

11. Marx defines surplus value as the difference between the value of the product and the value of labor power used directly and indirectly in its manufacture.

12. R. Prebisch, *The Economic Development of Latin America and its Principal Problems* (Lake Success, NY: United Nations, 1950).

13. H. Singer, 'The Distribution of Gains between Investing and Borrowing Countries,' *American Economic Review*, XL (1950) pp. 473–85.

14. This is not to say that the policy recommendations would be the same in the two cases. While Prebisch and Singer recommend industrial protection, the more recent Latin American writers would go further in proposing delinking from the capitalist system.

15. C. Furtado, 'The Concept of External Dependence in the Study of Underdevelopment,' in Charles K. Wilber (ed.), *The Political Economy of Development and Underdevelopment* (New York: Random House, 1973) pp. 118–23.

16. C. Furtado, 'Marx's Model in the Analysis of the Underdeveloped Economic Structures,' in *Marx and Contemporary Scientific Thought* (London: Mouton Publishers, 1970) pp. 407–14.

17. S. Amin, 'Some Thoughts on Self-Reliance Development, Collective Self-Reliance and the NIEO,' paper presented to the Conference on the Past and Prospects of the Economic World Order (Stockholm: Institute for International Economics, 1978); I. M. D. Little, *Economic Development. Theory, Policy, and International Relations* (New York: Basic Books for the Twentieth Century Fund, 1982).

18. Amin, *Le développement inégal.*

19. H. D. Evans, 'Trade, Production, and Self-Reliance,' in Dudley Seers (ed.), *Dependency Theory: A Critical Reassessment* (London: Frances Pinter, 1981) pp. 119–34.

20. Prebisch, *The Economic Development of Latin America and its Principal Problems.*

21. J. Spraos, *Inequalizing Trade?* (Oxford: Clarendon Press, 1983).

22. R. E. Lipsey, *Price and Quantity Trends in the Foreign Trade of the United States* (Princeton: Princeton University Press, 1963).

23. C. P. Kindleberger, *Terms of Trade, A European Case Study* (London: Chapman & Hall, 1956).

24. I. B. Kravis, and R. E. Lipsey, 'Prices and Terms of Trade for Developed Country Exports of Manufactured Goods,' in B. Csikós-Nagy, D. Hague, and G. Hall (eds), *The Economics of Relative Prices* (New York: St Martin's Press, 1984) pp. 415–45.

25. For a discussion of this issue, see Balassa 'The Terms of Trade Controversy and the Evolution of Soft Financing: Early Years in the UN. Comment,' in G. M. Meier and D. Seers (eds), *Pioneers in Development* (Oxford: Oxford University Press, 1984) pp. 304–11.

26. Between 1977 and 1985, the UN unit value index for manufactured goods exported by the developed countries increased by 23 percent. Assuming that the extent of the bias in the unit value index was the same as in the 1953–77 period, the increase in the prices of manufactured goods exported by the developed countries would be estimated at 11 percent, with a further downward adjustment needed for quality changes. In turn, the World Bank's price index for the nonfuel primary exports of developing countries declined by 12

percent. At the same time, the UN unit value index of manufactured goods exported by the developing countries, which came to exceed the value of their nonfuel exports, rose by 22 percent.

27. M. Michaely, *Trade, Income Levels, and Dependence* (Amsterdam: North-Holland, 1985).
28. More exactly, the calculations pertain to price changes for goods classified by income level, when the income level of exports (imports) is derived as an income-weighted average of exports by individual countries. The cited results refer to data for the lower half and the upper half of the distribution. The relevant formulas are provided in Michaely.
29. Essay 1 in this volume.
30. B. Balassa and Associates, *The Structure of Protection in Developing Countries* (Baltimore, Md.: Johns Hopkins University Press, 1971).
31. H. J. Bruton, 'The Import Substitution Strategy of Economic Development: A Survey,' *Pakistan Development Review*, X (1970) pp. 124–46.
32. World Bank, *World Development Report* 1981 (Washington, DC: 1981).
33. See Essay 4 in this volume.
34. B. Balassa, 'Adjustment Policies and Development Strategies in Sub-Saharan Africa, 1973–78,' in M. Syrquin, L. Taylor, and L. E. Westphal (eds), *Economic Structure and Performance*, Essays in Honor of Hollis B. Chenery (New York: Academic Press, 1984) pp. 317–40.
35. The latest data on US foreign direct investments are reported in US Department of Commerce, 'U.S. Direct Investment Abroad: Country and Industry Detail for Position and Balance of Payments Flows, 1984,' *Survey of Current Business*, LXV (1985) pp. 30–46 and on the US economy in *Economic Report of the President*, February 1986 (Washington, DC: US Government Printing Office, 1986).
36. The data derive from United Nations publications.
37. Data based on United Nations Industrial Development Organization, *Industrial Development Survey*, various issues.
38. Instituto Nacional de Estadisticas de Chile, *Censo Nacional* (Santiago, Chile: 1985).
39. G. P. Pfeffermann, 'Latin America and the Caribbean: Economic Performance and Policies,' *The Southwestern Review of Management and Economics*, II (1982) pp. 129–59.
40. See Essay 1 in this volume.
41. B. Balassa and Associates, *Development Strategies in Semi-Industrial Economies* (Baltimore, Md.: Johns Hopkins University Press, 1982).
42. See Essay 2 in this volume.

Essay 6   The Adding-Up Problem

INTRODUCTION

The 'Adding-Up Problem,' or the 'Fallacy of Composition,' has been with us for some time. In presenting the favorable economic results of countries following outward-oriented policies, or advocating the adoption of such policies in other countries, one often encounters the objection: 'But what would happen if everyone did the same?' The implicit, or explicit, contention is that there would not be enough markets, or that protectionist reactions would be triggered in the developed world, as a result of the onslaught of exports by the developing countries.

The argument was to be given professional respectability with the publication of a paper by William Cline.[1] Cline claimed that other developing countries could not match the economic performance of the East Asian countries, because market limitations in the developed countries would not permit a sevenfold rise in developing country manufactured exports, necessary in order to attain the East Asian 'norm in terms of the ratio of manufactured exports to GNP (with allowance made for differences in population size and per capita income). Recognizing that low income countries cannot be expected to match the East Asian performance for some time to come, Cline immediately modified his analysis, limiting it to seven developing countries (Argentina, Brazil, Colombia, Mexico, Indonesia, Israel, and Malaysia) and postulating a fourfold increase in developing country manufactured exports, so as to permit these countries to reach the East Asian 'norm.'

It was soon pointed out, however, that this estimate is also much exaggerated. Immediate reasons are the inclusion of Indonesia among countries with a potential for the rapid expansion of manufactured exports; the disregard of natural resources that require slower expansion of manufactured exports for economic growth, both because of the possibilities for primary exports and because of lower import needs; and the neglect of the potential for intra-LDC trade. Considering further the process of upgrading and export diversification as developing countries reach higher levels of industrialization, the possibilities for intra-industry trade between developed and developing countries, the use by the developing countries of increments in their export earnings to import from the developed countries, and the time element involved in any policy change, the Cline argument about the expansion of developing country manufactured

99

exports hurting against import constraints in the developed countries is practically emptied of its content.[2]

The question has been formulated in a different way by Sir Arthur Lewis.[3] While Cline couched his argument in static terms as he failed to admit economic growth in the developed countries, Lewis resurrected the postwar argument of export pessimism in a growth context. He suggested that developed country markets are not growing rapidly enough to accommodate a desirable rate of economic expansion in the developing countries.

A further question, raised in a somewhat different form by Cline, is whether satisfactory rates of overall export expansion may create protectionist reactions in developed country industries, which are of particular importance to the developing countries. This, in turn, leads to a consideration of the employment effects of the expansion of trade in manufactured goods between developed and developing countries.

The questions just stated will be addressed in the following. This will be done by reformulating the 'adding up' problem with reference to overall and sectoral import constraints. The analysis will be carried out in numerical terms, utilizing available information for recent periods.

Section I will consider the question if there is an overall constraint for developing country export expansion. This will be followed by an analysis of the sectoral and the geographical pattern of trade in manufactured goods between developed and developing countries (Sections II and III). Next, projections of the employment effects of this trade will be made and the implications of these projections will be drawn (Sections IV and V).

I AN OVERALL CONSTRAINT FOR DEVELOPING COUNTRY EXPORT EXPANSION?

In his Nobel Prize lecture, Sir Arthus Lewis suggested that a 6 percent rate of economic growth in the developing countries would require a 6 percent rate of expansion of their exports. He claimed, however, that the primary exports of these countries to the developed countries would rise by only 4 percent a year.[4]

Apart from the slowdown of economic growth in the developed countries, Lewis attributed this result to a historical relationship between the growth of industrial production and the exports of primary products, with an elasticity of 0.87 of the latter in regard to the former. In so doing he did not envisage the possibility that developing countries could gain export market shares in primary products or that they could rely on manufactured exports to promote their economic growth. Both of these assumptions are open to objections, however.

As Riedel correctly stated in a critique of Lewis's thesis, in primary products other than tropical beverages developing countries compete with developed countries and their market share should not be considered a datum. Correspondingly, the ratio between their primary exports and economic activity in the developed countries may change.[5]

This is, in fact, what happened following the quadrupling of petroleum prices in 1973. While the average rate of GDP growth in the developed countries fell from 4.7 percent in 1963–73 to 2.5 percent in 1973–84, the rate of growth of the non-fuel primary exports of the developing countries to the developed countries rose from 2.5 percent to 4.6 percent between the two periods.[6] The rise in the growth rate was especially large for foods and beverages (from 2.1 to 5.9 percent), followed by nonferrous metals (from 3.5 and 3.9 percent), with a small decline for industrial materials (from 2.9 to 2.8 percent).

Considering the entire 1963–84 period, and adjusting for changes in relative prices, a 1 percent increase in the gross domestic product of the developed countries appears to have been associated with a 0.5 percent increase in their imports of non-fuel primary products from the developing countries. But this was more than offset by a 1.9 percent rise in fuel exports and a 3.8 percent increase in manufactured imports for each 1 percent rise in GDP. All in all, the exports of the developing countries to the developed countries rose by 1.5 percent for each one percent increase in the latter's GDP (Table 1.2).

It follows that there is no overall trade constraint for economic growth in the developing countries as Lewis postulates. In fact, these countries have been particularly successful in increasing their non-fuel exports after 1973, with average annual export growth rates of 5.3 percent in 1963–73 and 8.3 percent in 1973–84 whereas economic growth rates in the developed countries fell by nearly one-half. The experience of this period disproves the existence of any constant relationship between import expansion and economic growth in the developed countries.

It is further apparent that the neglect of manufactured exports is a fatal omission in Lewis's argument. With their rapid expansion, manufactured goods have assumed increasing importance in the exports of the developing countries. They accounted for 7 percent of the total exports of these countries in 1963, 13 percent in 1973 and 40 percent in 1984, when the ratio reached 59 percent exclusive of fuels. In turn, developing countries account for only 23 percent of the world exports of nonfuel primary products.[7]

Correspondingly, particular interest attaches to the prospects for the manufactured exports of the developing countries. This will be the subject of the rest of the essay.[8]

II THE SECTORAL PATTERN OF TRADE IN MANUFACTURED GOODS

It has been customary to concentrate on the developing countries' exports of textiles, clothing, and shoes. But, while clothing and footwear exports continued to rise rapidly in recent years, such was not the case for textiles. This is shown in Table 6.1 that provides information on constant price growth rates of manufactured exports for the developing countries in thirty industrial categories for the periods 1963–73, 1973–83, and 1963–83.

The data, summarized for eight industry groups, indicate that textiles, clothing, and shoes had export growth rates below the developing country average in both 1963–73 and 1973–83. By contrast, engineering products had above-average growth rates in the first period and exceeded the average nearly twice in the second. Above-average export growth rates were exhibited also by the miscellaneous group of other industries in the first period and paper and paper products and nonmetallic products in the second.

Growth rates depend on the point of departure, hence interest attaches to absolute figures. These show that, among the thirty industrial categories, clothing continues to lead, with developing country exports of $18.2 billion in 1983. It is followed by radios and television sets including their parts and components)of $12.6 billion; other industries, $7.9 billion; spinning and weaving, $5.6 billion; basic chemicals, $5.0 billion; iron and steel and electrical machinery, $3.8 billion each; and footwear $3.7 billion.

Taken together, engineering products ($33.0 billion) surpassed textiles, clothing, and footwear ($32.1 billion) in the manufactured exports of the developing countries to the developed countries in 1983. Apart from other industries ($7.9 billion), major product categories include chemicals, $10.6 billion; wood products and furniture, $4.8 billion; iron and steel, $3.8 billion; nonmetallic products, $1.3 billion; and paper and paper products, $1.1 billion (Table 6.2).

These figures show the process of upgrading and diversification of developing country exports of manufactured goods that occurred during the past decade. They are also indicative of the increasing extent of intra-industry trade between developed and developing countries, which characterizes engineering products.

III THE GEOGRAPHICAL PATTERN OF TRADE IN MANUFACTURED GOODS

Further interest attaches to the geographical pattern of trade in manufactured products. For this purpose, developing countries have been divided into newly-industrializing countries (NICs), newly-exporting countries

TABLE 6.1 *Growth rates of manufactured exports of developing countries to developed countries*

Industry category		*1963–73*	*1973–83*	*1963–83*
32	Textile, apparel, and leather products	18.73	8.08	13.28
33	Wood products and furniture	16.25	2.75	9.29
34	Paper and paper products	11.53	9.81	10.67
35	Chemicals	19.27	6.78	12.85
36	Non-metallic products	17.94	8.87	13.32
37	Iron and steel	18.82	5.01	11.70
38	Engineering products	24.42	16.68	20.49
39	Other industries	25.55	0.71	12.44
3211	Spinning, weaving, etc.	12.86	2.17	7.38
321	–3211 Textile products	13.62	1.78	7.54
322	Wearing apparel	29.84	11.08	20.09
323	Leather and products	17.33	5.88	11.46
324	Footwear	28.05	18.05	22.95
331	Wood products	16.10	−0.10	7.70
332	Furniture, fixtures	19.52	21.70	20.60
3411	Pulp, paper etc.	9.63	9.57	9.60
341	–3411 Paper products	37.60	10.90	23.53
3511	Basic Chem. excluding fertilizers	16.26	6.31	11.17
3513	Synthetic resins, etc.	36.41	15.15	25.33
351	–3511/13 Other industrial chemical	24.30	4.26	13.84
3522	Drugs and medicines	24.38	4.89	14.22
352	–3522 Other chemical products	10.33	2.28	6.23
355	Rubber products	32.49	11.98	21.81
356	Plastic products, NEC	34.69	6.79	19.93
361	Pottery, China etc.	31.51	18.15	24.65
362	Glass and products	21.67	8.74	15.02
369	Non-metallic products, NEC	13.93	2.76	8.20
371	Iron and steel	18.82	5.01	11.70
381	Metal products	26.57	12.97	19.58
3825	Office, computing etc.	63.08	17.19	38.25
382	–3825 Machinery other	21.57	18.37	19.96
3832	Radio, television, etc.	33.39	19.79	26.40
383	–3832 Electrical machinery	39.61	13.48	25.87
3841	Shipbuilding, repair	13.25	12.41	12.83
3843	Motor vehicles	26.74	21.44	24.06
384	–3841/43 Transport equipment	9.76	10.52	10.14
385	Professional goods	31.18	17.87	24.34
390	Other industries	25.55	0.71	12.44
Total		20.19	8.54	14.21

SOURCE: United Nations' COMTRADE data-base.

TABLE 6.2 *Manufactured exports of developing countries to developed countries, 1963 and 1983: eight industry groups*
(1983 US$ million)

		NIC Latin America	NIC Far East	NEC Latin America	NEC N. Africa	NEC S. Asia	NEC Far East	Israel, S. Africa, Yugoslavia, Turkey	China	Other non-oil LDC	OPEC	All LDC
32 Textile, apparel, Leather products	1963	267.0	618.1	20.5	70.9	1000.5	40.6	200.8	122.1	139.7	175.6	2656.0
	1983	2249.5	16933.5	360.8	864.4	2645.2	1441.0	2372.9	3174.7	1664.7	441.1	32147.8
33 Wood products and furniture	1963	109.1	44.0	12.6	11.1	3.0	69.6	174.9	10.4	314.4	65.4	814.5
	1983	472.0	1718.5	16.0	8.0	23.2	1099.9	435.3	229.4	306.3	507.0	4815.8
34 Paper and paper products	1963	2.0	1.9	0.1	14.6	0.3	0.3	99.4	2.4	7.2	10.9	139.1
	1983	558.9	83.0	1.7	27.4	1.8	13.3	192.5	12.7	162.9	2.0	1056.2
35 Chemicals	1963	181.9	94.9	69.1	24.1	37.9	5.0	200.3	31.4	281.7	21.5	947.9
	1983	1452.0	3614.8	344.5	315.3	109.0	246.0	1379.7	706.9	1989.7	480.3	10638.1
36 Non-metallic products	1963	12.4	9.2	4.3	5.4	3.3	0.2	47.7	2.6	14.9	3.0	103.0
	1983	262.1	630.8	8.9	1.8	26.7	32.0	131.6	87.7	68.1	5.7	1255.5
37 Iron and steel	1963	60.8	4.5	0.6	3.9	7.0	0.0	220.2	12.1	90.1	21.8	421.1
	1983	1060.2	1363.2	27.6	4.7	20.8	26.1	783.6	16.4	375.8	171.1	3849.5
38 Engineering products	1963	36.8	104.3	6.4	15.1	57.5	4.2	159.1	3.1	336.1	70.9	793.7
	1983	5611.7	18245.8	74.2	139.5	302.8	3052.8	1569.9	320.8	2872.9	814.8	33005.3
39 Other industries	1963	33.7	256.5	8.2	4.6	69.1	7.8	230.4	12.1	123.2	15.6	761.1
	1983	209.2	3429.4	115.7	23.6	653.7	376.6	993.0	226.2	1806.5	112.5	7946.5
Total	1963	703.8	1133.6	121.9	149.8	1178.7	127.6	1332.8	196.1	1307.3	384.8	6636.5
	1983	11875.6	46019.1	949.5	1384.8	3783.2	6287.7	7858.5	4774.8	9246.9	2534.6	94714.6
Per cent	1963	10.6	17.1	1.8	2.3	17.8	1.9	20.1	3.0	19.7	5.8	100.0
	1983	12.5	48.6	1.0	1.5	4.0	6.6	8.3	5.0	9.8	2.7	100.0

SOURCE: United Nations' COMTRADE data-base.

(NECs), and less developed countries (LDCs), with a further breakdown based on their geographical location.

In an earlier study by the author, newly-industrializing countries were defined as countries having a share of manufacturing value added of 20 percent and higher in the gross domestic product in 1977 and per capita incomes of at least $1100 in 1978[9]. The same list of countries is obtained by applying the 20 percent benchmark in 1984 and using a per capita income figure of $1700 for that year.[10] (The only exception is Turkey that falls below the $1700 benchmark in 1984 but was nevertheless retained in the NIC group.)

The newly-exporting countries have been defined by the joint requirement that the share of manufacturing value added in GDP was at least 15 percent or manufactured goods accounted for at least 30 percent of total exports in 1984 *and* manufactured exports reached $250 million, i.e. 0.03 percent of world manufactured exports, and 0.2 percent of manufactured exports by the developing countries, in 1984.[11]

Among the newly-industrializing countries, the combined market share of the Far Eastern NICs (Hong Kong, Korea, Singapore, and Taiwan) in the manufactured exports of the developing countries rose from 17.1 percent in 1963 to 48.6 percent in 1983. The share of the Latin American NICs (Argentina, Brazil, Chile, Mexico, and Uruguay) increased to a much lesser extent, from 10.6 to 12.5 percent while that of the miscellaneous group, Israel, South Africa, Turkey, and Yugoslavia, declined from 20.1 to 8.3 percent (Table 6.2).

Among the newly exporting countries, only those of the Far East (Malaysia, Philippines, and Thailand) gained market shares, from 1.9 percent in 1963 to 6.6 percent in 1983. The losses were especially pronounced in the South Asian NECs (Bangladesh, India, Pakistan, and Sri Lanka), whose market share fell from 17.8 percent in 1963 to 4.0 percent in 1983. They were followed by the Latin American NECs (Columbia, Costa Rica, Guatemala, Peru, and Venezuela), with a decline from 1.8 to 1.0 percent, and the North African and Middle Eastern NECs (Egypt, Jordan, Morocco, and Tunisia), with a decrease from 2.3 to 1.5 percent.

Among the less developed countries, China made the largest gains, from 3.0 percent in 1963 to 5.0 percent in 1983, while the rest of the group lost ground (19.7 and 9.8 percent). Finally, the share of OPEC other than Indonesia and Venezuela declined from 5.8 to 2.7 percent.

The large variations in export performance among the three groups shows the importance of supply factors in the form of policy differences as against demand factors in the form of market constraints. Countries at similar levels of development faced essentially the same markets but performed very differently.

The adoption of outward oriented policies and the maintenance of these policies in response to external shocks contributed to the rapid growth of manufactured exports by the Far Eastern NICs. Rather than biasing the system of incentives against exports, these countries provided similar incentives to exports and import substitution and maintained realistic exchange rates.

Among the Latin American NICs, Brazil came the nearest to the policies followed by the Far Eastern NICs and it was largely responsible for increases in export market shares by the group. By contrast, Argentina and Mexico followed inward-oriented policies, biasing the system of incentives against exports, and had repeated periods of overvaluation, with considerable losses in export market shares. Finally, having earlier followed inward-oriented policies, Chile and Uruguay reformed the system of incentives in response to the quadrupling of petroleum prices but, given their small size, the subsequent gains in export market shares did not appreciably affect the results for the group.

Among the four other NICs, Israel and Yugoslavia reduced reliance on external markets after the mid-sixties. In turn, Turkey turned from an extreme case of inward orientation to outward-oriented policies in 1980. But, with little change occurring in South Africa's inward-oriented policies, the combined losses of export market shares by the group continued after 1973, albeit to a lesser extent than beforehand.

Among the newly-exporting countries, gains in export market shares in the Far Eastern NECs find their origin in the increasingly outward-oriented stance adopted by these countries. The other groups of NECs persisted in the application of inward-oriented policies, with consequent losses in market shares. The South Asian NECs,which suffered by far the largest losses in exports shares, are dominated by India which lost its earlier market position by turning inward.

Among less developed countries, its opening to the world economy helped China make gains in exports. The rest of the group consists of a large number of countries of different size; their evaluation would necessitate further geographical disaggregation which has not been attempted here.[12] Finally, losses of export market shares by OPEC countries may be explained by the 'Dutch disease,' owing to the rise of petroleum prices.

The expansion of manufactured exports by the Far Eastern NICs has involved a considerable upgrading and diversification of exports. While in 1963 textiles, clothing, and shoes, together with simple manufactured goods (wigs, toys, sports goods), accounted for 77 percent of the manufactured exports of these countries, the combined share of these products fell to 44 percent in 1983. In the same year, engineering products came to surpass textiles, clothing, and shoes, with a share of 40 percent, four-tenths of which consisted of radios and television sets and the rest chiefly of machinery, office, and computing equipment, and metal products (Table 6.2).

Apart from textiles, clothing, and shoes (38 percent), natural-resource based wood products and furniture (16 percent) and chemicals (26 percent) dominated the manufactured exports of the Latin American NICs in 1963 while engineering products had a share of only 5 percent. By 1983, engineering products accounted for 47 percent of the total, with radio and television sets, motor vehicles, and electrical machinery being the most important items, which originated to a large extent from Brazil.

The decline in the share of the miscellaneous group of NICs (Israel, South Africa, Turkey, and Yugoslavia) between 1963 and 1983 was accompanied by a doubling in the share of textiles, clothing, and shoes in their manufactured exports, from 15 percent to 30 percent. The shares of engineering products (from 9 to 20 percent) and chemicals (from 15 to 18 percent) increased also, and the declines were concentrated in wood products and furniture (from 13 to 6 percent) and in iron and steel (from 17 to 10 percent).

Outward orientation in the Far Eastern NECs also brought with it a decline in the shares of textiles, clothing, and shoes from 32 percent in 1963 to 23 percent in 1983, and an increase in the share of engineering products from 3 to 49 percent. In 1983, textiles, clothing and shoes accounted for the largest percentage of manufactured exports in the South Asian NICs (70 percent, although below the 85 percent figure in 1963), followed by China (68 percent), the North African and Middle Eastern NICs (62 percent) the Latin American NICs (38 percent), and OPEC (17 percent).[13]

The results indicate the process of upgrading and diversification that occurred in the export structure of the Far Eastern NICs and the Latin American NICs. And while textiles, clothing, and shoes retained their importance in the former group of countries, these products have also undergone considerable upgrading. This has involved shifting from grey fabrics to printed fabrics and from low-quality clothing to fashion garments.

The process of upgrading and diversification has also occurred in the Far Eastern NECs. Again, the policies applied had largely determined the outcome. At the same time, increased concentration in engineering products in these countries has contributed to intra-industry trade with the developed countries.

Intra-industry trade limits the cost of adjustment in the developed countries as it does not involve the inter-industry shift of resources. In fact, the international division of the production process in the form of increased sourcing of parts, components, and accessories improves the competitive position of developed country industries.

Diversification in developing country exports also limits the cost of adjustment in the developed countries, compared with concentration in particular industries. Similar considerations apply to the shift of particular exports, such as textiles, clothing, and shoes, from the NICs to the NECs as the developed countries are little affected by the replacement of one source of supply by another.

At the same time, an important aspect of adjustment in the developed countries is the employment effect of trade with the developing countries. This will be considered in the following. First, employment–output coefficients will be derived. Next, estimates on the prospective effects of trade in manufactured goods on employment in the developed countries will be presented.[14]

IV ESTIMATING LABOR COEFFICIENTS

In the present investigation, labor coefficients (the ratio of employment to output) have been estimated for individual countries in the 30 industrial category breakdown used in the tables. As a first step, average employment–output ratios for several years have been calculated for each country, for which data are available,[15] and the results have been converted into US dollars and expressed in terms of 1983 prices. The average labor coefficients thus obtained for particular industrial categories in the individual countries have next been regressed on average per capita incomes for the years 1979–81.[16]

The regression coefficients have the expected negative sign, ranging between −0.43 and −0.78, with a median of 0.60;[17] in the double-logarithmic form utilized in the estimation, the coefficients represent the elasticities of the employment–output ratios with respect to per capita incomes. All the regression coefficients are statistically significant at the 1 percent level while the adjusted coefficient of determination varies between 0.46 and 0.89 (Table 6.3).[18]

The estimated equations have been utilized to derive predicted values of the labor coefficients for particular industrial categories for each of the countries included in the investigation. Table 6.4 summarizes the average labor coefficients in trade in manufactured goods between developed and developing countries in 1983 in the 30 industrial category breakdown. The table shows that, in trade in manufactured products with the developing countries, the average labor coefficient was 14.4 for the exports and 18.0 for the imports of the developed countries.

The results obtained find their origin in differences in the labor-intensity of the exports and imports of the developed countries. For one thing, the developed countries have the lowest export–import ratios in industries with a relatively high labor content, such as clothing and shoes. For another thing, pulp and paper and processed chemicals, with the lowest labor coefficients, have relatively high export–import ratios in the developed countries.

There are a number of exceptions, however. They include basic chemicals that have one of the lowest labor coefficients but a barely above average export–import ratio for the developed countries. By contrast, motor vehicles have a below-average labor coefficient and an above-average export–import ratio. All in all, the Spearman rank correlation coefficient between average labor coefficients and the export–import ratios of the developed countries is -0.53, statistically significant at the 1 percent level.[19]

So far the discussion has concerned the average labor coefficients derived from developed country data. For reasons discussed earlier, labor coefficients for the developing countries are much higher than those for the developed countries. The coefficients estimated for the developing countries average 61.9 for their exports and 47.0 for their imports in trade in manufactured goods with the developed countries in 1983. At the same time, their inter-industry pattern is rather similar, although some differences are observed among industries, owing to differences in the elasticity of labor with respect to output.[20]

The results conform to the expected pattern of the developed countries exchanging capital-intensive products for labor-intensive products originating in the developing countries. It further appears that the labor-intensity of exports is correlated with the level of economic development.

Thus, the ratio of the relative labor-intensity of China's exports to that of its imports, denoted as the average employment coefficient (X/M) in Table 6.5, is 2.38; at the other extreme, the average ratio is 1.09 for Israel, South Africa, Turkey, and Yugoslavia (Table 6.5).[21]

China is followed by the South Asian countries, which have the lowest incomes among the NECs, with an average employment coefficient of 1.93. Latin American countries apart, we find a further progression in terms of labor coefficients as we move to the newly-exporting countries and, again, to the newly-industrializing countries. Thus, the average employment coefficient is 1.65 in the Far Eastern NECs, 1.62 in the North African and Middle Eastern NECs, and 1.57 for the Far Eastern NICs.

The relevant figures are 1.35 for the Latin American NECs and 1.22 for the Latin American NICs. The results conform to the findings of a research project under the direction of Anne Krueger, which showed a bias towards capital-intensive exports in Latin America.[22] This bias finds its origin in the protectionist policies applied by most of these countries that distort their trade pattern. By contrast, the relatively high labor intensity of exports by the Far Eastern NICs is again indicative of the fact that these countries have followed policies aimed at exploiting their comparative advantage in labor-intensive products.

Finally, the relative labor intensity of exports to imports varies little among the developed countries. The range is between 0.74 in the United States and 0.85 in Japan, corresponding approximately to the range of per capita incomes.

TABLE 6.3 Regression results for employment–output ratios

ISIC	Industry	Constant	t-value	Coefficient	t-value	R-square	N
3211	Spinning, weaving, etc.	1.775	5.80	−0.623	−15.90	0.8873	33
321 −3211	Textile products	1.629	4.37	−0.609	−12.84	0.8631	27
322	Wearing apparel	2.140	3.90	−0.617	−8.85	0.6424	44
323	Leather and products	0.680	1.05	−0.506	−6.17	0.5006	38
324	Footwear	1.618	3.18	−0.571	−8.89	0.6670	40
331	Wood products	3.127	4.92	−0.784	−9.73	0.7112	39
332	Furniture, fixtures	2.576	4.55	−0.697	−9.61	0.6955	41
3411	Pulp, paper etc.	1.291	3.14	−0.656	−12.56	0.8176	36
341 −3411	Paper products	0.562	1.14	−0.556	−8.91	0.7234	31
3511	Basic chem. excluding fertilizers	1.132	1.83	−0.667	−8.42	0.6858	33
3513	Synthetic resins, etc.	0.548	0.77	−0.598	−6.71	0.6202	28
351 −3511/13	Other industrial chemical	−0.536	−0.68	−0.505	−5.09	0.5672	20
3522	Drugs and medicines	−0.015	−0.04	−0.503	−9.55	0.7261	35
352 −3522	Other chemical prod.	0.828	1.93	−0.614	−11.14	0.8202	28
355	Rubber products	0.527	1.12	−0.513	−8.54	0.6428	41

356	Plastic products, NEC	1.568	3.69	−0.634	−11.71	0.7684	42
361	Pottery, China etc.	2.280	4.95	−0.641	−10.94	0.7625	38
362	Glass and products	1.733	4.68	−0.646	−13.78	0.8288	40
369	Non-metallic products, NEC	1.517	3.34	−0.656	−11.43	0.7827	37
371	Iron and steel	−0.656	−1.65	−0.429	−8.53	0.6364	42
381	Metal products	1.072	2.58	−0.563	−10.74	0.7506	39
3825	Office, computing etc.	1.324	1.20	−0.620	−4.56	0.4626	24
382 −3825	Machinery other	0.334	0.61	−0.490	−7.29	0.7035	23
3832	Radio, television, etc.	0.084	0.17	−0.410	−6.43	0.5285	37
383 −3832	Electrical machinery	0.220	0.75	−0.474	−12.63	0.8319	33
3841	Shipbuilding, repair	1.554	4.49	−0.617	−14.09	0.8495	36
3843	Motor vehicles	0.308	0.47	−0.536	−6.33	0.5271	36
384 −3841/43	Transport equipment	−0.105	−0.22	−0.437	−7.36	0.6634	28
385	Professional goods	1.176	2.87	−0.570	−11.24	0.8016	32
390	Other industries	0.500	0.71	−0.493	−5.50	0.4549	36

SOURCE: See text.

TABLE 6.4 Trade in manufactured goods between developed and developing countries

	Average labor coefficient				Developed countries total			
	Developed countries		Developing countries					
Industry category	Exports	Imports	Exports	Imports	Exports	Imports	Balance	X/M ratio
3211 Spinning, weaving, etc.	20.15	19.59	100.94	75.45	6870	5871	999	1.17
321 -3211 Textile products	19.27	18.07	105.55	73.69	2026	2160	-134	0.94
322 Wearing apparel	30.14	26.06	104.21	117.35	2141	19000	-16859	0.11
323 Leather and products	19.08	18.25	56.38	47.29	951	2618	-1667	0.36
324 Footwear	31.17	23.27	75.70	97.18	642	3839	-3197	0.17
331 Wood products	17.34	16.78	87.57	100.51	1624	3590	-1966	0.45
332 Furniture, fixtures	23.92	18.43	79.39	96.74	1372	1426	-54	0.96
3411 Pulp, paper etc.	8.37	9.00	34.67	39.93	4047	886	3160	4.56
341 -3411 Paper products	9.97	9.35	31.74	35.12	1078	214	864	5.04
3511 Basic chem. excluding fertilizers	6.74	6.81	35.49	33.14	15179	5235	9944	2.90
3513 Synthetic resins, etc.	7.13	6.86	19.80	27.68	8277	738	7539	11.21
351 -3511/13 Other industrial chemical	5.37	5.93	14.39	23.12	3409	474	2935	7.19
3522 Drugs and medicines	9.78	9.33	35.89	32.09	3892	457	3435	8.52

Code		1	2	3	4	5	6	7	8
352	-3522 Other chemical products	8.03	7.72	42.41	30.57	5045	663	4381	7.61
355	Rubber products	15.48	13.84	33.64	47.50	2239	1086	1152	2.06
356	Plastic products, NEC	14.46	12.36	35.37	55.54	1330	2434	-1103	0.55
361	Pottery, China etc.	29.34	24.13	100.78	106.94	728	519	209	1.40
362	Glass and products	15.70	13.45	47.47	60.19	1336	426	911	3.14
369	Non-metallic products, NEC	13.61	9.97	43.09	42.93	3649	363	3286	10.05
371	Iron and steel	10.38	9.50	22.17	28.66	16520	4010	12510	4.12
381	Metal products	17.30	14.73	46.33	55.03	11963	2832	9131	4.22
3825	Office, computing etc.	11.35	11.05	25.67	39.14	4598	2962	1636	1.55
382	-3825 Machinery other	15.16	14.41	36.57	46.39	47281	3377	43904	14.00
3832	Radio, television, etc.	24.19	22.71	47.99	56.93	19638	13106	6532	1.50
383	-3832 Electrical machinery	15.89	14.31	32.99	42.27	14519	3987	10532	3.64
3841	Shipbuilding, repair	16.42	15.32	49.61	86.48	10300	1630	8670	6.32
3843	Motor vehicles	9.79	9.32	25.89	31.17	24273	2143	22130	11.33
384	-3841/43 Transport equipment	15.29	16.71	45.83	45.56	12457	1992	10465	6.25
385	Professional goods	16.26	16.24	41.13	57.67	9440	2349	7091	4.02
390	Other industries	18.61	17.06	52.22	52.34	5067	8278	-3211	0.61
	Average and total	14.42	18.00	61.86	47.00	241890	98663	143277	2.45

SOURCE: See text.

114

TABLE 6.5 *Employment effects of trade in manufactured goods*

	Exports	Imports	Balance	X/M ratio	Average employment coefficient (X/M)
Developed countries					
United States	661.9	794.9	-133.1	0.83	0.74
EEC	1508.1	643.7	864.3	2.34	0.76
Japan	946.7	133.9	812.8	7.07	0.85
Other OECD	371.1	203.6	167.4	1.82	0.78
OECD total	3487.7	1776.2	1711.5	1.96	0.80
Developing countries					
NIC Latin America	483.6	561.9	-78.4	0.86	1.21
Far East	1852.0	985.6	866.5	1.88	1.57
NEC Latin America	49.0	188.0	-139.0	0.26	1.33
N. Africa and Middle East	116.4	579.3	-462.9	0.20	1.61
South Asia	671.9	820.8	-149.0	0.82	1.92
Far East	488.8	646.5	-157.7	0.76	1.67
Israel, S. Africa, Yugoslavia, Turkey	302.3	612.6	-310.3	0.49	1.34
China	901.1	679.5	221.5	1.33	2.38
Other Non-oil LDC	876.4	3495.9	-2619.4	0.25	1.20
OPEC	117.3	2798.1	-2680.8	0.04	1.22
All developing countries	5858.9	11368.4	-5509.4	0.52	1.32

SOURCE: See text.

V THE PROSPECTIVE EFFECTS OF MANUFACTURED TRADE ON EMPLOYMENT IN DEVELOPED AND IN DEVELOPING COUNTRIES

The next question concerns the possible impact that the future expansion of trade in manufactured products between developed and developing countries may have on employment in the two groups of countries.[23] In an earlier paper on the subject, the author suggested estimating employment effects for hypothetical cases of (A) a balanced and (B) a proportional expansion of trade in manufactured products.[24]

Balanced expansion of trade in manufactured products

In the first case, one evaluates the employment effects of equal increases in absolute values in the exports and in the imports of the developed countries in their trade in manufactured products with the developing countries. Under the stated assumptions, comparisons of average labor coefficients for exports and imports (import-competing goods) will indicate the employment effects of balanced trade expansion. These are shown in Table 6.5 for the developed and for the developing countries as well as for various country groups within each category. They were discussed previously and will be reinterpreted here in terms of employment gains and losses associated with the balanced expansion of trade in manufactured goods between developed and developing countries.

It is apparent that, in the event of equal absolute increases in the exports and imports of manufactured products of the developed countries in trade with the developing countries, the gain in employment through export expansion will fall short by 20 percent of the loss in employment in the import-competing industries of the developed countries. Employment losses would be below average in Japan and above-average in the United States. Within an overall gain of 32 percent for the developing countries, China and the countries of South Asia would make the largest employment gains, followed by the Far Eastern and North African and Middle Eastern NECs and the Far Eastern NICs while the Latin American NICs the other LDCs and the other NICs would have small gains and the employment effects of equal absolute increases in manufactured exports and imports would be nil for OPEC.

Equiproportionate increases in exports and imports

An alternative hypothesis postulates equiproportionate increases in exports and imports in trade in manufactured products between developed and developing countries (i.e. identical rates of change in exports and imports); for short, a proportional expansion of trade. The employment effects obtainable under this alternative can be indicated by reference to Table 6.5 that provides information on the labor content of manufactured exports, and of products competing with imports, in the trade of the developed countries with the developing countries. The estimates have been derived by multiplying export and import values in the year 1983 by the labor coefficients estimated for each country in the 30 industrial category breakdown.

The results show substantial positive employment effects for the developed countries, taken together, with the ratio of job gains through exports to jobs lost through imports being estimated at 2.0. The ratio is the highest, 7.1, for Japan that would derive benefits from its export surplus in manufacturing trade with the developing countries as well as from the relative labor intensity of its exports. The corresponding ratios are 2.3 for the European Common Market and 1.8 for the group of other developed countries. However, the United States would experience a small employment loss, with a ratio of 0.8, as its small export surplus in manufacturing trade with the developing countries would not compensate by the relative labor intensity of its imports.

Finally, the equiproportionate expansion of trade in manufactured goods with the developed countries would lead to considerable job losses for the developing countries, taken together, with the ratio of jobs gained through exports to the jobs lost through imports being 0.5. At the same time, the results need to be reinterpreted by reference to the situation existing in the developing countries. This will be done in the subsequent discussion of the employment effects of trade.

Alternatives (A) and (B) represent extreme cases, with a zero trade balance in manufactured goods assumed on the margin in the first case and an equiproportionate expansion of all manufactured trade flows in the second. Neither of these alternatives can be considered realistic.

For one thing, given the large export surplus of the developed countries in trade in manufactured products with the developing countries, substantial differences in export growth rates in favor of the latter (in the first year, the ratio of the two growth rates would have to approach 2.5) would be necessary for incremental changes in exports and imports to be equal. For another thing, given recent differences in export growth rates, one cannot expect equiproportionate changes in exports and imports to occur.

Continuation of past trends in trade in manufactured products

As an alternative to the two hypothetical cases discussed so far, the assumption has been made that past trends in trade in manufactured products would continue in the future. More exactly, the assumption is that the growth rates of exports and imports in manufactured trade between developed and developing countries in the 1983–93 period will equal the growth rates observed between 1973 and 1983.

Expressed in terms of constant prices, the manufactured exports of the developed countries to the developing countries rose by 4.4 percent a year between 1973 and 1983 while their manufactured imports from these countries grew by 8.5 percent. Rather than using these average figures, however, the projections have been made by extrapolating sectoral growth rates. At the same time, it has been assumed that the country composition of exports and imports would remain unchanged.

The results are intermediate between those obtained under the assumption of a balanced expansion and an equiproportionate expansion of trade. While the export–import ratio for the increment of manufactured trade for the developing countries is 1.0 under balanced expansion, and 2.4 in the event of equiproportionate expansion, of trade, it is 1.8 if past trends are projected to continue during the 1983–93 decade.

Tables 6.6 and 6.7 report the changes in employment that would result under the projected expansion of trade between developed and developing countries. The results show a net gain of 1093 thousand jobs in the developed countries in the 1983–93 period. Among individual sectors, gains would be obtained in the technologically more advanced industries, employing to a large extent skilled and technical labor, while losses would occur in industries using chiefly semi-skilled and unskilled labor, in particular clothing and footwear. But, these losses would occur over a ten-year period, thereby limiting the cost of adjustment. Also, experience indicates that there is considerable labor mobility, at least in the United States, within skill categories among individual industries.

As far as the developing countries are concerned, we cannot speak of employment losses in the non-existing industries of the OPEC countries. OPEC imports a number of manufactured products, in particular in the electrical and non-electrical industries, which are not produced domestically.

These considerations apply to a considerable extent also to the non-oil developing countries, which import a variety of commodities that are not produced domestically. More generally, economic growth in the developing countries will require more imports without necessarily replacing domestic production. At the same time, economic growth is promoted through the expansion of exports. Thus, attention should focus on the creation of 18 million jobs through the increased manufactured exports of the non-oil developing countries to the developed countries.

If present trends continue, more than one-third of these jobs would be created in the Far Eastern NICs. They would be approached by the newly-exporting countries and China, largely because of the higher labor coefficients observed in these countries which are at lower levels of

TABLE 6.6 *Employment effects in manufacturing trade, 1983–93: industry breakdown*

Industry category	Developed countries total				Developing countries total			
	Exports	Imports	Balance	X/M ratio	Exports	Imports	Balance	X/M ratio
3211 Spinning, weaving, etc.	181.7	142.6	39.2	1.27	705.0	680.5	24.6	1.04
321 –3211 Textile products	43.1	46.5	–3.4	0.93	261.0	164.9	96.1	1.58
322 Wearing apparel	140.7	1416.0	–1275.2	0.10	5435.7	547.9	4887.8	9.92
323 Leather and products	43.0	84.6	–41.6	0.51	250.7	106.5	144.3	2.35
324 Footwear	60.9	469.7	–408.8	0.13	1467.0	189.8	1277.1	7.73
331 Wood products	86.8	59.7	27.1	1.45	298.9	502.9	–204.1	0.59
332 Furniture, fixtures	132.1	187.3	–55.2	0.71	774.3	534.3	240.0	1.45
3411 Pulp, paper etc.	40.9	19.9	21.0	2.05	73.6	195.1	–121.5	0.38
341 –3411 Paper products	21.1	5.6	15.5	3.75	18.3	74.3	–56.0	0.25
3511 Basic chemicals excluding fertilizers	159.5	65.7	93.7	2.43	329.0	784.5	–455.5	0.42
3513 Synthetic resins, etc.	64.8	20.8	44.0	3.12	57.5	251.6	–194.1	0.23
351 –3511/13 Other industrial chemicals	14.1	4.3	9.8	3.29	9.9	60.5	–50.6	0.16
3522 Drugs and medicines	48.8	6.9	41.9	7.10	25.4	160.0	–134.6	0.16
352 –3522 Other chemical prod.	64.1	6.4	57.7	9.99	33.8	243.8	–210.0	0.14

355	Rubber products	56.0	46.6	9.4	1.20	108.8	172.0	−63.2	0.63
356	Plastic products, NEC	38.3	58.0	−19.7	0.66	159.4	147.2	12.3	1.08
361	Pottery, China, etc.	58.6	66.4	−7.8	0.88	266.1	213.5	52.6	1.25
362	Glass and products	33.4	13.2	−20.1	2.52	44.8	127.8	−83.0	0.35
369	Non-metallic products, NEC	135.5	4.8	130.8	28.53	19.7	427.5	−407.7	0.05
371	Iron and steel	167.9	62.1	105.8	2.71	139.1	463.5	−324.4	0.30
381	Metal products	404.7	141.2	263.5	2.87	426.5	1287.3	−860.8	0.33
3825	Office, computing, etc.	121.0	159.9	−38.9	0.76	356.7	417.5	−60.8	0.85
382 −3825	Machinery other	1015.8	262.8	753.0	3.87	640.0	3109.5	−2469.6	0.21
3832	Radio, television, etc.	2238.4	1810.6	427.7	1.24	3672.6	5266.9	−1594.3	0.70
383 −3832	Electrical machinery	443.3	202.2	241.1	2.19	447.4	1179.4	−732.0	0.38
3841	Shipbuilding, repair	181.5	80.4	101.1	2.26	250.1	956.0	−705.9	0.26
3843	Motor vehicles	402.8	139.4	263.4	2.89	371.7	1282.0	−911.1	0.29
384 −3841/43	Transport equipment	231.0	90.5	140.5	2.55	238.2	688.6	−450.4	0.35
385	Professional goods	343.1	197.4	145.7	1.74	480.0	1217.2	−737.2	0.39
390	Other industries	143.0	151.5	−8.6	0.94	445.3	402.0	−43.3	1.11
	Total employment	7115.8	6022.9	1092.8	1.18	17806.6	21855.2	−4048.6	0.81

SOURCE: See text.

TABLE 6.7 *Employment effects in manufacturing trade, 1983–93: country breakdown*

	Exports	Imports	Balance	X/M ratio
Developed countries				
United States	1428.5	3096.2	−1667.7	0.46
EEC	2962.3	1935.3	1027.1	1.53
Japan	2026.3	369.3	1657.0	5.49
Other OECD	698.7	622.2	76.5	1.12
OECD Total	7115.8	6022.9	1092.8	1.18
Developing countries				
NIC Latin America	1855.2	1146.5	708.7	1.62
Far East	6614.0	2263.2	4350.8	2.92
NEC Latin America	104.5	352.3	−247.8	0.30
N. Africa and Middle East	307.4	1132.8	−825.4	0.27
South Asia	1443.8	1398.6	45.2	1.03
Far East	1766.5	1542.7	223.8	1.15
Israel, S. Africa, Yugoslavia, Turkey	856.3	1164.1	−307.7	0.74
China	2240.5	1100.0	1140.5	2.04
Other Non-oil LDC	2358.5	6309.5	−3951.0	0.37
OPEC	259.9	5445.6	−5185.8	0.05
All developing countries	17806.6	21855.2	−4048.6	0.81

industrial development. Finally, the other non-oil developing countries would account for one-seventh, and the Latin American NICs for one-tenth, of newly-created jobs through export. One would expect, however, inter-regional changes to occur, with China and the NECs gaining, and the NICs losing, ground in the process.

CONCLUSIONS

This essay has presented empirical evidence pertaining to the 'adding up problem' or the 'fallacy of composition.' Having noted the inappropriateness of applying the East Asian 'norm' to other developing countries, the essay has considered the alleged existence of overall and sectoral import constraints for economic growth in the developing countries.

Sir Arthur Lewis postulated that economic growth in the developing countries is limited by a fixed relationship between their primary exports and economic growth in the developed countries and neglected their possibilities to increase manufactured exports. Against this pessimistic view, the essay put forward evidence on gains in primary export market shares in the developing countries and on the increasing importance of their manufactured exports.

In fact, following the quadrupling of oil prices, these countries more than compensated for declining rates of developed country growth by stepping up their nonfuel primary and manufactured exports. As a result, in the 1963–84 period, a 1 percent increase in the gross domestic product in the developed countries was accompanied by a 1.5 percent rise in the exports of the developing countries – nearly twice the figure Lewis postulated. It can be expected that the developing countries will further step up the supply of their manufactured exports if economic growth were to slacken in the developed countries.

Manufactured exports have assumed particular importance, accounting for 59 percent of the nonfuel exports and 40 percent of the total exports of the developing countries in 1984. Correspondingly, the future prospects for the manufactured exports of these countries offer especial interest.

Following a detailed review of changes in the sectoral and the geographical pattern of the manufactured exports of the developing countries, the essay has presented alternative estimates on the employment effects of future growth in these exports. Having considered the implications of a balanced and a proportional expansion of trade in manufactured goods between the developed and the developing countries, the assumption has been made that past trends in trade in manufactured products would continue in the future.

It has been shown that, under this assumption, the developed countries would obtain a net gain of 1.1 million jobs in the 1983–93 period. This would happen as employment gains in technologically advanced industries employing technical and skilled labor would more than offset losses in industries using chiefly semi-skilled and unskilled labor. At the same time, these losses would occur over a ten-year period, thereby limiting the cost of adjustment, and there are also possibilities for the inter-industry movement of labor.

Maintaining past rates of export growth would permit the emergence of new exporters of manufactured goods. This has occurred in recent years through the adoption of outward-oriented policies by the Far Eastern NECs and the appearance of China as a major new exporter of manufactured goods, even though developing country manufactured export growth rates were lower in the 1973–84 period than in the preceding decade.

At the same time, the burden of adjustment in the developed countries is eased by reason of the fact that economic development involves changes in export composition. As developing countries accumulate capital, they shift to the exportation of relatively more capital intensive products, thereby leaving room for countries that enter at a lower level. Now, as one developing country replaces another in the imports of particular commodities by the developed countries, the problem of adjustment in the latter does not arise.

Countries graduating at higher levels, in turn, undertake the exportation of commodities in industries characterized by intra-industry specialization, involving the exchange of parts, components, and accessories, such as engineering products. This represents an important change, compared with inter-industry specialization in textiles, clothing, and shoes where changes in product composition are limited. This is because adjustment may occur through changes in the pattern of production without the loss of employment.

In fact, one may go a step further in noting that outward orientation involves the upgrading and diversification of exports that limit pressure on particular industries and permit increased intra-industry specialization to the benefit of all participants. Thus, the argument of the proponents of the fallacy of composition thesis is turned on its head: the difficulties of adjustment in the developed countries can be reduced if more developing countries adopt outward-oriented policies, rather than persisting in exporting a limited number of simple manufactures.

This conclusion gains in force if one considers that the foreign exchange obtained through the exportation of manufactured goods is spent by the developing countries to purchase manufactured goods from the developed countries. Thus, the balance of trade does not change and, under outward orientation, the increment in foreign exchange is often utilized in the same industries via intra-industry specialization.

Finally, developing countries can also export to other developing countries. With the industrialization of outward-oriented countries, they can increasingly exchange manufactured goods with countries at lower levels of development, thereby providing an impetus to their economic growth without encroaching on developed country markets.

NOTES

1. W. R. Cline, 'Can the East Asian Model Be Generalized?' *World Development*, X (1982) pp. 71–90.
2. See Essay 4 in this volume.
3. W. A. Lewis, 'The Slowing Down of the Engine of Growth,' *American Economic Review*, LXX (1980) pp. 555–64.
4. For a discussion, see Essay 4 in this volume.
5. J. Riedel, 'Trade as the Engine of Growth in Developing Countries, Revisited,' *Economic Journal*, XCIV (1984) pp. 56–73.
6. Essay 1 in this volume.
7. Essay 1, Table 1.1.
8. The use of the International Standard Industrial Classification Scheme necessitates broadening the category of manufactured products somewhat to include also simple processed goods.
9. The following discussion derives from B. Balassa, 'Adjustment to External Shocks in Developing Countries,' in B. Csikós-Nagy, D. Hague, and G. Hall (eds), *The Economics of Relative Prices* (London: Macmillan, 1984) pp. 352–84. See also Essay 1 in this volume.

10. This is the lower limit for upper middle income countries in World Bank, *World Development Report 1986* (Washington, DC: 1986) Table 6.1.
11. Alternative definitions, see Essay 1 in this volume.
12. Note further that this category is derived as a residual: the difference between the imports of manufactured goods from the developing countries reported by the developed countries and the sum of exports reported by individual developing countries.
13. The group of other LDCs is not reported here because of the uncertainty relating to the figures.
14. For an earlier analysis, see B. Balassa, 'The Employment Effects of Trade in Manufactured Products between Developed and Developing Countries,' *Journal of Policy Modelling*, VIII (1986) pp. 371–90.
15. While a complete coverage of all the developed and developing countries under review could not be achieved, data have been obtained for 27 to 44 countries in particular industry categories.
16. Per capita incomes have been taken as an indicator of the relative price of labor in intercountry relationships. This has been done for lack of comparable information on wages in the individual countries.
17. The regression coefficients are generally higher than those estimated by Lydall who used the same equational form. But, Lydall's estimates are limited to nine 'genuine' manufacturing industries, only a few of which could be exactly identified with the industrial categories used in this paper. At the same time, Lydall does not report t-values and R^2s. Cf. H. F. Lydall, *Trade and Employment* (Geneva: International Labour Office, 1975) Table 13.
18. It may be observed that the coefficient of determination is the lowest for the miscellaneous category of 'other industries.'
19. The correlation has been estimated in regard to average labor coefficients for the exports of the developed countries; the corresponding rank correlation is -0.52 in regard to the average coefficient for imports. The two series of labor coefficients differ little among themselves, with a rank correlation coefficient of 0.99, as the only difference lies in the country composition of the exports and imports of the individual countries.
20. The Spearman rank correlation is 0.88 between labor coefficients for developed countries in their manufacturing exports to developing countries and the coefficients for the latter group of countries in their imports from the developed countries. The same result has been obtained in correlating labor coefficients for developed country imports and developing country exports.
21. We do not consider here the ratio of 1.18 for the miscellaneous group of other LDCs and the ratio of 1.00 for OPEC.
22. A. O. Krueger, *Trade and Employment in Developing Countries. 3. Synthesis and Conclusions* (Chicago: University of Chicago Press, 1983).
23. The estimates are limited to the direct employment effects of exports and imports. Indirect effects operating through input–output relationships have not been estimated because of the uncertainty involved as to the domestic or imported origin of the inputs.
24. B. Balassa, 'The Changing International Division of Labor in Manufactured Goods,' *Banca Nazionale del Lavoro, Quarterly Review*, XXXII (1979) pp. 243–85.

Part III
Agriculture and Economic Development

Essay 7   Economic Incentives and Agricultural Exports in Developing Countries

This essay will examine the effects of economic incentives on exports in general, and on agricultural exports in particular, in the developing countries. Section I will introduce a simple econometric model to estimate the effects of price incentives on exports. In Section II, the model will be applied to the exports of goods and nonfactor services and to merchandise exports. In Section III, the same model will be used to indicate the effects of price incentives on agricultural exports. Sections IV, V, and VI will present information on the responsiveness of merchandise and agricultural exports to incentives in the 1960–73, 1973–8, and 1978–81 periods, respectively, by making use of intercountry comparisons.

I MODELLING THE RESPONSE OF EXPORTS TO PRICE INCENTIVES

In this section, a simple model consisting of (foreign) export demand and (domestic) export supply equations will be put forward for estimating the effects of price incentives, and of other relevant variables, on exports. Foreign demand for a country's exports (X^F) will be affected by changes in its international competitiveness. This may be indicated by changes in the index of the real exchange rate, derived as the nominal exchange rate (R) adjusted for changes in the prices of traded goods (defined in terms of wholesale prices[1]) in foreign countries (P_T^F) and in the domestic economy (P_T^D).[2] Introducing foreign incomes (Y^F) as an additional variable affecting exports, we obtain equation (1).

$$X^F = f(R.P_T^F/P_T^D; Y^F) \tag{1}$$

In turn, the supply of a country's exports (X^D) will be affected by changes in relative incentives to traded *vs.* non-traded goods. This may be indicated by an index of relative prices in the domestic economy, derived as the ratio of domestic price indices for traded goods (P_T^D) and for nontraded goods (P_N^D).[3] Introducing a domestic capacity variable (C^D), we obtain equation (2). Finally, (3) represents the equilibrium condition.

$$X^D = g(P_T^D/P_N^D; C^D) \tag{2}$$

$$X^D = X^F \tag{3}$$

The reduced form equilibrium equation, derived from this system of equations, has been estimated by utilizing time-series data for 53 developing countries for the periods 1965–73 and 1974–82 as well as for the two periods combined. The first of the two periods was characterized by rapid growth in the world economy while the second included the two oil shocks and the ensuing recessions.[4] The choice of the countries has been dictated by data availabilities, including trade and national income statistics and domestic price indices.[5]

In view of the existence of an intercorrelation between exports and domestic capacity, the export–output ratio has been used as the dependent variable in the estimation. Separate estimates have been made for the exports of goods and nonfactor services as well as for merchandise exports, with the gross domestic product used as the output variable in both cases. In turn, the combined gross domestic product of the developed countries, the principal markets for the exports of developing countries, has been used as the foreign income variable.

Estimation has been done by expressing all variables in terms of rates of change between successive years and combining time-series observations for individual countries. Experimentation with lag structures has not been successful; hence, the reported estimates utilize data in an unlagged form.

In the event, the real exchange rate variable, but not the relative price variable for traded and nontraded goods, proved to be statistically significant in the estimation. This is not surprising since changes in the real exchange rate may practically instantaneously result in the redirection of production from domestic to foreign markets while the effects of changes in the relative prices of traded and nontraded goods are slower in coming and may affect exports and output in similar ways.[6]

II EFFECTS OF PRICE INCENTIVES ON EXPORTS

Table 7.1 reports the results of estimates for the exports of goods and nonfactor services and for merchandise exports, obtained by the use of the model described in Section I, for the 53 developing countries. The table shows the individual regression coefficients, their *t*-values, the number of observations, F-statistics, and the (adjusted) coefficient of determination.

TABLE 7.1 *Regression equations for export output ratios in developing countries* (*t*-values in parentheses)

	Constant	Real exchange rate	Foreign income	N	F	$\bar{R}^2$
I. 1965–73						
(a) Exports of goods and nonfactor services	−0.11 (−3.11)**	0.25 (3.19)**	2.69 (3.82)**	424	12.64	0.052
(b) Merchandise exports	−0.16 (−4.42)**	0.71 (8.50)**	3.75 (5.07)**	424	49.90	0.188
II. 1974–82						
(a) Exports of goods and nonfactor services	−0.22 (−1.97)*	0.58 (9.79)**	1.16 (3.11)**	424	54.92	0.203
(b) Merchandise exports	−0.03 (−1.77)*	0.78 (9.93)**	1.49 (2.98)**	424	55.84	0.206
III. 1965–82						
(a) Exports of goods and nonfactor services	−0.00 (0.25)	0.48 (9.84)**	0.51 (2.00)**	901	53.08	0.104
(b) Merchandise exports	0.00 (0.39)	0.77 (12.63)**	0.56 (1.76)+	901	84.59	0.157

NOTE: (a) The variables have been expressed in terms of rates of changes between successive years for individual countries combining time-series and cross-section observations.
(b) Levels of statistical significance: + 10%; * 5%; ** 1%.

SOURCE: World Bank data-base.

The estimates pertain to the 1965–73 and the 1974–82 periods and to the two periods combined.

The real exchange rate variable has the expected sign and it is statistically significant at the 1 percent level for the merchandise exports of the 53 developing countries, in all the equations. The foreign income variable also has the expected sign and it attains the 1 percent level of significance in the equations for the 1965–73 and the 1974–82 periods. However, its significance level declines to 5 percent in the equation for the exports of goods and nonfactor services and to 10 percent in the equation for merchandise exports in cases when the two periods are combined.

According to the estimates, a 1 percent change in the real exchange rate is associated with a 0.77 percent change in the ratio of merchandise exports to output over the entire 1965–82 period. The regression coefficient is slightly lower for the first period (0.71), and slightly higher for the second (0.78), but the difference is not significant statistically.

Larger differences have been obtained for the exports of goods and nonfactor services; the regression coefficient for the real exchange rate variable rises from 0.25 in 1965–73 to 0.58 in 1974–82; it takes the value of 0.48 for the entire period. The difference between the regression coefficients for the 1965–73 and 1974–82 periods is statistically significant at the 1 percent level, indicating a shift in the underlying function.

In view of the relative constancy of the regression coefficient of the real exchange rate variable in the case of merchandise exports, a shift appears to have occurred in regard to nonfactor services. At the same time, the weaker response obtained in regard to services may be explained by reference to the fact that some service items, such as license and management fees, are hardly responsive to exchange rate changes.

The regression coefficients of the foreign income variable declined between the two periods, irrespective of whether one considers the exports of goods and nonfactor services or goods alone. The coefficients are 2.69 for the exports of goods and nonfactor services and 3.75 for merchandise exports in the first period and 1.16 and 1.49, respectively, in the second, with estimated coefficients of 0.51 and 0.56 for the two periods combined. The differences are statistically significant at the 10 percent and the 5 percent level, respectively. It would appear, then, that the income elasticity of demand in the developed countries for the exports of the developing countries decreased in the period of external shocks.

These considerations may explain that the decline in the foreign income elasticity is larger for merchandise exports than for the exports of goods and nonfactor services. Nevertheless, the elasticity continues to be lower for goods and nonfactor services than for goods alone, indicating that some service items, such as dividends and interest, are not responsive to income changes in the developed countries.

Note finally that the coefficient of determination of the regression equations is low. This is not surprising, given that the variables are expressed in terms of rates of change; in particular, taking the rate of change of the export–output ratio tends to magnify the errors in the export and output data. Nevertheless, the F-statistics are uniformly high, indicating the existence of a significant and systematic relationship of the underlying economic variables.

III EFFECTS OF PRICE INCENTIVES ON AGRICULTURAL EXPORTS

The above equations have also been estimated for agriculture, with data on agricultural exports and production used in calculating the export–output ratio. In the case of agriculture, estimates have further been made for the ratio of net exports (exports less imports) to output. The estimates pertain to 52 developing countries (51 countries in the case of the net export equations), with the omissions being due to the lack of data on agricultural output and/or exports.

The results show the responsiveness of agricultural exports to changes in

TABLE 7.2 *Regression equations for agricultural exports in developing countries*

	Constant	Real exchange rate	Foreign income	N	F	$\bar{R}^2$
		A. *Export–output ratio*				
I. 1965–73	−0.05	0.55	1.69	416	7.10	0.029
	(−0.81)	(3.54)**	(1.22)			
II. 1974–82	−0.03	0.79	1.54	416	31.52	0.128
	(−1.57)	(7.44)**	(2.28)*			
III. 1965–82	−0.00	0.68	0.73	884	30.73	0.063
	(−0.21)	(7.47)**	(1.56)			
		B. *Net exports–output ratio*				
I. 1965–73	−0.17	0.42	−7.58	408	0.11	−0.004
	(−0.19)	(0.21)	(−0.42)			
II. 1974–82	−1.30	7.89	46.58	408	5.93	0.024
	(−2.14)*	(2.45)*	(2.25)*			
III. 1965–82	−0.65	4.96	14.00	867	4.02	0.007
	(−1.53)	(2.38)*	(1.30)			

NOTES: See Table 7.1.

the real exchange rate. In the equations for the developing country group, the estimated regression coefficients for agricultural exports are 0.55 for the 1960–73, 0.79 for the 1974–82, and 0.68 for the 1965–82 period. All the coefficients are statistically significant at the 1 percent level (Table 7.2). As in the case of merchandise exports, then, the regression coefficients estimated for the two periods combined lies between that for the first and for the second period, with coefficient values rising between the two.

A comparison of the results reported in Tables 7.1 and 7.2 indicate that the regression coefficients for agricultural exports exceed the coefficients estimated for the exports of goods and services by a considerable margin. At the same time, apart from the 1974–82 period, the coefficients are slightly lower than those for merchandise exports. The following comparisons will be limited to merchandise exports.

The regression coefficient for foreign incomes is shown to decline between the two periods in the case of agricultural exports. But, the differences are not significant statistically and the decline is much smaller than for merchandise exports, which include fuels where developing country exports decreased over time. Finally, the regression coefficient of the foreign income variable for the combined period is substantially lower than for the two periods, taken individually, although the level of significance of the estimates is low.

The coefficient of determination is lower for agricultural exports than for merchandise exports. The differences in the results may be explained by non-price factors, such as the weather, which affect agricultural production. Nevertheless, apart from the 1965–73 period, the F-statistics are high, in particular in the developing country equations.

The adjusted R^2s and the F-statistics are substantially lower in the equations utilizing the net export ratio as the dependent variable. This result may be explained in part by the fact that errors in the export and the import data are amplified when one takes the difference between the two and in part by the effects on imports of changes in foreign exchange receipts and in the availability of food aid.

The above considerations may also explain the fact that the statistical significance of the real exchange rate variable is lower in the net export equations than in the export equations. Nevertheless the variable is statistically significant at the 5 percent level for the 1974–82 and 1965–82 periods, although it is not significant for the 1965–73 period.

In the former two cases, the values of the regression coefficients are high – 7.9 and 5.0, respectively. In interpreting this result, it should be recognized that net export–output ratios tend to be small, and hence even a relatively small absolute change can lead to large changes in percentage terms. Finally, the coefficients of the foreign income variable are high, but their level of statistical significance is low.

IV INCENTIVES AND EXPORT PERFORMANCE: COUNTRY EXPERIENCES IN THE 1960–73 PERIOD[7]

A comparison of the experience of eleven semi-industrial countries provides additional evidence on the effects of incentives on agricultural exports in the 1960–73 period of rapid world economic growth. These countries were classified into four groups on the basis of the system of incentives applied during the period.

The countries of the first group, Korea, Singapore, and Taiwan, adopted outward-oriented policies in the early 1960s. These countries provided essentially a free trade regime to exports, further granting some export subsidies that insured similar treatment to exports and to import substitution in the industry sector. Nor was there discrimination against agricultural exports as agriculture and industry received similar incentives.

The second group, Argentina, Brazil, Colombia, and Mexico, adopted inward-oriented policies, entailing discrimination against exports as well as against agriculture in the postwar period. In the mid-1960s, Brazil and Colombia and, to a lesser extent, Argentina and Mexico reduced – but did not eliminate – the bias of the system of incentives against manufactured exports. The extent of discrimination remained especially pronounced against traditional agricultural exports while nontraditional exports received similar treatment as manufactured exports in Brazil and Colombia but not in Argentina and Mexico.

The third group, Israel and Yugoslavia, limited the bias of the incentive system against exports during the 1950s, but increased this bias afterwards.

TABLE 7.3 *Export growth rates, 1960–73*

	Merchandise exports			Agricultural exports		
	1960–66	*1966–73*	*1960–73*	*1960–66*	*1966–73*	*1960–73*
Korea	40.0	44.0	42.1	25.2	29.5	27.5
Singapore	28.5	28.5	28.5	2.9	19.2	11.4
Taiwan	23.5	35.5	29.8	15.6	16.3	16.0
Argentina	6.7	10.8	8.9	6.2	7.9	7.1
Brazil	5.4	19.9	13.0	4.5	16.7	10.9
Çolombia	1.5	12.7	7.4	1.0	11.1	6.3
Mexico	7.8	8.1	8.0	7.7	5.7	6.6
Israel	15.3	17.0	16.2	9.5	11.7	10.7
Yugoslavia	13.6	13.8	13.7	6.7	9.8	8.4
Chile	10.1	5.3	7.5	22.5	2.7	11.4
India	5.5	7.0	6.3	3.7	9.5	6.8

SOURCE: B. Balassa and Associates, *Development Strategies in Semi-Industrial Economies* (Baltimore, Md.: The Johns Hopkins University Press, 1982) Table 3.1.

Finally, inward-oriented policies continued to be applied in Chile and India, which are classified in the fourth group. Chile made some attempts to promote exports in the early 1960s but subsequently resumed its inward-oriented stance, from which India hardly deviated during the period under consideration.

Korea, Singapore, and Taiwan increased their manufactured exports several times faster than the developing country average during the 1960–73 period. The system of incentives applied also permitted them to raise agricultural exports at a rapid rate, averaging 28 percent in Korea, 16 percent in Taiwan, and 11 percent in Singapore that hardly has any agricultural base. Correspondingly, the total merchandise exports of the three countries rose at average annual rates of 42, 29, and 30 percent between 1960 and 1973[8] (Table 7.3).

At the other extreme, total exports as well as agricultural exports increased at average annual rates of less than 7 percent in India. And while export growth accelerated in Chile between 1960 and 1966 in response to the incentives provided, agricultural and manufactured exports changed little afterwards as the bias against exports greatly intensified.

Israel and Yugoslavia occupied an intermediate position in regard to export incentives as well as export performance. Between 1960 and 1973, their merchandise exports rose at average annual rates of 16 and 14 percent, respectively, while agricultural exports increased 11 and 8 percent a year.

Finally, in the second group, Brazil and Colombia experienced a considerable acceleration of the growth of both agricultural and manufactured exports after 1966 in response to increased incentives while smaller changes occurred in Argentina and in Mexico where the reform of the incentive system was less far-reaching. In the first two countries, the acceleration was particularly rapid in agricultural exports, with annual average increases of 17 and 11 percent, respectively, between 1966 and 1973. The corresponding figures were 8 percent for Argentina and 6 percent for Mexico. In all four cases, the rates of growth of manufactured exports, and hence of total merchandise exports, were higher but this occurred from a low base. Thus, the share of manufactured exports in industrial output did not surpass 4 percent in 1973 in Argentina and Brazil while it exceeded 40 percent in the countries of the first group.

V INCENTIVES AND EXPORT PERFORMANCE: COUNTRY EXPERIENCES IN THE 1973–8 PERIOD[9]

The 1973–8 period was characterized by external shocks in the form of the quadrupling of oil prices in 1973–4 and the world recession of 1974–5. At the same time, policy responses to external shocks differed to a considerable extent among newly-industrializing countries, defined as having per capita incomes between $1100 and $3000 in 1978 and a manufacturing share in GDP of 20 percent or higher in 1977, as well as among less developed countries that occupy the range between the newly-industrializing and the least developed countries.

Within the first group, Korea, Singapore, and Taiwan continued with their outward-oriented policies and were joined by Chile and Uruguay. In turn, after lesser or greater efforts made to reduce the bias of the incentive system against exports in the earlier period, Argentina, Brazil, Israel, Mexico, Portugal, Turkey, and Yugoslavia reaffirmed their inward-oriented policy stance.

Among less developed countries, Kenya, Mauritius, Thailand, and Tunisia applied relatively outward-oriented policies during the period under consideration. Conversely, inward orientation predominated in Egypt, India, Jamaica, Morocco, Peru, the Philippines, Tanzania, and Zambia.

The choice between outward and inward orientation was associated with differences in macroeconomic policies in both newly-industrializing and less developed economies. While outward-oriented countries adopted realistic exchange rates and limited reliance on foreign borrowing, most inward-oriented countries let their exchange rate appreciate, supported by foreign borrowing. At the same time, the borrowed funds were not generally used to promote efficient activities oriented towards exportation.

The policies applied greatly affected export performance in the countries under consideration. This is evidenced by changes in export market shares for each country's merchandise exports as well as for its agricultural exports. In each case the results reported in Tables 7.4 and 7.5 show the ratio of average export market shares in the 1974–8 period to the average for the 1971–3 base period.

All the outward-oriented NICs increased their export market shares in the period under consideration, with gains ranging from 3 to 53 percent. In turn, inward-oriented NICs experienced losses in market shares, the only exception being Brazil where the continuation of export subsidies led to moderate gains (Table 7.4). The losses were the largest in Portugal (39 percent), where the April 1974 Revolution also affected the results.

A similar picture emerges in the case of less developed countries. All outward-oriented LDCs gained export market shares, ranging from 8 to 21 percent. In turn, inward-oriented LDCs experienced losses of market shares, ranging from 9 to 29 percent, except that the Philippines had a small gain in response to incentives provided to manufactured exports.

The effects of the policies applied on export performance are also apparent in the averages calculated for the various groups. Thus, the outward-oriented newly-industrializing countries experienced an average gain of 18 percent in export market shares, compared with a loss of 8 percent for the inward-oriented NICs. In turn, the outward-oriented and the inward-oriented less developed countries had gains of 18 percent and losses of 10 percent, respectively (Table 7.5).

Tables 7.4 and 7.5 further provide information on the performance of individual countries and country groups in regard to traditional agricultural exports, defined as accounting for at least 1.5 percent of export value in 1971–3.[10] The results confirm the findings pertaining to total merchandise exports.

Among outward-oriented newly-industrializing countries, only one country,Uruguay, had traditional agricultural exports in the 1971–3 period, and it experienced increases in export market shares during the 1974–8 period. In turn, all inward-oriented NICs lost market shares in their traditional agricultural exports, ranging from 3 percent in Argentina to 33 percent in Yugoslavia.

The less developed countries show a broadly similar pattern. Among outward-oriented LDCs, Kenya and Thailand made gains of 24 and 17 percent, respectively, Tunisia experienced no change, and only Mauritius had losses in traditional agriculture exports (11 percent). By contrast, apart from India's unchanged position, all inward-oriented LDCs lost market shares, reaching 41 percent in the case of Egypt, where the appreciation of the real exchange rate was especially large.

For groups of countries, data are available for all traditional primary exports that include nonagricultural products as well. As shown in Table

TABLE 7.4 *Changes in export market shares: the newly industrializing countries*

Country	Merchandise exports		Traditional agricultural exports	
	1974–78	1979–81	1974–78	1979–81
Newly-industrializing countries				
Korea	153.4	167.4	—	—
Singapore	103.0	135.1	—	—
Taiwan	102.5	116.0	—	—
Chile	136.2	160.3	—	—
Uruguay	122.4	128.5	106.6	100.9
Argentina	99.3	93.7	96.8	92.0
Brazil	108.4	126.6	96.0	96.3
Israel	86.9	85.2	96.0	88.5
Mexico	79.1	92.2	78.3	68.9
Portugal	60.7	54.4	82.6	56.9
Turkey	91.6	103.8	78.1	73.7
Yugoslavia	91.1	87.2	67.1	39.6
Less developed countries				
Kenya	109.0	101.2	123.8	118.7
Mauritius	108.1	117.9	89.1	87.3
Thailand	121.0	145.6	116.5	123.7
Tunisia	114.3	142.3	100.0	80.3
India	91.0	62.6	100.7	90.4
Egypt	76.0	53.2	59.3	44.8
Jamaica	83.9	59.6	73.7	51.3
Morocco	85.2	86.7	77.6	61.3
Philippines	104.8	136.1	72.7	47.9
Peru	90.4	121.1	84.9	60.5
Tanzania	71.4	59.8	99.4	81.1
Zambia	87.4	77.9	—	—

NOTE: The results show the ratio of a country's export market share in the period under consideration to its share in the base period. For 1974–8, the base period is 1971–3; for 1979–81, it is 1976–8.

The average ratio for merchandise exports has been derived as the weighted average of the ratios calculated for traditional primary exports, defined as accounting for more than 1.5 percent in total exports in 1971–3, for nontraditional primary exports, for fuel exports, and for manufactured exports. For traditional agricultural exports, the average pertains to agricultural products within the traditional primary export group.

SOURCE: World Bank data tapes.

7.5, outward-oriented NICs had average gains of 24 percent, compared with losses of 10 percent for inward-oriented LDCs. Also, outward-oriented LDCs had gains of 14 percent while inward-oriented LDCs had losses of an equal magnitude.

TABLE 7.5 *Changes in export market shares: country groupings*

	Merchandise exports		Traditional primary exports	
	1974–8	*1979–81*	*1974–8*	*1979–81*
Country group				
Outward-oriented NICs	118.3	137.2	124.4	129.0
Outward-oriented LDCs	117.5	137.3	114.1	118.0
Outward-oriented NICs and LDCs	118.2	137.2	119.6	123.5
Inward-oriented NICs	91.9	96.1	90.5	88.0
Inward-oriented LDCs	89.8	80.8	86.3	78.6
Inward-oriented NICs and LDCs	91.2	91.3	88.7	84.2

NOTE: Table 7.4.

SOURCE: See Table 7.4.

VI INCENTIVES AND EXPORT PERFORMANCE: COUNTRY EXPERIENCES IN THE 1978–81 PERIOD[11]

In the 1978–81 period, developing countries suffered the effects of the two-and-a-half fold increase in oil prices, the ensuing recession in the developed countries, and the rapid rise in world interest rates. At the same time, as shown in Tables 7.4 and 7.5, the export performance of these countries again reflected the policies applied.[12]

All outward-oriented newly-industrializing countries gained market shares in total merchandise exports, ranging from 16 to 67 percent. In turn, apart from Brazil, which provided substantial export incentives, and Turkey, where important policy changes occurred in 1980, all inward-oriented NICs lost market shares, with Portugal showing the largest losses (46 percent).

The situation was similar in the case of the less developed countries. While outward-oriented LDCs gained export market shares, ranging from 1 to 45 percent, inward-oriented LDCs experienced losses of 13 to 47 percent, the exceptions being the Philippines and Peru. However, in the case of Peru, the discovery of oil reserves pushed the results into the plus column.

As far as country groups are concerned, the outward-oriented NICs and LDCs both increased their average market shares in merchandise exports by 37 percent. Conversely, inward-oriented NICs and LDCs experienced losses of 4 and 19 percent, respectively, although the results were improved by petroleum discoveries in Mexico in the first case and in Peru in the second.

All inward-oriented NICs lost market shares in traditional agricultural exports, ranging from 4 percent in Brazil to 40 percent in Yugoslavia. In turn, Uruguay, the only outward-oriented newly-industrializing country with traditional agricultural exports, had a small gain.

Also, all inward-oriented LDCs lost market shares in their traditional agricultural exports, with Egypt (55 percent), the Philippines (52 percent), and Jamaica (49 percent) incurring the largest losses. As in the previous period, Kenya (19 percent), and Thailand (24 percent) made gains among outward-oriented LDCs while Mauritius (13 percent) and Tunisia (20 percent) experienced losses.

Finally, gains in market shares in traditional primary exports averaged 29 percent in outward-oriented NICs and 18 percent in outward-oriented LDCs. Conversely, average losses were 12 percent in inward-oriented NICs and 21 percent in inward-oriented LDCs.

CONCLUSIONS

The findings of this essay indicate that exports in general, and agricultural exports in particular, strongly respond to price incentives. This conclusion has been established by an econometric analysis of data as well as by comparisons of the experience of countries at different levels of development and following different policies.

The econometric analysis shows the responsiveness of the exports of goods and nonfactor services, merchandise exports, and agricultural exports to changes in the real exchange. At the same time, the econometric estimates are subject to a downward bias, due in part to the use of ordinary least-squares (OLS) estimation techniques and in part to the absence of a lag structure in the estimates. Evidence on the downward-bias of OLS is provided in estimates for export demand and export supply functions for Greece and Korea.[13]

The country analyses further indicate that outward-oriented countries had a far better export performance in regard to merchandise exports as well as traditional agricultural exports than inward-oriented economies. This conclusion applies to all the periods under consideration (1963–73, 1973–8, and 1978–81) as well as to countries at different levels of development (newly-industrializing and less developed countries).

The findings obtained by different methods of investigation thus complement and reinforce each other, indicating the responsiveness of exports to price incentives as well as the advantage of outward-oriented policies. At the same time, they disprove the oft-voiced views that agricultural exports and exports would not respond to incentives.

NOTES

1. Wholesale price indices are superior to consumer price indices that include the prices of nontraded goods and are affected by price controls applied in a number of developing countries. The former, but not the latter, objection also applies to the use of GDP deflator in the calculations.
2. On alternative concepts of the real exchange rate, see B. Balassa, 'Effects of Exchange Rate Changes in Developing Countries', *Indian Journal of Economics* LVIII (1987) pp. 203–22.
3. Ideally, one would need to consider the price of value added (the effective rate of protection) rather than product prices.
4. Also, fixed exchange rates among major currencies prevailed in the first period while flexible exchange rates dominated in the second period. This will have relevance, however, primarily for those developing countries that fixed their currency values in terms of a single foreign currency.
5. Needless to say, the data are subject to considerable error. Nevertheless, there is no reason to assume that these errors would introduce a bias in the results.
6. Because of its lack of statistical significance, the relative price variable for traded and nontraded goods has been dropped from the estimating equations reported in the paper.
7. The discussion draws on B. Balassa and Associates, *Development Strategies in Semi-Industrial Economies* (Baltimore, Md.: The Johns Hopkins University Press, 1982) Ch. 3.
8. In the absence of appropriate deflators, the data refer to the dollar value of exports.
9. The discussion draws on the material presented in B. Balassa, 'Adjustment to External Shocks in Developing Countries,' B. Csikós-Nagy, D. Hague and G. Hill (eds), *The Economics of Relative Prices* (London: Macmillan, 1984) pp. 352–84 (cited as 1984a) and B. Balassa, 'Adjustment Policies in Developing Countries: A Reassessment,' *World Development* XII (1984) pp. 955–72 – the latter paper also describes the scheme of classification utilized in this essay.
10. This represents a subgroup of the traditional primary exports referred to earlier. In turn, it was not possible to separate nontraditional agricultural exports from other primary exports in the data.
11. The discussion draws on the material presented in Balassa, 'Adjustment Policies in Developing Countries: A Reassessment.'
12. The data relate to the ratio of average export market shares in the 1979–81 period to average shares in 1976–8 period.
13. B. Balassa, E. Voloudakis, P. Fylaktos, and S.T. Suh, 'Export Incentives and Export Growth in Developing Countries: An Econometric Investigation,' Development Research Department Discussion Paper No. 159 (Washington, D.C.: World Bank, 1985).

Essay 8   Incentive Policies and Agricultural Performance in Sub-Saharan Africa

This essay examines the experience of sub-Saharan Africa with economic incentives in general, and agricultural incentives in particular, and analyzes the effects of these incentives on economic performance. Section I of the essay reports on the findings of an econometric investigation on the responsiveness of exports to incentives. Section II reviews changes in the export market shares of sub-Saharan African countries pursuing different development strategies. Section III examines changes in export market shares for four sub-Saharan African countries, Tanzania, Kenya, Ghana, and the Ivory Coast. Sections IV and V provide a comparative analysis of agricultural policies and performance for two pairs of these countries: Tanzania and Kenya (Section IV) and Ghana and the Ivory Coast (Section V).

I THE RESPONSE OF EXPORTS TO PRICE INCENTIVES

Table 8.1 reports the results of estimates for the exports of goods and services and for merchandise exports, obtained by the use of a reduced form equilibrium equation, for 16 sub-Saharan African countries.[1] The estimates pertain to the 1965–82 period and to the 1965–73 and the 1974–82 subperiods.

The real exchange rate variable has the expected sign and it is statistically significant at the 1 percent level in the equations for the 1974–82 subperiod and the entire 1965–82 period but not for the 1965–73 subperiod. In the latter case, the regression coefficient is significant at the 10 percent level for the exports of goods and services and does not reach this level of significance for goods alone.

Limiting attention to the values taken by the regression coefficients which have a high level of statistical significance, we find that the coefficients vary between 0.78 and 1.01. Since the variables have been expressed in terms of rates of change, this means that a 1 percent change in the exchange rate is associated with a four-fifths to 1 percent change in the ratio of exports to output.

TABLE 8.1 *Regression equations for export–output ratios in sub-Saharan African countries (t-values in parentheses)*

	Constant	Real Exchange Rate	Foreign Income	N	F	R^2
I. 1965–73						
(a) Exports of goods and nonfactor services	−0.05 (−0.87)	0.37 (1.97)[+]	1.21 (1.07)	128	2.43	0.022
(b) Merchandise exports	−0.14 (−1.77)[+]	0.27 (1.04)	3.39 (2.17)*	128	2.81	0.028
II. 1974–82						
(a) Exports of goods and nonfactor services	−0.02 (1.13)	0.78 (6.60)**	0.95 (1.45)	128	24.44	0.270
(b) Merchandise exports	−0.02 (−0.65)	0.91 (4.07)**	1.79 (1.46)	128	10.28	0.127
III. 1965–82						
(a) Exports of goods and nonfactor services	0.01 (0.76)	0.88 (8.49)**	0.04 (0.08)	272	36.98	0.210
(b) Merchandise exports	0.02 (0.54)	1.01 (5.93)**	0.52 (0.71)	272	18.83	0.116

NOTE: (a) The variables have been expressed in terms of rates of change between successive years for individual countries combining time-series and cross-section observations.

(b) Levels of statistical significance: + 10%; * 5%; ** 1%.

SOURCE: World Bank data-base.

The coefficients for the real exchange rate variable are uniformly higher for the sub-Saharan African countries than for all developing countries, for which estimates are presented in Essay 7. For the 1974–82 subperiod and for the entire 1965–82 period, respectively, the differences between the two sets of estimates are 0.13 and 0.24 percentage points for merchandise exports and 0.20 and 0.40 percentage points for the exports of goods and services.

The results conflict with popular notions, according to which changes in the real exchange rate would have less of an effect on the exports of sub-Saharan African countries than for countries at higher levels of development. But, they are consistent with the observation that African countries, which let their exchange rate become greatly overvalued, experienced considerable losses in export market shares (Sections IV and V).

In contradistinction with the case of all developing countries, however, the level of significance of the foreign income variable is very low; it reaches 5 percent only in the case of merchandise exports in the 1965–73 period. This result may be explained by the high share in sub-Saharan exports of foods, the exportation of which responds little to income changes in the developed countries. Also, coffee exports, accounting for a large proportion of the exports of several sub-Saharan African countries,

TABLE 8.2 *Regression equations for agricultural exports in sub-Saharan African countries*

	Constant	Real Exchange Rate	Foreign Income	N	F	R^2
		A. *Export–output ratio*				
I. 1965–73	0.04	1.08	0.43	128	1.75	0.012
	(0.22)	(1.87)[+]	(0.13)			
II. 1974–82	–0.02	1.15	2.52	128	10.24	0.127
	(–0.36)	(4.00)**	(1.58)			
III. 1965–82	0.04	1.35	0.68	272	14.79	0.092
	(0.85)	(5.26)**	(0.61)			
		B. *Net exports–output ratio*				
I. 1965–73	1.65	–4.73	–42.65	128	0.42	–0.009
	(0.61)	(–0.52)	(–0.77)			
II. 1974–82	0.12	16.43	6.62	128	6.57	0.081
	(0.15)	(3.55)**	(0.26)			
III. 1965–82	0.07	11.47	–7.72	272	4.39	0.024
	(0.11)	(2.96)**	(–0.46)			

NOTES: See Table 8.1.

are determined by quotas under the International Coffee Agreement, which bear little relationship to changes in incomes in the developed countries.

Comparable estimates have been made for agriculture. The results again show the responsiveness of exports to changes in the real exchange rate. The regression coefficients for the export–output ratio range between 1.08 and 1.35; they are statistically significant at the 1 percent level for the 1974–82 subperiod and the entire 1965–82 period and at the 10 percent level for the 1965–73 subperiod (Table 8.2).

As in the case of merchandise exports, the regression coefficients of the real exchange rate variable for agricultural exports are uniformly higher for the sub-Saharan African countries than for all developing countries.[2] In fact, the differences are larger in the present case, ranging from one-half for the 1974–82 subperiod to a near doubling in the 1965–73 subperiod and the entire 1965–82 period.

At the same time, for the countries of sub-Saharan Africa, the regression coefficients for agriculture are substantially higher than for merchandise or for goods and services. This result again conflicts with conventional wisdom, which holds that agricultural exports are less responsive to prices than industrial exports.

In turn, the statistical significance of the foreign income variable does not even reach the 10 percent level for the countries of sub-Saharan Africa. This result may be explained by reference to the low income elasticity of demand for foodstuffs and, in particular, for tropical beverages as noted above in conjunction with merchandise exports.

The coefficient of determination is lower for agricultural exports than for merchandise exports or for the exports of goods and services. The differences in the results may be due to non-price factors, such as the weather, which affect agricultural production. Nevertheless, apart from the 1965–73 period, the F-statistics are high.

The adjusted R^2s and the F-statistics are substantially lower in the equation utilizing the net export ratio as the dependent variable. This result may be explained in part by the fact that errors in the export and the import data are amplified when one takes the difference between the two and in part by the effects on imports of changes in foreign exchange receipts and in the availability of food aid.

In the net export equation, the real exchange rate variable is statistically significant at the 1 percent level in the second subperiod as well as in the entire period. It takes values of 16.4 in 1974–82 and 11.5 in 1965–82. The results again provide evidence of the effects of changes in the real exchange rate on trade in agricultural products.

II ALTERNATIVE POLICIES AND EXPORT PERFORMANCE

In this section, we analyze the effects of alternative policies on export performance in the case of merchandise exports and agricultural exports. In so doing, alternative classification schemes have been used in regard to the policies applied by the countries of sub-Saharan Africa.

Distinction has first been made between market-oriented and interventionist countries on the basis of available information on the extent of public interventions in capital, labor, and foreign exchange markets. The first group includes Botswana, Cameroon, Ivory Coast, Kenya, Malawi, Mauritius, Niger, Togo, and Upper Volta while the second comprises Benin, Ethiopia, Ghana, Madagascar, Mali, Senegal, Sudan, Tanzania, Zaire, and Zambia. A three-fold classification scheme has also been utilized, with Botswana, Cameroon, Ivory Coast and Mauritius included in the group of private market economies, Benin, Ethiopia, Ghana, Madagascar, Mali, Tanzania and Zambia in the group of étatist countries, and Kenya, Malawi, Niger, Senegal, Sudan, Togo, Upper Volta, and Zaire in an intermediate group.

The policies applied greatly affected export performance in the countries under consideration. This is evidenced by changes in export market shares for each country's merchandise exports as well as for its agricultural exports. The results reported in Table 8.3 show the ratio of average export market shares in the 1974–78 period to the average for the 1971–73 base period.

The range of increases in average export shares was between 9 to 81 percent in market economies, except for Cameroon, Niger, and Togo that experienced declines of 4 to 22 percent. In turn, interventionist countries

TABLE 8.3 *Changes in export market shares in sub-Saharan African countries*

Country	Merchandise exports 1974–8	Traditional agricultural exports 1974–8
Botswana	181.2	120.7
Cameroon	96.0	107.7
Ivory Coast	118.9	134.9
Mauritius	108.1	89.1
Kenya	109.0	123.8
Malawi	152.3	150.1
Niger	77.8	47.1
Togo	9.1	61.6
Upper Volta	121.9	102.0
Senegal	103.2	119.3
Sudan	83.6	90.3
Zaire	76.9	63.1
Benin	41.8	35.8
Ethiopia	60.2	60.2
Ghana	72.8	79.7
Madagascar	82.4	88.9
Mali	106.6	89.1
Tanzania	71.4	99.4
Zambia	87.4	—

NOTE: The results show the ratio of a country's export market share in 1974–8 to its share in 1971–3.

The average ratio for merchandise exports has been derived as the weighted average of the ratios calculated for traditional primary exports, defined as accounting for more than 1.5 percent in total exports in 1971–3, taken individually for nontraditional primary exports, for fuel exports, and for manufactured exports. For traditional agricultural exports, the average pertains to agricultural products within the traditional primary export group.

SOURCE: World Bank data tapes.

generally lost export market shares, with the losses exceeding one-fourth in Benin, Ethiopia, Ghana, and Tanzania, where policy-induced distortions – in particular, the overvaluation of the exchange rate – were the most pronounced. Among the interventionist countries, only Mali and Senegal experienced small gains (13 to 7 percent) in export market shares.

The effects of the policies applied on export performance are also apparent in weighted averages calculated for the various groups. Thus, market-oriented countries had an average gain of 5 percent and interventionist countries an average loss of 19 percent in export market shares during the 1974–8 period. Using a three-fold classification scheme, and distinguishing among private market economies, intermediate, and étatist countries, the corresponding figures are +15, −10, and −24 percent.[3]

Table 8.3 further provides information on the performance of individual countries in regard to traditional agricultural exports, defined as accounting for at least 1.5 percent of export value in 1971–3. The results confirm the findings pertaining to total merchandise exports.

Apart from Mauritius, Niger, and Togo, private market economies in sub-Saharan Africa increased their market shares of traditional agricultural exports; the largest gains were observed in Malawi (50 percent), the Ivory Coast (35 percent), Kenya (25 percent), and Botswana (21 percent). In turn, apart from Senegal, all interventionist countries lost export market shares, with a nearly two-thirds loss in the case of Benin and over one-third in Ethiopia and Zaire. As shown in Table 8.3, the differences are even more pronounced if private market economies and étatist countries are compared.

All in all, market-oriented countries generally gained, and interventionist economies lost, export market shares during the 1973–8 period, when the former group of countries did not appreciably discriminate against exports and adopted realistic exchange rates while the latter group strongly biased the system of incentives against exports and let their exchange rate appreciate in real terms. The differences in policies, and in export performance, are even greater if comparisons are made between private market economies and étatist countries in a three-fold classification scheme that puts some countries in an intermediate group.[4]

These results are supported by the findings of a World Bank study on agricultural exports in Eastern and Southern Africa. According to the study, industrial protection and overvalued exchange rates adversely affected agricultural exports in this region during the 1965–83 period.[5]

Another Bank study found that, in sub-Saharan Africa, countries with a high degree of price discrimination against agriculture had an average agricultural growth rate of 0.8 percent in the 1970–81 period while the corresponding growth rates were 1.8 percent and 2.9 percent in countries with medium and low price discrimination against agriculture.[6] This result was confirmed by an econometric analysis of the relationship between the extent of price distortions and agricultural output growth in these countries.[7]

The same author examined the implications of overvalued exchange rates for the growth of agricultural production in sub-Saharan Africa. He found that, on the average, agricultural growth rates were higher in countries whose currency depreciated, than in countries whose currency appreciated, in real terms. In the 1970–81 period, the average annual growth rate of agricultural production was 2.6 percent in the first group and 1.5 percent in the second.[8]

III CHANGING EXPORT MARKET SHARES: THE EXPERIENCES OF FOUR SUB-SAHARAN AFRICAN COUNTRIES

Table 8.4 reports estimates on changes in export market shares for Tanzania, Kenya, Ghana, and the Ivory Coast for the 1974–8 and the 1979–81 periods. Changes in market shares have been expressed as the ratio of actual exports to hypothetical exports, calculated on the assumption that the country maintained its share in world markets in the 1971–3 and 1976–8 base periods, respectively.

Table 8.4 provides information on the traditional agricultural exports of the four countries, defined as accounting for at least 1.5 percent of their total merchandise exports in the base period. The table also shows weighted averages for these exports, the weights being each country's base period export values. Information is further provided on nontraditional primary exports, defined as primary products that individually accounted for less than 1.5 percent of total exports in the base period, which in their great bulk are agricultural commodities. Finally, the average for total merchandise exports has been calculated from data for traditional agricultural and nonagricultural primary exports,[9] nontraditional primary exports, fuel exports, and manufactured exports.

The data show a 1 percent average decrease in Tanzania's market shares in its traditional agricultural exports in 1974–8, followed by a 19 percent decline in 1979–81. This contrasts with increases of 24 percent and 19 percent in Kenya in the two periods, respectively.

Losses in market shares in Tanzania were much larger for annual crops than for tree crops (coffee and tea). The only major annual crop where Tanzania made gains in export market shares, tobacco, reached only one-half of its production target, despite large injections of capital. Among minor exports, cashew nuts and pyrethrum experienced a decline by two-thirds from peak levels.[10] In the exportation of coffee and tea, as well as in that of agava fiber, where the two countries are in competition, Kenya's export performance was much superior to that of Tanzania. The differences between the two countries are even greater in regard to nontraditional primary exports. While in Kenya average losses of 4 percent in 1974–8 gave place to a gain of 8 percent in 1979–81, Tanzania experienced losses of 44 percent in the first and 40 percent in the second period.

Tanzania also did less well than Kenya in the exportation of manufactured goods. As a result, Tanzania's average market share in merchandise exports fell by 29 percent in 1974–8, followed by a decline of 60 percent in 1979–81. Average gains for Kenya were 9 percent in the first period and 1 percent in the second, when it lost manufactured exports due largely to the closing of the Tanzanian border.

Among its traditional agricultural exports, data for 1974–8 period show

TABLE 8.4 *Changing export market shares: Tanzania, Kenya, the Ivory Coast, and Ghana*

	Tanzania		Kenya		Ivory Coast		Ghana
	1974–8	1979–81	1974–8	1979–81	1974–8	1979–81	1974–8
Merchandise exports	71.4	59.8	109.0	101.2	118.9	125.4	72.8
Nontraditional primary exports	56.4	60.0	96.0	108.0	116.1	214.8	76.2
Traditional agricultural exports	99.4	81.1	123.8	118.7	134.9	132.4	79.9
Coffee	104.9	94.6	130.5	121.2	140.1	109.1	
Tea	119.1	128.1	123.2	143.5			
Cotton	82.7	57.7			125.2	203.3	
Sisal	101.2	95.0	215.7	204.1			
Oilseed cake	57.7	33.7					
Tobacco	146.6	101.3					
Meat, prepared			92.0	23.9			
Maize			53.3	24.4			
Cocoa brans					139.4	205.1	81.1
Cocoa paste					87.1	39.7	
Cocoa butter					127.7	126.5	66.9
Bananas					89.6	72.9	
Palm oil					141.2	63.3	

NOTE: The results show the ratio of a country's export market share in the period under consideration to its share in the base period. For 1974–8 the base period is 1971–3; for 1979–81, it is 1976–8. On the method of calculating changes in market shares for merchandise exports, see Table 8.2.

SOURCE: World Bank data-base.

average losses in export market shares of 19 percent in cocoa beans and 33 percent in cocoa butter for Ghana. Ghana experienced even larger losses in its market shares in traditional nonagricultural exports and in nontraditional primary exports, bringing the decline in its average market share in merchandise exports to 27 percent. While there are no comparable data for the 1978–81 period, available information points to the continuation of these trends.

By contrast, the Ivory Coast increased its export market shares in cocoa butter and cocoa paste by 39 percent and 27 percent, respectively, in the 1974–8 period. And, while the two countries have similar climatic conditions, the Ivory Coast diversified its agricultural exports during the 1960s and made gains in the subsequent period in cotton and palm oil, although not in bananas.

Taken together, the Ivory Coast had an average gain of 35 percent in its traditional agricultural exports in 1974–8, compared with a loss of 20 percent for Ghana. The Ivory Coast also increased its market shares in nontraditional primary exports by 16 percent, compared with a loss of 24 percent for Ghana. And, the Ivory Coast made further gains in this commodity group in 1979–81, bringing the average gain for all merchandise exports to 25 percent, exceeding the 19 percent gain in 1974–8. In turn, Ghana experienced a 27 percent loss in merchandise exports in 1974–8; data for 1979–81 are not available.

IV AGRICULTURAL POLICIES AND PERFORMANCE IN TANZANIA AND KENYA[11]

An important factor contributing to losses in export market shares in Tanzania was the increasing overvaluation of the real exchange rate. Thus, Kenneth Meyers has estimated that the ratio of exports to agricultural value added in Tanzania would have been 18 percent higher in 1982 if the exchange rate remained at its 1973 level in real terms. Yet, the appreciation of the real exchange rate by 44 percent in the 1973–82 period followed an appreciation of 32 percent between 1965 and 1973.

Changes in the real exchange rate do not fully reflect the adverse effects of the incentive system on agricultural exports, which contributed to the decline in the ratio of exports to agricultural value added in Tanzania from 41 percent in 1973 to 14 percent in 1982. Another important influence was the increase in marketing margins of the parastatals that led to reductions in the ratio of producer to border prices, in particular for coffee and tea.

Exports were further discouraged as the prices of export crops declined by one-third, compared with the prices of domestic crops, between 1969–70 and 1979–80 in smallholder production. Yet, the average real price of domestic crops, derived by deflating the index of producer prices by the consumer price index, also decreased by 16 percent between 1970 and 1980.[12]

The adverse changes in the incentive system led to a fall of Tanzania's agricultural exports by 6.5 percent a year between 1970 and 1981. In turn, among domestic crops, marketed production declined at an average annual rate of 20.8 percent in the case of rice and 3.8 percent for wheat in the 1970–82 period. Also, while average increases were 3.6 percent a year for maize, production in 1981 and 1982 did not reach one-half of the peaks attained in 1978 and 1979.

At the same time, although it has been claimed that sales in informal markets rose rapidly in Tanzania, increases in imports indicate that domestic production was less and less able to provide for the needs of the population. Thus, despite foreign exchange shortages, the combined imports of maize, rice, and wheat averaged 275 000 tons in 1981–2, compared with an average of 50 000 tons in 1970–71.[13]

In Kenya, the ratio of agricultural exports to value added was 33 percent in 1973 and 31 percent in 1982. The relative constancy of this share may be largely attributed to the constancy of the real exchange rate and the lack of discrimination against exports in the agricultural sector. Thus, prices for export crops and domestic crops moved in a parallel fashion during the period; nor was there much variation among domestic crops. Also, the average real price of both export and domestic crops increased by 13 percent between 1972–3 and 1982–3.[14]

The system of incentives applied may explain that Kenyan agricultural exports rose by 2.6 percent a year between 1970 and 1981. In turn, marketed production increased at average annual rates of 2.3 percent in the case of maize, 2.1 percent in the case of rice, and 1.7 percent in the case of wheat.[15]

The situation is even more favorable if all domestic crops rather than only staple cereals are considered. Between 1972/73 and 1982/83, the production of domestic crops rose by 137 percent while the increase for all crops was 126 percent.[16]

Taking 1979/80 as the terminal year, comparisons may further be made with Tanzania. Between 1972/73 and 1979/80, the production of export crops rose by 18 percent and that of domestic crops by 104 percent in Kenya, with an average increase of 95 percent. In turn, between 1973/74 and 1979/80, the 23 percent decline in the production of export crops in Tanzania was barely compensated by the rise in the production of domestic crops, with an average increase of 8 percent.[17]

V AGRICULTURAL POLICIES AND PERFORMANCE IN GHANA AND THE IVORY COAST[18]

Changes in export market shares in Ghana and the Ivory Coast represent a continuation of trends since independence. Between 1963/64 and 1979/80, cocoa production fell from 443 000 to 275 000 metric tons in Ghana while it increased from 99 000 to 379 000 metric tons in the Ivory Coast. And, in Ghana, a further decline to 107 000 metric tons occurred by 1983–4.[19]

The results may be explained by reference to the price policies applied in the two countries. In 1984, Ghanaian cocoa farmers received 20 percent of the world market price while the corresponding ratio was 84 percent in the Ivory Coast.[20] Although the results for Ghana represent a deterioration of the situation from earlier periods, high taxes were levied on cocoa from the early 1960s onwards.

Relatively high producer prices provided incentives in the Ivory Coast for the expansion of cultivation, the upgrading of varieties through re-planting, and the careful husbanding of cocoa trees. In turn, in Ghana, a number of existing plantations were abandoned and new high-yielding cocoa varieties were not introduced in cases when replanting did occur.

Nor did Ghana experience a diversification of exports, so that the decline in the exports of cocoa was not compensated by increases in other agricultural exports. In fact, between 1970 and 1982, the ratio of exports to agricultural value added fell from 32 to 2 percent.

High industrial protection and the increasing overvaluation of the exchange rate contributed to these results. Thus, between 1975 and 1982, the real exchange rate appreciated by 80 percent in Ghana.

Import-substitution crops, in particular cereals, produced mainly on large farms, were protected by quantitative import restrictions. These crops, however, are at a comparative disadvantage in Ghana. Also, they suffered the consequences of the deterioration of physical infrastructure, in particular transportation facilities, and the scarcity of imported inputs, such as fertilizers and insecticides. Thus, the production of cereals declined by 62 percent between 1970 and 1983 while the production of starch staples fell by 40 percent.

These figures indicate the adverse effects of the policies applied on Ghanaian agriculture. While the intention had been to syphon off revenues from cocoa production to the benefit of other sectors of the economy, foreign exchange earnings decreased as a result, eventually leading to a decline in other production activities that were unable to obtain the necessary inputs.

By contrast, the Ivory Coast adopted a balanced system of incentives while encouraging the inflow of foreign capital and the immigration of labor from neighboring countries. As a result, agricultural production continued to rise at a rapid rate, with average increases of 3.8 percent in value added between 1970 and 1980. Within agriculture, the production of domestic crops and export crops grew in a parallel fashion, maintaining the share of exports at about three-fourths of the total.

With value added in manufacturing rising by 8.2 percent a year, the gross domestic product of the Ivory Coast increased at an average annual rate of 6.4 percent between 1970 and 1980, following a growth rate of 8.0 percent between 1960 and 1970. By contrast, increases of 2.2 percent a year in the 1960s gave place to an average annual decline of 0.5 percent in the 1970s in Ghana. Measured in terms of purchasing power parities, per capita incomes increased from $779 in 1960 to $1410 two decades later in the Ivory Coast while a decline from $1009 to $762 occurred in Ghana.[21]

Policy performance deteriorated in the Ivory Coast towards the end of the 1970s as high-cost investments were undertaken, in particular in sugar, and the exchange rate became increasingly overvalued as domestic inflation accelerated while the parity *vis-à-vis* the French franc was maintained in the framework of the Franc area. Important policy reforms were introduced in subsequent years, however, which are expected to lead to the resumption of rapid economic growth.

In Ghana, the Economic Recovery Program was launched in April 1983, involving a devaluation of the currency by 1900 percent, and the adoption of a flexible exchange rate system. Also, producer prices have been raised to a considerable extent. However, in the pursuit of self-sufficiency, the incentive system continues to favor import-substitution crops and further increases in cocoa prices would be necessary for the full exploitation of Ghana's production potential.

CONCLUSIONS

This essay has provided evidence on the effects of the policies applied on economic performance in sub-Saharan Africa, with emphasis given to agriculture. It has been shown that exports in general, and agricultural exports in particular, are highly responsive to changes in the real exchange rate. In fact, exports are more responsive to price incentives in sub-Saharan Africa than in developing countries in general.

It has further been shown that market-oriented countries generally gained, and interventionist countries lost, export market shares as the former, but not the latter, group of countries maintained realistic exchange rates and did not appreciably bias the system of incentives against exports. The differences in policies, and in export performance, are even greater if comparisons are made between private market economies and étatist countries in a three-fold classification scheme that puts some countries in an intermediate group.

Kenya and the Ivory Coast exemplify market-oriented, and Tanzania and Ghana interventionist, countries in sub-Saharan Africa. The essay has made pairwise comparisons between Kenya and Tanzania and between the Ivory Coast and Ghana, indicating the superiority of the market-oriented approach in promoting exports and agricultural production.

NOTES

1. The underlying model, and the derivation of the equation, are presented in Essay 7.
2. The results are shown in Essay 7.
3. B. Balassa, 'Adjustment Policies and Development Strategies in Sub-Saharan Africa, 1973–78,' M. Syrquin, L. Taylor, and L. E. Westphal (eds), *Economic Strategy and Performance*, Essays in Honor of Hollis B. Chenery (New York: Academic Press, 1984) pp. 317–40.
4. For a detailed discussion of the classification scheme utilized and the empirical results obtained, see Balassa.
5. R. Gulhati, B. Swadesh, and V. Atukorala, 'Exchange Rate Policies in Eastern and Southern Africa, 1965–1983,' World Bank Staff Working Paper No. 720 (Washington, DC: World Bank, 1985).
6. K. M. Cleaver, 'The Impact of Price and Exchange Rate Policies in Agriculture in Sub-Saharan Africa,' World Bank Staff Working Paper No. 728 (Washington, DC: World Bank, 1985).

7. Ibid.
8. Ibid.
9. Tanzania and Kenya did not have any traditional nonagricultural exports; this category includes sawn and veneer logs in the Ivory Coast and Ghana, sawn wood in the Ivory Coast, and sawn wood and aluminum in Ghana.
10. F. Ellis, 'Agricultural Price Policy in Tanzania,' *World Development*, XIII (1985) pp. 525–38.
11. Unless otherwise noted, the data originate in K. Meyers, 'Agricultural Policy and Performance in Tanzania' (Washington, DC: World Bank, 1986) mimeo and 'Agricultural Policy and Performance in Kenya' (Washington, DC: World Bank, 1985) mimeo.
12. Ellis, 'Agricultural Price Policy in Tanzania'.
13. U. Lele, C. Else, and H. McKonnen, 'How Different are Agricultural Pricing and Marketing Policies of Socialist and Market Oriented African Countries?' (Washington, DC: World Bank, 1985) mimeo.
14. C. L. Jabara, 'Agricultural Pricing Policy in Kenya,' *World Development*, XIII (1985) pp. 611–26.
15. Lele *et al.*, 'How Different are Agricultural Pricing and Marketing Policies of Socialist and Market Oriented African Countries?'
16. Jabara, 'Agricultural Pricing Policy in Kenya'.
17. Ellis 'Agricultural Price Policy in Tanzania'; Jabara, 'Agricultural Pricing Policy in Kenya'.
18. Unless otherwise noted, the data originate in L. Sherbourne, 'Agricultural Policy and Performance in Ghana' (Washington, DC: World Bank, 1985) mimeo and 'Agricultural Policy and Performance in the Ivory Coast' (Washington, DC: World Bank, 1985) mimeo.
19. J. D. Stryker and L. E. Brandt, 'Price Policy in Africa' (Washington, DC: Associates for International Resources and Development, 1985).
20. Ibid.
21. R. Summers and A. Heston, 'Improved International Comparisons of Real Product and Its Composition, 1950–80,' *Review of Income and Wealth*, XXX (1984) pp. 207–62.

Essay 9 Agricultural Policies and International Resource Allocation

INTRODUCTION

The essay will begin by describing the principal features of the common agricultural policy of the European Economic Community and indicating the effects of this policy on the level of agricultural self-sufficiency and on agricultural exports in the Community (Section I). This will be followed by a review of changes over time in average rates of agricultural protection in the EEC, Japan, and the United States (Section II). Information will further be provided on the welfare cost of industrial country agricultural protection (Section III) and on the possible effects of the removal of such protection on trade and economic welfare in the industrial and in the developing countries (Section IV). The essay will next consider the incentive policies applied by the developing countries and the potential welfare effects of these policies (Section V). Subsequently, the combined effects of agricultural protection in the industrial countries, developing countries, and the European socialist countries will be analyzed (Section VI). In the conclusions, the policy implications of the findings will be drawn.

I THE COMMON AGRICULTURAL POLICY AND LEVELS OF SELF-SUFFICIENCY IN THE EEC

The establishment of the common agricultural policy reflected the view that European integration should encompass all sectors and that eliminating intercountry differences in agricultural producer prices would improve economic efficiency in the EEC countries. It further responded to political exigencies as France, Italy, and the Netherlands apparently considered agricultural integration as a quid pro quo for industrial integration. Last but not least, the common agricultural policy was to ensure remunerative and stable prices for EEC producers and to favor them over nonmember country producers in supplying domestic consumption in the Community.

The stated objectives were to be served by establishing uniform prices for the major agricultural commodities within the European Common Market. Also, these prices were to be insulated from world market prices.

This has in fact been accomplished by the use of variable levies in the case of cereals and milk products, by a combination of tariffs and variable levies for meats, poultry, and eggs, and by seasonal tariffs for fruits and vegetables.

However, the full equalization of agricultural prices within the Community has not been attained as producers in strong currency countries have generally received higher prices than producers in weak currency countries. Such has been the case as changes in 'green' exchange rates applicable to agricultural commodities have regularly fallen behind changes in official exchange rates within the Community, effectively resulting in a combination of import (export) levies and subsidies in intra-EEC agricultural trade.

At the same time, in setting domestic producer prices above world market levels, and increasing them more or less regularly over time, the policies applied have not only safeguarded domestic markets for EEC producers but have led to surpluses in various commodities. Between 1967–71 and 1982–3, the extent of self-sufficiency in the Common Market increased from 82 to 159 percent for sugar, from 91 to 114 percent for butter, from 100 to 109 percent for other milk products, from 101 to 110 percent for poultry, from 90 to 105 percent for beef, and it reached 121 percent for soft wheat.

As a result, starting from a net import position, the Common Market has assumed a net export position in an increasing number of agricultural commodities. In 1982–3, its share in world agricultural exports, excluding intra-EEC trade, reached 19 percent in sugar, 47 percent in butter, 45 percent in cheese, 39 percent in poultry, 52 percent in eggs, 14 percent in beef and veal, and 17 percent in wheat.[1]

Exportation has been made profitable for EEC agricultural producers by paying them a subsidy. The subsidy was to be set as the difference between internal prices and world market prices. In fact, it has often been used to underbid traditional exporters, including developing countries, and the growing EEC exports have depressed world market prices.

Increases in exports, then, have importantly contributed to the rise in EEC expenditures on agricultural price support. The Common Market Commission reported that these expenditures rose from 2.6 billion ECUs (the accounting unit of the Community) in 1970 to 10.4 billion ECUs in 1980 and 22.2 billion ECUs in 1986, thereby constituting a considerable financial burden for the Common Market budget.

II CHANGES IN AGRICULTURAL PROTECTION IN THE INDUSTRIAL COUNTRIES

EEC agricultural exports have risen over time as production has continued to increase in the face of by-and-large stagnant consumption in the member countries. Production, in turn, has been promoted as the Community has maintained prices substantially above world market levels. In fact, the average rate of agricultural protection, expressed as the percentage excess of domestic over world market prices (the nominal rate of protection), increased from 30.2 percent in 1955 to 35.7 percent in 1980.[2]

Among the developed countries, increases in agricultural protection were much greater in Japan, with average rates of nominal protection rising from 17.5 percent in 1955 to 83.5 percent in 1980. The relevant figures are 2.4 percent and –0.1 percent respectively, in the United States.[3]

In the case of Japan, the results reflect increases in the relative income position of farmers in the face of the deterioration of agricultural productivity *vis-à-vis* manufacturing. Thus, from a ratio of 70 percent in the second half of the 1950s, per capita farm income reached the level of per capita income in manufacturing in 1975 and surpassed it by 19 percent in 1980 while there was a one percentage point difference in favor of manufacturing in terms of the annual rate of increase of labor productivity during the period.[4]

This has occurred as the price of rice was set on the basis of rising nonagricultural wages, reflecting higher productivity growth in the nonagricultural sectors, and support prices of other crops have been raised to ensure their profitability *vis-à-vis* rice. As a result, increases in agricultural prices have much exceeded the rise of the general wholesale price index. At the same time, import quotas on 22 agricultural commodities have limited purchasing from abroad.

Japan further grants subsidies to lower the consumer price of rice below the producer price and provides financial incentives to farmers to shift from rice to other crops. Increases in these expenditures raised agricultural support payments from 7.2 percent of gross output value in 1960 to 30.3 percent in 1980.[5] This figure does not include the cross-subsidization of domestic production by government import monopolies that reduced the consumer prices of wheat to one-third of the producer price which was 3.8 times the import price in 1980–82; the comparable figures were three-tenths and 4.3 for coarse grains (Table 9.1).

Despite the relatively high level of protection of dairy products, included in Table 9.1 but not in the figures cited earlier, the average protection of seven major agricultural commodities in 1980–82 was only 16 percent in the United States, compared with 144 percent in Japan and 54 percent in the European Common Market.[6] In subsequent years, however, the United States provided increasing agricultural support in response to the decline in world market prices.

TABLE 9.1 *Ratios of domestic to world market prices in the major developed countries, 1980–82*

	Japan		EC		USA	
	Producer price	Consumer price	Producer price	Consumer price	Producer price	Consumer price
Wheat	3.80	1.25	1.25	1.30	1.15	1.00
Coarse grains	4.30	1.30	1.40	1.40	1.00	1.00
Rice	3.30	2.90	1.40	1.40	1.30	1.00
Beef and lamb	4.00	4.00	1.90	1.90	1.00	1.00
Pork and poultry	1.50	1.50	1.25	1.25	1.00	1.00
Dairy products	2.90	2.90	1.75	1.80	2.00	2.00
Sugar	3.00	2.60	1.50	1.70	1.40	1.40
Weighted average	2.44	2.08	1.54	1.56	1.16	1.17

SOURCE: World Bank, *World Development Report 1986*, Table 6.1.

III THE WELFARE COST OF AGRICULTURAL PROTECTION IN THE INDUSTRIAL COUNTRIES

It has been estimated that in 1985 the cost of agricultural policies to the consumer and the taxpayer was 18 percent higher than the benefits the producers derived from protection in the European Common Market, while it was 221 percent higher in Japan and it was 6 percent lower in the United States. In the same year, the welfare cost of agricultural protection (consumer cost plus budgetary cost less producer benefit) was estimated at 0.9 percent of the gross national product in the EEC, 2.3 percent in Japan, and nil in the United States.[7]

But, the calculations understate the cost of agricultural protection and overstate the benefits that accrue to agricultural producers. For one thing, the estimates do not include the resources wasted in lobbying efforts by farmers and the cost of administering increasingly complicated agricultural support systems. For another thing, they do not allow for the fact that increases in profits to farmers remain temporary as profit rates tend to be equalized across industries.

Thus, in the long run, increases in land prices represent the only benefit to the agricultural sector or, rather, to the owners of the land. This has, in fact, occurred in the United States and the United Kingdom where the rate of return to agricultural land does not show a trend whereas the real price of land approximately doubled between 1950 and 1983.[8]

The impact of agricultural protection on land prices is particularly apparent in Japan. With protection rising at a rapid rate, farmland prices in Japan increased nine-and-a-half times between 1955 and 1983 while the wholesale price index rose only two-and-a-half times.[9] Higher land prices, in turn, represent a cost element for new farmers, thereby increasing pressure for higher protection. There has thus developed a vicious circle of increases in agricultural protection and land prices in Japan. At the same time, the high price of land has discouraged its use for other purposes, such as industry and housing.

The rising price of land, then, has augmented the extent of the misallocation of resources associated with agricultural protection. This misallocation has further entailed employing in agricultural pursuits capital and labor that could be used to greater advantage in other sectors. And while the mobility of labor may be limited in the short run, owing to age, education and social factors, this is not the case in the long run.

In fact, migration has reduced the agricultural labor force in the developed countries as the growth of labor productivity has exceeded that of output. But, new investments have been undertaken in agriculture, raising the level of production as well as economizing the labor. This misallocation of capital, resulting from the imposition of protective measures, could be avoided if agricultural protection were lowered, nay eliminated.

IV EFFECTS OF ELIMINATING AGRICULTURAL PROTECTION IN THE DEVELOPED COUNTRIES

The system of protection in the developed countries imposes a variety of costs on the developing countries. First of all, processing activities in these countries are discouraged as tariffs tend to be higher on processed agricultural products than on unprocessed goods. Thus, average tariffs facing developing country exports in the developed countries are 8.9 percent on fresh and 12.4 percent on prepared vegetables, 4.8 percent on fresh and 16.6 percent on prepared fruits, 2.7 percent on oilseed and oilcake and 8.1 percent on vegetable oils, 6.8 percent on coffee beans and 9.4 percent on processed coffee, and 2.6 percent on cocoa beans and 4.3 percent on processed cocoa.[10] The escalation of tariffs is further aggravated by the fact that the share of commodities subject to quantitative import restrictions is higher for processed than for unprocessed commodities.[11]

Apart from discrimination against processing activities, agricultural exporters among developing countries suffer losses as a result of agricultural protection in the developed countries. Against these losses one should set, however, the gains food-importing developing countries obtain as a result of lower world market prices, owing to the subsidization of exports by the developed countries.

The ensuing foreign exchange gains and losses have been estimated by various authors. The estimate covering the largest number (altogether 99) agricultural commodities was made for the case of a 50 percent reduction in

TABLE 9.2 *Effects on developing countries[a] of a 50 percent decrease in OECD tariff rates, 1975–7 (millions of 1980 dollars)*

Commodity	Absolute change
Change in export revenue	
Sugar	2108
Beverages and tobacco	686
Meats	655
Coffee	540
Vegetable oils	400
Cocoa	287
Temperate-zone fruits and vegetables	197
Oilseeds and oil nuts	109
Other commodities	883
Total increase of all exports	5866
Change in import costs	
Cereals	−876
Other commodities	−497
Total increase of all imports	−1373
Efficiency gains[b]	922

[a] Includes developing countries with populations of more than 4 million in mid-1985.
[b] Efficiency gains are estimates of the increase in the net sum of producer and consumer gains and losses, adjusted for tax revenue changes.

SOURCE: A. Valdés and J. Zietz, 'Agricultural Protection in OECD Countries: Its Cost to Less Developed Countries,' Research Report No. 21 (Washington, DC: International Food Research Institute, 1980) pp. 31, 47.

tariffs, including tariff-type measures such as variable levies, in the developed countries for the years 1975–7.[12] The results of the estimates are shown in Table 9.2, expressed in 1980 dollars.

It is apparent that increases in foreign exchange earnings for the agricultural exporting developing countries ($5.9 billion), attendant on a 50 percent reduction of agricultural tariffs in the developed countries, would much exceed increases in import costs to the food importing developing countries ($1.4 billion). As a result, a net gain in economic welfare of $0.9 billion to the developing countries would ensue.

The gains would be especially large for sugar, tobacco, coffee, cocoa, and oilseeds and oils that are produced in tropical areas. In turn, import costs would rise in the case of cereals and some other temperate zone foods, of which the developed countries are important exporters.

Subsequent estimates relate to selected agricultural commodities that are produced in the developed countries. Under alternative assumptions, increases in foreign exchange earnings for the developing countries, resulting from the elimination of tariff and nontariff protection in the developed countries, were estimated for 1979–81 in 1980 prices at $1.2–1.4 billion for wheat, $0.6–0.8 billion for maize, $4.4–5.8 billion for beef, and $2.2–5.1 billion for sugar; the corresponding figures for sugar at 1983 protection level are $3.4–7.4 billion. However, there would also be increases in import costs for the food importing developing countries, owing to the rise in world market prices, of $0.4–0.6 billion for wheat, $0.6–0.7 billion for maize, $0.3 billion for beef, and $0.3–0.5 billion for sugar.[13]

A more recent study estimated increases in the foreign exchange earnings of the developing countries, derived from the higher exports of wheat, coarse grains, rice, beef and lamb, pork and poultry, dairy products, and sugar, following the elimination of tariff and nontariff protection in the industrial countries, at $21.3 billion for 1985 in 1980 dollars. But, increases in import costs were to result in a net welfare loss if $11.8 billion for the developing countries.[14]

All these studies, and especially the Tyers–Anderson estimate, tend to understate potential increases in developing country exports. This is because the export supply elasticities they assume do not take account of the prospective expansion of supply in response to greater price stability and the elimination of the threat of the future imposition of protection by the developed countries, and they do not consider the possibility that the policy changes would induce developing countries to undertake the exportation of new products.

Also, except for the 1980 Valdés–Zietz study, the estimates include only products in which the developing countries compete with the developed countries. Yet, it is in tropical products where the developing countries would obtain unambiguous gains from developed country trade liberalization. Thus, just as in the Valdés–Zietz study, a fuller coverage of products would show larger increases in exports and welfare gains for the developing countries following the elimination of agricultural protection in the industrial countries.

V INCENTIVE POLICIES IN DEVELOPING COUNTRIES AND THE POSSIBLE EFFECTS OF TRADE LIBERALIZATION

Studies carried out under the direction of the author provided information on relative incentives to manufacturing industries and agriculture in a number of developing countries during the 1960s.[15] The countries in question may be divided into three groups on the basis of the policies applied during this period.

The first group includes Argentina, Brazil, Chile, Pakistan, and the Philippines, all of which highly protected their manufacturing industries and discriminated against agriculture to a considerable extent. Levels of industrial protection and discrimination against agriculture were lower in the countries of the second group, including Colombia, Israel, and Mexico. Finally, in Korea, Malaysia, and Singapore, manufacturing and agricultural activities received similar incentives, on the average.

Subsequent estimates showed little change in relative incentives to manufacturing and to agriculture in the case of Korea. At the same time, reforms undertaken in the second half of the 1960s reduced, to a lesser or greater extent, the protection of manufacturing activities and discrimination against agriculture in Brazil, Colombia, Mexico, and the Philippines whereas changes in the opposite direction occurred in Malaysia.[16] But, in several large Latin American countries, industrial protection and discrimination against agriculture was increased again in response to the external shocks of the post-1973 period while Korea began to protect domestic agriculture.

Thus, with few exceptions, the system of incentives has discriminated against agricultural activities in the countries in question. This conclusion applies to other developing countries as well. According to the 1986 *World Development Report* out of ten developing countries, agriculture is discriminated against in nine countries and it is favored in one country, Korea.[17]

One would, then, expect that overall trade liberalization would increase agricultural exports and reduce agricultural imports in the developing countries. The Tyers–Anderson study reaches the opposite conclusion, however. As shown in Table 9.3, according to these authors the developing countries would experience a decline in agricultural exports and an improvement in economic welfare, attendant on the liberalization of their agricultural trade. This conclusion may be explained by the use of an inappropriate methodology in the study.

Tyers and Anderson measure agricultural protection at the going exchange rate. This exchange rate is, however, affected by the measures of protection applied. The higher the average rate of protection, the more overvalued is the exchange rate compared with the free trade situation. Positive protection of agriculture at the going exchange rate, then, may correspond to negative net protection if adjustment is made for the protection-induced appreciation of the exchange rate. With industry being favored over agriculture in most developing countries, and often by a wide margin, this possibility becomes a certainty.

It follows that removing agricultural protection alone would reduce economic welfare in developing countries by increasing discrimination against agriculture. The correct conclusion is, then, exactly the opposite of that by Tyers and Anderson, who failed to consider the effects of the overvaluation of the exchange rate on the extent of agricultural protection.

This possibility is admitted by the authors in noting that 'for many other developing countries where exchange rates are grossly overvalued, GLS [grains, livestock and sugar' (and other tradable goods) producers are

TABLE 9.3 *Effects of trade liberalization on trade and welfare*
($ billion)

| | *Elimination of trade barriers on agricultural products by the* | | | | | | | |
| | *Developed countries* | | *Developing countries* | | *Developed and developing countries* | | *Developed, developing and European socialist countries* | |
	Export Earnings	*Economic Welfare*	*Export Earnings*	*Economic Welfare*	*Export Earnings*	*Economic Welfare*	*Export Earnings*	*Economic Welfare*
Effects on								
Developed countries	-38.6	48.5	16.3	-10.2	-26.1	45.9	-15.2	44.5
Developing countries	21.3	-11.8	-28.6	28.2	-6.1	18.3	5.0	16.4
European socialist countries	7.5	-11.1	7.1	-13.1	17.1	-23.1	-4.1	6.2
Together	-9.8	25.6	-5.2	4.9	-15.1	41.1	-16.2	67.1

SOURCE: R. Tyers and K. Anderson, 'Distortions in World Markets: a Quantitative Assessment,' Background Paper prepared for the World Development Report, 1986 (Washington, DC: World Bank, 1986) Tables 21, 30, 34, and 36.

being discouraged by a greater amount than the ratio in Table 9.3 suggest.'[18] But, apart from failing to make adjustments for overvaluation on the grounds that reliable estimates of exchange rate distortions are not available, the authors have neglected to indicate that for manufactured products the exchange rate adjustment would still leave positive net protection. A case in point is China and India where the authors report reduced agricultural exports and increased agricultural imports following the liberalization of trade, although the incentive system of these countries strongly discriminates against agriculture in favor of industry.

Thus, trade liberalization in the developing countries should lead to higher rather than to lower agricultural exports. At the same time, economic welfare would increase, owing to the elimination of price distortions and by reason of the positive correlation between export expansion and economic growth that has been observed in regard to agriculture, manufacturing, as well as for the national economy, taken as a whole.[19]

VI INCENTIVE POLICIES IN THE EUROPEAN SOCIALIST COUNTRIES AND THE EFFECTS OF GLOBAL TRADE LIBERALIZATION

Table 9.3 further shows that simultaneous trade liberalization by the industrial and the developing countries would produce larger overall welfare gains than trade liberalization by the two groups of countries, taken individually. At the same time, in this eventuality, the European socialist countries would increase their agricultural exports as against decreases for both the developed and the developing country groups. Increases in exports would be particularly important for pork and poultry, where the European socialist countries have an export surplus.

But, the estimates show a welfare loss, in the event of trade liberalization by the developed and the developing countries, for the European socialist countries. This is because of the higher prices these countries would pay for their imports of wheat, beef, and dairy products, the world market prices of which would rise following the liberalization of agricultural trade by the two groups of countries.

The situation would radically change if the European socialist countries also liberalized their own agricultural trade. According to the estimates reported in Table 9.3, global trade liberalization would reduce agricultural exports by the European socialist countries while increasing their economic welfare through the replacement of high-cost domestic production by lower-cost imports. At the same time, export losses for the developing countries would turn into gains.

In fact, as Table 9.4 shows, the developing countries would be the main

TABLE 9.4 *Effects on world trade shares[a] of global liberalization of agricultural trade, 1985*

	Wheat		Coarse grain		Rice		Ruminant meat		Nonruminant meat		Dairy products		Sugar	
	X	M	X	M	X	M	X	M	X	M	X	M	X	M
Before global liberalization														
Developed countries	93	7	82	33	31	11	68	43	50	7	94	6	28	28
European socialist countries	0	23	0	21	0	10	10	2	23	21	6	5	0	29
Developing countries	7	70	18	46	67	79	22	55	27	72	0	89	72	43
Following global liberalization														
Developed countries	92	6	81	30	12	38	41	73	5	42	83	10	4	20
European socialist countries	0	11	0	30	0	11	0	8	16	0	5	7	0	27
Developing countries	8	83	19	40	88	51	59	19	79	58	12	83	96	53

[a] X refers to the group's share of 'world' exports, M to its share of 'world' imports, where the 'world' total excludes trade within any of the country groups.

SOURCE: R. Tyers and K. Anderson, 'Distortions in World Markets: a Quantitative Assessment,' Background Paper prepared for the World Development Report, 1986 (Washington, DC: World Bank, 1986) Table 27.

beneficiaries of global trade liberalization in terms of increases in world market export shares. Increases would be especially large in beef and lamb (from 22 to 59 percent) and in pork and poultry (from 27 to 58 percent) but would occur in other commodities as well. In turn, the developed countries and, to a lesser extent, the European socialist countries would lose export market shares.

CONCLUSIONS

This essay has examined the effects of distortions in agricultural incentives in the developed, developing, and the European socialist countries. It has been shown that agricultural protection cum export subsidies in the developed countries imposes a considerable budgetary burden and economic cost on these countries while adversely affecting the agricultural exports of the developing countries, even though lowering the cost of food imports for several of these countries. The discrimination against agriculture associated with high industrial protection in the incentive systems of most of the developing countries further limits their agricultural exports. And, developing country exports encounter trade barriers in the European socialist countries as well.

Lowering agricultural protection in the developed and in the European socialist countries while reducing industrial protection in the developing countries would contribute to economic welfare overall by improving resource allocation in world agriculture as well as in world industry. The developed countries would obtain further benefits by reducing the budgetary burden of agricultural protection whereas in the developing countries export-based economic growth would receive a boost.

At the same time, overall benefits from policy changes would increase if such changes were undertaken simultaneously. The food-importing developing countries, too, would benefit if the price-raising effects of reduced developed country agricultural protection were mitigated through increased production by the agricultural-exporting developing countries, associated with reduced discrimination against agriculture in these countries which would tend to reduce prices.

The conclusions point to the desirability of multilateral trade negotiations that would permit simultaneous changes in policies. The Uruguay Round provides the appropriate forum for these negotiations and the nonsubsidizing agricultural exporters have constituted a pressure group to promote the success of negotiations in agriculture. With US support and the increasing recognition of the high cost of agricultural protection in the EEC, possibilities exist for making meaningful progress on trade liberalization in agriculture in the framework of multilateral trade negotiations for the first time in the postwar period.

At the same time, appropriate modalities would need to be established in order to overcome the opposition of vested interests and to ensure that progress is made in deprotecting agriculture. A particularly attractive possibility is to bind overall levels of agricultural support, defined in terms of nominal rates of protection, and to provide for reductions over time in the developed countries.[20] Similar procedures may be applied in developing countries, such as Korea, which protect their agriculture, whereas other developing countries could offer concessions in the form of reductions in industrial protection. And while apart from Hungary, a member of the group of nonsubsidizing agricultural exporters, European socialist countries are not members of GATT, it would be desirable if they also reduced their agricultural trade barriers.

NOTES

1. U. Koester and M. D. Bale, 'The Common Agricultural Policy of the European Community. A Blessing or a Curse for Developing Countries?' World Bank Staff Working Paper, Number 630 (Washington, DC: World Bank, 1984) Tables 1 and 2.
2. M. Honma, and Y. Hayami, 'Structure of Agricultural Protection in Industrial Countries,' *Journal of International Economics*, XX (1986), 115–291. Table 1 – The figures refer to the weighted average of nominal rates of protection for wheat, rye, barley, oats, maize, rice, sugar-beet, potatoes, beef, pork, chicken, eggs, and milk, calculated for the major EEC countries.
3. Ibid.
4. J. S. Hillman and R. A. Rothenberg, 'Wider Implications of Protecting Japan's Rice Farmers,' *The World Economy*, VIII (1985) pp. 47–8.
5. Organization for Economic Cooperation and Development *Country Economic Survey. Japan* (Paris: OECD, 1985).
6. The data includes wheat, coarse grains, rice, beef and lamb, pork and poultry, dairy products, and sugar.
7. R. Tyers and K. Anderson, 'Distortions in World Food Markets: A Quantitative Assessment,' Background Paper prepared for the *World Development Report, 1986* (Washington, DC: World Bank, 1986) mimeo.
8. World Bank, *World Development Report 1986* (Washington, DC: World Bank, 1986) Box 6.6.
9. Hillman and Rothenberg, 'Wider Implications of Protecting Japan's Rice Farmers', p. 54.
10. A. S. Yeats, 'The Influence of Trade and Commercial Barriers on the Industrial Processing of Natural Resources,' *World Development*, IX (1981) pp. 485–94.
11. World Bank, Box table 6.7.
12. A. Valdés, and J. Zietz, 'Agricultural Protection in OECD Countries: Its Cost to Less Developed Countries,' Research Report No. 21 (Washington, DC: International Food Research Institute, 1980).
13. J. Zietz and A. Valdés, 'The Costs of Protectionism to Developing Countries. An Analysis for Selected Agricultural Products,' World Bank Staff Working Paper Number 769 (Washington, DC: World Bank, 1986) Tables 1 and 2.

14. Tyers and Anderson, 'Distortions in World Food Markets.'
15. B. Balassa and Associates, *The Structure of Protection in Developing Countries* (Baltimore, Md.: The Johns Hopkins University Press, 1971) and *Development Strategies in Semi-Industrial Economies* (Baltimore, Md.: The Johns Hopkins University Press, 1982).
16. N. Roger, 'Trade Policy Regimes in Developing Countries' (Washington, DC: World Bank, 1985) mimeo.
17. World Bank, Table 4.1.
18. Tyers and Anderson, 'Distortions in World Food Markets,' p. 78 – The summary results are reproduced in Table 9.3 of the present essay.
19. Balassa and Associates, *Development Strategies in Semi-Industrial Economies*.
20. Valdés, 'Agriculture in the Uruguay Round: Interests of Developing Countries,' *The World Bank Economic Review*, I (1987) pp. 571–94.

Part IV
Public Enterprise and Policies in a Developing Country: Mexico

Essay 10   Public Enterprise in Developing Countries: Issues of Privatization

INTRODUCTION

There has been a sea change in attitudes towards public enterprise around the world in recent years. In Western Europe, the United Kingdom and, since April 1986, France have set out to privatize public enterprises on a large scale. In the case of France, this represents not only a reversal of the nationalizations undertaken by the previous socialist government in 1981, but companies nationalized in 1945 are also being privatized.

At the same time, there is little indication that the Labor party in Britain or the Socialist party in France would undo the denationalizations that are being carried out, if they were returned to power. Furthermore, in European countries with socialist-oriented governments, such as Austria, Finland, and Spain, several public enterprises are being privatized or their privatization is envisaged.

Attitudes have been changing in the developing countries as well. While many of these countries, whether their government professed itself to be socialist or not, had considered public enterprise as the mainstay of economic development, there has been an increasing disillusionment with public enterprise in recent years and proposals have been made for privatization in various areas.

This essay attempts to provide an explanation for the change in attitudes towards public enterprise in the developing countries, draw the lessons of developing country experience with public enterprises and with privatization, and indicate possible future changes. The discussion will be limited to manufacturing industries, excluding natural resource products which are often considered the preserve of the state; public utilities which as natural monopolies are owned or regulated by the state throughout the world; and services on which there are limited data.

Section I of the essay will provide information on the relative importance of public enterprises in the manufacturing sector of the developing countries. Section II will consider possible reasons for the trend towards privatization, with Section III concentrating on efficiency differences between public and private enterprises. In turn, Section IV will review the record of the developing countries with privatization and Section V will examine prospects for the future.

I PUBLIC ENTERPRISES IN THE MANUFACTURING SECTOR OF THE DEVELOPING COUNTRIES

Table 10.1 contains data on the relative shares of public enterprises in the manufacturing sector of the developing countries.[1] Apart from Ghana, where only gross output figures are available, the production data refer to value added and are, on the whole, internationally comparable.[2]

However, for a number of countries, there are investment but not production data. Investment data generally overstate the share of public enterprises, which tend to be in capital-intensive industries. Thus, in 1982, public enterprises accounted for 42 percent of the gross domestic product and for 66 percent of gross fixed investment in eight developing countries, on the average.[3]

In the 1970s, the share of public enterprises in the manufacturing sector of the industrial countries was the highest in Austria (23 percent), followed by Italy (19 percent), Portugal (12 percent), and France (11 percent). The French ratio reached 33 percent following the nationalizations of 1981, but it has been declining since as a result of denationalizations undertaken by the new government. At the other end of the spectrum, the ratio was practically nil in Belgium, 1 percent in Greece, 4 percent in Australia, and 5 percent in the United Kingdom in the late 1970s.[4]

Among developing countries, the share of public enterprises in the manufacturing sector exceeds 90 percent in Iraq and Syria; it was above this level in Egypt in the mid-1970s but declined to 80 percent by 1979. The share of public enterprises in the manufacturing sector is in the 50–60 percent range in Ethiopia and Burma.

All these countries, together with Tanzania, where the share of public enterprises rose from 15 percent in 1966–8 to 38 percent in 1974–7, profess themselves to be socialist. In turn, the share of public enterprises in the manufacturing sector is 33 percent in Ghana, 31 percent in Tunisia, and 30 percent in Turkey, which are considered mixed economies.

While India has also been influenced by socialist ideas, the share of public enterprises in its manufacturing sector (16 percent) is not much higher than in Korea (15 percent) and in Taiwan (12 percent). But, the direction of change has been different, with the share of public enterprises rising from 13 percent in 1970–73 to 16 percent in 1978 in India and declining from 56 percent in 1952 to 12 percent in 1985 in Taiwan.[5]

The share of public enterprises in the manufacturing sector does not

TABLE 10.1 *Relative shares of public enterprises in the manufacturing sector*

		Year	Relative share (percent)
Industrial countries			
Australia	GDP	1978–79	4.0
Austria	GDP	1970–75	23.0
Belgium	GDI	1978–79	0.4[a]
France	GDI	1971	11.4
Greece	GDP	1979	1.3[a]
Ireland	GDI	1974–7	9.4
Italy	GDI	1978	18.6
Portugal	GDP	1976	12.0[a]
United Kingdom	GDI	1978–81	5.3
Sub-Saharan Africa			
Ethiopia	GDP	1979–80	60.9
Ghana	GDP	1970	32.9
Ivory Coast	GDP	1979	25.2
Kenya	GDP	1970–73	13.1[a]
Senegal	GDP	1974	19.0
Sierra Leone	GDP	1979	14.2
Tanzania	GDP	1974–7	37.9
North Africa and Middle East			
Egypt	GDI	1979	80.4
Iraq	GDI	1975	96.7[a]
Morocco	GDI	1974–6	26.2
Syria	GDI	1975	95.9
Tunisia	GDP	1982	31.4
Turkey	GDP	1979	30.1
Yemen Arab Republic	GDI	1975–6	59.5
Asia			
Bangladesh	GDP	1981–2	46.1
Burma	GDP	1980	56.2
India	GDP	1978	15.7
Korea	GDP	1974–7	14.9
Nepal	GDP	1974–5	4.4
Pakistan	GDP	1974–5	7.8
Singapore	GDP	1972	14.2
Sri Lanka	GDP	1974	33.2
Taiwan	GDP	1985	12.0
Thailand	GDP	1970–73	5.2
Latin America			
Bolivia	GDP	1973–5	5.9
Venezuela	GDP	1985	16.2

NOTE: [a] including mining.

SOURCE: R. P. Short, 'The Role of Public Enterprise: An International Statistical Comparison,' and World Bank data files.

reach 10 percent in Nepal, Sri Lanka, and Thailand. It was below this level also in Pakistan in the mid-1970s, when a number of textile mills were nationalized under Bhutto's socialist-leaning government, some of which have since been reprivatized. In turn, the 46 percent share of public enterprises in the manufacturing sector of Bangladesh has been substantially reduced as a result of the denationalizations undertaken since that time.

In socialist developing countries, the tendency has been for public enterprises to dominate the manufacturing sector. In other developing countries, tobacco and, often, sugar, alcoholic beverages, and cement, are in public ownership. Such is frequently the case also for petroleum refining, pharmaceuticals, fertilizer, and iron and steel in countries where these industries exist. Furthermore, there are government printing presses in many developing countries and in a number of cases the public sector includes textile factories.

The existing situation reflects past decisions that have responded to a variety of considerations. In some industries, such as tobacco, sugar, and alcoholic beverages, public enterprises have been used to indirectly tax consumption. Industries such as steel are often in the public sector, because they are considered to be of strategic importance for economic development. There are again others, such as petroleum refining, fertilizer, and cement, where high capital requirements have led to the establishment of public enterprises. Elsewhere, the creation of public enterprises has been rationalized by reference to the alleged lack of private entrepreneurs. Finally, for social reasons, developing country governments have taken over private firms in difficulties in a number of industries.

II REASONS FOR PRIVATIZATION

Various reasons have been put forward to explain changes in attitudes towards privatization in recent years. It has been suggested that ideology, and changes thereof, has played an important role, in particular in France and the United Kingdom. Also, budgetary considerations have often been cited as reasons for privatization. Finally, it has been noted that private enterprises tend to be more efficient than their public counterparts.

While the relevance of ideology cannot be denied in the case of France and the United Kingdom, objective factors have importantly entered decision-making in these cases.[6] Furthermore, as noted in the introduction, there is little expectation that re-nationalization would be undertaken in the two countries in the event of a change in government and, in Western Europe, privatization is carried out by socialist-oriented governments as well. In developing countries also, privatization by-and-large cuts across the political spectrum, including for example Egypt and Tanzania, although it is not envisaged at this time in some Middle Eastern and African socialist countries.

As to budgetary considerations, in the 1974–7 period, for which data are available, public enterprises in developing countries had an overall deficit averaging 5.4 percent of their gross domestic product.[7] This result reflects the fact that the small current account surpluses of these enterprises, averaging 0.6 percent of GDP before depreciation and government transfers, financed only a fraction of their investments that accounted for the deficit on the capital account of public enterprises equal to 6.0 percent of the developing countries' GDP, on the average. In fact, the current account surplus of public enterprises in the developing countries did not even cover depreciation, averaging 1.1 percent of their GDP.

At the same time, the data overstate the current account surplus of the public enterprises as they do not allow for the credit preferences many of them receive. Also, the data include mineral-rich countries, such as Chile, Gambia, Guyana, Venezuela, and Zambia, where public enterprise revenues comprise substantial royalties from the sale of petroleum, copper, bauxite, and other minerals.

Budgetary subsidies and borrowing from the government financed, on the average, slightly over one-half of the overall deficit of public enterprises in the developing countries in the 1974–7 period, when these enterprises accounted for three-fourths of the public sector deficit. The rest of the financing was provided in more-or-less equal proportions by foreign and domestic borrowing, the latter from banks and in capital markets.

Foreign borrowing assumed particular importance after 1973, contributing substantially to the rising external indebtedness of the developing countries. Thus, in the three largest Latin American countries, Argentina, Brazil, and Mexico, public enterprises hold over one-half of the country's external debt.[8] It has also been reported that public enterprises contracted one-third of developing country borrowing on capital markets in 1976–8.[9]

Furthermore, public enterprises account for a large proportion of domestic bank credit. It has been noted that, for countries for which data are available, the average share of public enterprise credit in total domestic credit rose by 20 percentage points between the early 1970s and the end of the 1970s to a level of almost 30 percent.[10]

Public enterprises in developing countries, then, simultaneously increased their foreign and domestic borrowing during the 1970s. These results reflect the rising financial requirements of these enterprises, associated with their growing deficits.[11] With the drying up of foreign loans following the debt crisis of 1982, these deficits have come to be financed increasingly from domestic sources, thereby raising the spectre of 'crowding out' for the private sector.

Budgetary and, more generally, financial considerations have thus contributed to the change in attitudes towards public enterprises in the

developing countries. But, privatization will not reduce the financial burden that public enterprises represent, unless their performance can be
improved. In fact, there are cases, such as Tunisia, where private firms are
not willing to take over public enterprises unless the government undertakes their rationalization beforehand.

III THE RELATIVE EFFICIENCY OF PUBLIC AND PRIVATE ENTERPRISES

Budgetary and financial issues, then, lead to the question of the relative
efficiency of public and private enterprises. Efficiency comparisons should
ideally be made in cases where public and private enterprises carry out the
same economic activity. There are few such comparisons for the industrial
countries, and they generally relate to public utilities and service industries.

A recent study, which has taken particular care in selecting among
empirical investigations those which compare identical activities and use
appropriate indicators of efficiency, has found 17 cases where private
enterprises were more efficient than public enterprises, six where the
opposite was the case, and five where no difference could be discerned.[12]
The 28 cases investigated included only one manufacturing industry, steel,
where the private sector has been shown to be more efficient than the
public sector.

The virtual lack of efficiency comparisons for manufacturing industries in
the industrial countries is indicative of the fact that in these countries
public and private enterprise can be found side-by-side mostly in public
utilities and service industries. In developing countries, comparisons in the
service sector have been made for 33 development finance companies
(DFC). The study concludes that 'the private DFCs are markedly more
vigorous and efficient than state-owned institutions in mobilizing domestic
resources'[13] and generally have a much higher level of profitability.[14] At
the same time, for selected developing countries, information is available
on manufacturing enterprises in the public sector.

In the case of Brazil, it has been reported that the rate of return on
equity in public enterprises was one-half that in private enterprises in 1974
and in 1978. Also, in Israel, before-tax profits averaged 1.6 percent on
sales in public enterprises, compared with 11.6 percent in private enterprises, in 1976–8.[15] Finally, in India, public enterprises in the manufacturing sector earned a rate of return of just over 2 percent, while private firms
earned a rate of return of over 9 percent, in 1976.[16]

Yet, the profit figures overstate the efficiency of public enterprises that
pay very low, and even nil, interest on public loans in the three countries.
Also, no adjustment has been made for differences between market and

shadow prices. Such adjustments have been made in the case of public enterprises in 26 Egyptian manufacturing industries, for which financial and economic rates of return have been calculated for fiscal year 1980/81. The results show considerable differences between the two sets of calculations, reflecting the importance of price distortions in Egypt. They also indicate that, on balance, differences between market and shadow prices have raised financial over economic rates of return in Egyptian public enterprises. Thus, while only one-half of public industries had a financial rate of return of less than 10 percent, one-half of them had a negative rate of economic return.[17] Although comparisons with private firms are not available, this result puts the Egyptian public enterprises in the manufacturing sector in an unfavorable light.

Comparisons of various performance indicators for public and private firms have been made for Turkey. The results show that, in 1979, labor productivity was 30 percent higher in private than in public enterprises, even though the latter had a capital–labor ratio 50 percent higher.[18] Another study showed that, in 1976, public enterprises utilized 1 percent more labor and 44 percent more capital per unit of output than private enterprises in the Turkish manufacturing sector.[19]

These results are confirmed by estimates of economic rates of return for 123 Turkish manufacturing firms in 1981. In manufacturing, taken as a whole, the economic rate of return averaged -0.7 percent in public enterprises and 6.2 percent in private enterprises. Only in two sectors (iron and steel products and electrical machinery) out of 14 was the economic rate of return higher in the public than in the private sector; rates of return were equal for textiles.

At the same time, public enterprises were favored by the system of incentives applied. Thus, the effective rate of subsidy, indicating the combined effects of import protection, tax, and credit performances, averaged 31 percent in the public sector and 49 percent in the private sector. The incentive measures applied, then, benefited the largely inefficient public enterprises at the expense of private enterprises.[20]

Firm-by-firm comparisons of efficiency levels for Brazil, India, Indonesia, and Tanzania also show the superiority of private over public enterprises. In the case of the Brazilian plastics and steel industries, the level of technical efficiency was shown to be lower in public than in private firms.[21] In India, it was found that productivity in the fertilizer industry was lower in the public than in the private sector, and the differences were explained only in part by higher input costs due to the government imposing the use of high cost domestically-produced feedstock on public enterprises and by outdated technology stemming from the lack of renewal of old equipment.[22]

In the Indonesian manufacturing sector, production costs in public enterprises were shown to be generally higher than in private enterprises.[23]

In particular, 'by almost any indicator, the economic performance of the state mills has been inferior to that of private mills' in weaving.[24] Finally, a study of more than 300 firms in ten Tanzanian industries has found that 23 out of 32 public enterprises used both more capital and more labor than privately-owned firms in the same industry.[25]

A variety of factors account for the apparent poor performance of public enterprises in the manufacturing sector of the developing countries, some of which have been referred to already in regard to particular cases. A comparative study lists '(i) inadequate planning and poor feasibility studies resulting in ill-conceived investments; (ii) lack of skilled managers and administrators; (iii) centralized decision making; (iv) state intervention in the day-to-day operation of the firm; (v) unclear multiple objectives; and (vi) political patronage.'[26] One may add overmanning, the payment of excessively high wages and/or social benefits, slowness in decision-making, and the lack of the threat of bankruptcy. All these factors are related to two basic conditions: the absence of clear-cut objectives for managers and state intervention in firm decision making.

Profits are never the sole, and are often a subsidiary, objective of public enterprises in the developing countries. This means that there is little incentive to reduce costs and to improve technology. The situation is aggravated by the lack of the threat of bankruptcy, which provides the ultimate penalty for poor performance in private enterprise.

Public enterprises are also called upon to serve social goals, such as the regionalization of industry and increased employment, or political objectives, such as favoring the members of a particular race and party and augmenting military power. At the same time, the relative importance of economic, social, and political objectives is far from being unambiguous and it may show changes even in the lifetime of the same administration and, in particular, following changes in government.

The overmanning often observed in the public enterprises of developing countries may also be the result of demands by the supervising authorities to hire — or not to fire — labor. The lack of managerial independence further leads to slowness in decision making and to conflicts in sequential decisions. Finally, the dependence of managers on the government in power will induce them to pursue short-term objectives at the expense of long-term targets.

IV THE STATUS OF PRIVATIZATION IN DEVELOPING COUNTRIES

It may be suggested, then, that the observed shortcomings of public enterprises, resulting in their relatively low efficiency, have importantly motivated the movement towards privatization. But why the sudden change in attitudes? Has information not been available for a sufficiently long period on the performance of public enterprises?[27]

It may be claimed that evidence on the relative inefficiency of public enterprises has accumulated over time, increasing its weight and hence its effect on decision makers. Also, the increasing losses of public economic enterprises, which occurred parallel to the growing budgetary stringency associated with the debt crisis, have made governments recognize the cost of public enterprises to the budget and to the national economy. But, the principal reason may lie in changes in development strategies.

Privatization should be seen as part and parcel of the shift in development strategies initiated in a number of countries, involving greater outward orientation. This shift, necessitating improvements in efficiency, has led to proposals for privatization as private enterprise is considered to be better able to respond to the stick and carrot of competition, which is seen as a condition of improved efficiency.

This is the case, in particular, in regard to foreign markets where private enterprises are well placed to take the risks and reap the rewards of success in exporting. In fact, it has been shown that, in the 1970–81 period, export growth was negatively correlated with the share of public enterprises in the gross domestic product (GDP) and in gross domestic investment (GDI) of developing countries. The regression coefficient, estimated in a cross-section investigation of 21 countries in the first case and 38 countries in the second, is statistically significant at the 2 percent and the 1 percent level, respectively.[28]

In the same study, a negative correlation has been obtained between the share of public enterprise in GDP and in GDI, on the one hand, and the growth of GDP and that of GDI, on the other, although the results are not significant statistically. Statistically significant results have been obtained, however, in a multiple regression analysis of 73 developing countries, which included the GDP growth rate as dependent variable and per capita incomes, population, the domestic savings ratio, foreign aid, and the index of state intervention as explanatory variables.

The index of state intervention has been defined as a combination of the extent of state regulations in industry and the extent of nationalization. The regression coefficient of this variable has been consistently negative and highly significant, under the various specifications used in the study, for both the 1960–70 and the 1970–80 periods.[29]

One explanation for the observed negative relationship between state intervention and economic growth is the higher efficiency of private as against public investment. In fact, a study of 27 developing countries has shown the existence of a positive correlation between the share of private investment in the total and the rate of growth of GDP in the 1971–9 period.[30]

The next qestion concerns the privatization programs of developing countries and the extent to which these plans have been implemented. Table 10.2 provides information on planned sales to private interests and on sales actually accomplished, as well as on closings and liquidations and on leases and management contracts with private interests. The table excludes the sale of 133 enterprises in Chile during the 1970s, representing more than one-fourth of the net worth of the 250 largest Chilean private firms;[31] the privatization of jute and textile mills, representing some 40 percent of capacity and about 1000 smaller businesses in 1982 in Bangladesh; and the reprivatization of some 2000 rice, flour, and cotton mills in Pakistan following the nationalizations of the 1970s.[32]

The table shows that limited progress has been made so far in implementing privatization programs in the developing countries. The opposition of vested interests, the poor financial situation of the enterprises to be privatized, the political obstacles to their rationalization and the limited availability of private capital, have all contributed to the delays that have been encountered.

In fact, a considerable number of actions have involved the closing-down of inefficient public enterprises rather than their sale and, more often than not, the sales have entailed reprivatization rather than the divestiture of firms that were originally established as public enterprises. Finally, as shown in Table 10.2, there have been relatively few instances of leasing or management contracts.

V PROSPECTS FOR THE FUTURE

Just as in recent years, the closing-down option will have to be invoked in the future in cases where the conditions of a public enterprise are beyond repair. At the same time, the political obstacles to closing down large firms may be surmounted through their division into smaller units, some of which will be viable and others not.

As to privatization, it should be emphasized that selling some of the shares of a public enterprise while retaining control in the public sector, as in the case of Petrobas in Brazil, does not constitute privatization. Rather, such sales reduce the availability of finance for the private sector, thereby contributing to 'crowding-out.'

Privatization should be defined as involving the transfer of control. It may not mean selling all shares to private interests, in particular in countries where the availability of domestic capital is limited. It has been reported, for example, that in Zambia 50:50 joint ventures are invariably managed by the private partner.[33]

At the same time, one would have to create the appropriate conditions for privatization. This would necessitate, first of all, establishing clear and unambiguous procedural rules and applying these rules in practice. The rules should provide for the valuation of the enterprises to be privatized by an independent body, which may use auctioning or other methods appropriate for the conditions of the country concerned. This will permit both to avoid underpricing (as it happened in Chile after 1974) and to avoid putting an unreasonable value on assets of questionable productivity (there may be need, in fact, to set a notional price as it was done in one case in Canada).

It may also be desirable for the state to undertake the rationalization of the enterprise prior to privatization, so as to eliminate its excessive debt and to reduce overmanning. It may not be expected that firms whose debt exceeds the value of assets would be taken over by private interests. Reductions in the labor force should also be effected before privatization, unless agreement is reached with the labor unions on a timetable for subsequent reductions in manning levels.

Domestic financial limitations may hinder privatization in developing countries, in particular in low-income countries. At the same time, combining privatization with democratization may bring fruit in, for example, selling state-owned farms to peasants and selling public trading companies, engaged in the marketing of agricultural produce and inputs, to producers – just as the council houses have been sold to their occupants in Britain. These cases have been noted in regard to sub-Saharan Africa, where possibilities exist also in privatizing local industry and fishing[34] notwithstanding the stringency of domestic financial limitations.

Furthermore, the example of France indicates that privatization may be used to revitalize the stock market.[35] It is also the intention of Pakistani policy makers to use privatization as a means to strengthen the stock market. And, the sale of bonds secured by revenues from the sale of the Bosphorus Bridge and the Keban Dam are said to have contributed to the revitalization of the bond market in Turkey.

In indebted countries, debt-equity conversions offer potentialities for privatization, involving the country's own nationals who have funds abroad as well as foreigners. More generally, the domestic financing of privatization may be complemented by foreign financing. Apart from well-established cases of national interest, there is no reason to discriminate against foreign capital in the process of privatization.

Consideration may nevertheless be given to leasing or management contracts as alternatives to privatization, with the contracts awarded through auctions, an option that has long been proposed.[36] It has been used more recently in socialist countries, such as Hungary, where ideological considerations limit the sale of public assets.

At the same time, for privatization to succeed, certain policy conditions need to be met. In particular, there is need for policy reform in developing countries where the system of incentives is biased against exports and in favor of import substitution. While reform efforts have contributed to the process of privatization in these countries, the success of privatization is

TABLE 10.2 The status of privatization in developing countries

Region/Country	Total Number of public enterprises	Targeted Sales	Actual sales		Closures and liquidations		Leases and management contracts	
			Total	of which manufacturing	Total	of which manufacturing	Total	of which manufacturing
Africa								
Cameroon	80	12	—	—	5	5	6–10	5–9
Guinea	65	43	—	—	16	16	1	3
Ivory Coast	113	20	4	2	10	3	3	—
Kenya	180	20	—	—	5	3	—	—
Liberia	23	7	—	—	—	—	1	—
Madagascar	130	15	—	—	5	—	5	—
Mali	54	11	2	1	9	4	1	—
Mauritania	108	10	1	—	4	3	—	—
Niger	54	24	—	—	3	1	—	—
Senegal	104	10	5	3	25	24	—	—
Sierra Leone	26	10	—	—	1	—	4	—
Sudan	136	n.a.	7	7	10	8	—	—
Togo	73	40	—	—	9	9	7	3
Uganda	130	67	—	—	—	—	3	—
Zaire	138	37	11	—	3	—	3	—

Latin America								
Argentina	100	27	—	—	12	—	—	—
Brazil	547	155	17	9	9	—	—	—
Chile	27	23	n.a.	n.a.	—	n.a.	—	—
Costa Rica	39	14	1	1	—	n.a.	—	—
Honduras	81	66	12	n.a.	3	n.a.	14	3
Jamaica	320	41	6	n.a.	1	n.a.	—	—
Mexico	845	236	33	n.a.	10	—	—	—
Panama	45	5	1	—	2	—	—	—
Peru	142	60–70	3	n.a	3	—	—	—
Asia								
Bangladesh	778	n.a.	217	70	—	—	1	—
India	217	29	—	—	—	—	—	—
Malaysia	150	—	4	n.a.	—	—	—	—
Pakistan	112	—	6	6	—	—	—	—
Philippines	86	41	1	n.a.	—	—	—	—
Singapore	n.a.	—	—	2	—	—	—	—
Sri Lanka	43	—	11	2	—	—	5	5
Thailand	70	—	3	3	2	—	1	1
Turkey	65	10	2	—	—	—	—	—

SOURCES: E. Berg and M. M. Shirley, 'Divestiture in Developing Countries', Tables 1 to 6; R. Hemming and P. Massoor, 'Privatization and Public Enterprises' Appendix 1; *Far Eastern Economic Review*, 2 April 1987 (for Singapore); *Financial Times*, 10 February 1987 (for Chile); and *Financial Times*, 5 May 1986 (for Turkey).

conditioned on the full implementation of these reforms.

There is further need to strengthen and, where it is lacking, to establish competition in order to derive the benefits of privatization. Without competition, profit maximization by the newly-established private firms may not serve the national interest.[37] In fact, it has been shown that the superiority of private enterprises over public enterprises is the most evident in competitive industries.[38]

For similar reasons, in the absence of privatization, establishing competitive conditions for public enterprises would lead to improvements in efficiency. Such a direction is being taken by the Hungarian policy makers. But this can be successfully done only if the management of public enterprises is made independent of the government and it is given appropriate incentives to maximize profits.

The independence of managers can be ensured if they are made responsible to a board of directors, in which the government representatives are in a minority. At the same time, linking the remuneration of management to the firm's profits and establishing the possibility of bankruptcy would provide the carrot and the stick of competition, provided that provisions are simultaneously made for free entry and/or the breaking up of large firms and for import liberalization. Also, the existing privileges of public enterprises in matters of credit and taxation should be eliminated, putting them on an equal footing with private firms.

The question remains, however, if one can establish truly competitive conditions for public enterprises while maintaining public ownership. This question has been much debated in Hungary and while there are some examples of highly efficient public enterprises in developing countries, e.g. in Brazil, a knowledgeable observer of the African scene has expressed scepticism as to the prospects for industrial development via public enterprise.[39]

CONCLUSIONS

This essay has noted the significant role public enterprises play in the manufacturing sector of the developing countries. These enterprises have often been considered the mainstay of economic development and have assumed particular importance in industries that are seen as being of strategic importance for industrialization as well as in highly capital-intensive industries.

Over time, public enterprises have come to constitute an increasing financial burden for the developing countries, however. Also, with the drying up of foreign loans, their deficits have been increasingly financed from domestic sources, thereby raising the spectre of 'crowding out' the private sector.

The poor financial performance of public enterprises to a large extent reflects their relative inefficiency *vis-à-vis* private enterprises, which is documented by the experience of a number of developing countries. Privatization, then, may be regarded as a response to perceived differences in efficiency between private and public enterprises. And, while it is given urgency by the difficult financial situation of public enterprises, it is part and parcel of the shift in development strategies initiated in a number of developing countries, involving greater outward orientation, which requires improved efficiency.

At the same time, for privatization to be successful, it is necessary to establish the conditions of competition. One would further need to overcome the obstacles to privatization in the form of the opposition of vested interests, the poor financial situation of the enterprises to be privatized, the political obstacles to rationalization, and the limitations of domestic private capital.

It has been suggested that, in the absence of privatization, consideration be given to leasing or management contracts, to closing down firms where the conditions are without repair, and to improving the operation of public enterprises. Effecting such improvements, in turn, would require complete independence and improved incentives for managers while exposing them to domestic and foreign competition. The question remains, however, if this can be accomplished while maintaining public ownership.

NOTES

1. For purposes of comparison, the table also includes data for the industrial countries, whenever available.
2. In several cases, mining is included with manufacturing. But, in the countries in question mining is generally of little importance and hence it can be disregarded in the discussion.
3. The data include mining and manufacturing. M. A. Ayub and S. O. Hegstad, 'Public Industrial Enterprises. Determinants of Performance,' *Industry and Finance Series, Volume 17* (Washington, DC: World Bank, 1986) p. 17.
4. This explains that, apart from British Telecom, the British denationalizations have related largely to public utilities and transportation.
5. During the period under consideration, no change occurred in Korea.
6. In the case of France, expectations for increased efficiency and reduced bureaucratic interference have been given as reasons for privatization (cf. B. Balassa, 'French Economic Policy Since March 1986,' Essay 18 in this volume).
7. Unless otherwise noted, the data derive from R. P. Short, 'The Role of Public Enterprise: An International Statistical Comparison,' in R. H. Floyd, C. S. Gray, and R. P. Short (eds), *Public Enterprise in Mixed Economies* (Washington, DC: International Monetary Fund, 1984) pp. 110–96.
8. B. Balassa, G. M. Bueno, P. Kuczynski, and M. H. Simonsen, *Toward Renewed Economic Growth in Latin America* (Washington, DC: Institute for International Economics, 1986) Table 4.4.

9. World Bank, *Borrowing in International Capital Markets* (Washington, DC: 1980).
10. Short, 'The Role of Public Enterprise,' p. 176.
11. Ibid.; Balassa, Bueno, Kuczynski, and Simonsen, *Toward Renewed Economic Growth in Latin America*, Ch. 4.
12. Within the last group there was one case where public enterprise may be slightly favored. G. Yarrow, 'Privatization in Theory and Practice,' *Economic Policy*, I (1986) pp. 323–70.
13. D. L. Gordon, 'Development Finance Companies, State and Privately Owned,' World Bank Staff Working Paper No. 578 (Washington, DC, 1983), p. 38.
14. Ibid., p. 32.
15. Ayub and Hegstad, 'Public Industrial Enterprises,' p. 15.
16. A. M. Choksi, 'State Intervention in the Industrialization of Developing Countries. Selected Issues,' World Bank Staff Working Paper No. 341 (Washington, DC, 1979) pp. 23–4.
17. M. M. Shirley, 'Managing State-Owned Enterprises,' World Bank Staff Working Paper No. 577 (Washington, DC, 1983) p. 33.
18. Ibid., p. 16.
19. A. O. Krueger, and B. Tuncer, 'Estimating Total Factor Productivity Growth in a Developing Country,' World Bank Staff Working Paper No. 422 (Washington, DC, 1980) p. 43.
20. F. Yagci, 'Protection and Incentives in Turkish Manufacturing. An Evaluation of Policies and their Impact in 1981,' World Bank Staff Working Paper No. 660 (Washington, DC, 1984) pp. 86 and 97.
21. W. G. Tyler, 'Technical Efficiency in Production in a Developing Country: An Empirical Examination of the Brazilian Plastics and Steel Industries,' *Oxford Economic Papers*, XXXI (1979) pp. 477–95.
22. M. Gupta, 'Productivity Performance of the Public and the Private Sectors in India: A Case Study of the Fertilizer Industry,' *Indian Economic Review*, XVII (1982) pp. 165–86.
23. R. Funkhouser, and P. W. MacAvoy, 'A Sample of Observations on Comparative Prices in Public and Private Enterprise,' *Journal of Public Economics*, XI (1979) pp. 353–68.
24. H. Hill, 'State Enterprises in a Competitive Industry: An Indonesian Case Study,' *World Development*, X (1982) pp. 1015–23.
25. F. S. Perkins, 'Technology Choice, Industrialization, and Development Experiences in Tanzania,' *Journal of Developing Studies*, XIX (1983) pp. 213–47.
26. Choksi, 'State Intervention in the Industrialization of Developing Countries,' p. iv.
27. In this connection, reference may be made to a statement by Adam Smith in *The Wealth of Nations*, according to which 'In every great monarchy in Europe the sale of the crown lands would produce a very large sum of money, which, if applied to the payment of the public debts, would deliver from mortgage a much greater revenue than any which those lands have ever afforded to the crown. . . . When the crown lands had become private property, they would, in the course of a few years, become well improved and well cultivated.' (cited in Yarrow, p. 324).
28. P. Nunnenkamp, 'State Enterprise in Developing Countries,' *Intereconomics*, XXI (1986) pp. 186–97.
29. R. D. Singh, 'State Intervention, Foreign Economic Aid, Savings and Growth in LDCs: Some Recent Evidence,' *Kyklos*, XXXVIII (1985) pp. 216–32.

30. M. I. Blejer, and M. S. Khan, 'Private Investment in Developing Countries,' *Finance and Development*, XXI (1984) pp. 26–9.
31. Shirley, 'Managing State-Owned Enterprises,' pp. 57–8.
32. P. Young, 'Privatization in LDCs: A Solution that Works,' *Journal of Economic Growth*, I (1986) pp. 24–30.
33. E. Berg, and M. M. Shirley, 'Divestiture in Developing Countries' (Washington, DC: World Bank, 1986) mimeo.
34. It has been reported that, after collectively purchased motor boats had been sold to fishermen, the share of boats in operating conditions rose from 15 percent to 85 percent, with corresponding increases in output. E. Berg, 'Private Sector Potential in Africa,' *Journal of Economic Growth*, I (1986) pp. 17–23.
35. The success of the present French government to do so has disproved the contention of the supporters of the socialist government that the French stock market would not be able to absorb the shares offered in the course of privatizing large enterprises (cf. Essay 18 in this volume).
36. H. Demsetz, 'Why Regulate Utilities?' *Journal of Law and Economics*, XI (1968) pp. 55–65.
37. As suggested in the case of the United Kingdom efficiency may conceivably deteriorate rather than improve as a result. J. A. Kay and D. J. Thompson, 'Privatization: A Policy in Search of a Rationale,' *Economic Journal*, XCVI (1986) pp. 18–32.
38. Yarrow, 'Privatization in Theory and Practice.'
39. 'To an African Government contemplating the creation of a substantial public sector as a means of promoting industrialization the advice of this writer would have to be: don't do it; there are better ways of stimulating industrial growth. A large industrial public sector will contribute little to dynamic industrial growth, will tend to become a drain on public finances, will require a net inflow of resources to cover its capital requirements and will discourage the growth of private industry' (T. Killick, 'The Role of the Public Sector in the Industrialization of African Developing Countries,' *Industry and Development*, no. 7 (New York: United Nations, 1983) p. 87.

Essay 11 Economic Prospects and Policies in Mexico

INTRODUCTION

This essay sets out to examine Mexico's possibilities in the world economy in general and in the North American area in particular, and to consider the choice of policies that may be applied to exploit its possibilities to best advantage. As an introduction to the discussion, Section I will review the policies applied in Mexico during the 1973–83 decade of external shocks. In turn, Section II will examine the extent to which Mexico has exploited its comparative advantage in trade in manufactured goods. Finally, Section III will focus on policies that may permit Mexico to cope with its debt problem and to ensure rapid and sustained economic growth in the future.

I THE POLICIES APPLIED IN PERIODS OF EXTERNAL SHOCKS, 1973–83

The author has estimated the balance-of-payments effects of external shocks, and of the policies applied, for the 1973–8 and the 1978–83 periods.[1] External shocks have been defined as large, unanticipated changes in world economic conditions. They include shifts in the terms of trade, associated to a large extent with changes in oil prices, and the slowdown in the growth of world export demand, associated with world recessions. In the second period, increases in interest rates in world financial markets also come under this heading.

The methodology applied involves estimating the balance-of-payments effects of external shocks, including terms of trade and export volume effects and, in the second period, interest rate effects, as well as those of the policies applied, including additional net external financing, export promotion, import substitution, and deflationary measures. The base year for the calculations pertaining to the 1973–8 period is the average of the years 1971–3; it is the average of the years 1976–8 for the 1978–83 period.

This essay reports the estimates made for Mexico. Table 11.1 shows the balance-of-payments effects of external shocks, and of the policies, applied on an annual basis. The annual data are of particular interest because of the changes that occurred in Mexico's petroleum exports. In the following discussion, the two periods of external shocks will be separately considered.

TABLE 11.1 *Balance-of-payments effects of external shocks and of the policies applied: Mexico*

	1974	1975	1976	1977	1978	Average 1974–8	1979	1980	1981	1982	1983	Average 1979–83
External shocks (as percent of GNP)												
Terms of trade effects	1.1	1.9	0.8	-0.1	0.0	0.7	0.8	-0.9	-2.5	-5.7	-5.8	-2.9
Pure	-0.7	-0.5	-1.2	-1.8	-2.4	-1.4	-0.1	-3.3	-5.4	-5.8	-0.9	-3.2
Unbalanced	1.9	2.4	2.0	1.7	2.4	2.1	0.9	2.4	2.9	0.1	-4.9	0.3
Export volume effects	0.2	0.5	0.3	0.7	0.7	0.5	0.1	0.5	0.8	1.1	1.5	0.8
Interest rate effects	—	—	—	—	—	—	1.3	2.1	3.5	4.6	2.4	2.8
Total	1.3	2.4	1.2	0.6	0.6	1.2	2.1	1.7	1.7	-0.1	-2.0	0.7
Total less unbalanced terms of trade effects	-0.5	0.1	-0.9	-1.1	-1.7	-0.9	1.2	-0.7	-1.2	-0.1	-2.9	0.4
The policies applied (as percent of external shocks)												
Additional net external financing	240.2	151.5	140.5	-94.7	-16.9	123.1	127.4	222.3	313.2	-4413.9	-646.3	-129.2
Export promotion	-47.1	-28.1	-112.3	-206.3	-66.7	-70.4	-61.0	131.1	171.9	4860.7	274.2	467.4
Import substitution	-84.3	-21.4	55.6	322.6	137.3	33.5	-76.9	-231.6	-361.7	-1028.7	186.8	-269.1
Effects of deflationary policies	-8.8	-1.9	16.2	78.5	46.3	13.8	-11.4	-21.8	-23.4	481.9	85.2	31.0
Additional net external financing/GNP	3.2	3.7	1.6	-0.5	-0.1	1.5	2.7	3.7	5.3	-3.4	-12.7	-0.9
Export promotion/exports	-17.7	-21.1	-42.0	-38.1	-10.4	-24.7	19.8	31.4	38.9	44.2	50.2	38.9
Import substitution/imports	-13.4	-6.6	9.6	33.4	12.6	5.7	-17.3	-33.0	-43.6	-9.1	88.7	-18.7
Lower GNP growth effects/imports	-1.4	-0.6	2.8	8.1	4.3	2.4	-2.5	-3.1	-2.8	4.3	40.5	2.2

NOTE: Interest rate effects were assumed to be zero in the 1974–8 period.

SOURCE: World Bank data-base.

1973–8

With its trade balance in petroleum turning positive following domestic discoveries, pure terms of trade effects became increasingly favorable for Mexico during the first period of external shocks.[2] Towards the end of the period, they came to offset the adverse unbalanced terms of trade effects that find their origin in Mexico's large deficit in merchandise trade more than compensating for increases in the adverse volume effects owing to the world recession and the subsequent slow growth of the world economy. Correspondingly, after rising from 1.3 percent in 1974 to 2.4 percent in 1975, the negative balance-of-payments effects of external shocks decreased to 0.6 percent of the gross national product in 1978 (the results become favorable if unbalanced terms of trade effects are excluded from the calculations, with a gain of 1.7 percent).

In view of the small magnitude of external shocks during the first period, it may not be appropriate to speak of policy responses to these shocks in Mexico. In fact, the policies applied were largely autonomous, with the expansionary measures applied by President Echevarria until 1976 followed by deflationary policies in 1977 and expansionary measures being again taken in 1978 under President López Portillo. Nevertheless, the methodology applied retains its usefulness as it permits examining quantitatively the effects of the policies applied in a consistent framework.

The expansionary measures applied by President Echevarria involved increasing the share of public expenditure in the gross domestic product from 17 percent in 1971–3 to 28 percent in 1976. With the lack of a commensurate rise in revenues, the deficit of the public sector reached 9 percent of GDP in 1976, compared with 2 percent in 1971–3.[3] The deficit was increasingly financed by foreign borrowing that provided more than one-half of the net financial requirements of the public sector in 1976.

Foreign borrowing made it possible for Mexico to maintain the exchange rate at 12.50 pesos to the US dollar until September 1976, even though domestic prices rose more rapidly than foreign prices (Table 11.2). The resulting deterioration in Mexico's competitive position led to declines in export market shares that came to represent a loss of 28 percent in export value in 1977. The loss was even larger, 35 percent, if one excludes the exports of petroleum from newly-found deposits. It declined to 22 percent (excluding petroleum) in 1978, reflecting the effects of the devaluations of the peso undertaken in September 1976 and in the course of 1977 (Table 11.3).

In the 1974–8 period, taken as a whole, a decline of 20 percent occurred in Mexico's average export market share, excluding petroleum. In particular, its market share in the manufactured exports of the developing countries fell by one-half between 1971–3 and 1977 and rebounded only

TABLE 11.2 Changes in real exchange rates in Mexico
(1976–8 = 100)

	1976	1977	1978	1979	1980	1981	1982	1983	1984	1985
					(annual estimates)					
Exchange rate										
Peso/US$	15.43	22.57	22.77	22.81	22.95	24.51	56.40	120.09	167.83	256.87
Index	76.2	111.4	112.4	112.6	113.3	121.0	278.5	592.9	828.6	1268.2
Wholesale price index	74.1	104.7	121.1	143.4	178.4	222.1	346.6	718.9	1224.4	1880.2
US wholesale price index	93.6	99.3	107.1	120.5	137.5	150.1	153.1	155.0	158.7	157.9
Index of relative price *vis-à-vis* US	79.8	106.2	114.1	119.9	130.7	149.1	228.2	467.0	777.7	1200.1
Real exchange rate *vis-à-vis* US	94.9	105.8	99.3	94.6	87.4	81.9	120.0	128.7	107.9	105.4
Real effective exchange rate	93.8	105.3	100.9	96.3	88.4	79.7	114.7	121.5	100.6	98.3

TABLE 11.2 (cont'd)

	1983				1984				1985				1986	
	I	II	III	IV	I	II	III	IV	I	II	III	IV	I	II
					(quarterly estimates)									
Exchange rate														
Peso/US$	102.0	114.2	126.1	138.0	150.0	161.9	173.7	185.7	200.6	218.6	274.8	333.6	423.6	522.2
Index	503.7	563.8	622.6	681.5	740.4	799.2	857.7	917.0	990.2	1079.1	1356.5	1647.0	2091.5	2577.8
Wholesale price index	563.5	683.7	771.7	856.6	1020.5	1180.2	1279.9	1417.2	1599.0	1786.2	1935.5	2200.3	2674.8	3113.4
US wholesale price index	153.7	154.2	155.7	156.5	158.2	159.3	158.9	158.5	158.1	158.3	157.2	158.2	155.8	152.8
Index of relative price *vis-à-vis* US	369.6	446.9	499.6	551.9	650.2	747.0	812.1	901.5	1019.5	1137.7	1241.0	1402.3	1731.9	2053.7
Real exchange rate *vis-à-vis* US	137.3	127.3	125.5	124.5	114.8	107.8	106.4	102.5	97.9	95.6	110.0	118.4	121.6	126.5
Real effective exchange rate	130.8	120.4	117.8	116.9	107.7	101.2	98.7	94.7	89.6	88.1	102.8	112.7	118.3	124.6

NOTE: The real effective exchange rate has been calculated by weighting with the composition of Mexico's trade in 1976–8. The estimates are averages of monthly estimates, so that there are some small discrepancies if one wishes to translate one row into another in the table.

SOURCE: World Bank data-base.

TABLE 11.3 *Changes in export market shares in Mexico*

	1974	1975	1976	1977	1978	Average 1974–8	1979	1980	1981	1982	1983	Average 1979–83
Fuel exports	10.8	347.6	348.5	578.0	1277.9	509.0	137.2	330.7	543.4	762.4	864.3	476.1
Non-fuel primary exports	-7.3	-9.4	-17.5	-17.9	2.6	-9.8	-1.1	-2.0	2.5	-8.6	-2.0	-2.3
Manufacturing exports	-24.5	-36.3	-49.7	-50.0	-43.6	-41.9	-8.4	-30.1	-41.1	-27.0	18.3	-16.3
Total exports	-15.1	-17.5	-29.6	-27.6	-9.5	-19.8	24.7	45.7	63.7	79.1	100.7	63.8
Total exports other than fuels	-15.4	-21.8	-33.9	-34.5	-22.2	-25.9	-3.9	-13.6	-16.4	-16.4	7.3	-8.3

SOURCE: World Bank data-base.

slightly in 1978. Mexico further experienced losses in primary exports, especially in cattle, meat, and sugar.

The appreciation of the real exchange rate also gave rise to negative import substitution in Mexico, represented by an increase in the income elasticity of import demand. Import substitution turned positive in 1976 in response to the tightening of import controls and increases in tariffs, with the devaluation of the exchange rate providing further incentives to the replacement of imports by domestic production.

Finally, the application of expansionary measures contributed to the acceleration of the growth of imports in the early part of the period, followed by a deceleration as deflationary measures were applied. However, the effects of these measures were partially undone in 1978, when expansionary policies were again adopted under President López Portillo.

All in all, the policies applied discriminated against exports, owing both to the overvaluation of the exchange rate and increased import protection. The adverse effects of the resulting losses in export market shares on Mexico's balance of payments were only partly offset by import substitution. At the same time, notwithstanding the virtual absence of external shocks, Mexico accumulated foreign debt that came to attain 33 percent of the gross national product in 1978, compared with 9 percent in 1971–3, on the average.

1978–83

Favorable pure balance-of-payments effects increased further after 1979, exceeding the adverse unbalanced terms-of-trade effects by widening margins. As a result, despite the rise of the unfavorable export volume effects, the balance-of-payments impact of external shocks other than interest rate effects became increasingly positive, reaching 4.6 percent in 1982. (Unbalanced terms-of-trade-effects were practically nil in that year.)

Petroleum prices declined in 1983 but this was compensated by the fact that unbalanced terms-of-trade effects turned favorable as Mexico drastically cut its imports in response to the debt crisis. At the same time, given its high and rising indebtedness, Mexico experienced large adverse interest rate effects as world interest rates rose.

Increases in oil revenues fueled the expansionary policies adopted by President López Portillo. These revenues did not suffice, however, to finance the rising public expenditures, in particular public investment, and transfer payments. By 1981, the share of public expenditures in the gross domestic product reached 47 percent and the public sector deficit came to amount to 13 percent of GDP.

The financing of the large public sector deficit, in turn, required foreign borrowing. This borrowing permitted maintaining the exchange rate in the range of 22.5 to 24.5 pesos to the dollar between 1977 and 1981, notwith-standing the acceleration of inflation resulting from the application of expansionary policies. As a result, by the fourth quarter of 1981, the exchange rate appreciated in real terms by 35 percent *vis-à-vis* the cur-rencies of Mexico's trading partners, compared with the 1976–8 average.

Borrowing abroad reinforced the adverse effects of increased petroleum exports on the non-oil tradable goods sector. Even in the absence of foreign borrowing, the balance of payments would have been equilibrated at an exchange rate unfavorable for non-oil exports and import substitu-tion. The foreign financing of the current deficit, amounting to 5 percent of the gross domestic product in 1983, further aggravated the situation for the non-oil tradable sector.

As a result, Mexico suffered a 16 percent loss in export market shares between 1976–8 and 1981, excluding fuels. The losses were concentrated in manufactured goods, where Mexico experienced a 41 percent decline in export market shares. In turn, the slight gain of 3 percent in nonfuel primary exports is explained by increased United States demand for fruits and vegetables while Mexico suffered considerable losses in the exports of cattle and meat.

Mexico further experienced negative import substitution, reflecting in part the overvaluation of the exchange rate and in part the spillover effects of rapid economic expansion. Also, the expansionary fiscal policies applied contributed directly to the rise of imports as shown by the negative macroeconomic effects in Table 11.1.

The situation changed in August 1982, when Mexico ceased to be creditworthy for commercial bank lending. Additional net external financing turned strongly negative and imports were reduced to a considerable extent. Substantial declines in imports occurred as a result of the direct and indirect effects of deflationary policies, the application of import controls, and a large devaluation of the exchange rate.

The large devaluations undertaken in the course of 1982 and 1983 contributed to the expansion of exports and, in 1983, Mexico had a gain in its market shares for non-fuel exports. This was the result of an increase of 18 percent, compared with the 1976–8 average, in the exports of manufac-tured goods, and a 2 percent loss in nonfuel primary exports. Increases in export market shares contributed to the financing of interest payments on the foreign debt without, however, appreciably affecting Mexico's external debt. Thus, Mexico remained saddled with a large foreign debt that was the result of the excessively expansionary policies applied during much of the period under consideration.

II EXPLOITING MEXICO'S COMPARATIVE ADVANTAGE IN MANUFACTURED GOODS

Having reviewed the policies applied during the 1973–83 decade, and the effects of these policies, the essay will next analyze the pattern of Mexico's comparative advantage in manufactured goods. This will be done by utilizing a two-stage procedure.[4]

In the first stage, indices of revealed comparative advantage, calculated as tha ratio of a country's share in the world exports of individual commodity categories to its share in the world exports of all manufactured goods, were regressed on variables representing the capital intensity of the individual commodity categories. The calculations have been made for 38 developed and developing countries by using a stock as well as a flow concept of capital, both of which include physical and human capital.[5]

The estimating equation is shown in (1), where x_{ij} is the index of revealed comparative advantage of country j in commodity category i, k_i is the ratio of capital to labor (capital intensity) for commodity category i, and the ß coefficient for country j indicates the percentage change in the country's comparative advantage index associated with a one percentage change in capital intensity. A positive (negative) ß coefficient thus shows that a country has a comparative advantage in capital (labor) intensive commodities, while the numerical magnitude of the ß coefficient indicates the extent of the country's comparative advantage in capital (labor) intensive commodities.

$$\log x_{ij} = \log \alpha_j + \text{ß}_j \log k_i \tag{1}$$

Next, the hypothesis was tested that intercountry differences in the ß-coefficients can be explained by differences in country characteristics that determine the pattern of comparative advantage. This test was performed by regressing the ß-coefficients estimated for the individual countries on variables representing their physical (*GDICAP*) and human (*HMIND*) endowments in an intercountry framework.

$$\text{ß}_j = f(GDICAP_j, HMIND_j) \tag{2}$$

The estimates made for 1971 show that intercountry differences in the structure of exports are in large part explained by differences in physical and human capital endowments, both of which are highly significant statistically. These results were reconfirmed by estimates for the year 1979.[6]

In the present case the focus of interest is Mexico. In both 1971 and 1979, the ß-coefficients for Mexico had the expected negative sign. For 1971, the coefficients, estimated by utilizing equation (1), were −0.47 and

−0.29 using the stock and the flow measures of capital, respectively. Coefficient values increased between 1971 and 1979; they reached −0.19 using the stock measure and −0.09 using the flow measure of capital. These changes may be explained by the fact that the accumulation of physical and human capital in Mexico between 1971 and 1979 much exceeded the average; it was surpassed by only four countries during the period.

Considerable differences remained, however, in Mexico's relative position in terms of physical as compared with human capital. In 1971, Mexico was in 26th place in regard to the former and 33rd place in regard to the latter, whereas the corresponding rankings were 22nd and 31st in 1979. The results indicate the existence of a bias in Mexico's capital endowment inasmuch as the accumulated physical capital was not accompanied by corresponding changes in human capital. This fact reflects a weaker educational effort in Mexico compared with other countries, in particular those of the Far East. Thus, in 1979, Mexico was ahead of Korea and Taiwan in terms of physical capital but it was considerably behind them in terms of human capital.

At the same time, the ß-coefficients derived in the first stage equation (or the *actual* coefficients) are considerably higher than those obtained in the second stage equation (or the *expected* coefficients), indicating that Mexico's manufactured exports were much more capital-intensive than expected on the basis of its physical and human capital endowment relative to other countries. Nor did this relationship change appreciably between 1971 and 1979. In 1971, the expected ß-coefficient, estimated from equation (2), was −0.93 using the stock measure, and −0.84 using the flow measure, of capital; the corresponding coefficients were −0.98 and −0.88 in 1979.

The explanation for this persistent deviation appears to lie in the policies applied, which did not permit exploiting Mexico's comparative advantage in manufactured goods indicated by the expected ß-coefficient derived in cross-country relationships. High import protection, low duties on capital equipment, the repeated overvaluation of the peso, and distortions in factor prices, with low interest rates and social legislation favoring capital-intensive activities, contributed to the exportation of commodities that were substantially more capital intensive than warranted by Mexico's physical and human capital endowment. It is apparent that these policies have imposed a considerable cost on the Mexican economy by distorting production and trade patterns.

The observed large deviation between the actual and the expected values of the ß-coefficients for Mexico makes it difficult to undertake projections for the future. Two possible alternatives present themselves; postulating that Mexico will asymptotically approach the cross-country relationship between capital endowments and the relative capital intensity of exports or assuming that the observed deviations from the cross-country pattern will persist over time. In the first case, one may utilize equation (2) to estimate the ß-coefficients corresponding to Mexico's physical and human capital endowment for some future year; in the second case, the estimate is adjusted for deviations between actual and expected values of the ß-coefficients in the base year, 1979.

Projections were made for the year 2000 by postulating that Mexico would reach Spain's 1979 physical capital endowment, representing an increase by nine-tenths compared with 1979 values in Mexico, and Argentina's 1979 human capital endowment, representing an approximate doubling compared with 1979 values in Mexico. These projections reflect the assumption that Mexico would reduce, but not eliminate, its lag in the accumulation of human capital.

Utilizing equation (2), Mexico's expected ß-coefficients in the year 2000 would reach -0.61 using the stock and -0.53 using the flow measure of capital.[7] While these expected values are considerably lower than those estimated for 1979 from the same equation, they continue to exceed the actual values of the ß-coefficients for 1979, estimated from equation (1). At the same time, they call for emphasis on labor-intensive exports in Mexico.

It should not be assumed, however, that labor intensity is synonymous with the textile, clothing, and shoes industries, which the UN Economic Commission for Latin America called 'vegetative industries.' While Mexico has possibilities for expanding its clothing and shoe exports, textiles have increasingly become a capital-intensive industry and there are other labor-intensive activities that hold considerable promise for Mexico.

These activities include, first of all, agriculture that was once a net exporting sector but, with an increased bias of the incentive system against exports and against agriculture in general, became a net importer. With appropriate incentives, Mexico can exploit its comparative advantages in agriculture that is a labor-intensive sector.

Agriculture, in turn, can provide the basis for the expansion of agro-industry, including traditional processed foods as well as new products derived from agriculture. Examples are dehydrated fruits and vegetables, prepared food, and feed supplements, involving the extraction of protein from sugar-cane and other low-valued products.

Mexico also has considerable potential in tourism, in border trade, and in maquila industries. The last point, in turn, leads to the question of Mexico's comparative advantages in labor-intensive products. Apart from products using largely unskilled labor, such as leather goods, sisal products, toys, and sporting goods, Mexico has a potential in products using semi-skilled labor, such as machinery and transport equipment, where it can participate in the international division of the production process by manufacturing labor-intensive parts and components as well as undertaking assembly activities. This would, however, require a far-reaching policy reform in the short and medium run and an increased educational effort in the medium and longer run. The next section of the chapter will deal with the requirements of such a policy reform.

III POLICY REFORMS FOR STRUCTURAL ADJUSTMENT AND ECONOMIC GROWTH

Economic policies in Mexico would have to serve the double objectives of coping with the debt situation, which was aggravated by the precipitous decline in oil prices, and promoting economic growth. The former requires generating sufficient foreign exchange to pay interest on Mexico's large external debt. The latter necessitates a reorientation of Mexico's development strategy as neither import substitution nor oil can provide an adequate impetus for economic growth. Import substitution-orientation brought diminishing returns and increasingly smaller net foreign exchange earnings in highly protected domestic markets from the mid-sixties onwards while the deterioration of markets does not augur well for the oil sector.

This is not to say that the opportunities for efficient import substitution would have been exhausted in Mexico. In the manufacturing sector, such possibilities exist in conjunction with exports through the exploitation of economies of scale and through participation in the international division of the production process. In agriculture, Mexico's natural advantages would permit the reversal of its unfavorable trade balance through exports and import substitution if appropriate policies are followed.

The precondition for economic growth through exports and efficient import substitution is a shift towards an outward-oriented development strategy that provides similar incentives to exports and to import substitution as well as to manufactured and to primary activities, with exceptions made for infant industries. The change in development strategy, in turn, needs to be linked to appropriate policies for servicing the foreign debt.

Two broad alternatives present themselves: an expenditure-reducing, or deflationary, policy and an expenditure-switching, or output-increasing, policy. The choice between these alternatives is exemplified by recent experiences of Hungary and Turkey, both of which encountered debt problems as early as 1979.

Hungary adopted a deflationary policy that bore heavily on investment, reinforced price and import controls, and let its exchange rate appreciate in real terms, leading to losses in export market shares, with the slow growth of the economy (about 2 percent a year) being threatened by increases in imports as structural adjustment has not occurred. In turn, output-increasing policies in the form of a large devaluation, the provision of export subsidies, and the liberalization of prices and imports have contributed to structural adjustment in Turkey, with exports doubling between 1980 and 1983 under difficult world market conditions, economic growth rates averaging 4–5 percent, and the country again becoming creditworthy for lending on commercial terms.[8]

Exchange rate policy

Structural adjustment through the adoption of output-increasing policies
would thus permit simultaneously to deal with the debt problem and to
promote economic growth in Mexico. The cornerstone of such a policy is
the adoption of an appropriate exchange rate policy.

As noted in Section I, several years of overvaluation of the Mexican peso
were followed by substantial devaluations in 1982 and 1983. These devaluations brought the real exchange rate *vis-à-vis* Mexico's principal trading
partners above its 1978 level.[9] The real exchange rate appreciated again in
1984 and the first half of 1985, however, as Mexico failed to devalue
sufficiently to compensate for domestic inflation. Thus, in the second
quarter of 1985, the peso showed a 13 percent appreciation in real terms
compared to 1978 (Table 11.2).

These changes in exchange rates had a considerable effect on Mexico's
exports. While the dollar value of non-fuel exports rose by 36 percent
between the first half of 1982 and the first half of 1984 as the exchange rate
depreciated, this increase was followed by a 11 percent decline over the
next twelve months period as the peso appreciated in real terms.

Substantial devaluations were again undertaken after June 1985. By the
end of the year, Mexico's real exchange rate stood 11 percent above its
1978 level and a depreciation of 25 percent occurred by mid-1986. At the
same time, the difference between the free market and the official exchange rate declined to 5 percent from over 60 percent in mid-1986.

The devaluation of the peso compared with its 1978 level was necessary
because of the changes that have occurred since. To begin with, a shift
occurred from large external borrowing to the payment of substantial
interest charges. Also, Mexico having accepted the obligation to abolish
export subsidies under a bilateral agreement with the United States in early
1985, the exchange rate becomes the principal instrument of export promotion. Finally, in order to encourage exports, Mexico would have to reduce
the existing anti-export bias of the system of incentives that can be
accomplished by lowering import protection *pari passu* with the devaluation of the exchange rate.

It would further be desirable to unify the free and the official exchange
rates. While the difference between the two rates decreased to a considerable extent in the course of 1985, this is largely explained by extreme
tightening of monetary policy that led to the repatriation of funds held
abroad. Under a less restrictive policy, the difference in the rates would
increase again, inviting evasion through the underinvoicing of exports and
the overinvoicing of imports, providing inducement for capital flight in
expectation of a further devaluation of the official exchange rate, and
favoring sectors that can utilize the free exchange rate (tourism) over
sectors utilizing the official rate (domestic manufacturing).

There would further be need for maintaining stability and predictability in the real exchange rate, thereby reducing uncertainty that discouraged exports in recent years. Stability and predictability would be served by setting automatic rules, so as to avoid that the exchange rate would get out of line again in the future.

Trade policy

The Programa Nacional de Fomento Industrial y Comercio Exterior (PRONAFICE) states the need 'to favor efficient import substitution and to promote exports in Mexico' (p. 119). The program suggests that these objectives may be attained by rationalizing protection, promoting exports in a sustained manner, developing the border areas and free trade zones, and entering into international negotiations in order to consolidate existing markets and to open new ones.

The decision to enter GATT is an important step towards the fulfilment of the last-mentioned objective. It would have to be followed by further steps, with Mexico taking an active role in the new round of multilateral trade negotiations. This is necessary both because the participation of the newly-industrializing countries, such as Mexico, is a precondition of the success of the negotiations and because joint action by these countries may ensure favorable treatment for them.

The further development of border zones and free trade areas is also desirable. Mexico may promote these arrangements while simultaneously pursuing the objectives of industrial decentralization and the geographical diversification by providing infrastructure for port-based regional development oriented towards Western Europe, the Far East, and Latin America.

At the same time, efforts would need to be made to increase links between these areas and the rest of the national economy. This should not be done by imposing domestic content requirements on producers in border zones and free trade areas, but by providing the suppliers of domestic products with the same privileges as if they were exporting directly and permitting producers in border zones and free trade areas to sell in domestic markets on the payment of duties on imported components.

Under the bilateral agreement signed with the United States, Mexico cannot provide direct export subsidies. Reducing the anti-export bias of the system of incentives, then, would necessitate lowering import protection. This would also provide incentives to reduce costs and to improve technology in import-competing industries. As stated in PRONAFICE, 'excessive and permanent protection cannot be the norm of the policy applied as it gives rise to a super-protected industry that in many cases is hardly efficient' (p. 119).

While Mexico's precarious balance-of-payments situation does not permit precipitated action, additional measures will need to be taken to eliminate excessive protection and to reduce the bias against manufactured and primary exports and against primary production in general. This will be necessary in order to meet PROFINACE's target of 15–18 percent annual increases in non-oil exports and to carry out its recommendation 'to favor agricultural and mineral production which create more employment per invested capital and could limit migration from the country to the cities' (p. 122).

The stated objectives would be served by liberalizing imports *pari passu* with the devaluation of the exchange rate. This would amount to a compensated devaluation, under which exports receive the full benefits of the change in the exchange rate while the resulting increases in import prices are offset by reductions in protection. In particular, it would be desirable to abolish the import prohibitions that provide powerful incentives for the domestic production of luxury goods; to further reduce the scope of quantitative import restrictions that adversely affect domestic production; to eliminate the use of official import reference prices that have in practice similar effects as import restrictions; and to reduce all the tariff rates in excess of 40 percent that unduly raise domestic prices.

The described measures would need to be followed by the further reduction and rationalization of import protection. This should be done according to a timetable determined in advance, so as to prepare domestic producers for the changes and to provide incentives for adjustment. The timetable would include eliminating the remaining quantitative import restrictions, lowering tariffs to a maximum of 15–20 percent, and reducing tariff disparities. In fact, as shown in PROFINACE (Table 6.1.3), effective protection on value added now varies between negative rates for agriculture and minerals to up to 3500 percent in some manufactured goods.

Additional incentives may be provided to new activities on a temporary basis and on a degressive scale. Such incentives should preferably take the form of production subsidies, so as to simultaneously encourage exports and import substitution. They should be available to all new activities, with the selection made by the market rather than by bureaucrats who can have only limited knowledge of the opportunities available.

Further questions arise about the appropriateness of sectoral programs, of which two are in operation at present and six more are envisaged. The implementation of sectoral programs runs counter to the effort at reducing protection. National content requirements increase protection while the fulfilment of export targets may substantially raise costs for the domestic user.

These considerations may explain that Brazil has eliminated export targets for domestic as well as for foreign enterprises operating in its territory. In fact, Brazil has done well in exporting manufactured goods, including automobiles, while Mexico has not succeeded to do so, despite the proximity of the United States. Mexico may profitably follow the Brazilian example by foregoing the establishment of new sectoral programs and phasing out the existing ones.

The roles of the public and private sectors

Under the Echeverria (1972–6) and the López Portillo (1977–82) presidencies, the role of the public sector increased greatly in Mexico. The public sector enlarged the scope of its regulatory activities; raised the extent of its participation in the productive sphere; increased the amount of budgetary transfers; and augmented its claims on financial resources.

Increases in regulations took various forms. Labor legislation limited the scope of the enterprise to reduce its work-force; the procedures involved in establishing new enterprises became more onerous; after an interlude of trade liberalization, import restrictions were tightened again; and the scope of price control increased to a considerable extent.

The extent of public participation in the production process also rose substantially. Public enterprises assumed importance in the steel and chemical industries, as well as in the production of trucks, buses, tractors, railway cars, agricultural machinery, paper, and sugar. The government established a large number of enterprises and took over private firms threatened by bankruptcy. As a result, the number of public enterprises, including decentralized agencies, grew from 84 in 1970 to 964 in 1982.

Also, the government greatly enlarged the activities of the State Marketing and Price Stabilization Board (CONASUPO). While the original purpose was to provide basic staples at relatively low prices, CONASUPO was subsequently transformed into a vast retail trade network operating at a high cost. Finally, in late 1982, the commercial banks were nationalized.

The growing importance of public enterprises and of the public sector in general is apparent, first of all, in the rise of the share of public investment from 7.2 percent of the gross domestic product in 1973 to 10.9 percent in 1982. The increase was even larger in investments by public enterprises that came to account for two-thirds of public investment in 1982.

Furthermore, the share of current expenditures by the public sector rose from 17.9 to 36.3 percent of GDP between 1973 and 1982.[10] Much of the increase in current expenditures involved transfers including consumer subsidies, the financing of the losses of public enterprises, and allocations to state and local governments, rising from 2.2 percent of GDP in 1973 to 11.3 percent in 1982.[11] Administrative expenditures also increased rapidly as the bureaucracy proliferated.

Notwithstanding increases in oil revenue, the rise in public expenditures led to a large public sector deficit. The deficit in the budget of the central government rose from 4.0 percent of GDP in 1973 to 15.4 percent in 1982 and the deficit of the entire public sector exceeded 18 percent in that year.

The figures include interest charges that rose rapidly as the public debt accumulated.

For a time, the public sector deficit was financed in large part by foreign loans. With the exhaustion of borrowing possibilities abroad and the increased budgetary cost of servicing the debt, domestic financial resources were increasingly drawn upon. As a result, the share of financial resources made available to the private sector declined over time.

Large public deficits also contributed to high real interest rates and to inflation. Real interest rates are in the 20–25 percent range, creating considerable hardship for private firms, and the rate of inflation again reached 80 percent. These adverse consequences occurred, notwithstanding reductions in the deficit of the public sector after 1982, bringing it slightly below 10 percent of GDP.

Considerations of macroeconomic equilibrium and the need to provide financial resources to the private sector call for further reducing the public sector deficit. Such reductions become cumulative, creating a virtuous circle, as lower deficits lead to lower interest rates by decongesting financial markets that, in turn, reduce the budget deficit, which reflects in large part the high interest cost of domestic borrowing.

Reducing the deficit of the public sector should preferably take the form of lowering expenditures, rather than increasing taxes that would again limit the availability of financial resources to the private sector. While steps were taken in this direction, more would need to be done. Even before the deregulations proposed below take effect, the size of the government bureaucracy could be reduced by eliminating certain functions and by not replacing government workers who depart for reasons of age, health, or for the private sector. Improvements in the operations of public enterprises would give rise to further savings.

There would also be need to lower consumption subsidies that led to the pricing of a number of goods and services much below the cost of production. An extreme case is the availability of free telephones in the streets of Mexico City. Subsidies for public transport and for many products sold by CONASUPO are also high.

The deficit may be further reduced by phasing out preferential credits. Apart from their budgetary costs, these credits introduce considerable distortions in the allocation of capital. At the same time, it would be desirable to increasingly link domestic interest rates to foreign rates, with allowance made for a risk premium.

While these measures would represent a first step towards the remonetization of the economy following a decline in the ratio of the broadly defined money supply to the gross domestic product,[12] additional steps would need to be taken to ensure improvements in financial intermediation. These steps would include the development of short-term and long-term financial markets. Mexico may also follow the example of Portugal in permitting the establishment of private financial institutions that can perform commercial banking functions in competition with the nationalized banks. Furthermore, the December 1984 regulations on investment finance would need to be liberalized in order to encourage the establishment of investment companies and, in particular, venture companies. Finally, the practice of the government unilaterally setting interest rates on Treasury certificates (CETES) should be discontinued.

In addition to banking, the private sector would need to be given a greater role in manufacturing and in commerce. While the government may wish to retain ownership in petroleum and basic petrochemicals, it should reconsider its role as a producer in the competitive sector. This would mean extending and, to a considerable extent amplifying, the government's present privatization program. At the same time, on the British example, one would need to apply a well-thoughtout plan to ensure that privatization is carried out in an orderly manner.

The remaining public firms in the competitive sector should be transformed into independent enterprises, that are to be given the objective of maximizing profits, with the manager being made responsible for profits and losses. This would necessitate separating the financial operations of these enterprises from the government budget and eliminating the paraphernalia of bureaucratic control, such as annual operation programs, disbursement authorizations, and monthly operational reports. It would further be desirable to strengthen the role of the board of directors while ensuring their independence from the government administration.

The proposed measures would contribute to cost reductions, thereby reducing the burden on the government budget in financing the losses of public enterprises. At the same time, these enterprises should be put on an equal footing with private firms by eliminating their privileges in regard to credit and budgetary allocations, to be replaced by the payment of dividends.

There is room for improvement in the production of public services as well. Considerable operational savings could be effected in the railways, where efficiency by international standards is low. Improvements may also be made in electricity generation and distribution, and in postal and telephone services. Apart from budgetary savings, such improvements would benefit productive activities in the private sector.

At the same time, existing regulations pertaining to the private sector would need to be greatly simplified, so as to serve the needs of a modern economy. This would involve liberalizing prices and labor legislation which introduced considerable rigidities in the economic system. There is further need for drastically reducing the scope of discretionary decision making which tend to discourage in particular small and medium-size enterprises, with adverse effects on employment. Finally, fundamental property rights should be ensured and internationally acceptable rules for patents and copyrights established.

The modernization of existing regulations would make Mexico more attractive for foreign direct investment. At the same time, regulations affecting foreign investment more directly would need to be reviewed, including the length of the procedures involved in dealing with applications, the 51 percent Mexican ownership rule, and the admissibility of international arbitration.

Mexico may have been the gainer in the IBM case, where it obtained considerable concessions in response to accepting 100 percent foreign ownership. However, the length of the procedure, approximately two years, and the reversals observed during this period created mistrust on the part of other potential investors, so that in the long run Mexico may well have been the loser.

In general, there would be need for simplifying the procedures involved in handling applications for foreign investment. Also, the conditions under which such investments are permitted should be clarified and greater flexibility introduced in accepting majority foreign ownership in investments oriented towards export markets.

The refusal to accept Chrysler's proposal for truck manufacturing in partnership with a Mexican firm, only a month after the IBM decision, also raises queries. It seems to reflect the view that the national market is divided among domestic firms (three in the present case) without considering the possibilities for exportation, even though the Chrysler proposal would have entailed a considerable foreign exchange gain for Mexico. In fact, truck manufacturing is a labor intensive activity and, on the example of Turkey, Mexico could become a net exporter.

It would further be desirable for Mexico to devise an arrangement, by which it would accept international arbitration. This could be done by generalizing the agreements reached with Chile and Ecuador, under which the parties may appeal to international fora if remedies on the national level have been exhausted. Participation in the Multilateral Investment Guarantee Agency administered by the World Bank would also increase Mexico's attractiveness for foreign direct investment.

In this connection, it should be emphasized that, in adopting an outward-oriented policy stance, Mexico needs foreign investment to provide technical, managerial, and marketing expertise. Also, foreign direct investment creates new employment opportunities and provides foreign exchange, thereby easing the debt situation.

CONCLUSIONS

This essay reviewed the policies applied in Mexico during the 1973–83 decade of external shocks and examined the extent to which Mexico exploits its comparative advantage in manufacturing industries. It further made recommendations for policy reform designed to serve the double objectives of coping with the debt situation and promoting economic growth in Mexico.

The cornerstone of such a reform is the adoption of an aggressive exchange rate policy, accompanied by import liberalization. This would entail, in particular, the abolition of the import prohibitions introduced in September 1985, reductions in the scope of quantitative import restrictions, elimination of the use of official import reference prices, and reductions in tariffs in excess of 40 percent.

The net effects of these measures would be to promote exports as well as efficient import substitution, in particular in the agricultural sector that is not protected. The existing bias of the incentive system against exports would need to be reduced further in subsequent years through the elimination of quantitative import restrictions as well as reductions and rationalization of tariffs. And while additional incentives may be provided to new activities on a temporary basis, sectoral programs do not appear to be appropriate vehicle for doing this.

It would further be desirable to limit the scope of the public sector in the Mexican economy. This would involve reducing the public sector deficit, chiefly by lowering expenditures; liberalizing financial markets, involving also the establishment of private financial institutions; undertaking denationalizations outside basic industries; ensuring the independence of the remaining firms in the competitive sector; improving operations in the production of public services, with a view to lowering costs and promoting the development of a modern economy; and reforming existing regulations to conform to the needs of a modern economy. Finally, regulations concerning foreign direct investment would need to be reviewed so as to increase Mexico's attractiveness for foreign investment.

Re-establishing confidence on the part of the private sector is of particular importance. This would require providing for stability and predictability in exchange rates and in the system of incentives in general. It would further necessitate drastically reducing the scope of discretionary decision making by public authorities.

Inflation is a source of uncertainty for business decisions. Present rates of inflation could not be maintained for a protracted period without causing economic dislocation. Nor can one expect to reduce inflation rates to earlier levels through traditional means of macroeconomic policy.

These considerations point to the need for monetary reform. Proposals for such a reform have been made recently. Their implementation, however, requires establishing an appropriate climate, with an understanding on the part of government, business, and labor on the principles of the reform.

NOTES

1. B. Balassa, 'Policy Responses to External Shocks in Selected Latin American Countries,' *Quarterly Review of Economics and Business*, XXI (1981) pp. 131–64, Republished as Essay 3 in Bela Balassa *The Newly Industrializing Countries in the World Economy* (New York; Pergamon Press, 1981) pp. 83–108, and 'Policy Responses to Exogenous Shocks in Developing Countries,' Essay 3 in this volume. These papers also describe the methodology applied.
2. Pure terms of trade effects have been calculated on the assumption that the balance of trade, expressed in base year prices, was in equilibrium; in turn, unbalanced trade effects indicate the impact of price changes on the deficit (surplus) in the balance of trade.
3. The data represent a revision compared with B. Balassa, 'Trade Policy in Mexico,' *World Development*, XI (1983) pp. 795–812. Republished as Essay 7 in Bela Balassa, *Change and Challenge in the World Economy* (London: Macmillan, 1985) pp. 131–56. The following discussion relies on this paper as well as on Balassa, 'Policy Responses to External Shocks in Selected Latin American Countries.'
4. The procedure is described in B. Balassa, 'The Changing Pattern of Comparative Advantage in Manufactured Goods,' *Review of Economics and Statistics*, LXI (1979) pp. 259–66.
5. The stock measure has been derived by adding to the value of the physical capital stock, established as the depreciated value of investments undertaken over the past fifteen years, the present value of the difference between average and unskilled wages, taken to represent investment in human capital. In turn, the flow measure of capital has been defined as value added less the unskilled wage. In all cases, the ratio of capital to worker has been used in the calculations. The data derive from US statistics.
6. B. Balassa, 'Comparative Advantage in Manufactured Goods Revisited,' *Review of Economics and Statistics*, LXVIII (1986) pp. 315–19.
7. These projections pertain to a situation that would obtain if Mexico's physical and human capital endowments would increase without changes in other countries.
8. B. Balassa, 'The "New Growth Path" in Hungary,' Essay 13 in this volume.
9. For purposes of the following discussion, comparisons are made with 1978, in part to allow for the effects of the 1977 devaluation on domestic prices and in part because this was the first year of substantial petroleum production in Mexico. Note that, in accordance with the method of calculation of Table 11.2, an increase in the real exchange rate represents a depreciation.
10. Inter-American Development Bank, *External Debt and Economic Development in Latin America* (Washington, DC, 1984).
11. International Monetary Fund, *Government Finance Statistics Yearbook, 1985* (Washington, DC, 1986).
12. Between December 1981 and December 1985 the real value of money and quasi-money combined (M4) declined by 30 percent to its lowest level since 1978, although GDP increased by 28 percent during the seven-year period.

Essay 12 Mexico's Debt Problem and Policies for the Future

INTRODUCTION

Mexico has been a central actor in the debt saga that has unfolded in recent years. In August 1982, the suspension of the servicing of its external debt precipitated the debt crisis. Subsequently, Mexico became the first recipient of an IMF loan package arranged with the participation of government and commercial bank creditors.

At the same time, the Mexican government took strong adjustment measures. The currency was repeatedly devalued, leading to substantial depreciation in real terms, i.e. adjusted for inflation at home and abroad by the use of trade weights, and the budget deficit cut to a considerable extent. The measures applied gave rise to a substantial surplus in the current account balance and to a decline in the debt–export ratio in 1983.

Mexico was highly praised at the time as a 'good debtor' and its adjustment record was considered an example for other countries. There followed, however, the expansionary policies of the mid-1984 to mid-1985 period, leading up to elections in several important states, with rising current public expenditures in relation to GDP and the appreciation of the exchange rate in real terms (Table 11.2).

The resulting deterioration of the debt situation again led to the application of adjustment measures, with currency devaluations and reductions in budgetary expenditures in real terms in the second half of 1985. However, as luck would have it, Mexico was hit by the precipitous fall in petroleum prices that was only partly offset by declines in international interest rates. Large devaluations again followed, but political considerations limited reductions in public expenditures as a tug of war ensued between different tendencies within the government.

While various scenarios were considered in dealing with the debt situation, including the suspension of interest payments, on 22 July 1986 an agreement was reached with the International Monetary Fund and the World Bank. Following a description of the new agreement and public policies for its implementation (Section I), the discussion will concern the choice of policies aimed to effectively utilize the available resources for promoting stable economic growth in Mexico (Section II).

I THE NEW AGREEMENT AND PUBLIC POLICIES

The 22 July 1986 Agreement

The July 22 agreement calls for a loan package totalling $12.2 billion during the rest of 1986 and in 1987. It includes $1.6 billion from the International Monetary Fund, $1.9 billion from the World Bank, $0.4 billion from the Inter-American Development Bank, $1.5 and $0.8 billion in the form of international export credits and US farm credits, respectively, and an expected $6.0 billion from the commercial banks.

The agreement has two new features that represent a sharing of risks between Mexico and the international financial community. It provides financing on a contingency basis if a further decline in the price of petroleum occurs or if the growth of manufacturing production in Mexico falls below target levels.

Contingency financing is triggered in the event that the price of oil declined below $9 per barrel. The shortfall would be initially financed in its entirety from external sources, with repayments taking place in subsequent periods. The IMF would contribute to the financing of the shortfall and the commercial banks are also asked to participate. In turn, if the price of petroleum exceeded $14, external financing would be commensurately reduced.

Contingency financing is also triggered in the event that the rate of increase of manufacturing output fell below an agreed upon level, provided that Mexico fulfilled all conditions under the loan. The additional financing would be provided by the World Bank for pre-appraised public sector investment projects.

The use of the concept of 'operational balance,' derived by adjusting the public sector deficit for the inflationary component of interest payments on the domestic debt, also represents an innovation for Mexico, even though such a concept was earlier employed in IMF negotiations with Brazil. For 1986, the public sector borrowing requirement is estimated to equal 17 percent of Mexico's gross domestic product while the operational deficit would amount to 2 percent of GDP.

In contrast with other IMF agreements, the agreement with Mexico does not include an inflation target. Nevertheless, inflation enters implicitly since the public sector borrowing requirement is set in nominal terms, so that the acceleration of inflation would not permit observing this target unless expenditures were cut in real terms.

The program of adjustment

In his letter of 22 July to Jacques de Larosière, then the Managing Director of the IMF, subsequently distributed to commercial banks, the Secretary of

Finance and Public Credit of Mexico, Gustavo Petricioli, announced the adoption of a 'an economic program of growth-oriented adjustment and structural reform.' The program is said to have been framed in a medium-term horizon and to encompass both demand management measures and supply-oriented structural policies.

A 3 percent reduction in the deficit of the public sector, excluding interest payments on the external and the internal debt, is envisaged over an eighteen-month period. The reduction would involve increases in tax receipts (1.3 percent of GDP), increases in public enterprise prices and utility tariffs (1.2 percent of GDP), and reductions in public expenditures (0.5 percent of GDP, reflecting a decrease of 1.0 percent in current expenditures and an increase of 0.5 percent in capital expenditures).

In regard to public enterprises, it is envisaged to continue the process of selling or closing nonstrategic and nonpriority firms. Furthermore, industrial reconversion plans will be carried out in several industries, including fertilizer and steel. At the same time, measures are to be introduced to facilitate foreign direct investment in Mexico.

In the monetary area, flexible interest rate policies will be employed and compulsory reserve requirements for commercial banks reduced somewhat under the proposed policies. Also, the Mexican government plans to apply flexible exchange rate policies, aimed to lower the differential between the free market and official exchange rates, with a view to its eventual elimination.

In the trade area, tariff rates will be limited to the the 0–30 percent range by October 1988, with temporary tariff surcharges applied in particular cases. Furthermore, the scope of imports subject to import licensing are scheduled to be reduced by 5 percentage points in relation to production value by the end of 1986, and official reference prices for imports eliminated by December 1987. At the same time, policies of export promotion will be stepped up.

The proposed measures represent the first step towards the adoption of a policy oriented towards promoting stable economic growth in Mexico. In the following, possible additional steps will be considered in the areas covered by the program.

Reforming the tax system

The Mexican government proposes to increase tax receipts in an amount equal to 1.3 percent of the gross domestic product by limiting the deductibility of interest payments from the base of the corporate income tax and reducing the lag between the accrual and the collection of taxes, the aim being to re-establish the earlier ratio of tax revenues to the gross domestic product. In fact, after having risen from 9.6 percent in 1975 to 10.7 percent in 1981, the share of non-oil-related taxes declined to 8.9 percent of GDP in 1985. The comparable ratios for income taxes were 4.5, 5.8, and 4.2 percent.[1]

For the medium term, further changes would be necessary to ensure that the tax system promotes economic growth in Mexico. In this connection, consideration needs to be given to the effects of inflation on tax obligations and payments and to the rationality of the system of taxes, abstracting from the effects of inflation.

Under the present system of corporate taxation, inventory investment is favored over fixed investment and debt financing is favored over equity financing. This is because the application of the LIFO (last-in-first-out) system provides full adjustment for inflation in regard to inventories, but depreciation is fully adjusted only if the firm's liabilities do not exceed its monetary assets. In the opposite case, the difference between the adjusted value of liabilities and monetary assets is deducted from the adjusted value of depreciation. Furthermore, nominal interest payments are fully deductible, although this would change under the proposed program.

While limiting the deductibility of interest payments will increase corporate tax liabilities, in the absence of changes in the valuation of assets and liabilities profits will be overstated, thereby discouraging corporate savings and investment. The situation is aggravated by the nondeductibility of compulsory profit sharing arrangements with employees.

Also, while the proposed measures will reduce the lag between the accrual and the payment of taxes, the lack of annual adjustment in income tax rates leads to bracket creep. In fact, the maximum tax rate of 55 percent is presently reached at an annual income level of less than 30 000 dollars. The high effective rate of taxation, in turn, tends to discourage domestic savings, work effort, and risk taking.

Thus, until inflation is brought under control, raising domestic savings and investments would necessitate making adjustment for inflation in calculating tax obligations. In taxing corporate income, the assets and liabilities of firms should be annually revalued. In taxing personal incomes, tax brackets should be changed *pari passu* with inflation. It should not be assumed that such adjustments would excessively burden tax administration as they have been routinely made in Brazil.

The proposed changes would alleviate the adverse effects of inflation on direct taxation in Mexico. But, even if inflation were to be eliminated, certain features of the tax system would need reform. In particular, in order to encourage savings, a shift from taxing incomes to taxing consumption would be desirable. Such a shift could be accomplished by increasing the share of indirect taxes and reducing that of direct taxes.

The income distributional consequences of such a change may be neutralized by imposing excise taxes on luxuries and semi-luxuries. At any rate, under conditions existing in Mexico, such taxes are likely to be more effective in pursuing income distributional objectives than progressive income taxes. The latter are often evaded or, in the case of fixed income recipients where evasion is difficult, inducement is provided for emigration.

As regards indirect taxation, under inflationary conditions tax and tariff rebates to exporters should be adjusted for inflation so as to avoid losses to exporters. Also, irrespective of inflation, the number of rates of the value added tax should be reduced and the scope of value added taxation extended to a greater number of businesses.

Adjusting public service prices and utility tariffs

Planned increases in public service prices and utility tariffs would raise budgetary revenues by 1.2 percent of GDP between 1985 and the end of 1987, with much of the increase occurring in 1986. In this connection, reference has been made to the rise of subway fares in Mexico City from Mex$1 to Mex$20 in August 1986.

However, the new subway fare hardly exceeds 3 US cents, which is very low compared with fares in other countries and with wages and salaries in Mexico. The situation is similar for bus tickets, in particular in Mexico City where fares are one-fifth of the price of a ride in smaller cities. Also, following the decline in the value of the coin used as telephone token in Mexico City, telephones have been altered so that no coin is now required.

Among public utilities, electricity is underpriced, with rates of about 2.5 US cents per kilowatt, a little over one-half of their level in real terms in 1960, and the government power company reportedly receiving a subsidy of $735 million in 1985.[2] The extent of underpricing is even greater for water, especially in Mexico City, where the cost of pumping water from distant low-lying valleys is ten times higher than in cities with more accessible reservoirs and most users pay a flat rate, irrespective of the amount consumed.

While the cited information relates to particular prices and tariffs, data on changes in average prices for public and private consumption also indicate the increasing underpricing of public services and utilities. Whereas the price index for public consumption rose somewhat more (a 3.9 fold increase) than that for private consumption (a 3.3 fold increase) between 1975 and 1981, the situation was reversed afterwards as a 3.8 fold increase occurred in the former and a 5.1 fold increase in the latter between 1981 and 1985.

Thus, although budgetary stringency would have required increases in the relative prices of public services, the opposite has happened. And, for the 1975–85 period, taken as a whole, the price index stands at 1460 for public consumption and 1660 for private consumption.

Apart from reducing the budget deficit, higher public service prices and utility tariffs would provide inducement to economize with resources that are wasted at excessively low prices and decrease investment requirements. It would also reduce the attractiveness of Mexico City whose inhabitants are the main beneficiaries of low service prices and utility tariffs. At the same time, congestion in Mexico City imposes rising costs on the national economy and leads to demands for infrastructural investments.

Current public expenditures

The government proposes to reduce current public expenditures, other than interest payments on the external and internal debt of the public sector, in an amount equal to 1.0 percent of the gross domestic product in 1987. To put this reduction in perspective, changes in earlier years may be reviewed.

The ratio of current public expenditures other than interest payments to GDP remained approximately unchanged between 1981 and 1985, after having increased by 1.4 percentage points between 1975 and 1981. In his budget speech to the Mexican Congress on 15 November 1985, President Miguel de la Madrid announced that these expenditures would be cut in an amount equal to 1.8 percent of GDP in 1986.[3] According to calculations presented by the Secretary of the Finance and Public Credit, however, the actual decline is only 0.5 percent of GDP. The original projections have not been met either for public consumption or for current transfers.[4]

At the same time, national income statistics show that public consumption continued to rise at a rate exceeding that of private consumption and the gross domestic product following the onset of the debt crisis. Thus, while private consumption declined by 3 percent between 1981 and 1985, public consumption rose by 9 percent, thereby increasing its constant price share in GDP from 9.1 to 9.9 percent. These changes represent an acceleration of earlier tendencies as private consumption grew by 45 percent and public consumption by 53 percent between 1975 and 1981, with the latter's share in GDP rising from 8.9 to 9.1 percent; increases for the entire period were 42 and 67 percent, respectively.

The growth of public consumption is linked to the rise of public employment. Between 1981 and 1984, the number of employees in the public sector increased from 3.5 to 4.2 million; with private employment declining from 16.5 to 15.9 million, the share of the public sector in total employment rose from 17.5 to 21.5 percent during this period. Compared with these increases, the oft-cited elimination of 25 000 public sector jobs in 1985 appears rather small.

Current transfers increased at a lower rate than public consumption between 1981 and 1985 and were cut to a greater extent in 1986. This reduction represents in large part decreases in subsidies through the State Marketing and Price Stabilization Board (CONASUPO). Still, considerable subsidies remain and in 1986 current transfers may amount to 7–8 percent of the gross domestic product.

Finally, government contributions to state enterprises rose more rapidly than public consumption and transfers between 1981 and 1985. And, in 1986, the expenditures of these enterprises are expected to increase rather than declining as originally projected.

II POLICIES FOR IMPROVED RESOURCE ALLOCATION AND ECONOMIC GROWTH

Public enterprises

The rise in public enterprise expenditures on goods and services reflects in part upward adjustments of spending targets and in part a lack of observance of these targets. Also, increases in employment have been greater, and cuts in real wages smaller, in public enterprises than in the federal government after the onset of the debt crisis.

These developments followed the rapid expansion of the public enterprise sector in Mexico in earlier years. Between 1970 and 1982, the number of state-owned enterprises increased from 39 to 677, of which 621 are majority-owned. In the same period, the number of decentralized agencies increased from 45 to 95 and 192 trust funds were established. Using a broader definition of public enterprises, then, their number increased from 84 in 1970 to 964 in 1982.

As a result of these changes, public enterprises came to range across practically all sectors of the Mexican economy. Such enterprises were established at the federal, state, and local levels; bankrupt private firms were taken over by the government; and the nationalization of the banks in December 1982 brought a large number of private firms owned by the banks into the public sector.

In February 1985, it was decided to merge 14 public enterprises, to transfer the same number to the states, to liquidate 148 entities, and to sell 112 firms, mostly rather small. By mid-1986, none of the mergers and transfers were accomplished, 32 firms were liquidated, and 44 sold to private interests. While the delays in mergers are largely explained by administrative difficulties, the states have postponed transfers because of their own financial problems, liquidation procedures have been held up due to accounting considerations and because of the reluctance to fire workers,[5] and the sale of public enterprises has encountered economic as well as political problems.

While profitable hotels in Mexico City and Cancun have easily found buyers, private firms are reluctant to purchase public enterprises that have accumulated losses, contain inefficient units, and have excess labor. According to an executive of a Mexican bank, 'who would want to invest his money in a bankrupt company or in a company with irresolvable labor problems.'[6]

In turn, the government is under pressure from the public sector labor unions to prevent the new owners from taking rationalization measures. The conflicts that make the sale of public enterprises difficult may be indicated by reference to a reported statement of an adviser to President de la Madrid, according to whom 'some businessmen say they will take these companies over only if they can shut half the place down, cancel labor contracts and fire half the workers. We cannot allow that.'[7] Yet, rationalization would need to be undertaken for the firms to become viable entities.

Rationalization would also be necessary in firms whose privatization is not presently envisaged. Particular importance attaches to steel and fertilizer, whose production represents inputs for other industries, mostly in the private sector. State-owned SICARTSA on the Pacific Coast is reportedly producing steel at twice the cost of a comparable Korean mill and incurred losses of $245 million in 1985. The losses of FERTIMEX, the fertilizer manufacturer, amounted to $295 million in the same year.

The results point to the need to carry out the government's announced intention for the reconversion of these industries. At the same time, questions arise about the desirability of continuing investments in the second stage of SICARTSA, even on a selective basis as envisaged. Similar considerations apply to public investments in fertilizer.

The government is reviewing the operation of CONASUPO that commercializes a substantial part of agricultural production in Mexico. It reportedly has excessive administrative costs that have contributed to a $930 million deficit in 1985. It would be desirable to increasingly transfer CONASUPO's operations to the private sector that can better perform the trading functions than a large bureaucracy. This conclusion applies also to manufacturing activities in the competitive sector, i.e. outside public utilities and natural resource products, even though sales at realistic prices will often mean selling below book value.

Public investment

In the public sector, the brunt of austerity was borne by public investment. According to national income statistics, public investment declined by 44 percent between 1981 and 1985, approximately regaining its 1975 level. This compares with a 23 percent fall in private investment that remained 28 percent above the 1975 level in 1985.

A further substantial cut in public investment occurred in 1986, much exceeding in magnitude the originally planned reduction. In turn, an increase equal to 0.5 percent of GDP is planned for 1987. While the projected growth of public investment may be warranted following the large declines of recent years, it would need to be ensured that the funds are put to productive use. In fact, Mexico could gain considerably more by improving the allocation of public investment than from foreseeable increases in the future.

To begin with, public investment needs could be reduced by lowering the growth of demand for public services and utilities through the setting of realistic prices. This conclusion applies, in particular, to electricity and, in Mexico City, to water. The experience of other developing countries indicates that considerable savings can be effected if realistic prices are adopted.

Also, there are several public sector projects that could be postponed without materially affecting economic activity in Mexico. They include transport projects, such as the metrorail system in the Federal District and the Manzanilla and Frontier Road projects, as well as public investments in several manufacturing industries, including fertilizers, petrochemicals, and steel. It turn, there would be need to invest in export-oriented infrastructure, such as the Altamira port, as well as highway and rail links to the ports.

At the same time, in order to ensure that public investments meet economic criteria, appropriate procedures would need to be adopted for project preparation and approval. The implementation of investment projects should be preceded by adequate feasibility studies, with a uniform methodology utilized for economic project evaluation. Also, the approval process should be undertaken in the framework of multi-year investment budgeting, with co-ordination at the federal, state, and local levels.

Disincentives to the private sector

Combining current and capital expenditures, with the exclusion of interest payments on the external and internal debt of the public sector, the data show a decline in public expenditures from 30.0 percent to 22.3 percent of GDP between 1981 and 1985, falling slightly below the 1975 figure of 24.1 percent. Apart from the fall in public investment, the reduction in capital transfers accounts for this decline.

In the same period, current public revenues increased from 20.4 to 24.9 percent of GDP, much surpassing the 1975 figure of 16.4 percent. But, the increase was entirely due to the rise in PEMEX receipts, and the ratio of non-petroleum revenues to the gross domestic product declined slightly.

Taken together, and excluding all interest payments on the public debt, there was a surplus in the budget of the public sector equal to 2.6 percent of GDP in 1985, compared with deficits of 7.7 percent in 1975 and 9.5 percent in 1981. Including interest on the foreign debt and real (inflation-adjusted) interest on the domestic debt of the public sector, in turn, results in a deficit equal to 2.0 percent of GDP in 1985 and 1986.

The latter concept of operational deficit, exclusive of the inflationary component of interest payments on the domestic public debt estimated at 7.2 percent of GDP in 1985 and 13.7 percent in 1986, indicates the use of physical resources by the public sector, which is relevant from the point of view of the balance of payments. However, the domestic financing needs of the public sector are indicated by its borrowing requirement that equalled 10 percent of GDP in 1985 and 17 percent in 1986.

In particular, the rising financing needs of the public sector have limited the availability of credit to the private sector. The commercial banks' marginal reserve requirement is 100 percent, with the ratio being 93 percent if account is taken of loans provided to housing, exports, and agriculture in the framework of preferential arrangements. In fact, the average share of the public sector in domestic credit has been rising rapidly over time. It was only slightly above 20 percent in the early 1970s, surpassed 30 percent in 1975, reached 50 percent in 1978, exceeded 70 percent in 1982, and approached 80 percent in 1985.

This 'crowding out' has created increasing difficulties for the private sector. And while alternative sources of financing have developed, real interest rates have risen to 20–25 percent a year. Furthermore, the private sector bears the consequences of payment delays on the part of public sector enterprises, preferential treatment granted to these enterprises, price control, and bureaucratic procedures.

In conjunction with budgetary stringency, payment delays by public enterprises have increased substantially in recent years. With the public sector union resisting cuts in employment and reductions in real wages, the effects of spending ceilings on public enterprises have been felt to a considerable extent by private firms.

Also, public enterprises receive preferential treatment in granting credits; they do not pay taxes; and receive subsidies from the public budget. Private enterprises are put at a disadvantage, in particular, in areas such as steel and the marketing of agricultural produce.

In the absence of subsidies, for example, maintaining the price of steel at low levels has adversely affected the operations of the private ALFA group. At the same time, the unfavorable effects of price control on the private sector have been aggravated by rapid inflation because of delays in granting price increases, especially in the case of public necessities. Also, in some instances, political considerations and in others bribery have entered the process of decision making on prices.

More generally, the private sector suffers from the extensive bureaucratization of the Mexican administrative apparatus.[8] This has involved considerable costs and has contributed to the centralization of the power of decision making in Mexico City. As Alfredo Sandoval Gonzalez, the president of COPARMEX, the association of business firms, noted 'to try to get a price increase for products, or an import license, or anything that requires government permission, a businessman must come to Mexico City if he wants quick action.'[9]

While larger firms may be equipped to deal with the bureaucracy, the endless *trámites* (bureaucratic hurdles) have hindered the development of small and medium-size businesses that do not have the necessary connections and may not be able to support the costs involved. Yet, these businesses have the potential to provide a wide range of goods and services and to create new jobs.

In order to foster economic growth and employment in Mexico, it would be necessary to simplify the system of regulations and to limit discretionary decision making while strengthening property and contractual rights. Employment would also be promoted by liberalizing restrictive labor regulations that have limited hiring in the past. Furthermore, attaining higher rates of growth of output and employment would necessitate removing the disadvantages under which the private sector operates, including payment delays on the part of public sector enterprises, the preferential treatment of these enterprises, and price control.

Changes in the regulations would need to be accompanied by increasing the availability of credit to the private sector. This, in turn, requires lowering the financial requirements of the public sector. While the government plans to equilibrate the operational balance in 1987, it would be appropriate to aim at a surplus of several percent of the gross domestic product.

Such a target is both necessary and attainable. It is necessary to ensure the expansion of private sector activities for promoting economic growth and employment. It is attainable through further increases in public service prices and utility tariffs, reductions in the size of public administration, and improvements in the operation of public enterprises. At the same time, the sales of such enterprises should not be 'counted' as budgetary improvements, since they involve the use of private funds.

Monetary reform

Reductions in the deficit of the public sector would also ease inflationary pressures in Mexico. As noted in a recent annual report of the Banco de Mexico, 'credit stringency would not correct inflationary effects that originate in the persistence of excessive public sector deficits . . .'[10]

In fact, a vicious circle is created as public sector deficits, defined in the traditional sense, augment inflationary pressures that contribute to higher interest rates which, in turn, add to the deficit and so on. Also, despite the lack of indexing, 'inertial' inflation is generated as income recipients attempt to maintain their real income position and the prices of tradable goods are raised through devaluations intended to offset the adverse effects of inflation on international competitiveness.

Price increases have reached 80 percent a year in Mexico and show a tendency to accelerate. Such high inflation rates cannot fail to adversely affect economic activity by creating uncertainty about the course of incomes,

encouraging speculative activities at the expense of production, and discouraging investments with a longer-term pay-off. Furthermore, inefficiencies are created as differing rates of price adjustment to inflation lead
to variations in relative prices.

Inflation also interferes with the process of financial intermediation. This
has occurred in Mexico as the acceleration of inflation has reduced demand
for financial assets. Thus, after rising from 24.7 percent in 1977 to 33.5
percent in 1982, the ration of M2 (money and quasi-money) to the gross
domestic product declined to 27.1 percent in 1985. And, the Banco de
Mexico reports that M5, the widest monetary aggregate, declined by 9
percent in real terms between December 1984 and December 1985, representing largely a fall in financial savings in the face of inflation-induced
uncertainty.[11]

The adverse economic effects of inflation may be reduced by indexation.
Such is the case, in particular, as far as taxation and financial obligations
are concerned. At the same time, the indexation of wages and prices tends
to accelerate inflation. This happened in Brazil, where reducing the period
of wage adjustment from 12 months to 6 months contributed to an
approximate doubling of the rate of inflation in 1979. Inflation also accel-
erates under indexation in response to external shocks.

Correspondingly, consideration should be given to monetary reform.[12]
At the same time, Mexico could learn from the experience of Argentina
and Brazil as to the need for creating the conditions necessary for the
reform. In this connection, it has been suggested that monetary reform
may be undertaken once in a lifetime, so that its effective preparation is a
crucial necessity.[13]

The conditions include, in particular, a surplus in the operational budget
of the public sector; removing distortions in relative prices, by raising the
public service prices, utility tariffs, and the prices of goods produced by the
private sector that have been kept down artificially by price control; and
liberalizing imports. The latter point will be discussed below.

Trade and exchange rate policy

Under the government's program, the scope of imports subject to licensing
were to be reduced by 5 percentage points in relation to production value
by the end of 1986, official reference prices to be eliminated by December
1987, and import tariffs to be reduced in steps 0–30 percent range by
October 1988, with temporary tariff surcharges applied in particular cases.
Also, policies of export promotion will be stepped up.

To proceed in the reverse order, the government took a number of
export promoting measures in the first half of 1986, and further progress in
this regard is desirable. Also, in April 1986, the government made tariff

changes covering more than one-third of imports. It lowered the tariff ceiling to 45 percent; reduced tariff rates of 10 to 40 percent by 2.5 percentage points on a large number of commodities; and eliminated the 5 percent rate, with tariffs raised to 10 percent on most products and eliminated on others.

These reductions, averaging about one-half of one percent on import value, followed tariff increases undertaken in conjunction with the reduction in the scope of import licensing in July 1985. According to calculations made at the Colegio de Mexico, the increases fully offset the reduction in protection on items that were freed from import licenses.[14] Furthermore, the government greatly expanded the scope of import reference prices that provide additional protection. And while the action was rationalized on anti-dumping grounds, this would not explain the use of import reference prices for 1171 tariff positions, covering over one-sixth of production.

The elimination of official reference prices by December 1987 is thus welcome while it should be ensured that the new anti-dumping legislation is not used for protective purposes. At the same time, the proposed elimination of import licensing on 5 percent of the value of production from the present 55 percent[15] will not suffice to establish a competitive economy in Mexico.

In this connection, it should be recalled that, with few interruptions, the scope of commodities subject to import licensing was rising throughout the postwar period, reaching a peak of 100 percent in 1981–82 before measures of liberalization were taken. With practically unlimited protection under import licensing, incentives were not provided for the establishment of efficient industries and for subsequent improvements in efficiency.

Estimates by Mexican economists indicate that the cost of production is particularly high for iron and steel, capital goods, automobiles, and consumer durables that continue to be subject to import licenses. Also, according to calculations made at the Colegio de Mexico, the international competitiveness of these sectors deteriorated between 1970 and 1982.

For the manufacturing sector, taken as a whole, total factor productivity declined by 0.7 percent a year during this period as against increases in developed countries and in developing countries such as Korea, Thailand, and Turkey. Among individual industries, there appears to be a positive correlation between exposure to international competition and productivity change, with export-oriented industries generally experiencing improvements, and industries protected by import licenses a deterioration, in efficiency.

These considerations point to the importance of import liberalization in Mexico. Its industries need foreign competition to provide inducement for productivity improvements and for product specialization. Trade liberalization will also promote exports that are at a disadvantage *vis-à-vis* import substitution behind protection. There is no reason, for example, why Mexico would not develop automobile exports under an appropriate incentive system.

The automobile industry provides an example of sectoral agreements providing quantitative import restrictions. Similar considerations apply to the sectoral agreement on pharmaceuticals. A revision of these agreements, entailing the liberalization of imports, would be desirable. Tariffs up to 30 percent should suffice to protect these industries as well as other activities in the manufacturing sector, with additional protection provided to infant industries on a declining scale.

A *sine qua non* of the elimination of quantitative restrictions is the establishment of a realistic exchange rate. Mexico's real effective exchange rate, calculated by the use of trade weights in adjusting nominal exchange rates for changes in wholesale prices at home and abroad, appreciated by 20 percent between 1976–8 and 1981. There followed a depreciation of 52 percent in real terms in the subsequent two years, an appreciation of 27 percent between 1983 and the second quarter of 1985, and a depreciation of 44 percent over the following twelve months (Table 11.1). In the second quarter of 1986, the average real effective exchange rate for the year 1983 was re-established, representing a depreciation of 27 percent compared with the 1976–8 average.

Maintaining the present level of real effective exchange rate should permit the liberalization of imports. At the same time, import liberalization would lower domestic prices, hence the importance of undertaking it simultaneously with monetary reform. One may, then, avoid the widespread imposition of price and wage controls that accompanied monetary reforms in Argentina and Brazil.

Additional devaluations would be desirable, however, if the difference between the parallel market rate and the official exchange rate exceeded 5–10 percent. In fact, in line with the statement by the Secretary of Finance and Public Credit, progress should be made towards the unification of the two exchange rates as the higher parallel market rate provides incentives for capital flight and the under-invoicing of exports.

Foreign direct investment

The decline in foreign direct investment in Mexico from $2.5 billion in 1981 to $0.4 billion in 1984 compares unfavorably with other major Latin American countries. Foreign direct investment increased again, to $0.5 billion, in 1985 but a further decline occurred in the first half of 1986. The government plans to improve the situation by simplifying administrative procedures. At the same time, it plans to pursue its policy of selectivity in the existing legal framework. This means requiring majority participation by Mexican nationals.

Also, Adolfo Hegwish Fernández-Castello, the Undersecretary for the Regulations of Foreign Investment and Technology Transfer, reported to have said that 'the government would not provide incentives, stimulus, or special privileges to attract foreign capital while it offers a climate of stability and peace, captive markets, and efficient infrastructure in exchange for the investors to align themselves with national objectives.'[16] Apart from a possible overstatement of the advantages Mexico offers, the reference to captive markets appear to neglect the possibilities for export expansion on the part of foreign investors in Mexico.

If the export orientation of Mexican industry is desired, a more accommodating stance towards foreign direct investment would be desirable. An additional consideration is that direct investment offers advantages over loan capital. For one thing, it provides access to foreign technical, managerial and marketing expertise. For another thing, the investor rather than the host country bears the commercial risk and payments are linked to business conditions, hence to the host country's ability to pay.

In fact, it would be desirable to encourage a shift from loan capital to foreign participation in Mexican firms. Regulations to this effect are being formulated in Brazil, with foreigners empowered to pay the country's debt at a discount and use the full amount in domestic currency to invest, with the proviso that a resale cannot be effected within a certain period of time.

It would further be desirable to liberalize ownership rules in Mexico and to simplify administrative procedures, with foreign investment being automatically accepted once a certain time has elapsed following the date of the application. At the same time, the liberalization of imports would ensure that foreign investment conforms to national objectives. Finally, Mexico may join other Latin America and Far Eastern countries to participate in the Multilateral Investment Guarantee Agency being established under World Bank auspices.

CONCLUSIONS

This essay has set out to examine the conditions under which Mexico's recent agreement with the International Monetary Fund may be translated into stable economic growth. Thus, its objective has been to conform to de la Madrid's dictum, according to which 'Mexico has the capacity to simultaneously grow and pay [interest on its debt].'

Emphasis has been given to the need for increasing the resources available for investment and improving the productivity of these resources. Savings may be increased by alleviating the adverse effects of inflation on direct taxation and increasingly taxing consumption rather than savings. Encouraging productive investment would further require establishing stability that may be accomplished through monetary reform. This, in turn, presupposes reducing the share of current public expenditures in the gross domestic product, remedying distortions in public service prices and utility tariffs, and liberalizing imports.

Reducing current public expenditures and increasing public sector prices would also be necessary in order to provide private enterprise with the funds needed for their activities. For the private sector and, in particular, small and medium scale enterprises to realize their potential for economic growth and employment, existing regulations would also need to be simplified, the scope of discretionary decision-making reduced, and prices liberalized. At the same time, private enterprises should be put on the same footing as public enterprises, and the movement towards privatization speeded up.

In turn, the liberalization of imports would provide inducement for productivity improvements and product specialization and reduce the anti-export bias of the system of incentives. A more accommodating stance towards foreign direct investment would also contribute to technological change and to export expansion.

The recommendations made in the essay are interdependent. There is need to encourage domestic savings, to provide for the credit needs of private enterprise, and to promote foreign direct investment in order to support export expansion and efficient import substitution following the liberalization of imports. In turn, import liberalization would ensure that foreign direct investment conforms to national objectives and would permit the liberalization of prices, which is needed for the efficient allocation of resources and the promotion of private industry.

NOTES

1. Unless otherwise noted, the date cited originate from official Mexican sources.
2. *International Herald Tribune*, 12–13 July 1968.
3. 'Criterios Generales de Politica Económica para la Iniciativa de Ley de Ingresos y el Proyecto de Presupuesto de Egresos de la Federación, correspondientes a 1986' (Mexico, DF: Presidencia de la República, 1985) Table 4.
4. The results repeat those of 1985, when actual expenditures exceeded programmed expenditure by an amount equal to 0.7 percent of GDP. They seem to conflict with the statement made by Carlos Salinas de Gortari, the Secretary of Programming and the Budget, who announced plans to cut the federal budget by $1 billion, suggesting that 'this reduction in public spending . . . has no precedent in the history of the country and very few points of comparison at the international level' (Associated Press–Dow Jones News Service, 15 April 1986). It may be added that $1 billion is equivalent to about two-thirds of 1 percent of Mexican GDP.
5. However, the closing down of Fundidora Monterrey, involving the elimination of 9000 jobs in May 1986, was an important decision.
6. *New York Times*, 16 February 1986.

7. *International Herald Tribune*, 12–13 July 1986. The same source provides information on losses by FERTIMEX and CONASUPO cited below.

8. An apt description of the situation is provided by *The Economist*: 'At every level of society, economic decisions must be filtered through numerous layers of bureaucracy. The simplest commercial activities are smothered in rules and regulations; success depends heavily on the goodwill of bureaucrats. This has bred a fixing mentality, not just among the influence-peddlers, but among their clients, too. Its most obvious result is tolerance of corruption.' (5 April 1986, p. 21).

9. *The Wall Street Journal*, 4 October 1985.

10. Banco de Mexico, *Informe Anual, 1985* (Mexico, DF, 1986) p. 25. The report also refers to the insufficient availability of external resources that has since been remedied.

11. *Informe Anual*, p. 37.

12. A proposal to this effect was in fact made by a group of Mexican economists in May 1986.

13. This point was made by Guillermo Ortiz, the Executive Director for Mexico at the IMF, at a meeting of the Institute for International Economics, held on 15 May 1986 in Washington, DC.

14. According to information received from the Undersecretary for Trade at the Ministry of Industry and Commerce, the unweighted average of tariffs on these items rose from 10.7 to 24.3 percent while their weighted average increased from 9.3 to 16.5 percent.

15. However, one-fifth of the total consists of petroleum and its derivatives that account for about one-tenth of GDP.

16. *Vanguardia*, 27 February 1986.

Part V
Reform Efforts in Socialist Countries

Essay 13   The 'New Growth Path' in Hungary

INTRODUCTION

This essay will analyze changes in economic policies in Hungary that began with the December 1978 resolution of the Central Committee of the Hungarian Socialist Workers' Party (for short, Party resolution). The impetus for policy change was provided by Hungary's growing indebtedness, with its deficit in convertible currency trade reaching $1.2 billion in 1978, equivalent to 6.7 percent of the gross domestic product.[1]

Changes in economic policies had the double objective of remedying the disequilibrium in Hungary's balance of payments and re-establishing the reform process that began in 1968 but was subverted in various respects after 1972. The new policies have been given the collective name 'the new growth path' that has been chosen as the title of the essay.

Section I of the essay will briefly review the policies that led to Hungary's rising indebtedness in the 1973–8 period and analyze the subsequent process of adjustment. Section II will examine the principal determinants of Hungary's export performance in recent years while Sections III and IV will consider possible reforms for accelerating the growth of exports and of national income in the future.

I ADJUSTMENT POLICIES AND THE DEBT CRISIS

With its large exposure to foreign trade, the unfavorable balance-of-payments effects of external shocks through the deterioration of the terms of trade and the export shortfall associated with the slowdown of economic activity abroad averaged 10.5 percent of Hungary's gross domestic product in the 1973–8 period.[2] Over two-thirds of this loss occurred in trade with private market economies, which will be the subject of the following discussion. This is in part because Hungary's rising debt *vis-à-vis* private market economies was the principal factor motivating the stabilization measures taken following the December 1978 Party resolution and in part because of the constraint foreign exchange earnings in convertible currencies represent for economic expansion in Hungary.[3]

Hungary responded to the external shocks of the 1973–8 period by borrowing abroad. This was done in an effort to maintain earlier rates of growth of domestic consumption and investment, notwithstanding the deterioration of the external situation. Domestic investment rose particularly rapidly, doubling between 1973 and 1978, while consumption increased by one-fourth. Thus, Hungary did not make use of macroeconomic policies to reduce the imbalance in its external accounts that resulted from external shocks. And while some import substitution did occur, it was offset several times by losses in export market shares. These losses, representing an average decline of 18 percent in Hungary's share in the imports of private market economies,[4] amounted to $316 million in 1978. In the same year, import substitution associated with a slight decline in the income elasticity of import demand *vis-à-vis* the 1963–73 period was $63 million.[5]

Losses in export market shares represented a reversal of trends observed in the previous period. In particular, Hungary's share in the imports of developed countries, accounting for three-fourths of its exports to private market economies, increased from 0.22 percent in 1965 to 0.28 percent in 1973, but declined again to 0.22 percent in 1979.[6] While Hungary was adversely affected by restrictions imposed in 1974 on its cattle exports by the European Common Market,[7] the principal reasons for this reversal can be found in changes in the policies applied.

The introduction of the new economic mechanism of 1 January 1968 represented a break with the centralized system of economic planning, under which production targets were set and materials allocated centrally and domestic prices were divorced from world market prices. The establishment of market relationships among firms and the adoption of a single commercial exchange rate (called foreign exchange conversion ratio at the time), supplemented by export subsidies, gave considerable impetus to exports to private market economies in the years following.

In turn, the measures of recentralization applied following the November 1972 Party resolution and, especially, the attempts made to isolate the Hungarian economy from external events after 1973, reduced the incentives to export. Profits derived from exporting were lowered through reductions in export subsidies and by *ex post* transfers to the state budget. These changes, together with the buoyancy of domestic markets, tended to discourage export expansion and the transformation of the export structure in response to the changing pattern of foreign demand.[8]

The December 1978 Party resolution called for a return to the principles of the 1968 reforms, including the decentralization of the system of decision-making and the linking of domestic to world market prices. At the same time, recognizing the fact that Hungary could not continue indefinitely accumulating convertible-currency debt, which increased from $900 million at the end of 1973 to $4600 at the end of 1978 in net terms,[9] the resolution called for re-equilibrating the balance of trade in convertible currencies.

Equilibrium in the balance of trade was restored by 1981, notwithstanding the adverse effects of increases in petroleum prices in 1979–80, the world economic slowdown, and the rise in interest rates on world financial markets. The adjustment, however, was not brought about by output-increasing policies in the form of export expansion and import substitution, but through the application of restrictive macroeconomic policy measures.

In fact, in its trade with private market economies, Hungary experienced little import substitution between 1978 and 1981, and this was increasingly offset by losses in export market shares. By 1981, Hungary's average market shares in the imports of these economies declined by 15 percent, giving rise to a foreign exchange loss of $511 million, whereas the balance-of-payments gain from import substitution was only $123 million.[10]

During this period, Hungary suffered the adverse effects of the cessation of its cattle exports to the Common Market, but this was compensated by increases in meat exports. Furthermore, while exports of pig iron to the EEC halted, this was more than offset by higher exports of iron and steel products. At the same time, limitations on the exports of textile products to the Common Market apply to most socialist and developing countries and not only to Hungary. Finally, although individual EEC member countries impose quotas on certain manufactured goods imported from Hungary, these quotas reportedly affect only 3–4 percent of Hungary's manufactured exports to the Common Market.[11] It would thus appear that one can attribute no more than a fraction of the losses in Hungary's market shares to discrimination against its exports.

Restrictive macroeconomic policies, in turn, bore on investment rather than on consumption. Between 1978 and 1981, gross domestic investment fell by 21.3 percent in Hungary, with net investment declining by 40.7 percent. By contrast, domestic consumption increased by altogether 6.0 percent during the period. With the gross domestic product rising by a total of 4.5 percent between 1978 and 1981, the share of domestic consumption in GDP increased, partly offsetting the effects of reduced investment on Hungary's balance of payments.

The situation was aggravated in subsequent years as Hungary suffered the consequences of the events in Poland that brought into question the creditworthiness of the socialist countries for foreign private loans. There ensued the virtual cessation of commercial bank lending and the partial withdrawal of liquid funds, mostly by Middle Eastern countries, from the Hungarian National Bank.

In view of Hungary's debt payment obligations, the government's objective was changed from the re-equilibration of the balance of trade in convertible currencies to achieving a substantial surplus. This in fact occurred in 1984, when a $0.7 billion surplus in convertible currency trade was attained. The adjustment entailed the continued application of restrictive macroeconomic policies, again involving reductions in investment rather than consumption, supplemented by import restrictions while

Hungary continued to lose export market shares. In turn, the expansionary measures taken contributed to the decline in this surplus to $0.3 billion in 1985.

Gross domestic investment fell by 15.7 percent between 1981 and 1985, with net investment declining by 47.4 percent whereas consumption increased by 4.7 percent. At the same time, increased import restrictions in convertible currency trade reduced the ratio of imports to the gross domestic product. Thus, a 6.1 percent rise in Hungary's GDP between 1981 and 1985 was accompanied by a 3.4 percent decline in its imports from private market economies. In this way, 'forced' import substitution occurred in Hungary.

Changes in Hungarian exports may be evaluated by making comparisons with the export performance of other countries at similar levels of economic development. This has been done in regard to the exports of newly-industrializing developing countries (NICs), including Argentina, Brazil, Chile, Israel, Korea, Mexico, Portugal, Singapore, Taiwan, Turkey, Uruguay, Hungary, and Yugoslavia, to the developed countries.

Using import data reported by the developed countries,[12] estimates have been made of hypothetical exports, defined as the exports that would have taken place had Hungary maintained its 1981 market share in the imports of each of the developed countries from the NICs. Under this hypothesis, the current dollar value of Hungary's exports to developed country markets would have increased from $2.4 billion in 1981 to $3.0 billion in 1985. In actual fact, exports were $2.5 billion, representing a decline in market shares of 14 percent and a loss of $0.5 billion in absolute terms.

The result for Hungary contrasts with that for the outward-oriented NICs, such as the Far Eastern countries, which gained export market shares during the period. This contrast represents a continuation of earlier trends, with the outward-oriented newly-industrializing countries gaining and Hungary as well as inward oriented NICs losing export market shares both in the 1973–8 and the 1979–81 periods.[13]

Comparison may further be made with Turkey that used to be considered an extreme case of an inward-oriented country. This comparison is of especial interest, both because Turkey encountered debt servicing difficulties at about the same time as Hungary and because, in contradistinction with Hungary, the policies applied led to increases in Turkey's export market shares. While Turkish exports to the developed countries would have increased from $2.2 billion in 1981 to $2.7 billion in 1985 under the assumption of unchanged market shares, actual exports reached $3.8 billion, representing a gain of 41 percent or $1.1 billion.

The contrast is even greater if total exports to private market economies rather than only to the developed countries are considered, largely because of Turkey's success in entering Middle Eastern markets. Between 1981 and 1985, Turkey raised the dollar value of its exports to private market economies by 35 percent whereas a decline of 1 percent occurred in Hungary. In the same period, Turkey's imports from private market economies rose by 37 percent and those of Hungary declined by 13 percent.

The observed increases in Turkish imports point to the fact that the rapid growth of exports permitted limiting the use of deflationary measures. Correspondingly, Turkey's gross domestic product increased by 26.3 percent between 1981 and 1985, compared with 5.8 percent for Hungary. Economic growth in Turkey was also aided by the rapid rise of construction abroad whereas Hungary was largely unsuccessful with foreign construction.[14]

The rapid growth of the exports of goods and services in Turkey can be attributed to the effects of the wide-ranging economic reform introduced in January 1980.[15] The reform included a substantial devaluation, the provision of export incentives, the liberalization of imports, as well as the freeing of the prices of a wide-range of products, followed by interest rate reform. From the point of view of export performance, the first three of these measures offer particular interest.

Changes in exchange rates have been evaluated by adjusting trade-weighted (effective) exchange rates for changes in domestic and in foreign wholesale prices.[16] The real effective exchange rate thus derived, calculated on a 1976–8 basis, appreciated by 9 percent in 1979, the year before the reforms were implemented. However, the rate depreciated by 32 percent in 1980, with further devaluations occurring after 1981. By 1985, Turkey's real effective exchange rate depreciated by 41 percent compared with its 1976–8 level.

Turkey has also provided export incentives in the form of preferential credits and tax rebates, with additional rebates granted to trading companies.[17] Furthermore, exporters have been given the right to import their inputs duty free even if a domestic substitute is available. Finally, imports have been liberalized, thereby reducing the protection of domestic markets and encouraging efficient production and exports.[18]

In turn, various influences have contributed to the poor performance of Hungarian exports. They include the appreciation of the exchange rate in real terms, the introduction of the so-called competitive pricing rules, relative risks and rewards for exporting to private market economies *vis-à-vis* domestic sales and exports to socialist countries, the system of wage determination, the taxation of profits, the remuneration of managers, access to funds for export-oriented investments, the availability of labor, and the imposition of import restrictions on inputs used directly or indirectly in exporting.

II FACTORS AFFECTING HUNGARY'S EXPORT PERFORMANCE

After an initial depreciation, the Hungarian forint appreciated in real terms to a considerable extent. On a 1976–8 basis, the index of the real effective exchange rate rose to 109 in 1979, declining to 94 in 1980, 85 in 1981, and 83 in 1982, increasing slightly to 88 in 1984 and estimated at 86 in 1985. The figure for 1985 represents a 16 percent real appreciation of the forint compared with 1978, the year when policy changes were introduced, even though the external shocks suffered and the objective of turning the trade deficit into a surplus would have called for a devaluation (Table 13.1).

The cited results may appear surprising in view of the frequent references made in Hungary to the devaluation of the forint. Thus, according to an official of Foreign Trade Ministry, 'after the revaluations of the years 1980 and 1981, the forint was devalued by 27 percent, compared to the average of convertible currencies, between 1981 and 1984.'[19] The explanation for this apparent discrepancy may be found in the inappropriate weighting of foreign currencies in Hungary's currency basket, with a much greater weight given to the US dollar than warranted by its importance in Hungary's trade.[20] Yet, from the point of view of evaluating changes in the competitive position of Hungary, the country composition of its trade is relevant.

As the dollar was rising rapidly in recent years *vis-à-vis* other major currencies, its excessive weight in the currency basket limited the extent of devaluation of the forint. Thus, the trade-weighted nominal effective devaluation in Hungary was only 7 percent between 1981 and 1984, compared with the 27 percent figure cited above.[21] The extent of the devaluation was 6 percent if changes in foreign currency values are averaged by using Hungary's exports, rather than exports and imports, as weights. At the same time, weighting by exports will be relevant for explaining changes in Hungary's export market shares.

Compared with 1978, Hungary's nominal effective exchange rate appreciated by 22 or 26 percent by 1985, depending on whether export and import, or only export, weights are used in the calculations. The corresponding figure is 16 to 19 percent for the real effective exchange rate, depending on the choice of weights, reflecting the fact that wholesale prices (in effect, producer prices) rose less in Hungary than in its partner countries, on the average (Table 13.1).

Table 13.1 also shows data on changes in the nominal and in the real value of the forint *vis-à-vis* Hungary's principal trading partners and, for comparison, the United States. As is apparent, the forint appreciated in real terms by 28 percent *vis-à-vis* the German mark, 17 percent *vis-à-vis* the Austrian shilling, and 5 percent *vis-à-vis* the Italian lira between 1978 and

TABLE 13.1 *Real exchange rates in Hungary, 1978–86*
(1976–8 = 100)

	1978	1979	1980	1981	1982	1983	1984	1985	1986
Bilateral real exchange rates adjusted by									
WPI									
Austria	104.3	108.4	96.4	84.0	82.5	87.0	87.5	86.1	98.9
Germany	105.3	111.0	95.5	82.2	82.6	87.9	87.7	86.0	101.2
Italy	102.6	111.1	102.6	90.1	87.9	94.8	97.7	95.7	108.7
USA	98.3	101.5	91.9	99.5	103.5	115.6	172.9	126.2	109.7
Yugoslavia	97.7	99.7	78.4	78.6	69.6	55.1	57.1	53.6	68.1
CPI									
Austria	105.6	102.4	94.4	82.6	81.1	86.4	85.2	82.9	99.4
Germany	105.5	103.7	92.4	79.7	78.0	83.1	79.3	76.4	89.9
Italy	104.0	105.0	103.6	94.1	91.9	101.8	101.4	99.3	117.1
USA	97.1	93.1	88.5	98.6	104.5	117.0	126.8	128.0	113.5
Yugoslavia	101.6	104.2	88.1	87.5	79.9	65.9	64.4	61.1	71.9
Real effective exchange rates									
Export and import weights									
WPI	103.3	108.5	93.9	85.4	83.4	85.9	88.2	86.4	97.6
CPI	104.4	102.7	93.8	86.4	83.7	86.2	84.4	82.2	93.9
Export weights									
WPI	103.1	108.7	93.9	84.7	82.3	83.8	85.6	83.7	95.9
CPI	104.4	103.6	94.9	86.7	83.7	85.7	83.8	81.5	94.0

NOTE: An increase (decrease) in the index represents a depreciation (appreciation) of the real exchange rate.

SOURCE: World Bank.

1985. And while a 32 percent depreciation occurred *vis-à-vis* the US dollar, Hungary's trade with the United States represented less than 5 percent of its trade with private market economies in the base period.

The revaluation of the exchange rate in real terms adversely affected Hungarian exports by reducing their profitability and by limiting the possibility of increasing their volume through price cutting. At the same time, the introduction of so-called competitive pricing in January 1980 tended to discourage industrial firms from increasing their convertible currency exports and even encouraged them to reduce such exports. This was the case because prices on domestic sales could be raised only if export prices increased *and* export profitability improved in convertible currency trade. In eliminating exports with below-average prices and/or profitability, then, the firm could raise domestic prices under the rules. Moreover, some firms endeavored to keep their convertible currency exports below 5 percent of their total sales, in which case the competitive pricing rules did not apply to them.

There is evidence that the introduction of competitive pricing rules unfavorably affected the volume of manufactured exports in 1980.[22] Nor did attempts made in subsequent years to remedy the situation by modifying the rules suffice to remove these adverse consequences. In fact, they were reinforced by the increased overvaluation of the exchange rate, which broadened the range of products that were unprofitable for the firm but profitable for the national economy.

While the application of competitive pricing rules adversely affected the profitability of exporting firms, under conditions of excess demand existing in the domestic market firms with less than 5 percent convertible currency exports had greater possibilities to improve their profitability by raising prices or by changing their product composition towards higher-priced products. This conclusion is supported by available empirical evidence.

To begin with, industrial firms that had less than nine-tenths of the average rate of profit, calculated on capital investment and wages combined, accounted for 49 percent of convertible currency exports in 1979, 53 percent in 1980, 57 percent in 1981, and 59 percent in 1982.[23] In the latter year, in the iron and steel, machinery, chemical, and light industries, firms with profit rates of less than 5 percent on fixed capital exported 13, 24, 28, and 13 percent of their output for convertible currencies while export shares averaged 9, 11, 7, and 8 percent for firms with profit rates in excess of 20 percent.[24] It has further been reported that all firms showing losses were subject to competitive pricing rules[25] and that highly indebted firms had twice the average share of convertible currency exports in their output.[26]

But, even if a firm could conceivably increase its profits by raising the prices, or expanding the volume, of exports to private market economies, these exports involved a considerable risk, which practically did not exist in the case of domestic sales and exports to socialist countries. There was a risk not only because of fluctuations in foreign demand and prices, but because of the possibility that the higher quality requirements of developed country markets led to the rejection of the merchandise.

Variations in profits obtained in exporting to private market economies had implications for wage setting. While in years of good profits increases in wages were limited by the highly progressive taxation of wage increments, in bad years firms could not raise wages, thus risking the departure of workers, in particular skilled workers and technicians. Nor could firms set up wage reserves with confidence, since such reserves were repeatedly confiscated by the state. Also, firms feared that fluctuations in profits would meet with adverse reception on the part of the supervising authority and that high profits may be taken away from them as it happened in several instances.

These considerations point to a tendency on the part of the firm to be risk averse. And, even apart from the risk involved, the prospects of profits derived from exporting might not have created sufficient encouragement for the firm to expand exports. Several reasons may be adduced in support of this conclusion.

To begin with, the firm producing for exports could not adequately remunerate its high-performing workers because of the progressivity of taxes on wage increments, with only about Ft. 4–5 of a profit increment of Ft. 100 allocable to such increases.[27] This fact created particular difficulties in manufacturing high-quality products, which are in demand in developed countries. These products require better work performance and/or higher quality labor, the remuneration of which would have necessitated raising average wages that was subject to very high taxes.

Furthermore, on the average, the profit tax and other taxes payable from the firm's profits amounted to about 80 percent of profits in recent years while government financial support accounted for 40–45 percent of profits.[28] As these ratios varied from firm to firm, the profits obtained after redistribution became to a large extent divorced from the pre-distribution profits.[29]

Nor could post-redistribution profits be freely utilized by management as they were divided between the profit-sharing and the investment funds. And, apart from confiscating the reserves for wage increases derived from the profit-sharing fund, limitations were repeatedly imposed on the use of the investment fund.

Finally, the sharing of the managers in increases in profits was limited. This was the case, firstly, because of the overall limitations imposed on the payment of bonuses after 1972; secondly, because of the importance given to considerations other than profits in the bonus scheme; and thirdly, because of the latitude of the supervising ministries to modify the bonus conditions.

In fact, according to one observer, 'the incomes of the managers – within the strict limits on income differentiation – have little to do with their work, their performance, and their abilities.'[30] At the same time, the deciding role played by supervising ministries in setting bonuses, and the subjective elements involved in these decisions, meant that the managers reportedly expressed more of an interest in pleasing the cadres of the ministries than improving the performance of the firm.[31]

At the same time, exports were adversely affected by limited access to financing. To begin with, the special fund of bank credits that had earlier been made available for investment in export activities was increasingly allocated to import-substituting projects. Yet, in the latter case, differences in quality and in specifications made it difficult to provide an objective appraisal of economic benefits, which may be measured in terms of net foreign exchange receipts in the case of exports.

Also, the time limits set for the repayment of loans for investments in export activities were reduced to a considerable extent. While three years had earlier been allotted for implementing the investment and five years for recouping the amount invested, in 1981 the total time limit for repayment was set at four years. This regulation benefited agriculture and food processing at the expense of manufacturing industries and favored capacity-increasing investments over the introduction of new products and technological change. Nor were the credits provided as a part of an investment program of the firm, aimed at structural change.[32]

More generally, manufactured exports suffered from the reduction of investment funds that was more pronounced in the industrial sector than the average decline on the national economy level. Also, in the allocation of industrial investment funds preference was given to central investments in energy and heavy industry over enterprise investments in the light and machinery industries, which give promise for exports.

Thus, within the industrial total, the combined investment share of mining, electricity generation, and iron and steel increased from 32.9 percent in 1978 to 49.3 percent in 1984 whereas that of the light and machinery industries declined from 28.9 to 22.0 percent. Yet, the average age of machinery is 16 years in Hungary's manufacturing industries and product composition is far from up to date, with new products accounting for only 3–4 percent of output each year,[33] which represents a deterioration compared with the situation existing earlier.

A further consideration is that export credits, and other export incentives, were provided to direct but not to indirect exporters. As a result, firms manufacturing intermediate products often undertook direct exports, even though from the point of view of the national economy exporting in processed form would have been desirable.

One-half of the firms exporting to private market economies indicated that the lack of manpower limited the possibilities for increasing exports. But import restrictions were considered to be a more important source of difficulties. Thus, it happened that by the time the import license was obtained higher prices had to be paid for the input or the would-be purchaser of the final product did not accept the delay that had occurred. More generally, the imposition of import restrictions discouraged exports by creating uncertainty for the firm.[34]

It was attempted to offset the inadequacies of the incentive system by the government reaching agreements with some large firms on export targets, providing certain advantages in return. The poor export results cited earlier indicate, however, that these attempts were far from being fully successful. At the same time, such a procedure tends to freeze the existing export pattern and does not ensure the efficient choice of export activities. Moreover, it increases the scope of *ad hoc* interventions.[35]

The last point leads to the general observation that while the December 1978 Party resolution simultaneously aimed at re-establishing external equilibrium and returning to the principles of the 1968 reform, in practice these objectives came into conflict. More often than not, the conflicts were resolved in favor of the former objective, so that there were increasing interventions in the firms' activities.

Such interventions originated with the Economic Committee, the Ministry of Finance, the Materials and Price Board, as well as the sectoral ministries. They involved *ex ante* actions, such as instructing the firm to undertake or not to undertake certain activities as well as *ex post* actions, such as the withdrawal of investment and wage funds from the firm. Apart from creating mistrust on the part of firms, these actions induced firm managers to curry favor with the supervising authorities that often appeared to be the easiest way to pursue the firm's objectives.

The adverse consequences of the increased scope of *ad hoc* interventions were well stated by János Hoós, the Vice-President of the Planning Office:

> The overall direction of economic activities has lost its transparency; its automaticity decreased to a considerable extent and there are adverse consequences in the price system and in the regulation of incomes. As a result, firms are not sensitive to costs and they do not have appropriate incentives. This is expressed in the fact that in practice every firm can obtain – if in no other way than through government support – the revenues it needs for continued operation. . . . The situation has been aggravated by the import limitations and export obligations resulting from short-term problems of equilibrium, which have led practically to production instructions. For all these reasons, firms cannot optimize their decisions and rationally combine their resources.[36]

III THE EXCHANGE RATE, PRODUCT PRICES, AND COMPETITION

According to Lajos Faluvégi, Deputy Prime Minister and President of the Planning Office, the pre-condition of renewed economic expansion in Hungary is that productive activities be increasingly oriented towards exports. Preliminary targets for the 1985–90 period call for exports to rise at an average annual rate of 3.5–4.0 percent. Faluvégi notes that reaching this target would permit the growth of national income to attain 3 percent a year during the period while imports would increase 3 to 5 percent a year.[37]

The export target appears rather modest. According to the World Bank's average projection, the manufactured exports of the developing countries would rise by 8 percent a year between 1985 and 1990.[38] Also, Hungary has considerable possibilities for expanding and upgrading its food exports, provided that export markets are diversified.

Setting aside the growth of foreign demand, Hungary could theoretically increase its exports to private market economies by 65 percent if it regained the market shares lost between 1971–3 and 1984 in its trade with these economies. And while regaining market shares takes time, this objective would need to be pursued through the adoption of appropriate policies.

The question arises, then, how can Hungary accelerate its export growth to private market economies. More generally, the question is how can Hungarian firms improve their international competitiveness to permit increasing exports as well as efficiently replacing imports, so as to ease the foreign exchange constraint that limits the growth possibilities of the national economy.

The first condition is to adopt a realistic exchange rate. As shown above, the forint appreciated in real terms by approximately 15 percent between 1978 and 1985. Yet, the external shocks Hungary suffered, and the objective of turning the trade deficit into a surplus, would have necessitated a devaluation.

While adjusting the exchange rate adds to inflation, in providing tax rebates to exports and imposing taxes on imports, the introduction of a value added tax would have the same effects as a devaluation without any inflationary consequences, provided that the tax were to replace profit taxes as suggested below. However, reducing profit taxes by one-half would permit but a 3.5–4.0 percent adjustment,[39] which would go only part of the way to undo the appreciation of the real exchange rate.

The Hungarian authorities wish to keep the rate of inflation within a 6–7 percent range. In recent years, reductions in consumption subsidies was the principal factor contributing to price increases. In early 1985, the resulting increases reached the presumed annual limit, leading to a virtual freeze on producer prices for the rest of the year.

Although reducing consumer subsidies is desirable in the long term, the rationalization of producer prices is a more immediate objective, when the process of rationalization involves, first of all, setting realistic exchange rates. At the same time, the inflationary effects of a devaluation may be mitigated by simultaneously lowering tariffs. Apart from compensating for the increases in import protection associated with the imposition of the value added tax, one may provide partial compensation for the effects of the devaluation through tariff reductions.[40]

Lowering tariffs parallel with a devaluation would lessen the bias against exports that results from import protection. The bias against exports may be further reduced by increasing export incentives and extending the incentives received by direct exporters to indirect exporters (the manufacturing of domestic inputs for export production) as well.

To begin with, it would be desirable to ensure the automatic and duty free importation of inputs used directly or indirectly for export production. This provision conforms to GATT rules and hence does not invoke retaliation on the part of importers. It has been used to good effect by successful exporting countries in the Far East and, more recently, Turkey.

On the example of these countries, it would further be desirable to extend the credit facilities available to direct exporters to indirect exporters as well while increasing the volume, and improving the terms, of these credits. In particular, providing longer-term credits would contribute to investment in export activities.

Hungary may also follow the example of successful exporting countries in improving the organization of foreign trade. Apart from generalizing the right of direct exportation to all industrial firms, and extending it to agricultural cooperatives, it would be desirable to encourage the establishment of trading companies. Producers, then, would be free to choose among the alternatives of direct exporting, selling through the traditional specialized exporting firms, and utilizing the services of trading companies.

Trading companies have played an important role in the rapid expansion of exports in Japan, subsequently in Korea, and more recently in Turkey. At the same time, experience indicates that, in order to become important factors in exporting, trading companies need incentives, foreign exchange allocation, and capital.

The described measures would provide inducements for exports as well as for efficient import substitution, particularly in industries producing inputs for exports. At the same time, for these inducements to have the desired effects, additional measures would need to be taken to establish rational prices, to provide the carrot and the stick of competition, and to ensure the incentive effects of profits.

Note has been taken above of the use of 'constructed' prices in domestic markets that unfavorably affected industrial exports. To overcome the deficiencies of this price scheme, it was decided to introduce 'genuine' market prices in Hungary. This was to be done first for firms that undertook certain obligations in the framework of the so-called 'price club,' established in 1984, subsequently extended to over one-third of industrial firms in 1985, with further extensions planned in later years.

Membership in the price club required the fulfilment of three conditions: (a) supply-demand balance in domestic markets; (b) domestic prices not to exceed import prices,[41] and (c) potential for export expansion. It was further stated that the extension of the new price scheme was conditioned on equating domestic supply and demand, with domestic prices being bounded by import prices.

In practice, however, there is little domestic competition in Hungary that would ensure the establishment of genuine market prices. Also, as noted by the head of the department responsible for price control in the Materials and Price Board, in the absence of import competition, comparisons of domestic and import prices have considerable information requirements. Thus,

> one needs to take account of the product's physical and chemical characteristics, its specifications, durability, the variability of product

characteristics, packaging, the rate of delivery, the accepted delivery time, as well as other conditions of sale, such as the size of the order and the servicing, transportation, and financial conditions.[42]

This is a formidable set of requirements and, in his earlier review of criticisms of the so-called competitive price scheme, the then President of the Materials and Price Board, Béla Csikós-Nagy, expressed the view that a 'price scheme based on import prices is a practical impossibility.'[43] Csikós-Nagy added that

> of the several millions of products manufactured in Hungary only a few ten thousand are imported. Thus, not actual but constructed foreign prices would be in the center of price determination, and the comparisons of domestic and foreign semi-manufactures and finished goods would burden price setting with problems that cannot find a solution.[44]

The same point was subsequently made by the head of the department responsible for price setting at the Materials and Price Board:

> How can an import price that does not exist and is not known in the home market serve as a ceiling for domestic prices? This would be possible under import competition, when the producer is provided with the importing alternative . . . and the potential import price provides a limit to the domestic price. But if the seller knows that he does not have to meet competition from abroad, what is the limit? . . . Without real competition, the import price ceiling cannot provide a limit for the domestic price.[45]

At the same time, in the absence of effective domestic and import competition,[46] the freeing of prices raises the danger of monopolistic or oligopolistic price determination. This danger has in fact been invoked in rationalizing the increased role of the Materials and Price Board in setting prices in conjunction with the introduction of so-called genuine market prices.

It appears, then, that the lack of competition in Hungary has not permitted the establishment of genuine market prices and has led to increased price controls. It is further apparent that in a small country, a situation approximated by Hungary, the efficient allocation of resources would require adopting world market prices and specializing in response of these prices.

While one may set world market prices for standardized products, which have well-defined specifications, most manufactured goods are differentiated products where import competition would be needed to align domestic prices to world market prices. Under present conditions, this is not in the realm of possibilities for Hungary. Such being the case, one should first take measures to intensify domestic competition, with the gradual opening of the domestic market to imports.

In 1980–81, several trusts and large enterprises were broken up, leading to the establishment of 167 new firms. Still, Hungary continues to have a very centralized industrial structure. To increase competition, it would be necessary to continue the process of deconcentration, by breaking up firms that have several factories producing identical or similar commodities. Such is the case, in particular, in the steel, machinery, textiles, clothing, and shoe industries as well as in construction and commerce.

Breaking up large firms is a necessary but not a sufficient condition for effective competition. The break-up of the food canning trust has not led to price competition in the industry, for example. Rather, the newly-established firms have colluded in setting prices, which have then been reviewed by the Materials and Price Board. Central price setting, however, does not provide an appropriate solution as noneconomic considerations, such as the desire to limit price increases, affect the outcome.

A more appropriate solution would be to establish anti-trust legislation and to rely on the courts to ensure that cartels are not formed. While this would require a transformation of the way the courts presently operate, it would represent an extension of the role currently being assigned to them in the economic sphere in handling cases of bankruptcy. At the same time, such an arrangement would permit limiting interference in the firms' activities by central authorities.

The courts may also be given a role in breaking up large firms that have monopoly or quasi-monopoly positions in Hungary. Moreover, in order to minimize the possibilities for interventions on the part of the ministries, one may wish to transfer their newly-acquired responsibility for supervising the legality of the firms' actions to the courts.

Domestic competition could further be increased if the measures taken in 1981 and 1982 were followed by additional steps to provide inducements for the establishment of small and medium-size enterprises. These enterprises could also play a role in replacing imported parts and components by domestic production and embark on direct exportation. Appropriate measures may include increasing the number of workers that can be hired by private firms, reducing the taxes that were recently increased on such firms, and eliminating the additional taxes imposed on workers' organizations supplying state-owned enterprises.

At the same time, steps would need to be taken to gradually introduce import competition. János Deák, the Director of the Institute of Market Research, suggested that this be done by liberalizing during the 1985–90 period the imports of products and product groups, where exports are profitable at the existing exchange rate, followed by further import liberalization in cases where international competition can be established during the next five year period. Deák also suggests closing down activities that could not become internationally competitive.[47]

The implementation of this proposal would permit the gradual liberalization of imports while limiting the cost of adjustment in the domestic economy, when an additional criterion for import liberalization may be the existence of monopoly positions. At the same time, it should not be assumed that foreign competition would necessarily lead to the demise of domestic firms that presently produce at costs in excess of import prices. This is because of the possibilities for improving operating efficiency in Hungarian firms through improved utilization of the capital stock and through reductions in what has been called intra-plant unemployment.

In fact, increased competition from imports would elicit cost reductions through the rationalization of operations and provide inducements for technological change. It would also make exports to private markets more attractive relative to production for domestic markets by lessening the advantages that sellers have over buyers in Hungary. In turn, if particular plants or firms continue to make losses in a competitive environment, they would need to be closed down. While decisions on closing plants may be taken by firm management, the involvement of the courts in bankruptcy proceedings would provide for the orderly closing down of firms.

IV FACTOR PRICES AND INSTITUTIONAL CHANGE

Further consideration needs to be given to the pricing of productive factors. Several important measures have been taken in this regard in 1985. They include the introduction of a 10 percent tax on labor and a 3 percent tax on own capital for most manufacturing industries, compensated by a net reduction in the profit tax by 3–4 percentage points. At the same time, a number of firms have adopted new wage regulations that treat wage costs as any other cost item and make the ability of firms to pay wages dependent on its income.[48]

The tax on wages is intended to internalize the cost of some of the social policies that are presently financed from the government budget; the tax on own capital provides a payment to the state for the ownership of capital. Both of these changes contribute to the efficient pricing of primary factors while increasing the incentive effects of profits.

In turn, the newly-introduced wage (earnings) regulations improve rationality in firm decision-making by treating all cost items equally. They represent a break with the system of incremental wage regulations, under which increases in wages are financed from increases in profits. Under the incremental wage system, the ability of the firm to raise wages is dependent on its original starting position and inefficiently managed firms could raise wages by effecting some improvements in their operations while highly efficient firms could do so to a lesser extent as their scope for productivity improvements was more limited. Furthermore, as noted above, the incremental wage system has contributed to risk aversion and has slowed the process of technological change for the sake of providing steady wage increases.

At present, the new earnings regulations apply only to a minority of firms that have accepted its introduction; other firms continue to employ the incremental wage system or increases in wages are determined centrally. In view of its described advantages, the application of the new regulations should be extended over a wider sphere.

Under the new earnings regulations, firms that cannot pay the competitive wage will lose labor to other firms. At the same time, the mobility of labor would need to be accompanied by the mobility of capital. This, however, would necessitate adopting appropriate tax and credit policies.

The imposition of taxes on labor and capital increases the interfirm variability of profits. But, for profits to have sufficient incentive effects, the payments made to the budget from profits would have to be reduced. The recent lowering of the profit tax rate represents the first step in this direction. It would need to be followed by a more substantial reduction in profit tax rates, say by one-half, with the revenue loss offset through the introduction of the value added tax. As noted above, the introduction of the value added tax would also improve the international competitiveness of Hungarian exports.

While lowering profit tax rates would increase the amount of funds successful firms have available for investment, firms exhibiting poor performance would have to draw on their amortization funds to finance their losses, thereby leading to the reallocation of capital. Providing credits on the basis of profitability considerations alone would also contribute to the allocation of capital to efficient activities. This, in turn, would require placing increased reliance on commercial principles in bank lending.

The recent establishment of financial institutions and commercial banks represent steps in this direction. Making profitability the dominant consideration for the commercial banks would further call for the establishment of a competitive banking structure.

At the same time, the availability of investment funds to manufacturing enterprises would need to be increased, with additional funds devoted to infrastructural investment aimed in particular at improving transportation and communication facilities. This may be accomplished by devoting an increasing part of the increment in national income to new investments, encouraging private savings, promoting foreign direct investment, raising the share of the industries of transformation in total industrial investment, and reducing the scope of central investments and of central interventions in firm decision-making on investment.

Hungary's recent experience with the issue of bonds indicates the responsiveness of savers to interest rates. Establishing positive real interest rates on savings deposits can be expected to attract further private savings.

The same effect may be achieved by permitting private individuals to buy shares in small and medium-size firms while encouraging the establishment of such firms.

Promoting foreign direct investment would benefit Hungary through the inflow of capital as well as through the increased availability of technological and marketing know-how. Particular importance attaches to the latter factors as, more often than not, the purchase of foreign licenses has not led to continued efforts to improve technology in Hungarian firms and marketing expertise is needed to ensure the success of the export effort.

Increasing the share of the industries of transformation in total investment would involve reducing allocations to energy and to basic industries. Among other things, it would be desirable to renegotiate the agreement on the joint Hungarian–Czechoslovakian hydroelectric installation on the Danube that would require substantial funds and bring limited benefit as well as potential environmental damage.

The funds available for firm investments may further be increased by limiting the scope of central investments. Such a shift would permit orienting investments toward high profitability uses by relying on firms to make choices on the basis of their evaluation of market possibilities domestically and abroad. This will also increase the responsibility of the firm for its own actions while the central interventions practiced today represent an undesirable division of responsibilities.[49]

At the same time, the introduction of bankruptcy proceedings would need to be accompanied by the strengthening of financial discipline,[50] thereby replacing the 'soft' by a 'hard' budget constraint for the firm. In this way, one may reduce the presently excessive demand for investment credit on the part of firms, with interest rates used to equilibrate credit markets. Also, firms would have more incentive to make placement with banks which would again contribute to the reallocation of capital.

Distortions in product and in factor markets have been said to motivate case-by-case interventions by the supervising authorities that have taken the form of fixing prices, establishing export obligations, setting targets for domestic sales, and modifying *ex post* the firm's retained profits. Such interventions have grown in scope in recent years as 'manual guidance' has been utilized to re-establish macroeconomic equilibrium.

Reducing distortions in product and factor markets and re-establishing macroeconomic equilibrium would lessen the rationale (or the excuse) for case-by-case interventions. At the same time, the institutional changes under way aim at limiting the opportunities for interventions. Thus, following the earlier consolidation of the industrial ministries into one, sectoral departments have been abolished, the only exception being the energy sector. Furthermore, apart from about one hundred of the largest industrial firms, the ministry only retains veto power over the choice of the firm's manager who is elected by the council or the collective of the firm.

These institutional changes are to be welcomed. But, fears have been expressed that the newly-acquired responsibilities of the Material and Price Board for 'market surveillance' would mean the displacement rather than the abolition of case-by-case interventions. And, while the new legislation provides possibilities for the firm to present its case at the courts for compensation in the event that the Board's actions adversely affect its profits, its dependence on the Board in regard to price setting may make this little more than a theoretical possibility.

The above considerations again point to the importance of freeing prices which, as noted before, is dependent on the establishment of the conditions of competition. At the same time, there would be need to reduce the scope of fiscal redistribution that takes the form of *ex ante* regulations and *ex post* decisions on a case-by-case basis. As noted above, financial support accounted for 40–45 percent of firm profits, representing a counterpart to the various taxes that took away over 80 percent of the profits.

Apart from actions to assist firms in difficulties, the bulk of financial support has aimed at offsetting the high production costs for firms that cannot profitably export at the existing exchange rate. The adoption of a rational exchange rate would reduce the need for such support, both by shifting upward the threshold of export profitability and by providing possibilities to replace high-cost export products through the expansion of low-cost exports.

Correspondingly, fiscal support for exports could be reduced and ultimately eliminated. This had been repeatedly envisaged in the past without, however, establishing the conditions for its elimination through the adoption of a rational exchange rate. More generally, all financial interventions should be limited to cases when government actions affect the firm's profits, thereby increasing the financial responsibility of the firm for its own actions.[51] This purpose would further be served by penalizing firms that delay payments to their firms.[52]

Note has been taken above of the changes in the system of appointing managers. Under the new regulations introduced in 1985, in the majority of firms the chief executive will be chosen by an enterprise council that is elected by the workers of the firm. In smaller enterprises, generally those having less than 500 workers, the chief executive will be elected by the general assembly of the workers' collective. Finally, in the largest one hundred industrial firms, the supervising ministry will continue to appoint the chief executive for the time being.

The following discussion will concentrate on the case of firms that have enterprise councils, which account for approximately two-thirds of all industrial firms and for a similar proportion of industrial workers. In turn, only about 2 to 3 percent of the workers will be in firms where the general assembly elects the chief executive, representing about one-sixth of industrial firms. The remaining one-sixth of industrial firms, employing nearly one-third of the workers, will remain under the administrative control of the supervising ministry.[53]

Apart from selecting the chief executive, the enterprise council will define the annual plan, approve the annual financial statement, determine the utilization of profits, set up subsidiaries, and decide on the division of the firm into independent units. On the whole, the council will fulfil the function of the board of directors of capitalist firms, with the important exception that the supervising ministry will retain veto power over the choice of managers and its agreement will be necessary for closing down the firm.

At the same time, while in capitalist countries the board of directors represents the shareholders of the firm, in Hungary the council will be composed of the firm's workers. This represents a change compared with the original proposal that called for majority participation by representatives of organizations, such as the supervising ministry, the banks, the Chamber of Commerce, as well as outside experts.

The changes made in the composition of the council make them resemble the Yugoslav system of workers' management. As it is well known, this system has involved a bias against hiring new workers who would reduce the average product of labor, which is the relevant consideration for the workers' collective that does not equate wages to the marginal product of labor. Also, Yugoslav firms have showed a preference for increasing wages and social benefits over new investment.

There is a danger that enterprise councils in Hungary will follow the Yugoslav example. This danger is enhanced by reason of the fact that the trade unions are playing an important role in selecting the members of the council. Another danger is that the chief executive would dominate the proceedings, thereby perpetuating his stewardship. Such a danger exists since the council will include members of the management team who are appointed by the chief executive.

The above considerations indicate the advantages of the original proposal to have a majority of outside members on the enterprise council. This is not to suggest to have representatives of the supervising ministry on the council, since this would mean combining ownership and regulatory functions. A more appropriate alternative would be to establish an agency, consisting of legal, economic, and accounting experts, that would represent the state *qua* owner on the enterprise council. But, in order to avoid that such an agency assume excessive powers, its minority participation on the council would be desirable. A possible formula may be to have one-third of the members represent the agency, one-third the other outside organizations referred to above, and one-third the firm's employees on the enterprise council.

One may envisage establishing the described form of enterprise council initially for industrial firms that have remained under administrative control. Eventually, however, all enterprise councils established under the present regulations should be so transformed. Finally, in the case of firms established by banks, a procedure that is supposed to be applied in the future, the banks' representative may have a larger representation on the enterprise councils.

CONCLUSIONS

Following a brief review of the policies applied in response to external shocks, this essay has examined Hungary's adjustment experience in the 1978–85 period. It has been shown that Hungary succeeded in transforming a deficit in convertible currency trade into a surplus during the period. But, this involved the adoption of deflationary policies, bearing chiefly on investment activity, as well as import controls, while Hungary lost export market shares and the rate of economic growth averaged only 1.6 percent a year.

Apart from effecting a shift in Hungary's convertible currency balance, it was envisaged to re-establish the reform process that had begun in 1968. Among the measures initially taken, the introduction of the so-called competitive price scheme in January 1980 did not fulfil its promise and the system of wage setting continued to reflect the application of the basis principle; i.e. increments in wages linked to changes in the firm's performance.

In the early 1980s, organizational changes were also made in consolidating the three industrial ministries into one, breaking up trusts and a number of large enterprises, and providing for new organizational forms in the public as well as in the private sectors.[54] While the last-mentioned changes have been given considerable attention, in 1984 the combined output of the new organizations did not attain 2 percent of the output of state enterprises. In turn, although the break-up of trusts and large enterprises created the potential for competition, collusive actions on the part of the newly-established firms hindered the exploitation of this potential. Finally, until 1985, retaining the sectoral departments of the industrial ministry limited changes in its operating procedures.

At the same time, the exigencies of turning a deficit into a surplus in convertible currency trade and the requirements of the reform effort repeatedly came into conflict and, more often than not, this conflict was resolved in favor of the former objective. This involved limiting the firm's freedom of actions, both through binding regulations and through case-by-case interventions.

In turn, the changes introduced in 1985, in particular the establishment of enterprise councils, changes in the tax system, the new wage regulations, and the shift away from the so-called competitive price scheme, represent important reform efforts. But, for these measures to have their full effect, further actions would need to be taken to rationalize product and factor prices and to increase the freedom of action by the firm. More generally, one should create a situation where the firm responds to market signals rather than to ever-changing regulations and interventions. This, in turn, calls for establishing the conditions for effective competition in the domestic economy and, eventually, through imports.

These changes are necessary for the structural transformation of the Hungarian economy that has been hindered by the practice of overregulations and 'manual guidance.' Such transformation will require investments, more exactly efficient investments that conform to market conditions. In this respect, too, greater scope needs to be given to decision-making by the firm that has to take the risks and enjoy the reward of its actions. One may, then, ensure that 'the new growth path' lives up to its name as adjustment occurs through exports and efficient import substitution, thereby leading to higher rates of economic expansion.

NOTES

1. Trade is defined to include services other than investment income; unless otherwise noted, all data originate in official Hungarian statistical sources.
2. The terms of trade loss is measured by taking the difference between Hungary's imports and exports valued in actual prices and in the prices of the 1971–3 base period; the export shortfall is derived by taking the difference between Hungary's actual exports and its hypothetical exports, calculated on the assumption that trends observed in world trade in 1963–73 continued *and* Hungary maintained its 1971–3 export market shares in this trade.
3. Private market economies provided markets for 39 percent of Hungary's exports and supplied 48 percent of its imports during the period under consideration, with socialist countries accounting for the remainder. About 15 percent of Hungary's trade with socialist countries was settled in convertible currencies but the volume of this trade was circumscribed by state-to-state trade agreements.
4. Changes in Hungary's market shares have been calculated with respect to the imports of nonfuel primary products, fuels, and manufactured goods by private market economies in the years 1971–3.
5. B. Balassa, and L. Tyson, 'Adjustment to External Shocks in Socialist and Private Market Economies,' in Luigi Pasinetti and Peter Lloyd (eds), *Structural Change, Economic Interdependence and World Development Vol. 3. Structural Change and Adjustment in the World Economy* (London: Macmillan, 1987) pp. 123–48.
6. I. Lakos, 'A magyar kivitel eredményei a fejlett tőkés országokban' (The Achievements of Hungarian Exports in the Developed Capitalist Countries), *Külgazdaság* (External Economy), XXV (1981) pp. 22–35.
7. Between 1973 and 1978, Hungary's cattle exports to the European Common Market declined from $133 million to $43 million. But, in the same period, Hungary's meat exports to the Common Market increased from $84 million to $149 million.

8. B. Balassa, 'The Hungarian Economic Reform, 1968–81,' *Banca Nazionale del Lavoro Quarterly Review*, XXXVI (1983) pp. 163–84 and Essay 12 in Bela Balassa, *Change and Challenge in the World Economy* (London: Macmillan, 1985) pp. 261–81.

9. Ibid.

10. Changes in export market shares in the commodity groups listed above have been calculated with respect to the 1976–8 period; in turn, the base period for estimating changes in the income elasticity of import demand has remained 1963–73.

11. *Financial Times*, 1 May 1984.

12. The data are expressed in current dollars at fob prices for the United States, Canada, Australia, and New Zealand and at cif prices for Japan and the countries of Western Europe. They originate in International Monetary Fund, *Direction of Trade Statistics*. Lack of information on the commodity composition of exports did not permit applying the methodology utilized in regard to the 1973–8 and 1978–81 periods.

13. Balassa and Tyson, 'Adjustment to External Shocks in Socialist and Private Market Economies.'

14. *Financial Times*, 10 October 1983.

15. In fact, the dollar value of Turkish exports increased by 75 percent between 1980 and 1981, permitting increases in imports of 18 percent while simultaneously improving the balance of payments to a considerable extent. In the same year, the dollar value of exports fell by 6 percent, and that of imports by 2 percent, in Hungary.

16. The data derive from International Monetary Fund, *Direction of Trade Statistics* and *International Financial Statistics*.

17. In 1981, exporters received an extra amount equal to 5 percent of export value if their exports reached $4 million a year and 10 percent if exports attained $15 million. And although these rebates have subsequently been reduced, they provided a strong push for the establishment of trading companies that spearheaded the export expansion.

18. For a detailed discussion of the situation existing in 1981, see Balassa, 1982; subsequent developments are discussed in Balassa 1983c.

19. I. Dunai, 'A kǔlgazdasági tevékenység állami irányítása, szabályozása' (The State Guidance and Regulation of Foreign Trade Activities), in M. Pulai and F. Vissi (eds), *Gazdaságirányítás 1985* (The Guidance of the Economy) (Budapest: Kǒzgazdasági és Jogi Kǒnyvkiadó, 1984) p. 94.

20. This has been the case in some developing countries as well, reflecting a confusion between the use of the dollar in denominating exports and imports and the share of trade with the United States. In turn, adjustments in the currency basket to appropriately reflect the geographical composition of trade have led to considerable devaluations in several countries in recent years.

21. Among Hungary's principal trading partners, the forint was devalued by 9 percent *vis-à-vis* the German mark and by 11 percent *vis-à-vis* the Austrian shilling while it was revalued by 9 percent *vis-à-vis* the Italian lira; at the same time, a devaluation of 40 percent occurred *vis-à-vis* the US dollar.

22. B. Balassa, 'Reforming the New Economic Mechanism in Hungary,' *Journal of Comparative Economics*, VII (1983) pp. 253–76 and Essay 13 in *Change and Challenge in the World Economy*, pp. 282–309. Hungarian translation in *Kǒzgazdasági Szemle* (Economic Review), XXX (1983) pp. 826–42.

23. B. Kevevári, 'A tǒkeallokációs mechanizmus fejlesztésének lehetǒségei' (Possibilities for Developing the Mechanism of Capital Allocation), *Pénzǔgyi Szemle* (Financial Review), XXVIII (1984) p. 486.

24. M. Pető, 'Alacsony és magas jövedelmezőség' (Low and High Profitability), *Figyelő* (Observer), 15 December 1983, p. 3.
25. A. Juhász, 'Versenyképesség és árrendszer' (Competitiveness and the Price Regulations), *Közgazdasági Szemle* (Economic Review), XXX (1983) p. 956.
26. J. Deák, 'Az iparvállalatok teljesitmény- és exportösztönzésének tapasztalatai a legutóbbi években' (Experiences with Incentives for the Performance and Exports of Industrial Firms in Recent Years), *Ipargazdasági Szemle* (Industrial Review), XIV (1983) p. 36.
27. L. Faluvégi, 'Cazdasági hatékonyság – gazdaságirányitás' (Economic Efficiency – Economic Management), *Közgasdasági Szemle* (Economic Review), XXXI (1984) p. 1078.
28. This and the subsequent points apply to domestic sales as well.
29. In an empirical investigation covering all state enterprises, it has been shown that in 1979 and in 1980 the correlation between pre- and post-redistribution profits in Hungarian industry was practically nil (J. Kornai and A. Matits, 'A kőltségvetési korlát puhaságáról – vállalati adatok alapján' (On the Softness of the Budget Constraint – on the Basis of Firm Data), *Gazdaság* (Economy), XVII (1983) pp. 7–28.
30. L. Héthy, *Gazdaságpolitika és érdekeltség* (Economic Policy and Economic Interests) (Budapest: Kossuth Kőnyvkiadó, 1983) p. 65.
31. This is the conclusion of a survey of managers conducted by the Labor Research Institute as reported in *Figyelő* (Observer), 21 October 1982.
32. I. Garamvölgyi, 'Hogyan tovább? Az exportfejlesztésben' (How to Proceed? In Promoting Exports), *Figyelő* (Observer), 10 March 1982, pp. 1, 11, and T. Draviczky, 'Beruházási hitelezés, export-nővelés vagy más?' (Investment Credits, Export Development or Something Else?), *Figyelő* (Observer), 2 August 1982, p. 1.
33. Interview given by Andrea Deák, then Chief Economist of the Industry Ministry, as reported in *Figyelő* (Observer), 22 December 1983, p. 11.
34. These are the conclusions of a survey, the results of which are reported in *Figyelő* (Observer), 5 January 1984, p. 12; the difficulties exporters encountered because of the existence of import restrictions were also voiced in interviews by firm managers, reported in *Figyelő* (Observer), 30 August 1984, p. 5.
35. The dangers of providing preferential treatment to large exporters, irrespective of the cost of earning foreign exchange, are noted in Török, 1985.
36. J. Hoós, *Az új nővekedési pálya feltételei és kővetelményei* (The Conditions and Requirements of the New Growth Path) (Budapest: Kőzgazdasági és Jogi Kőnyvkiadó, 1985), p. 115.
37. Faluvégi, p. 1029.
38. World Bank, *World Development Report 1985* (Washington, DC: World Bank 1985).
39. I. Vincze, 'Az értéknővekmény-adó' (The Value Added Tax), *Figyelő* (Observer), 8 September 1984, p. 3.
40. Adjusting tariffs to the same extent as the exchange rate would leave import prices unchanged, and the resulting compensated devaluation would be equivalent to an (implicit) export subsidy. However, with tariffs being relatively low in Hungary, full compensation could not be envisaged.
41. Import prices (or world market prices) refer to the prices prevailing in private market economies. The prices of goods sold to, or purchased from, socialist countries are adjusted by the use of compensating taxes and subsidies to approximate prices prevailing in the (capitalist) world market.
42. Interview reported in *Figyelő* (Observer), 4 October 1984, pp. 1, 7.

43. B. Csikós-Nagy, 'Az árrendszer továbbfejlesztése' (The Further Development of the Price System), *Pénzügyi Szemle* (Financial Review), XXVII (1983) p. 732.
44. Ibid., p. 732.
45. L. Rácz, 'Import korlát – vagy versenyár' (Import Limitation – or Competitive Price?) *Figyelő* (Observer), 29 March 1984, p. 4.
46. The importance of competition is emphasized in B. Csikós-Nagy *Arpolitikánk időszerü kérdései, 1985–1988* (Timely Questions of Our Price Policy, 1985–1988) (Budapest: Közgazdasági és Jogi Könyvkiadó, 1985) p. 38.
47. J. Deák, 'A kůlkereskedelmi egyensúly és as export-import szabályozás' (The Equilibrium of Foreign Trade and Export-Import Regulations), *Kůlgazdaság* (Foreign Economy), XXVII) (1983) pp. 3–14.
48. Pulai and Vissi describe these changes and indicate the need for further improvements in the system of incentives, some of which are taken up below.
49. This point is emphasized in L. Kismarty, 'A beruházási döntési rendszer korszerüsitéséről' (On the Modernization of the System of Decision-Making on Investments) *Pénzügyi Szemle* (Financial Review), XXIX (1985) pp. 361–7.
50. On the question of financial discipline, see further below.
51. The institution of a list of firms operating with low efficiency, with a view to induce these firms to improve their operations, represents a step in this direction. However, a variety of exceptions continue to be made, providing scope for bargaining. M. Laki, 'A gazdaságirányitás és a vállalati valóság' (The Guidance of the National Economy and Firm Reality), *Kůlgazdaság* (External Economy), XXIX (1985) pp. 41–58.
52. Recent increases in firm-to-firm indebtedness and the lengthening of payment delays are reported in D. Jánossy, 'Fizetőképesség. Vállalatok feketelistán' (Ability to Pay. Firms on the Blacklist), *Figyelő* (Observer), 30 May 1985, p. 3.
53. J. Deák, 'Az iparvállalatok átszervezésének menetrendje' (The Program of the Reorganization of Industrial Firms), *Figyelő* (Observer), 7 February 1985, p. 3.
54. Balassa, 'Reforming the New Economic Mechanism in Hungary.'

Essay 14 Next Steps in the Hungarian Economic Reform

INTRODUCTION

This essay will analyze the policies that may be employed to improve the performance of the Hungarian economy. After indicating the need for a restrictive macroeconomic policy and for the efficient promotion of exports, the essay will concentrate on the conditions existing in factor markets. Recommendations will be made for modifying the relative prices of labor and capital and improving the operation of markets for these productive factors in Hungary.

Section I of the essay will review the macroeconomic situation in Hungary and make recommendations for policy changes. Section II will examine the system of incentives applied, with special reference to labor and capital markets. Labor markets will be the subject of section III while Section IV will analyze changes in the volume of investment and its allocation and Section V will focus on capital markets.

I THE MACROECONOMIC SITUATION

In response to the external shocks – slowdown in external demand and deterioration in the terms of trade – of the 1974–8 period, Hungary borrowed extensively abroad, with a view to ensure continued rapid increases in domestic consumption and investment. Owing to the deterioration of export performance and the virtual lack of import substitution[1] foreign borrowing led to the accumulation of a substantial convertible currency debt. Thus, apart from Poland, Hungary's per capita debt surpassed that of any other socialist and developing country in 1978.[2]

In order to improve the situation, the authorities set out to eliminate Hungary's $1.2 billion annual deficit in convertible currency trade. This objective, attained in 1981, was transformed to a goal of a $500–600 million trade surplus in convertible currencies, to permit financing interest payments on the debt, in the aftermath of the Polish debt crisis.

In fact, Hungary's trade surplus in convertible currencies came to exceed $0.5 billion in 1982 and $0.7 billion two years later. The burden of the adjustment was borne by gross domestic investment, which fell by 31 percent between 1978 and 1984 while domestic consumption rose by 9 percent, only slightly less than the 11 percent increase in the gross domestic product during the period.[3]

The improvement in the balance of trade between 1978 and 1984 did not reflect improved export competitiveness as Hungary's export market shares declined to a considerable extent during the period.[4] Rather, it reflected decreases in imports, brought about by cuts in investment activity and by increasingly severe import restrictions.

As the adverse economic effects of these restrictions, *inter alia* on exports, came to be recognized, steps were taken towards the liberalization of imports. The (partial) release of pent-up import demand, accompanied by expansionary monetary and fiscal policies, contributed to the deterioration of Hungary's balance of trade in convertible currencies, with the trade surplus declining to $0.3 billion in 1985.

As to the expansionary measures applied, the National Bank of Hungary provided increased working capital to firms that raised wages over and above the rise in prices, as well as credits to the government that augmented its producer and consumer subsidies, thereby adding to the budget deficit. Correspondingly, domestic consumption rose by 2 percent in 1985, notwithstanding a slight decline in GDP, whereas gross domestic investment decreased by an additional 3 percent.

Hungary's trade balance deteriorated again in 1986 as a 2 to 3 percent rise in consumption, associated with increases in real wages and other incomes, was accompanied by little change in investment, raising the growth of aggregate expenditure above that of GDP (1.5 percent) by a substantial margin. The doubling of the budget deficit, exceeding 4 percent of GDP, and an accommodating monetary policy importantly contributed to these results and Hungary incurred a $0.2 billion deficit in convertible currency trade.

The decrease in the volume of convertible currency exports between 1984 and 1986, in the face of increases in the total imports of Hungary's main trading partners among private market economies, was an important factor in the deterioration of the trade balance. Hungary's continued poor export performance, in turn, was the result of a variety of influences.[5]

To begin with, Hungary's export competitiveness deteriorated to a considerable extent. Calculated by the use of export weights, between 1978 and 1985 the forint appreciated in real terms by 19 percent if the exchange rates are adjusted for changes in wholesale prices, and by 22 percent if the adjustment is made by the use of consumer price indices (Table 13.1).[6]

Furthermore, the fall in investment, accompanied by a substantial decline in the investment share of industries in which Hungary has a comparative advantage,[7] did not permit the transformation of the structure of exports and the upgrading of their technological level.[8] The higher profitability and the lower risk of sales in domestic and in CMEA markets, and the uncertainties associated with increased reliance on case-by-case interventions by the authorities, have further discouraged exports.[9]

Yet, increases in exports is a necessary condition for renewed economic growth in Hungary. Possibilities for efficient import substitution have been well-nigh exhausted in Hungary's small domestic market. Thus, while economizing with raw materials (particularly energy) would bring import savings, economic growth will require the increased availability of foreign exchange through exports as Hungary cannot continue borrowing abroad.

Several measures were taken to promote exports to private market economies in 1986. They include the depreciation of the export exchange rate by 15 percent in real terms, irrespective of whether the wholesale or the consumer price index is used as deflator (Table 13.1); the establishment of four trading houses, together with the elimination of restrictions on the export profile of 38 foreign trade enterprises and the simplification of procedures for obtaining trading rights by industrial firms; increases in profit tax rebates for export-oriented investments from 33 to 50 percent; the elimination of the 15 percent accumulation tax on export-oriented investments, and the concentration of medium-term credits in such investments; reduced interest rates on short-term export credits; wage preferences to firms increasing their exports; and, last but not least, moral suasion.

Incentives to exports to private market economies are warranted as long as import protection and trade arrangements with socialist countries raise the profitability of sales in domestic and in CMEA markets above that obtainable in these exports. But, the preferential treatment of increments in exports, calculated annually, may discourage exports in years when increases cannot be achieved, so as to show a larger rise afterwards. There have also been reports that products which are exported in response to government pressure are imported by other firms at higher prices.[10]

Furthermore, it is feared that firms will be artificially maintained in life in order to avoid a decline in exports and that the exclusive concentration on export-oriented investments will not ensure the efficient allocation of investment funds.[11] At the same time, the provision of credits for export-oriented investments involves a bargaining process concerning the amount of exports pledged for a five-year period and there is uncertainty as to the exports actually undertaken. The bargaining extends to firm-specific measures aimed to maintain and to expand exports with little regard to cost.

The efficient way to promote exports involves establishing an equilibrium exchange rate that provides incentives to exports across the board and permits eliminating measures which safeguard and extend high-cost exports. Furthermore, in raising import prices, the devaluation will serve as a restraint on purchases from private market economies.

It would be desirable to establish the new exchange rate instantaneously, so as to reduce uncertainty that led to postponing exports in the past. In setting the new rate, account should be taken of the fact that the exchange rate for exports, adjusted for changes in wholesale prices, in 1986 represented a 7 percent appreciation in real terms compared with 1978 (10 percent if adjusted by the consumer price index), albeit the shift from borrowing abroad to servicing the external debt would have required a devaluation (Table 13.1).

A customary objection to devaluation in Hungary is its inflationary impact. At the same time, such an effect is necessary in order to offset increases in real incomes in 1985 and 1986, which were not commensurate with changes in domestic production and led to higher imports. Nevertheless, measures would need to be taken to limit the inflationary effect of an once-for-all devaluation and to avoid that it gives rise to an inflationary spiral.

Firms operating under the so-called competitive price system should not be allowed to raise prices on domestic sales in proportion with the rise in export prices that would result from an once-for-all devaluation; nor should prices be adjusted on CMEA sales. Apart from reducing its inflationary effects, this is necessary to enhance the effectiveness of the devaluation that requires increasing the profitability of sales in Western – as against domestic and CMEA – markets through changes in relative prices. And, most importantly, the government should reverse the expansionary monetary and fiscal policies followed in 1985 and in 1986.

II THE SYSTEM OF INCENTIVES

A more general issue concerns the deterioration of the efficiency of Hungarian industry. While total factor productivity, expressing changes in the combined productivity of labor and capital, increased at an average annual rate of 2.8 percent between 1968 and 1978, it fell by 0.6 percent a year between 1969 and 1982 and showed only small improvements in subsequent years.[12]

The increased use of firm-specific interventions after 1978 contributed to the deterioration of efficiency in the Hungarian industry. Poorly-performing enterprises received government support in the form of reductions in taxes, easing of credit conditions, price increases, preferential wage arrangements, and straight subsidies while good performance often led to additional charges. In order to improve the operation of the market mechanism in Hungary, and to enhance the effectiveness of the devaluation, it would be necessary to narrow the scope of firm-specific measures, with a view to their elimination over time, thereby hardening the budget constraint for the firm.

It has been suggested however that, under present conditions, the removal of firm-specific support would result in the bankruptcy of 40–50 percent of Hungarian firms. This has been said to be the case because of the lack of effective labor and capital markets in Hungary.[13]

The statement assumes that firms could not improve the use of their existing resources (increased operational efficiency or the utilization of internal reserves according to the Hungarian terminology). Such is hardly the case, given the low productivity of labor and capital in Hungarian industry that is linked in part to poor work performance and in part to excess labor, hired because of the fear of labor shortages, and the application of a wage system that encouraged lowering average wages through the employment of low-skill labor in the past. At the same time, the soft budget constraint for the firm did not provide a penalty for excessive hiring.

There are examples of substantial improvements in operational efficiency even in private market economies (e.g. Fiat in Italy and Chrysler in the United States) where efficiency levels are relatively high. There have also been cases where improvements have occurred in Hungarian firms in response to the threat of closing down. This has happened in the Hungarian Cable Works, although not in Kontakta, a producer of parts and components, where continued firm-specific support has limited the incentives to do so.[14]

But, unless possibilities exist for increasing production, which may not be the case in poorly-performing firms, improvements in operational efficiency will entail reducing the firm's labor force. This should not be considered undesirable to the extent that the firm sheds labor whose productivity is below its cost. And, the workers thus freed would be available for other activities, where labor shortages exist.

An additional consideration is that the relative prices of labor and capital are distorted in Hungary. The introduction of the 10 percent tax on labor in 1985 provides only a partial offset for the cost of social benefits financed from the government budget. In turn, the cost of capital is augmented by high real interest rates and the price-raising effects of high customs duties on imported machinery, with the accumulation tax further increasing the cost of new investment.

According to one calculation, the profitability of new investments fell from over 30 percent in 1969 to 10 percent in the late 1970s and to nil in 1980–81, with a slight increase to 2 percent in 1982–3.[15] The low profitability of new investments, in turn, entailed a decline in the average profitability of capital in Hungarian industry from over 20 percent to below 15 percent during this period.[16] with after-tax profits amounting only to 4 percent of gross value added in 1985.[17]

In view of the declining profitability of investments, it may come as a surprise to outside observers that there has been excess demand for investment funds in Hungary throughout the period. The solution to this puzzle lies in the existence of a soft budget constraint. Firms have correctly anticipated that they can have recourse to price increases and various other forms of government support to compensate for the low profitability of their investments.

There is thus need to harden the budget constraint for the firm. Also, the relative prices of labor and capital would need to be adjusted. This may be accomplished through changes in the tax system. For one thing, taxes on labor would have to be raised to finance the social benefits provided by the government; for another thing, it would be desirable to reduce duties on capital goods and to eliminate the accumulation tax.

Further changes in the existing regulations would be necessary in order to ensure the adequate operation of labor and capital markets in Hungary. Orderly adjustment requires improvements in the operation of labor markets while capital markets need to provide funds for firms which can sufficiently upgrade their operations to become profitable. Labor and capital markets have the additional function of ensuring the flow of resources from low-profitability to high-profitability activities. The measures that may be taken to improve the operation of these markets will be considered below.

III LABOR MARKETS

Since the mid-1970s the wage bill of Hungarian enterprises in the material-producing sectors has increased substantially relative to profits, with the differences rising to a considerable extent after 1978. Thus, while in 1975 the wage bill approximately equalled profits, the former exceeded the latter by about 40 percent in 1984.[18]

This result may be explained by pressures to raise wages as a result of the excess demand for labor under the soft budget constraint. The hardening of the budget constraint would reduce the labor needs of firms which can improve their operations, and labor will also be released by firms which cannot make the necessary improvements and will close down. One should not fear, however, that these changes would lead to wholesale unemployment.

To begin with, unfilled vacancies exceed 50 000, compared with a loss of altogether 15 000 jobs in 1985, when the intervention of the official labor placement bureau was necessary in only 700 cases to find jobs for the displaced workers.[19] At the same time, the number of unfilled vacancies are understated in Hungary as only a minority of firms utilizes the services of a labor placement bureau, preferring the use of informal channels instead. Furthermore, there is a tendency to underestimate labor mobility by focusing on job opportunities in a particular geographical location and in a particular occupation.

Thus, one should encourage geographical as well as occupational labor mobility. As to the former, there is need to reduce the cost of movement just as the cost of migration is partly financed by the state in certain private market economies through tax allowances. As to the latter, budgetary contributions to the cost of training should be accompanied by assistance to firms that undertake on-the-job training.

Small private firms could also create considerable employment if the conditions for their operation and, in particular, the regulations on the number of workers they can hire, are liberalized. These firms can importantly contribute to providing for the needs of the population and increase competition in Hungarian industry.

The introduction of a six months period of wage payment in the event of the loss of a job, compared with the regular period of one month, and the payment of unemployment compensation for an additional six months by firms that close down some or all of their operations, will ease the transition for workers that have become superfluous. But, notwithstanding the conditions contained in the relevant regulations, there is the danger that the payment of 100 percent of wages for six months, 75 percent for the next three months, and 60 percent for the last three months will induce people to postpone taking a job while working in the second economy as has been the case in Western European countries.

The hardening of the budget constraint would further provide inducement to firms to resist claims for large wage increases. It should also limit wage demands in firms making profits, thereby alleviating the disparities that have arisen as such firms may have raised wages by as much as 18 percent in 1985 and 1986 combined whereas increases were as little as 2–3 percent in firms making losses which are under central wage determination.[20]

In this connection, it should be emphasized that in private market economies wages do not depend on the profitability of the firm. While there may be differences in wages in accordance with differences in labor efficiency, wages tend to be equalized for equivalent work through the operation of the labor market.

This would also happen in a socialist market economy under a hard budget constraint, where profit maximization is the objective of the firm and there is an effective labor (and capital) market. Under these conditions, there would be a tendency towards the equalization of wages as firms would not wish to pay higher wages for equivalent work than others. At the same time, firms that are unprofitable at the going wage would cease their operations.

One would, then, have a situation approaching that of the vgm-s, the acronym for a workers' collective in the firm that undertakes certain tasks after hours for the payment of a fixed sum. More generally, the principle of compensation for work actually performed, applied in the vgm-s, could find application to work done during regular working hours. In this way, one could ensure the profitability of the firm while paying higher wages for more efficient work as is done in the vgm-s.[21]

The introduction of income taxes paid on all personal incomes, irrespective of source, as proposed in the 19–20 November 1986 resolution of the Central Committee of the Hungarian Socialist Workers' Party, would entail partially replacing existing taxes on wages at the firm level. Tax rates would need to be set so as to establish macroeconomic balance in consumer goods markets, which was to have been accomplished so far largely through the taxation of wages at the firm level, and with limited results because the regulations could not be made watertight.

The situation is complicated by reason of the fact that in most firms management is responsible to the workers' collective in Hungary. Now, the danger of excessive wage increases exists in firms making high profits as workers will wish to share in these profits. At the same time, paying dividends to workers may be objected to on the grounds that they are not the owners of the firm. Correspondingly, for the time being, the application of some rules limiting wage increases may be necessary.[22]

IV THE VOLUME OF INVESTMENT AND ITS ALLOCATION

The discussion of capital markets may be prefaced by reference to the availability of investment funds and their allocation in Hungary. The volume of gross domestic investment fell by one-third between 1978 and 1985, with gross fixed investment declining by one-fifth as a considerable decumulation of inventories occurred. However, there was a much larger decline in net investment, i.e., after allowance made for depreciation; net investment did not reach one-third of the 1978 level and hardly exceeded six-tenths of the 1970 level in 1985.

Industry's share of gross fixed investment fell between 1978 and 1985 from 36.9 to 33.2 percent, expressed in terms of constant prices, while the share of agriculture declined from 13.4 to 11.0 percent and that of transportation and communication decreased from 11.6 to 11.3 percent. In the same period, the share of public and private investment in housing rose from 15.9 to 19.2 percent.

Within industry, substantial increases occurred in the investment shares of mining (chiefly coal) and electrical energy, with the former rising from 10.5 to 22.2 percent and the latter from 14.6 to 20.6 percent between 1978 and 1985. As the steel and chemical industries approximately maintained their share in industrial investment (23.6 percent in 1978 and 23.1 percent in 1985), the declines were concentrated in the industries of transformation, in particular engineering (from 18.6 to 12.1 percent) and light industry (from 10.1 to 6.1 percent). By comparison, production shares in 1985 were 12.8 percent for mining and electrical energy, 29.0 percent for steel and chemicals, and 40.8 percent for engineering and light industry.

Yet, it is in the engineering and light industries[23] where Hungary has a comparative advantage, by reason of the availability of relatively low-cost skilled and technical labor. These industries have also experienced increases in total factor productivity in the 1980–84 period while total factor productivity fell in the production of coal, electrical energy, and steel.[24]

The described pattern of investment allocation has thus contributed to the deterioration of the efficiency of Hungarian industry noted in Section II above. Together with the reduction in total industrial investment and the limitations imposed on the importation of machinery from developed countries, it has also led to a decline in the technological level of the Hungarian engineering and light industries *vis-à-vis* private market economies. In this connection, two examples may be of interest.

In contrast to the rapid developments that occurred in private market economies, the growth in the use of numerically-controlled machine tools has slowed down to a considerable extent in Hungary after 1980. Also, the competitiveness of Hungarian industry has suffered as, 'with few exceptions, it has not been possible to establish flexible machinery complexes due to the purchase of numerically controlled machine tools at different times, with different technical levels, programming requirements, and completeness and from different countries and firms, and of different types'[25] when the limited and uncertain availability of investment funds and foreign exchange, contributed to this outcome.

In the textile industry, the average age of Hungarian machinery has been rising and it much exceeds that observed in private market economies. Also, the constraints imposed on new investment and, in particular, on the importation of foreign machinery, has not permitted the vertical integration of operations required by modern production. Correspondingly, labor productivity in the Hungarian textile industry does not reach one-seventh of labor productivity in the developed countries.[26]

For the period of the VIIth Five Year Plan (1986–90), the combined investment share of mining and electrical energy is projected at 42 percent. This compares with relative shares of 27 percent in the 1976–80 and 38 percent in the 1981–85 periods of the Vth and VIth Five Year Plans, respectively, expressed in terms of current prices.[27]

In the case of coal, three alternatives have been put forward, involving prospective annual production volumes of 29, 24, and 17 million tons, compared with 26 million tons in 1985. Even the second alternative would necessitate substantial investments, however, owing to the need for mechanization, as there are few miners to replace those who retire and Hungary has had to import miners from Poland whose number has reached 6–7000. At the same time, domestic production costs exceed the price at which coal can be obtained from Western Germany by 50–60 percent;[28] they reportedly are about 80 percent above the domestic price of coal in Hungary.

The decline in the price of petroleum to $16–18 per barrel on the world market further points to the need for reducing the investment allocation of

Hungarian coal industry. In this connection note that, after having raised the production target to 20 million tons immediately following the May 1981 elections, the French socialist government reduced this target to 11–12 million tons at a time when the oil price was $28 per barrel.[29]

Apart from lowering the investment allocation of the coal industry, the adoption of the 17 million ton production target would permit closing down several high-cost mines in the Northern part of Hungary. Even if the present oil price will not last beyond 4–5 years, nuclear capacity may be brought on stream in the meantime, while making further efforts to lower energy requirements. In fact, Hungary's energy use reportedly exceeds that of private market economies by a considerable margin.

Among the 16 countries for which data are available, in 1983 Hungary led with 49.5 megajoules per dollar of GNP, followed by China (40.5), Romania, the Soviet Union, and Czechoslovakia (between 30 and 40), East Germany, Poland, and Yugoslavia (between 20 and 30), the United States, the United Kingdom, Italy, and West Germany (between 10 and 20), and Japan, Sweden, and France (between 8 and 10).[30] And, while these comparisons are distorted by the choice of exchange rate conversion ratios, and the use of more realistic conversion ratios puts Hungary below other socialist countries as far as energy consumption is concerned, the high density of population should reduce Hungary's transportation needs below that of most other countries.

Lowering energy use per unit of output would require raising energy prices. Fuel oil prices are between one-half and one-third lower in Hungary than in major Western European countries[31] and the consumer prices of household electricity, heating oil and natural gas are greatly subsidized. At the same time, the latter uses are very responsive to price; thus, for the 1970–84 period, the long-term price elasticities of demand were estimated at 1.6 to 2.0, 0.9 to 1.1, and 4.5 to 5.3 in these three uses, respectively.[32]

It would further be necessary to de-emphasize heavy industry, in which Hungary has a comparative disadvantage, owing to the lack of domestic raw materials and the limited availability of capital. Within heavy industry, it would be desirable to reconsider the decision to maintain steel production at present levels, which would involve continued exports at high subsidies. France again provides an example as, following an increase in 1981, production targets were reduced considerably in 1984.[33]

In Hungary, this would involve adopting earlier proposals to reduce capacity by closing down a high-cost steel mill. In this connection, note that, with 57 percent of its steel produced by the inefficient open hearth process and only 11 percent by recycling electric arc, the Soviet Union alone among major steel producing countries has more outdated steel plants than Hungary, where these ratios are 51 and 13 percent. The open hearth process is used to produce 29 to 45 percent of steel in other socialist countries and India, which has extensively applied Soviet technology, but account for less than 10 percent of output in private market economies. At the same time, the share of the electric arc process ranges from 15 to 31 percent in socialist countries and India and between 19 and 61 percent in private market economies.[34]

It would further be desirable to reduce the investment allocation of the heavy chemical industry that was excessively promoted in the 1970s despite its high energy cost. In turn, improvements in the technological level of Hungarian industry and the transformation of the export structure would necessitate increasing investments in the engineering and light industries.

Investments would also be needed to upgrade the food industry, where outdated processing facilities, packaging, and canning have adversely affected the competitiveness of Hungarian products in recent years. And, Hungary has considerable possibilities in developing an integrated industry of aluminium and aluminium products.

However, doubts may be expressed about the desirability of establishing a car assembly facility in Hungary. Apart from the fact that the proposed assembly of 100 000 automobiles a year would not provide the economies of scale necessary for international competitiveness, the proposed project would involve the use of scarce foreign exchange without offsetting exports of parts, components and accessories.

On the example of several other small European countries, a more appropriate solution would be to engage in the production of car parts for assembly abroad, the proceeds of which could be used to purchase automobiles for convertible currencies. And while it has been suggested that the quality of domestic steel is not appropriate for this purpose, high-quality steel could be imported. This would also be necessary for upgrading Hungarian exports of machinery and machine tools. At the same time, it would permit reducing domestic steel production which not only involves high costs but is very energy intensive, requiring on the margin imports for convertible currencies.

There is further need to improve infrastructure, including transportation facilities and, in particular, communications. While Hungary was one of the pioneers in establishing a telephone network, this is now woefully inadequate for meeting the needs of modern industry. This conclusion applies, a fortiori, to the new branches of telecommunications.[35]

The investment needs of modernizing the industries of transformation and providing for the necessary infrastructure may exceed the possible savings attainable in reducing investment plans for basic industries. It would be desirable, therefore, to increase the share of investment in the gross domestic product in Hungary.

It may be objected that, despite recent declines, this share is still relatively high, 25 percent, compared with an average of 21 percent in developed countries and 23 percent in developing countries.[36] But, the Hungarian investment share is overstated by reason of the overestimation of the prices of capital goods relative to consumer products and services that are widely subsidized.

According to one estimate, the adjusted share of gross domestic investment in GDP is 22–23 percent in Hungary.[37] Furthermore, according to official data, the share of net investment in national income did not reach 18 percent in 1985 in terms of current prices and it was only 10 percent in terms of 1980 prices, which still overestimate the share of investment.[38] And whereas the gross investment figure matters for the introduction of new technology, net investment is relevant from the point of view of increases in productive capacity.

The shortage of investment funds, and the lack of possibilities for foreign borrowing, puts a premium on foreign direct investment in Hungary. Such investment has the further advantage of bringing technological, managerial and marketing know-how to Hungarian industry. Also, it is superior to bank loans as it does not involve a fixed income obligation and it is preferable to the purchase of licenses as it ensures the continuous upgrading of technology.

Apart from the two newly-established banks, foreign direct investments totalled only $35 million at the end of 1985, and industrial investments did not exceed $10 million in total. This is explained by the requirements of majority participation of domestic interests, the high rate of taxation, the high duties on imported machinery, the complicated accounting requirements, and the bureaucratic difficulties of granting permission for foreign participation. Also, Hungarian firms that wished to have a foreign partner were reportedly discouraged by the authorities prior to 1986.[39]

The regulations introduced on 1 January 1986 have eased the requirements of majority domestic ownership, reduced the rate of taxation, postponed the payment of duties in imported machinery by five years, strengthened the accounting procedures, and simplified the process of granting permission. Nevertheless, problems remain, including the lack of free utilization of the paid-in foreign exchange contribution of the foreign partner, import licensing, and price control.

The changes in the regulations reportedly led to considerable increases in foreign direct investment in 1986, with concentration in manufacturing industry and banking. Further simplifications of the regulations would be desirable in order to attract foreign direct investment in substantial amounts. More importantly, there is need for the government authorities to make a concerted effort to promote foreign direct investment.

V CAPITAL MARKETS

The shift of investment activity from heavy industry towards the industries of transformation should entail reducing the directive role of the state in investment decisions, thereby reversing recent tendencies toward central-ization. The adverse effects of these tendencies have often been noted in Hungary. In fact, during the 1981–4 period, the state provided 24 percent of investment funds for low-profitability firms, which had an average profit rate fo 1.2 percent, while providing only 4 percent of investment funds for high-profitability firms, which had an average profit rate of 16.3 percent. As a result of government interventions, the rate of investment by the two groups of firms was practically the same, notwithstanding the observed large differences in profitability.[40]

The decentralization of investment decisions would link investments to firm profitability as envisaged by the 19–20 November 1986 Party resolu-tion. In turn, profits would need to be linked more closely to enterprise performance through changes in exchange rates and the hardening the budget constraint for the firm, as suggested above. It would further be desirable to provide incentives for household savings, to promote the use of these savings in efficient investments, and to ensure the movement of funds from low-profitability to high-profitability firms.

Interest rates on savings deposits have traditionally been negative in real terms in Hungary. This is not the case for bonds that have recently been issued for purchase by households. The tax-free interest rate on bonds is 11 percent, compared with 3 to 7 percent on savings deposits. At the same time, experience indicates that bond purchases by households have not been at the expense of savings deposits that are used essentially as a down payment for housing.

In order to step up investment activity, it would be desirable to substan-tially increase bond issues to households, which totalled 5.3 billion forints by mid-1986. This would require facilitating the issue of bonds by indi-vidual firms, as well as improving existing procedures for the trading of bonds.

At present, the government provides a guarantee to bond holders, with identical rates of interest paid on all bonds. Removing the guarantee or, initially, differentiating the guarantee fee, would make the desirability of the bond dependent on the creditworthiness of the issuer, resulting in differences in interest rates depending on risk. There would further be need to establish a secondary market for bonds where transactions are executed under an auction system. The newly-established banks could act as brokers in this market, taking positions in bonds for which they served as underwriters.

Bond issues may also provide a vehicle for the movement of funds among firms. In 1986, only bonds valued at 3.0 billion forints were subscribed by other firms. Rather, firms tend to use their profits and amortization funds in self-investment, with little regard to yield as they expect to be bailed out by the government in the event that the investments sour. The taxing of interest paid on bonds and low interest rates on deposits with the banks also favor self-investment.

The hardening of the budget constraint, together with the elimination of taxes on interest paid on bonds and higher interest rates on bank deposits, would encourage firms with poor investment prospects to lend the funds they have rather than to invest them. The establishment of an active capital market would thus contribute to the flow of funds from low-productivity to high-productivity uses. It would also permit firms in difficulties to borrow money in order to improve their operations, provided that they have favorable prospects for the future.

In fact, it would be desirable to permit the issue of securities of varying maturities by the firms, with bonds providing for their investment needs and commercial paper for working capital.[41] In this connection, reference may be made to the experience of China that has recently allowed the issue of commercial paper by state enterprises.

Beyond their role in the bond market, the newly-established commercial banks would perform important functions of financial intermediation in Hungary. At the same time, for the banking system to operate efficiently, one should ensure that the banks act on the basis of business principles and there is sufficient competition among them. Various measures would need to be taken in order to establish the conditions for the pursuit of these objectives.

To begin with, the banks should be free to decide on their lending operations, thus limiting the role of plan priorities and central guidelines. This suggests the need to increasingly regulate bank lending through reserve requirements, with the refinancing by the National Bank envisaged at present assuming a subsidiary role. Also, the banks should be given the right to collect time and savings deposits that is not actually the case.

Furthermore, the banks should be made fully responsible for profits and losses in their operations, and their profits should be subject to taxes at the same rate as the profits of industrial enterprises. These measures would aim at providing them with incentives to maximize profits.

Finally, competition would need to be ensured by reducing size differences among the commercial banks and avoiding specialization according to industries and regions. For the same reason, it would be desirable to establish additional commercial banks, including those with foreign participation.

It would further be desirable to increase the autonomy of the five financial institutions that have been created to foster innovation in Hungary. These institutions should be provided with their own funds and their decision-making power over centrally-allocated funds increased.

The next question concerns the practical application of the bankruptcy law, under which firms may be rehabilitated or closed down as conditions warrant. Apart from the liquidation during the 1970s of the Hungarian hat-making factory, the products of which ceased to be demanded, there are only two recent cases where a state enterprise has been closed down in Hungary. And, while 47 firms are under review in the application of the new bankruptcy law, which became effective on 1 September 1986, these are mostly small firms and co-operatives.[42]

Yet, the problems have been concentrated in large state enterprises. In 1982, 11 large firms accounted for 80 percent of accumulated losses of state enterprises and in 1984 there were 11 large enterprises (the two lists overlap to a considerable extent) that experienced losses over several years.[24] This is hardly surprising, given that the establishment of large firms in Hungary did not respond to economic imperatives but was the result of industrial concentration undertaken on non-economic grounds prior to, as well as following, the implementation of the 1968 reforms.

In recent years, steps have been taken to break up large firms, which had a quasi-monopoly position. But the government has continued to favor large firms of low profitability with investment funds. Thus, in the 1982–4 period, the 73 largest firms had an average profit rate of 5.4 percent but, with the government providing 37 percent of their investment funds, had a higher rate of investment than the next group of large firms, which had an average profit rate of 7.2 percent and received 17 percent of their investment funds from the state, and small and medium-size firms, which had an average profit rate of 8.1 percent and received 9.5 percent of their investment funds from the state. As a result, the rate of investment of the 73 largest firms exceeded that of the other two groups.[44]

Breaking-up large firms would permit separating well-operating units from those that cannot be made profitable. At the same time, in limiting closings to certain units within individual firms, one can avoid the political dilemma involved in the bankruptcy of large enterprises.

Much attention has been given recently to the rehabilitation of firms that are in difficulties. In this connection, it should be noted that in the past such efforts have remained temporary and the problems have re-emerged soon afterwards.[45] At the same time, the budgetary cost has been substantial, amounting to over Ft 10 billion a year. As noted by Gyula Csáki, a Deputy Finance Minister, these unfavorable results find their origin in the emphasis on financial rescue operations, generally subject to bargaining between the firms and the government without an overall plan for the rehabilitation of the firms' productive activity.[46]

The new bankruptcy law provides for the preparation of an overall plan to rehabilitate firms in difficulties. Nevertheless, as an informed observer noted, the danger exists that rehabilitation becomes a slogan that is invoked by every firm in difficulty in order to obtain financing, thereby imposing a large burden on the government budget and on the national economy.[47] Yet, in view of Hungary's overall financial limitations, there is a choice between making financing available for the development of efficient enterprises and for trying to save inefficient ones. Correspondingly, emphasis would need to be given to the use of the firm's own resources in effecting improvements in its operations.

An additional consideration is that continuing losses of inefficient enterprises represent a considerable drain on resources. Closing-down enterprises would thus contribute to the reallocation of resources to more efficient uses. At the same time, the sale of the assets of closed-down enterprises may not only bring financial returns but permit a more productive use of these assets.

And, once bankruptcy proceedings are initiated, other firms may reinforce their efforts to improve operations and to avoid excessive wage increases.[28] Thus, while it has been suggested to keep such proceedings *in camera*, there is rather need to give them considerable publicity so as to increase their 'educational' effect.

CONCLUSIONS

This essay has reviewed the macroeconomic situation and made recommendations for a restrictive macroeconomic policy and for the efficient promotion of exports in Hungary. Note has further been taken of the need to harden the budget constraint facing the firm by limiting, and over time eliminating, firm-specific financial support that is to be replaced by overall macroeconomic policies regulating aggregate demand. This should be accompanied by measures taken to ensure the adequate operation of labor and capital markets while adjusting the relative prices of these factors of production.

In regard to labor markets, emphasis has been given to measures aimed at ensuring labor mobility and avoiding excessive wage increases. In turn, a variety of measures may be used to increase the availability and to ensure the efficient use of capital in Hungary.

Investment activity may be stepped up by limiting wage increases, broadening the availability of financial instruments to households, and extending recent measures aimed at attracting foreign direct investments. At the same time, there is need to reorient investment activity from the energy sector and heavy industry towards the industries of transformation, with greater scope given to firm decision-making in the process.

The efficient allocation of investments would further be promoted by broadening the scope for the flow of financial resources among firms through the bond market and via the banks. At the same time, it should be ensured that the banks act as profit-making institutions and there is sufficient competition among them.

Closing-down inefficient firms would also free financial resources for more efficient uses while care should be exercised that the rehabilitation of poorly-functioning firms is not done at the expense of efficient enterprises. Rather, the emphasis should be on the use of the firms' own resources in effecting improvements in operations.

Another important issue is the need to establish 'property interest,' with a view to increasing the value of the firm.[49] This raises the question of valuation by financial markets as well as ownership rights. An analysis of these questions is left for a later occasion.

NOTES

1. B. Balassa, 'The Hungarian Economic Reform, 1968–82,' *Banca Nazionale del Lavoro Quarterly Review*, XXXVI (1983) pp. 163–84 and Essay 12 in Bela Balassa *Change and Challenge in the World Economy* (London: Macmillan, 1985) pp. 261–8.
2. The relevant figure for Hungary was $545 per head, compared with $571 in Poland, $506 in Yugoslavia, $501 in Mexico, $379 in Brazil, $337 in Argentina, $272 in Turkey and $232 in Romania. The data derive from international sources and refer to gross public and private debt.
3. Unless otherwise noted, all data originate in official Hungarian sources.
4. Essay 13 in this volume.
5. In addition to the factors noted below, reference may be made to the loss of food exports due to Chernobyl that may have amounted to $80 million in 1986.
6. While the results are explained in part by the depreciation of the Yugoslav dollar, the Hungarian forint appreciated to a considerable extent *vis-à-vis* the German mark and the Austrian shilling as well.
7. See Section IV below.
8. In particular, Hungary's market share in the developed countries' imports of machinery and equipment fell from 1.25 percent in 1980 to less than 0.8 percent in 1985. *Figyelő* (Observer), 26 June 1986, p. 9. The same source notes that, owing to the low degree of technical sophistication of Hungary's manufactured exports, average unit values declined while increases were experienced elsewhere.
9. Evidence on the latter point is provided in Essay 13 in this volume, where note has been taken of several additional factors contributing to losses in export market shares.
10. *Figyelő* (Observer), 25 September 1986.
11. According to one author, 'it is an error to assume that we can increase our export capacity by promoting exclusively export-oriented investments. The experience of the last several years indicates that such actions could help the situation of external equilibrium only for a short time. The permanent improvement of our [competitive] position is possible only through the *overall improvement* of conditions in our national economy.' I. Barta, 'A beruházási szféra feloldásra váró ellentmondásai' (The Contradictions of the Investment Sphere Requiring a Solution), *Közgazdasági Szemle* (Economic Review), XXXXIII (1986) p. 840 (italics in the original).
12. L. Csernenszky, and K. Demeter, 'A struktúra változása – a változás strukturája' (Transformation of Structure and Structure of Transformation), *Figyelő* (Observer), 19 June 1986, p. 7.
13. M. Tardos, 'A szabályozott piac kialakitásának feltételei' (Conditions for the Development of a Regulated Market), *Közgazdasági Szemle* (Economic Review), XXXII (1985) pp. 1290–92.
14. *Figyelő* (Observer) 21 August 1986, p. 6 and 5 December 1985, p. 4.
15. A. Kunvári, 'Miért jutott holtpontra beruházásaink jövedelmezősége?' (Why

has the Profitability of our Investments Reached the Zero Point?), *Közgazdasági Szemle* (Economic Review), XXXIII (1986) p. 828.

16. Ibid., p. 828.
17. Ibid.
18. Ibid., p. 832.
19. K. Gulyás, 'Válás magyar módra' (Divorce Hungarian Style), *Figyelő* (Observer), 18 September 1986, pp. 1, 6.
20. G. Révész, 'Bérezés an 1980-as évek Magyarországán' (Wage Setting in the Hungary of the 1980s), *Közgazdasági Szemle* (Economic Review), XXXIII (1986) pp. 809–24.
21. This point is made in O. Pirityi, 'Viszaforditható-e a folyamat?' (Could One Reverse the Tendency?), *Figyelő* (Observer), 6 March 1986, p. 5.
22. It is a different question that one should avoid the error of announcing in advance that above a certain annual wage increment the wage tax will become practically prohibitive in the following period, thereby inducing excessive wage increases before the end of the year. This occurred in Hungary, leading to average increases in wage payments of 17.2 percent, including year-end bonuses, in November–December 1985, compared with the corresponding period of the previous year, as against the year earlier figure of 9.0 percent. Cf. *Figyelő* (Observer), 6 March 1986, p. 3.
23. It may be added that while the Common Market countries limit the importation of textiles and clothing, Hungary has considerable possibilities for upgrading these exports and to export elsewhere.
24. Csernenszky and Demeter, 'A struktura változása – a változás strukturája,' p. 3.
25. Z. Nádudvari, 'Számvezérlésű szerszámgépek. Fejlett technika-félállásban' (Numerically-Controlled Machine Tools. Developed Technology-Halfway), *Figyelő* (Observer), 16 October 1986, p. 7.
26. *Figyelő* (Observer) 2 October 1986.
27. However, according to the figures cited in the Five Year Plan document, the investment share of mining and electrical energy was 43 percent in terms of 1984 prices in 1981–5.
28. Interview by Ferenc Vissi, the Deputy President of the Material and Price Board, reported in *Figyelő* (Observer), 6 March 1986, p. 3.
29. See Essay 17 in this volume.
30. W. V. Chandler, 'The Changing Role of Market in National Economies,' Worldwatch Paper 72 (Washington, DC; Worldwatch Institute, 1986) Table 2.
31. Ibid., Table 10.
32. I. Dobozi, 'An Empirical Estimation of Price Responsiveness of Hungarian Economy: The Case of Energy Demand,' paper prepared for the Tenth U.S. – Hungarian Economic Roundtable held on 1–5 December 1986 in Budapest.
33. Essay 17 in this volume.
34. Chandler, 'The Changing Role of Market in National Economies,' Table 3.
35. As stated in a summary of articles dealing with telephones, 'a service industry that is one of the most dynamic (if not the most dynamic) in the world has gotten to the brink of bankruptcy in our country in recent years. The neglect of the development of infrastructure over several decades greatly contributed to this desperate situation,' *Figyelő* (Observer), 7 August 1986, p. 3.
36. World Bank, *World Development Report 1986* (Washington, DC; 1986) Table 5.
37. Barta, 'A beruházási szféra feloldásra váró ellentmondásai,' p. 836.
38. According to the same author, the 12 percent share of net investment in 1984

in constant prices was only 8 percent if adjustment is made for price distortions (Barta, p. 836).

39. Interview by Béla Csikós-Nagy in *Figyelő* (Observer), 16 January 1986.
40. E. Várhegyi, 'Utolsó pár előre fuss?' (From Last to be First), *Figyelő* (Observer), 4 December 1986, p. 5. As discussed further below this has meant promoting large firms of low profitability.
41. The proposed changes would also permit alleviating the constraints imposed on the firm by the central regulation of working capital that has been justly criticized. Cf. O. Gadó, 'Meg kell szüntetni a tartós készlet mérési módszerének kőzponti előirását' (Need to Abolish the Central Determination of the Measurement of Inventory Needs) *Figyelő* (Observer), 16 October 1986, p. 3.
42. *Figyelő* (Observer) 19 September 1986.
43. G. Lamberger, E. Szalai, and E. Voszka, 'Válságkezelés és vállalalatmegszűntetések' (Crisis Management and the Closing Down of Firms), *Valóság* (Reality), XXIX (1986) pp. 24–31.
44. Várhegyi, 'Utolsó pár előre fuss?', p. 5.
45. M. Laki, 'A gazdaságirányitós és a vállalati valság' (The Guidance of the National Economy and Level Crisis), *Kűlgazdaság* (External Economy), XXIX (1985) pp. 41–58.
46. *Figyelő* (Observer), 11 September, p. 1.
47. G. Varga, 'Tiszta vizet a pohárba' (Put Clear Water in the Glass), *Figyelő* (Observer), 20 March 1986, p. 3.
48. This will not happen as long as firms can confidently expect government support. Thus, it has been reported that two large firms in difficulties raised wage costs by about 10 percent in 1985. Cf. *Figyelő* (Observer), 5 December 1985, p. 4 and 25 September 1986, p. 7.
49. For perceptive analyses, see Tardos and J. Bársony, 'A vagyonérdekeltség kialakitásának problémái' (Problems Related to Interest in Enterprise Property), *Kőzgazdasági Szemle* (Economic Review), XXXIII (1986) pp. 435–53.

Essay 15   China's Economic Reforms in a Comparative Perspective

INTRODUCTION

This essay will briefly review the economic reforms introduced in China after 1978, analyze the performance of Chinese agriculture and industry following the reforms, and examine prospective changes in the future. In regard to the individual topics, the experience of European socialist countries and, in particular, that of Hungary will be noted, based largely on the writings of the author.[1]

Section I will discuss the experience of agriculture with economic reform. Following a brief statement on industrial reform and performance (Section II), planning and markets (Section III), competition and profit incentives (Section IV), price reform (Section V), and wages and bonuses (Section VI) will receive detailed consideration. Finally, in Section VII the macroeconomic requirements of the reform will be examined.

I AGRICULTURAL REFORMS AND PERFORMANCE

As in the case of Hungary, the first major reforms in China were introduced in agriculture. After 1978, agricultural prices were substantially raised, resulting in improvements in agriculture's terms of trade. Also, mandatory quotas for sown area and output were eliminated and purchase (compulsory procurement) quotas reduced, with the sale of above-quota output on free markets and increased possibilities were provided for undertaking so-called sideline activities. Finally, the commune system gave place to family responsibility systems, among which the bao gan dao hu[2] has come to dominate, accounting for 94 percent of peasant households in 1984.

There are similarities as well as differences in the agricultural reforms introduced in China and in Hungary. Agricultural prices were raised in both cases; however, Hungary abolished the system of compulsory delivery as early as 1957. But, it retained the co-operatives as basic farming units while giving greater scope to household plots, with production on these plots accounting for one-third of agricultural output. Finally, similar to the case of China, Hungary encouraged the expansion of the sideline activities.

There are several reasons for the observed differences in the institutional structure. The Hungarian farming cooperatives are relatively small, possess considerable flexibility, and provide performance incentives to their members whereas the Chinese communes were huge, unwieldy units. Also, the high degree of mechanization in Hungarian agriculture has necessitated the maintenance of large production units that has not been the case in China.

In response to the reforms, per capita grain production in China rose by one-sixth between 1978 and 1985, although the acreage devoted to the cultivation of grains declined. As grains accounted for a large proportion of total acreage, land under other crops increased considerably, notwithstanding some decline in the total sown area.[3] With rising yields, the per capita output of cotton rose by two-thirds, that of oilseeds, sugar, and tobacco approximately doubled, and substantial increases were observed also in the case of minor crops. Assisted further by the expansion of livestock raising and sideline activities, per capita gross agricultural output grew by two-thirds, with crop output per head rising by two-fifths during the 1978–85 period.[4] According to one estimate, about one-half of the increase in farm output (crops and livestock) between 1978 and 1984 can be attributed to increases in inputs and one-half to the growth of total factor productivity, which had fallen in the preceding 26 years.[5]

The rapid rise of agricultural output was achieved, even though the share of agriculture in budget allocation for new investment and for current expenditures fell during the period and the agricultural credit system restrained investment, with increases in rural deposits substantially exceeding the rise in lending to agriculture.[6] Also, due to uncertainty about land tenure, private investments in agriculture concentrated in housing.

It has been suggested that increases in prices might have led to the rise in output even in the absence of organizational changes.[7] But, in Soviet Central Asia, cited as evidence in support of this proposition, increases in agricultural production were much smaller than in China. And, the observed rise in yields could not have been accomplished under the commune system, where the link between performance and rewards was lacking. This conclusion is supported by the findings of a cross-section investigation, which shows that the growth of agricultural production was positively correlated with the extent to which the family responsibility system was applied in individual provinces in the early 1980s.[8]

The reduction in the number of agricultural commodities under compulsory procurement from 29 to 10 in 1984, followed by the replacement of compulsory procurement quotas by purchases under contract for grains and cotton, represent a further easing of controls although the state will continue to set the purchase price under the contracts. Zhao Ziyang, the Premier of the State Council, announced that agricultural prices and purchase quotas will be further liberalized in the future, with a view to developing exports.[9] In this connection, comparisons of domestic agricultural prices with world market prices offer an interest.

According to a study of the Research Institute of Prices, in 1984 the average purchase prices for 18 major agricultural products were, on the average, 26 percent lower than world market prices, with large disparities shown among commodities. Thus, average prices paid for wheat were 22 percent and for oil and fat 17 percent higher than prices on the world market while cotton and jute prices were 28 percent and average prices for animal products 48 percent lower than world market prices.[10]

In 1985, prices for pigmeat were raised to a considerable extent, so as to encourage production through improved profitability that was compromised as a result of earlier increases in the prices of feed grains. This change conforms to the price relationships found on the world market. Further changes in this direction would be desirable to permit the exploitation of China's comparative advantage in agricultural products, with account taken of the possible effects of Chinese exports and imports on world market prices.

Thus, China could export rice if its quality improved, although large exports would depress the world market price. Rapid expansion of Chinese exports of cotton, jute, and tea may also lower world market prices somewhat. However, for all remaining products, in particular for potential new exports, world market prices will provide an appropriate guide.

In the statement referred to above, the Premier of the State Council noted the possibility that in the coastal areas, where considerable potential exists for exports, as well as in areas suitable for forestry and animal husbandry, peasants may in the future pay a tax instead of delivering grain to the state. This alternative may be generalized by freeing markets for all agricultural products and replacing sales to the state at below-market prices, which represent an implicit tax, by a land tax.[11]

Such changes would contribute to the growth of agricultural output and incomes through increased intraregional and interregional specialization, complemented by international trade. This is of particular importance since the large gains in yields, obtained chiefly through increased work effort, better organization, and improved marketing, could not be duplicated in the future. At the same time, the introduction of a land tax would also permit reducing interregional income inequalities that result from differences in the quality of land both within and among regions.[12]

The development of Chinese agriculture would further require the increased availability of modern inputs, such as fertilizer, agricultural machinery, and improved seeds, as well as credit and support services. While higher agricultural prices would permit peasants to pay for modern inputs without the granting of input subsidies that tend to encourage their excessive use, improvements in infrastructure and the provision of extension services and research have to be a governmental responsibility as the social benefits exceed the benefits to the individual peasants.

Finally, there is need to encourage investments by the peasants themselves. This would require changing existing land tenure arrangements. Short of the privatization of land, granting its use for a period of, say, 30–40 years and permitting the transfer of the contract would provide inducements to investment.

II INDUSTRIAL REFORMS AND PERFORMANCE

The expression 'responsibility system,' originally applied to agriculture, has come to be employed in reference to state-owned industry as well. It is used to refer to the increased role of material incentives, including profit retention schemes and productivity-based bonuses, the enhanced power of managers *vis-à-vis* party officials in the affairs of the firm, and the greater latitude given to the firm for making its own production and investment decisions, with above-quota output sold to consumers either directly or indirectly through commercial channels.

But, whereas under the family responsibility system there is a direct link between performance and reward, in state-owned industry the link is indirect through profit allocation and bonus schemes, when profits are affected by factors extraneous to the firm, in particular prices, and profit retention by the firm depends on the norm established by the supervisory authorities. Also, with reductions in the scope of compulsory deliveries, together with the encouragement of sideline activities, the scope of market-oriented activities has been greater in agriculture than in industry, and the share of these activities in industry has varied considerably among firms. By contrast, Hungary abolished plan targets on 1 January 1968.

Following an initial slowdown, the growth of industrial output accelerated in China.[13] At the same time, while greater reliance on markets has encouraged production for the needs of the population, the pursuit of profits has often led to changes in the product mix that did not conform to demand. Also, there is conflicting evidence in regard to changes in the efficiency of industry in China.

According to one study, the ratio of value added net of depreciation to output value increased by 6 percent between 1978 and 1981.[14] However, other researchers found a decline rather than an increase in the share of value added in industrial output for the same period, with value added rising by 19.4 percent and output volume by 22.9 percent, both expressed in 1970 prices.[15] Also, available estimates show that total factor productivity in state-owned industry declined between 1978 and 1983 as the 28.4 percent growth in net output involved a 49.3 percent increase in capital and a 16.7 percent rise in employment.[16]

III PLANNING AND MARKETS

In contradistinction to Hungary, after 1978 China maintained plan targets for its state-owned firms. While planning has subsequently been liberalized, the products remaining subject to mandatory plans continue to represent a substantial segment of industry, with estimates ranging from 20 percent upwards. The products in question include coal, crude oil, petroleum products, rolled steel, nonferrous metals, timber, cement, electricity, chemical materials and fertilizer, synthetic fibers, cigarettes, newsprint, imported machinery and equipment, as well as munitions. For these products, the state continues to set production quotas and prices, although above-quota sales are permitted at so-called floating prices.

The 20 October 1984 Decision of the Central Committee stated that 'other products and economic activities [i.e. those not subject to mandatory quotas] . . . should either come under guidance planning or be left entirely to the operation of the market, as the case may require.'[17] However, the meaning of guidance planning has not been clarified, and a large number of products, which do not come under mandatory planning, are subject to quota allocation for part of their output, with the rest marketed outside the plan at floating prices.

The two-tier system of sales and prices increases the freedom of decision-making for the firm, but may have adverse effects on the national economy. Since raising the quota allocation of inputs and reducing that of output may affect the firm's profits to a much greater extent than any improvements in production, bargaining and influence-peddling are at a premium. Nor should it be assumed that profitability at the prices of above-quotas sales represents social profitability, in part because these prices differ from equilibrium prices that would obtain in the absence of quotas, and in part because the prices of capital and labor do not reflect scarcity relationships.

In order for China to reap the benefits of a market-oriented economy, it would have to reduce the number of commodities subject to mandatory planning, and to phase out quotas on all other products, relying on indirect policy instruments, such as taxes and monetary policy to guide enterprises. Furthermore, one should reaffirm the freedom of decision-making for the enterprise *vis-à-vis* the various surrogates for the central planning authorities, including the industrial bureaus and corporations as well as the 'guiding' role assigned to localities, which have assumed importance in recent years. As one observer noted:

In the early stages of reform implementation the position of enterprises was enhanced and the 'excessive' control previously exercised by their immediate supervisors criticized. . . . Starting in 1980 and especially with the campaign to promote ERSs [economic responsibility systems] of

1981, the orientation of reforms shifted to the next higher level in the industrial management – the bureaus and corporations. Under the ERS these organizations commonly determine all of the key financial provisions of incentive schemes affecting their subordinate enterprises.[18]

According to the same author,

> there are good economic reasons why in many cases decentralization should not proceed all the way down to the enterprise level. In particular, decentralization of investment decisions and control over investment funds to enterprises is likely to generate an inefficient and duplicative pattern of investment, in the absence of effective financial intermediation of the banking system.[19]

Decision-making on investment should not be divorced, however, from responsibility for profits and losses since otherwise profitability considerations will not appropriately enter into investment decisions. In this connection, the experience of Hungary offers an interest.

At the time of the introduction of the economic reform, it was decided to decentralize investment decisions in manufacturing industries, except for large investments that substantially added to capacity in a particular industry and for the establishment of new enterprises. In subsequent years, however, there were increased government interventions in investment decisions in linking the provision of budget support to state preferences.

Eventually, it came to be understood that the sharing of responsibility for the investment decision was not conducive to efficiency, and firms were provided with the opportunity to request government aid in the event that the investment proved to be unprofitable. Correspondingly, steps have been taken to restore decision-making authority on investment to the enterprise.

China is well-advised to follow Hungary's example in linking investment decisions to responsibility for profits and losses at the firm level, with government organizations retaining decision-making authority only over large investments in basic industries and the establishment of enterprises of nation-wide importance. Thus, the recent inclusion of investments by collective and individual enterprises in the overall state plan[20] represents a backward step. Rather than relying on central interventions, duplication in investment may be avoided through competition and rational pricing.

At the same time, to the extent that the industrial bureaus and corporations combine firms manufacturing particular products, as in the case of shipbuilding and the automotive industry, competition will be reduced. In any case, the industrial bureaus and corporations, established through the transformation of government offices, have remained administrative organizations imposed on the enterprises. In order to free enterprise decision

making from undue interference, similar organizations have been eliminated in Hungary.

Nor does the regional decentralization of administrative organizations
represent an appropriate solution. Localities have played an important role
in recent years in setting profit conditions for the enterprise and, under a
recent State Council decision, the Ministry of Machine Building Industry
will delegate its management power to the major cities where subordinate
enterprises are located. Apart from the division of decision-making authority, the problem associated with this arrangement is that local interests
may predominate over the national interest.[21]

In the event, there have been repeated reports of the localities setting
barriers to incoming products and to the sale of raw materials in other
regions. Not unlike the case of the Soviet Union at the time of the
regionalization of decision-making, such actions aim at increasing regional
self-sufficiency. This objective has also been served by investments undertaken by localities, which have assumed increasing importance notwithstanding the central government's exhortations to the contrary.

In presenting the Sixth Five Year Plan, the Premier of the State Council
underlined the need that 'no locality or department shall make investment
in fixed assets outside the plan without prior approval by the appropriate
higher authorities.'[22] As unplanned investments nevertheless increased
rapidly, the need for checking their growth was repeatedly stated. Yet, in
the first seven months of 1985, unplanned investments were 95 percent
higher than in the corresponding period in 1984, bringing the average
increase of new fixed investments (in Chinese parlance, investments in
capital construction) to 45 percent, although planned investments rose by
only 9 percent.[23]

Investments by localities, undertaken to the neglect of national economic considerations, have led to considerable duplication of capacity.
The financing of these investments has been accomplished in part by
withdrawing funds from enterprises and in part by borrowing from the
local branches of banks. Increasing the freedom of action of the enterprises
would limit the availability of the first of these sources of funds while the
second may be dealt with through the reform of the banking system,
discussed below.

IV COMPETITION AND PROFIT INCENTIVES

Freeing enterprises from the dominance of the central and local authorities
is a necessary step towards assuring that they bear 'complete responsibility
for profits and losses' and that 'all enterprises compete on an equal footing'
– the stated objectives of the Seventh Five Year.[24] This is because instructions and interventions by supervisory organizations cannot fail to affect

the economic performance of the firm and the conditions under which it operates.

In this connection, it should be emphasized that the firm's profits and the conditions of competition depend to a considerable extent on its relationships with the supervising organizations and on its bargaining power in obtaining favorable treatment in the allocation of materials, the extent of above-quota sales, and the setting of profit targets (compensating taxes). Hierarchical differences among the supervising organizations have been further sources of differentiation among enterprises.[25]

Competition has also been limited by the desire of industrial bureaus and corporations to safeguard all firms under their jurisdiction. Protection at the provincial and local level, referred to earlier, has represented another limitation to competition. According to one observer 'barriers to inter-regional trade erected by local and provincial governments may well be the most serious obstacle to the development of competition and resulting benefits like efficiency improvements and increased regional special-ization.'[26]

Apart from removing obstacles to competition, the pursuit of the stated objectives would require that the director of the enterprise be given full power to manage the firm's affairs. Thus far, directors have been freed from the tutelage of party committees in about one-third of the industrial firms; the rest should follow under the decision of the Central Committee, which calls for establishing 'a system of the director or manager assuming full responsibility' for the firm.[27] This objective was reconfirmed by Premier Zhao Ziyang in his report on the Seventh Five-Year Plan[28] and a new directive to this effect was promulgated on 1 October 1986.[29]

Responsibility for the firm's operations means making the manager financially interested in the profits and losses of the enterprise. In addition to decision-making power over the distribution of enterprise funds, the director, and management in general, should share in the profits of the firm in the form of bonuses and in the losses through reductions in compensa-tion. At the same time, unless they can be rehabilitated, enterprises experiencing continuing losses would have to be eventually closed down.

The need for closing down enterprises that could not meet the test of the market has been recognized in the Decision of the Central Committee, according to which 'our enterprises are put to the test of direct judgment by consumers in the market place so that only the best survive'.[30] But while a considerable number of collective enterprises have closed their doors in recent years, this has reportedly been the case for only one state-owned firm.

At the same time, there would be need to introduce bankruptcy legisla-tion regulating the conditions and the modalities of closing down firms as has already been done in Hungary. However, for profits and losses to reflect enterprise performance in the context of the national economy, prices need to express resource scarcities. This, in turn, leads to the question of the rationality of prices and the need for price reform in China.

V PRICE REFORM

Official prices in China are the result of governmental decisions taken at different points of time and for different purposes. They correspond neither to production costs nor to market conditions, and the few adjustments made since 1978 have changed the situation but little. Yet, price distortions favor some enterprises and penalize others; provide the wrong signals for production and investment; and entail a cost for the national economy.

To begin with, price distortions exist in input-output relationships. For example, the revenue derived from exporting one ton of granular active charcoal is $800 while exporting the fuel necessary for its production would bring $1680.[31] More generally, prices are low for energy and raw materials and high for finished products, compared with world market prices. On the average, the domestic prices of petroleum and petroleum products are 78 percent, and the prices of metallurgical products 47 percent, below world market prices. In turn, the prices for 21 chemical products are, on the average, 80 percent higher than world market prices and the prices of steel-based products also tend to be higher.[32]

Distortions in the relative prices of inputs and outputs encourage the excessive use of energy and raw materials and discourage increasing their production. Furthermore, distortions in the prices of substitute products raise the economic cost of providing for domestic consumption. For example, despite the adjustments made in 1982, the domestic prices of cotton yarn and raw silk are 35 to 74 percent lower, and the prices of polyester and polyamide filaments 97 to 113 percent higher, than world market prices.[33]

Furthermore, artificial differences in the prices of the enterprise's products have an adverse impact on the users, and hence on the national economy, in reducing product variety and compelling users to buy products that do not fully conform to their needs. This is of particular importance in the case of intermediate products, where the unavailability of the requisite variety adds to costs and reduces product quality.

It has been reported, for example, that a zinc smelter has abandoned the production of Grade 2 electrolytic zinc that had a similar cost but a lower price than Grade I zinc. For the same reason, a cement factory has ceased to produce lower grades of cement.[34] Also, steel products do not conform to requirements because of artificial differences in their prices. Thus, it has been reported that the profit margin is ten times as high on hot-rolled steel than on cold-rolled steel,[35] thereby favoring the production of the former over the latter.

Finally, high-quality product varieties are in excess demand, and low-quality varieties in excess supply, leading to shortages in the first case and to the accumulation of unsold inventories in the second. Prices do not perform their equilibrating function as the maximum price differential for consumer goods of different qualities has been set at 15 percent.[36]

These considerations indicate the need for price reform. Such reform is necessary, first of all, to ensure that profits and losses reflect the enterprise's performance rather than the vagaries of the price system. The setting of profit quotas and, more recently, the imposition of differential taxes on profits, designed to compensate for profit differentials that are unrelated to performance, cannot adequately cope with the situation.

To begin with, compensating taxes are levied on existing profits that may result from favorable prices but may also reflect superior performance. Also, the setting of these taxes is subject to bargaining and may depend on the favoritism shown by the supervising organizations in regard to particular enterprises. And while periodic price adjustments are made for unfavorable changes in the underlying conditions of the enterprise, e.g. increases in the prices of inputs, an asymmetry is introduced by the fact that enterprises tend to conceal favorable changes in these conditions.[37]

Apart from eliminating the effects of price distortions on profits, the price reform would channel the energies of the enterprise from trying to obtain better treatment by the supervisory organizations to improving performance. It would further contribute to the objective of having enterprises compete on an equal footing. In turn, the appropriate valuation of fixed capital, with realistic charges made for their use, would permit eliminating differences in profits due to the age and the technical level of machinery in the enterprise.

Establishing realistic prices would also avoid the enterprise choosing to manufacture products on the basis of their favorable prices. At the same time, greater price differentiation is necessary to establish equilibrium in product markets by providing appropriate signals for consumers as well as for producers.

Greater price differentiation would bring about an increase in demand for low-quality varieties, and a decrease in demand for high-quality varieties, of a particular product. This is of especial importance in regard to imports that have been encouraged by relatively low prices of high-quality products.[38] Appropriate pricing provides a better way to limit the imports of consumer goods than controls, which invite evasion through smuggling and bribery.

Greater price differentiation would also encourage the manufacture of high-quality products and discourage that of low-quality products. Apart from contributing to product upgrading, this would permit avoiding a situation when new capacity is created by existing firms, as well as by firms entering the industry, to manufacture outdated products for which there is little demand, in response to misleading price signals.

Market-clearing prices would thus permit demand to guide production decisions. Furthermore, apart from providing incentives for energy and material savings, establishing appropriate price relationships as between inputs and outputs would encourage low-cost transformation activities while discouraging high-cost activities. More generally, rational prices would contribute to efficient resource allocation through changes in consumption, production, and trade.

The existing two-tier system of prices provides a basis for establishing market-clearing prices in China. In this connection, the interdependence of pricing and competition should be emphasized, when the possibilities for effective competition depend on the size of the domestic market. Comparisons with Hungary offer an interest in this regard.

At the time of the introduction of the reform, Hungarian industry was greatly concentrated, with monopoly positions existing in some industries and oligopolistic market structures in others. In order to increase the scope of market prices, efforts were made to establish competition by breaking up trusts and large enterprises. Still, in a number of industries, the extent of competition is limited by the smallness of Hungary's domestic market, necessitating import competition.

While population is not an appropriate measure of market size, China's gross domestic product is fifteen times that of Hungary and its manufacturing sector is about twelve times larger. Furthermore, China has much more state-owned enterprises than Hungary and individual enterprises are also assuming a greater role. Correspondingly, China has important advantages over Hungary in its possibilities to establish domestic competition in manufacturing industries that is a pre-condition for the market determination of prices. At the same time, competition should also extend to commercial activities, including the establishment of multiple channels in wholesale and retail trade and the creation of trading companies operating across provincial boundaries.

In some basic industries shortages cannot be eliminated overnight, owing to the lack of sufficient capacity. In these cases, mandatory targets and price fixing would need to be maintained on a temporary basis. But, the number of such products should be kept to a minimum, lest difficulties are created for the expansion of market-relations in the rest of the economy. At the same time, world market prices would provide an appropriate standard for setting the prices of these commodities. Placing increased reliance on world market prices, in turn, necessitates establishing a realistic exchange rate.

The proposals made here would entail the establishment of a mixed price system in Chinese industry, with the market-determination of prices in industries where planning targets are abolished and the central price fixing retained in industries under mandatory planning, with links established to world market prices in the latter case. Apart from standardized products, world market prices could not be readily utilized in China because the varieties produced there generally differ in quality and specifications from those available abroad. At any rate, as the author earlier noted, given its large market and relatively low level of industrial development, it would seem appropriate for China to have domestic prices of differentiated products reflect domestic scarcities rather than world market relationships for such products.[39] This contrasts with the case of Hungary, in whose small market domestic competition needs to be complemented by import competition, involving reliance on world market price relationships.

VI WAGES AND BONUSES

The long-standing custom of providing practically equal wages to every worker, regardless of productivity, expressed by the saying of 'everybody eating from the same big pot' gave place to a bonus system after 1978. Bonuses were supposed to reward performance and be paid from increases in profits. In fact, however, bonuses were often provided indiscriminately to all workers, and even in the absence of profits, thereby contributing to general wage increases.

In order to combat these tendencies, in May 1984 the government introduced a tax on enterprises whose yearly bonus awards exceeded a certain level. The tax was set at 30 percent in cases when bonuses equalled two-and-a-half to four months' wages; 100 percent on bonuses between four and six months' wages; and 300 percent above this limit.[40]

The imposition of the tax on bonuses encountered practical difficulties of collection, however. Also, enterprises increased basic wages, in the place of providing bonuses, in order to escape the tax. Increases were undertaken, in part in response to worker demands and in part to establish a high base for the newly-announced system of taxing increments in wages and bonuses from their 1984 level.

In the event, the growth of labor compensation accelerated, with the total wage bill of enterprises rising by 19 percent in 1984 over the previous year's level.[41] The government's exhortations notwithstanding, a further increase of 22 percent occurred between 1984 and 1985.[42] These figures do not include increases in compensation in kind, such as clothes and free lunches, which have assumed considerable importance.[43]

Apart from the need to soak up the resulting excess purchasing power, to be discussed below, questions arise about the appropriateness of the wage regulations actually applied in China. It is evident that the combination of hourly wages and bonuses has contributed to wage inflation. Nor do exhortations suffice to deal with the situation in the framework of the present wage system. Thus, the cited increases occurred notwithstanding the fact that, in his report to the Fifth National People's Congress on 20 November 1981, Premier Zhao Ziyang demanded that 'the present practice of handing out bonuses indiscriminately should be strictly checked and bonuses payable in 1982 limited to the 1981 level.[44]

Furthermore, one may object to linking labor compensation to profits, which depend on managerial decisions rather than on the performance of individual workers. It would be more appropriate to generalize the use of the piece-wage system that links wages directly to the worker's performance as it is increasingly done in Hungary. The use of such a system was proposed by Ma Hong, one of China's leading economists.[45] Yet, piece wages are utilized today in less than one-tenth of Chinese industry.

On the example of Hungary, it would further be desirable to tax wage increments above a certain level. One such alternative would involve taxing increase in the wage bill in excess of the rate of increases in profit taxes paid to the state;[46] another would entail taxing wage increments in excess of a predetermined rate. The former of the two alternatives has the disadvantage that, under the present irrational price system, increases in profits do not necessarily reflect improved performance; in turn, the latter alternative does not take account of changes in the firm's productive activity. A possible compromise would be to tax increments in the wage bill in excess of increases in the firm's value added.

But the latter method, too, has the shortcoming that it takes the previous year's wages and output as the basis, although these may not represent an appropriate ratio of wages to output. And while enterprises have been told that 'they must see to it that all irrational factors in their total payrolls of last year are eliminated,'[47] the practical application of these instructions will encounter difficulties.

The ultimate objective should be to consider wages as a cost element that is done under the new wage regulations a number of Hungarian firms have introduced in 1985. This, in turn, would necessitate progressive taxation for income recipients, for which the taxes on wage incomes above a certain level, introduced recently in China, provide a basis.

There will further be need to promote the movement of labor, permitting workers to leave their jobs and reducing the work-force if conditions warrant. Steps in this direction were taken in September 1986 through the introduction of the contract system for newly-hired employees, regulations concerning the dismissal of workers who violate labor discipline, and a system of unemployment compensation.[48]

VII MACROECONOMIC PRECONDITIONS

We have seen that China experienced rapid increases in investment activity and in wage and bonus payments in 1984 and in 1985. These increases were supported by the expansion of bank loans. The loans financed a substantial proportion of unplanned investment undertaken by the localities. Also, the easy availability of financing allowed enterprises to increase wages and bonuses as they could finance investment from bank borrowing and may even have used borrowed funds directly to raise labor compensation.

The observed developments reflected the lack of ability of the People's Bank, newly becoming the central bank of China, to control the money supply. Thus, the local branches of the specialized banks (the Agricultural Bank, the People's Construction Bank, and the newly-established Industrial and Commercial Bank), and of the People's Bank itself, reportedly did the bidding of the localities rather than following instructions from the People's Bank. Furthermore, it has been reported that, in response to the suggestion that 'the amount of credit funds at the disposal of the specialized banks be determined with the amount of loans granted in 1984 as a base figure for 1985, . . . some monetary units . . . vied in granting loans so as to increase the base figures of credit.'[49]

In order to remedy the situation, the State Council decided to 'introduce a unified credit and monetary policy, strengthen the regulatory functions of the People's Bank of China over macroeconomic activities, and firmly control the amount of credit and cash in circulation. . . . The People's Bank of China will fix in a unified manner currency issue ceiling for its branches . . .'[50] The practical implementation of these measures is an urgent priority, so as to provide the macroeconomic conditions for the successful application of the reforms.

In fact, the interdependence of macroeconomic policies and economic reform has come to be emphasized in China. Attention has further been given on the need to improve the financial structure. Thus, in his report on the Seventh Five-Year Plan, Premier Zhao Ziyang speaks of the need 'to give full play to the role of the banking system in raising funds, guiding the flow of funds, making better use of them, and regulating social demand.'[51]

In the meantime, it would be necessary to raise interest rates for loans as well as for deposits. While China has made progress in raising interest rates in recent years, the 4.8 percent interest rate on investment loans provides inducement for using borrowed funds in preference to profits to finance new investments and it permits undertaking investment projects that have low economic rates of return. Also, deposit rates are negative in real terms, thereby discouraging savings.

Higher deposit rates, then, would syphon off some of the excess purchasing power created by rapid increases in wages and bonuses. The increased use of financial instruments sold to individuals by enterprises would have similar effects. It would further be desirable to encourage the movement of funds among enterprises, so as to ensure the better allocation of savings.

CONCLUSIONS

The economic reforms introduced since 1978 have led to considerable increases in production and in living standards in China. The growth in agricultural output permitted raising food consumption and upgrading its pattern, with substantial increases in the consumption of meat, dairy products, fruits, and vegetables; the growth of industrial output made it possible to ease shortages and to expand the consumption of high-quality products; and average floor space per person increased by about two-fifths in both urban and rural areas. Also, national income per head rose by 6.6 percent a year between 1978 and 1984, compared with an increase of 3.9 percent in the 1953–78 period.[52]

At the same time, the greater use of prices and markets should not carry the blame for excessive investments and increases in labor compensation or for profiteering and corruption. For one thing, excessive money creation has importantly contributed to rapid increases in investments and in wages and bonuses, with the delegation of decision-making power to the localities adding to the former and inadequate financial restraint on enterprises to the latter. For another thing, profiteering and corruption flourishes in a situation when controls on prices and markets continue.

These considerations, then, call for adopting appropriate macroeconomic polices and simultaneously extending the reform effort. In fact, the former is a precondition for the latter; in particular, the application of price and wage reforms is hindered by the existence of excess demand in China.

To establish macroeconomic equilibrium, China would have to utilize the tools of fiscal and monetary policy. While recent developments show success in eliminating the budget deficit, much remains to be done to establish an effective monetary policy that would aim at avoiding excessive credit expansion. Also, there is need to modernize the financial system and to set realistic interest rates.

In extending the reform effort, one should reduce the decision-making power of the localities and increase that of enterprises while freeing prices and markets. Also, measures should be taken to establish the conditions for effective competition, to give full responsibility to the manager for the firm's operations, to reform the system of prices, and to improve the wage and bonus system.

Although it has often been argued that social and political considerations advise caution in the implementation of the reforms, the example of Hungary indicates the potential benefits of simultaneous actions on a broad front. This is because reforms in various areas are interdependent and only their simultaneous introduction can assure full success.

NOTES

1. B. Balassa, 'The Hungarian Economic Reform, 1968–81,' *Banca Nazionale del Lavoro, Quarterly Review*, XXXIV (1981) pp. 163–84 and Essay 12 in Bela Balassa, *Change and Challenge in the World Economy*, pp. 216–81; B. Balassa, 'Reforming the New Economic Mechanism in Hungary,' *Journal of Comparative Economics*, VII (1983) pp. 253–66 and Essay 13 in *Change and Challenge in the World Economy*, pp. 282–309 (London: Macmillan, 1985); and Essays 13 and 14 in this volume.
2. Under this system, land (adjusted for quality) is divided equally among households in per capita terms, or on the basis of the number of able-bodied workers per household. The obligations of individual households are limited to the payment of taxes, the fulfilment of purchase quotas, and contributions to social welfare funds. These obligations have been defined in absolute terms, rather than as a proportion of output, thereby providing incentives for increasing production.
3. In the 1979–83 period, for which data are available, the area devoted to grains was reduced by 4 percent, that under other crops increased by 20 percent, while the total sown area declined by 3 percent. E. Lim *et al.*, *China: Long Term Development Issues and Options* (Baltimore, Md.: The Johns Hopkins University Press, 1985) Annex 2, p. 11.
4. H. Ma, *New Strategy for China's Economy* (Beijing: New World Press, 1983), Table 1 and 'Communique on the Statistics of 1985 Economic and Social Development,' State Statistical Bureau, 28 February 1986.
5. D. G. Johnson, 'Economic Reforms in the People's Republic of China,' *Economic Development and Cultural Change* (forthcoming), Table 2.
6. N. R. Lardy, 'Prospects and Some Policy Problems of Agricultural Development in China,' *American Journal of Agricultural Economics*, LXVIII (1986) pp. 165–82.
7. A. R. Khan, and E. Lee, *Agrarian Policies and Institutions in China after Mao* (Bangkok: International Labour Organization, Asian Employment Programme, 1983) p. 52.
8. J. Y. Lin, 'The Household Responsibility System in China's Agricultural Reform: A Theoretical and Empirical Study,' *Economic Development and Cultural Change* (forthcoming).
9. *Beijing Review*, 18 February 1985, p. 16.
10. F. Dong, 'The Reform of Economic Structure in China,' paper prepared for the Seminar on Economic Reforms, held in Paris 29 July–2 August 1985 and organized by the Economic Development Institute of the World Bank, mimeo, p. 26.
11. There is today a rudimentary land tax in the form of an output tax that has changed little over the years, but the revenue it provides is rather small, considerably below 2 percent of value added in agriculture (Lardy, 1986). At the same time, the experience of other countries indicates that the difficulties of establishing a land tax can be overcome. Such a tax has long been used in

Hungary, where the elimination of compulsory procurement in 1957 has led to higher output through increased specialization and exports.

12. B. Balassa, 'Economic Reform in China,' *Banca Nazionale del Lavoro, Quarterly Review*, XXXV (1982), pp. 307–33 and Essay 14 in *Change and Challenge in the World Economy* (London: Macmillan, 1986) pp. 310–36.

13. 'Communique on the Fulfilment of China's 1984 National Economic Plan,' State Statistical Bureau, 3 March 1985 and 'Communique on the Statistics of the 1985 Economic and Social Development,' State Statistical Bureau, 28 February 1986.

14. W. Byrd, 'Economic Reform and Efficiency in Chinese State-Owned Industry' (Washington, DC; World Bank, 1982) mimeo, Table 2.

15. Ma, *New Strategy for China's Economy*, Table 1 and T. G. Rawski, 'Productivity, Incentives, and Reform in China's Industrial Sector,' paper prepared for the Annual Meetings of the Association for Asian Studies, held in Washington, DC on 23 March 1984, mimeo.

16. G. Tidrick, 'Productivity Growth and Technological Change in Chinese Industry,' World Bank Staff Working Paper No. 761 (Washington, DC, 1986) Table 2.

17. 'Decision of the Central Committee of the Communist Party of China on the Reform of Economic Structures,' 20 October 1984, p. VIII.

18. Byrd, 'Economic Reform and Efficiency in Chinese State-Owned Industry,' p. 14.

19. Ibid., p. 15.

20. *Beijing Review*, 31 March 1986, p. 26.

21. This was noted in the October 1984 Decision of the Central Committee that exhorted 'city governments to separate their functions from those of enterprises . . . and not repeat the past practice of mainly depending on administrative means to control enterprises so as to avoid creating new barriers between departments and regions' ('Decision,' p. X).

22. 'Report on the Sixth Five Year Plan,' delivered by Zhao Ziyang, Premier of the State Council at the Fifth Session of the Fifth National People's Congress on 30 November 1982.

23. *Beijing Review*, 16 September 1985, p. 2.

24. 'Proposal of the Central Committee of the Chinese Communist Party for the Seventh Five-Year Plan for National Economic and Social Development,' adopted at the National Conference of the Communist Party of China on 23 September 1985.

25. According to an informed observer, there is a distinction between enterprises directly under the central government and local enterprises (including provincial enterprises, county enterprises, etc.), a distinction between key enterprises and non-key enterprises, and even distinctions between ministerial, departmental and board categories. 'All these different enterprises were treated differently in terms of funds, materials, labor (including technical personnel), product marketing, foreign-directed economic activities, raw materials prices, and so on.' F. Dong, 'Questions on Increasing the Vitality of Enterprises under the System of Ownership by the Whole People' (Beijing: Institute of Economics, Chinese Academy of Social Sciences, 1985) mimeo.

26. F. Byrd, 'The Role and Impact of Markets,' in G. Tidrick and C. Jiyan (eds), *China's Industrial Reform* (New York: Oxford University Press, 1987) p. 45.

27. 'Decision,' p. XI.

28. 'Report on the Seventh Five Year Plan,' delivered by Zhao Ziyang, Premier of the State Council at the Fourth Session of Sixth National People's Congress on 25 March 1986, p. xii.

29. *Beijing Review*, 1 November 1986, p. 4.
30. 'Decision,' p. X.
31. P. K. Chang, and S. K. Lin, 'China's Modernization: Stability, Efficiency, and the Price Mechanism,' in M. Dutta (ed.), *Asia-Pacific Economies: Promises and Challenges* (Greenwich, Conn.: JAI Press, 1987) pp. 103–18.
32. Dong, 'The Reform of Economic Structure in China,' p. 26.
33. Ibid.
34. W. Byrd, 'The Role and Impact of Markets,' p. 47.
35. *The Economist*, 27 October 1984.
36. The adverse economic effects of the regulations applied have been well-expressed by Tian Jiyun, the Vice-Premier of the State Council: 'Fine-quality products cannot have their prices raised and poor-quality goods cannot have their prices reduced. Therefore, the supply of fine-quality products falls short of demand, but production cannot be developed because of the low price. Poor-quality products do not sell well and they get stock-piled, but their production cannot be reduced.' ('Price System Due for Reform,' *Beijing Review*, 29 January 1985, p. 2).
37. Byrd, 'Economic Reform and Efficiency in Chinese State-Owned Industry,' pp. 19–20.
38. In the first half of 1985, China imported more consumer goods than it did in all of 1984 when these commodities already reached one-fifth of total imports (*Beijing Review*, 29 July 1985, p. 2). Compared with the same period of the previous year, imports of television sets from Japan increased four times, reaching an annual rate of $1.0 billion in the first half of 1985 (*The Economist*, 10 August 1985). Further increases occurred in subsequent months, leading to the subsequent introduction of restrictions.
39. Balassa, 'Economic Reform in China.'
40. *Beijing Review*, 25 June 1984, p. 4.
41. 'The Current Economic Situation and the Reform of the Economic Structure,' Report of the Work of the Government Delivered by Zhao Ziyang, the Premier of the State Council, at the Third Session of the Sixth National People's Congress on 27 March 1985.
42. *Beijing Review*, 23 December 1985, p. 23.
43. Ibid., 22 April 1985, pp. 4–5.
44. Ibid., 21 December 1981, p. 21.
45. 'When the system of time wages plus bonuses was carried out in the past, bonuses were often divided equally among workers and staff members. The principle of distribution according to work was not followed. Only by implementing the general piece-rate wage system, or alternatively, piece-rate wages for output which exceeds the quota can we really adhere to the principle of more income for more work, less income for less work and no income for no work.' (Ma, pp. 107–8).
46. 'The Current Economic Situation,' p. X.
47. Ibid.
48. *Beijing Review*, 15 September 1986, pp. 37–8.
49. 'The Current Economic Situation,' p. VII.
50. Ibid., p. XI.
51. 'Report on the Seventh Five Year Plan,' p. XIII.
52. *Beijing Review*, 10 March 1986, p. 14.

Part VI
Economic Policies in France

Essay 16 Five Years of Socialist Economic Policy in France: A Balance Sheet

INTRODUCTION

Nearly five years have elapsed since François Mitterrand assumed the presidency of the French Republic and a socialist-dominated assembly was elected. There have been considerable changes in the rhetoric as well as in the policy measures taken during this period. While references to 'class warfare' and to the need for a 'radical break with capitalism' were made in Mitterrand's speeches prior to the 1981 elections, he subsequently spoke about 'the community of a mixed economy'[1] and, finally, in his televised statement of 15 January 1984, stated that 'it is the enterprise that creates wealth, it is the enterprise that creates employment, it is the enterprise that determines our living standard and our place in the world hierarchy.'

Changes in policies have followed changes in the rhetoric. Apart from the nationalizations, the emphasis of economic policy-making after May 1981 was on taking expansionary measures in tandem with the redistribution of incomes. The adverse consequences of these measures for the balance of payments and inflation have subsequently led to the application of restrictive measures and to limitations on wage and price increases.

What have been, then, the consequences of the policies initially applied and of the subsequent reversal of these policies? Have the restrictive measures run their course and what are the policy conditions of a favorable economic performance in France for the future? These are the questions to which the present essay seeks answers.

Section I of the essay will examine the changing course of economic policies under the socialist government. Section II will focus on developments regarding prices and wages, Section III on profits and investment, and Section IV on unemployment. Section II will analyze changes in the public sector deficit and in the fiscal burden while Section VI will concern macroeconomic policies and foreign trade. Finally, Section VIII will consider policy perspectives for the future.

291

I THE CHANGING COURSE OF POLICIES

The newly-elected socialist government took expansionary measures at a time when the French economy began to overcome the effects of the second oil crisis and other major industrial countries concentrated their efforts on reducing inflation. But the character of the measures applied may have been more important than their magnitude, representing a contrast with those taken following the first oil crisis.

Whereas the measures adopted after the first oil shock were temporary, reverting to the initial situation following their expiration, the 1981–2 measures were to be of a permanent character. Also, while the measures of the earlier period increasingly took the form of tax reductions and incentives to productive investment, the 1981–2 measures involved increasing taxes and limiting the scope of investment incentives introduced by the preceding government. Higher taxes were designed to finance an extensive social program, which further required deficit financing. Thus, the budget of the administrations went from a surplus of 0.2 percent of GDP in 1980 to a deficit of 2.7 percent two years later.

In addition to higher social charges, the enterprises had to bear the burden of the redistributive measures taken outside the budget, including a 25 percent increase in the minimum wage, the addition of a fifth week of paid vacations, the reduction of working hours from 40 to 39 hours a week with full compensation, and provisions for early retirement. Furthermore, reflecting the effects of the rise in minimum wages and the accommodating stance taken by the government towards wage demands by the unions, the quarterly increase in the hourly wage rate, which fell from a peak of 4.2 percent in the second quarter of 1980 to 2.8 percent in the first quarter of 1981, reached 4.7 percent (a compound annual rate of increase of 20 percent) a year later.

Given the increases in labor costs, firms had little incentive to provide for the increased demand generated by the expansionary measures applied while exports declined in absolute terms. There ensued a deterioration in the French balance of payments, with the current account deficit reaching 3 percent of GDP in 1982, following the surpluses of the years 1978 and 1979 and the deficits of 1.4 percent of GDP in 1980 (due to the tripling of oil prices) and less than 1 percent in the first half of 1981.

The current account deficit of $16.8 billion in the years 1981–2 was financed by borrowing abroad, allowing for a 5.1 percent rise in consumption that much exceeded the 2.3 percent increase of GDP during the period. Private and public consumption grew at approximately equal rates, fueled by wage increases as well as by increased social benefits in the first case and the rise of public employment in the second. At the same time, inflation accelerated while it declined abroad.

To remedy the balance-of-payments situation, three devaluations were undertaken in the space of eighteen months. The October 1981 devaluation was not accompanied by significant macroeconomic measures; the devaluation of June 1982 was followed by a price and wage freeze, but the budget deficit continued to rise; only in conjunction with the devaluation of March 1983 did the French government institute an austerity policy, involving restrictive monetary measures and limiting the rise of budgetary expenditures. At the same time, 'backward' wage indexation was eliminated.

II WAGES AND PRICES

Under backward indexation, the rate of inflation of the preceding period effectively served as a floor for wage increases. In turn, the wage norms announced by the government (5 percent for 1984, 4.5 percent for 1985, and 3.7 percent for 1986)[2] were based on expected inflation. Although the norms were only indicative for the private sector, a considerable deceleration of wage increases occurred.

While the hourly wage rate rose by 16.3 percent in 1981, the increase was 12.5 percent in 1982, 9.7 percent in 1983, 6.4 percent in 1984, and 5.2 percent in 1985. Allowing for the effects of price increases, productivity growth, and unemployment, INSEE attributes 2.2 percentage points of the deceleration of wage increases between mid-1983 and mid-1984 to changes in the method of wage indexation.

The deceleration of wage increases contributed to the fall in inflation rates, with the rate of increase of the consumer price index declining from 13.9 percent in 1981 to 4.7 percent in 1985. Following increases after May 1981, differences in inflation rates *vis-à-vis* other major industrial countries have narrowed as a result. Weighted by France's exports to its eight principal trading partners, the differential was 2.4 percent in 1980, it rose to 3.1 percent in 1983 and declined to 1.0 percent in 1985.

The question arises, however, whether and to what extent prices have been artificially kept down by controls, which apply to practically all services and distributive margins and to four-fifths of the industrial products included in the consumer price index. According to an econometric investigation by INSEE, the prices of services would have risen to a greater extent in the absence of controls but such would not have been the case for industrial products; according to other calculations, average industrial prices would be 1 to 2 percent higher without controls.

III PROFITS AND INVESTMENT

In any case, increases in prices would permit re-establishing the profitability of enterprises at earlier levels. Edmond Malinvaud estimated the rate of profit on net capital, adjusting for the amortization of physical assets (revalued each year) and for decreases in the real value of the debt due to inflation. Having fluctuated between 6 and 7 percent during the 1960s, the net rate of profit of nonfinancial enterprises exceeded 7 percent at the beginning of the 1970s. Following the first oil shock, the rate declined to 4.4 percent in 1976; it rose again to 5.6 percent in 1979, only to decline to 4.5 percent in 1980 in the wake of the second oil crisis. The policy measures applied by the socialist government led to further decreases to 3.0 percent in 1981 and 1.9 percent in 1982 and, despite the deceleration of wage increases, even the 1981 figure was not attained in 1984.[3]

Malinvaud suggested that, in order to obtain an indicator of profitability, the real rate of interest should be subtracted from the net rate of profit, and that the minimum rate of profitability to assure the productive investment necessary for economic growth in France is about 4 percent. Apart for the second half of the 1960s, this rate was attained between 1962 and 1976 and it was regained again in 1979 following declines in the intervening years. However, after falling to 1.1 percent in 1980, the rate of profitability turned negative in 1982 and, despite some improvement, remained negative in 1983 and in 1984 (Table 16.1).

As long as the rate of interest exceeds the rate of profit, firms will be inclined to reduce their indebtedness instead of investing. This conclusion is strengthened if one considers that since 1980 gross business savings have been consistently less than amortization while they exceeded amortization by one-third to two-thirds between 1962 and 1973 and surpassed it again in 1979 following a negative outcome in the intervening years.

The results reported in the December 1985 by the OECD[4] further show that France failed to match the performance of the other major industrial countries in rebuilding profit margins. As a result, in 1985, the gross rate of return on capital in French manufacturing was surpassed by 11 percentage points in Japan, 5 percentage points in the United States, and 4 percentage points in Germany.

The contrast in profit performance was translated into a contrast in investment performance. In the 1980–85 period, productive investment declined by 1 percent in France, compared with increases of 39 percent in Japan, 31 percent in the United States, and 3 percent in Germany, where a further increase by over 8 percent is estimated for 1986; the figure was 29 percent in the United Kingdom, where investments were concentrated outside the manufacturing sector whose profit performance remained poor.

TABLE 16.1 *The profitability of nonfinancial enterprises (billions of francs and percent)*

	1979	1980	1981	1982	1983	1984
Gross savings	135	133	120	136	164	205
Distributed profits	44	48	57	65	67	74
Depreciation	127	147	172	208	227	233
Reduction of debt	65	77	89	71	97	62
Net profits	117	111	94	64	101	108
Net capital	2100	2472	3092	3392	3739	(4000)
Net profit rate	5.6	4.5	3.0	1.9	2.7	2.7
Real interest rate	1.2	3.4	4.2	5.5	4.3	5.1
Profitability	4.4	1.1	−1.2	−3.6	−1.6	−2.4

SOURCE: Edmond Malinvaud, 'Mise à jour' (Paris: Institut National de la Statistique et des Etudes Economiques, 1985), mimeo.

In turn, both private and public consumption increased more rapidly than domestic final demand in France while the opposite was the case in the other major industrial countries, the only exception being Germany. At the same time, France underperformed the United States, Japan, and the United Kingdom as far as the growth of GDP is concerned, notwithstanding a spurt of economic activity in 1981–2. Also, Germany caught up with France in terms of cumulative GDP growth by 1985 and is expected to surpass it in 1986.

For reasons adduced earlier, the spurt of economic activity in France in 1981–2 did not extend to industry. In fact, French industrial production declined in absolute terms in both 1981 and 1982 and it was slightly below the 1980 level in 1985. This compares with increases of 15 percent in the United States, 22 percent in Japan, 5 percent in Germany, and 3 percent in the United Kingdom.

IV UNEMPLOYMENT

Notwithstanding its poor industrial performance, between 1980 and 1983 unemployment rates rose less in France than in the other countries under consideration, the exception being Japan. But, increases in unemployment accelerated in subsequent years while Germany and the United Kingdom experienced a deceleration and the United States and Japan an absolute decline. By 1985, the French unemployment rate exceeded the German, US, and Japanese figures. And, although the rate was lower than in the United Kingdom, France surpassed all four countries in the duration of unemployment and youth unemployment in 1984, with 42 percent of the unemployed having been out of work for more than 12 months (compared with 33 percent in 1980) and 26 percent of the young in the 15–24 age group being unemployed (15 percent in 1980).

At the same time, questions have been raised about the comparability of the unemployment statistics over time. These questions relate both to the so-called 'social treatment' and the 'statistical treatment' of unemployment. The effects of social measures taken between 1980 and 1983 on the number of unemployed were estimated at 608 000, including reductions in working hours (40 000), creation of public employment (135 000), aids to the maintenance and promotion of employment (115 000), early retirement and retirement at 60 years (244 000), youth training (10 000), and several specific measures (64 000).[5]

Although its high cost and the recognition of the adverse effects of increasingly excluding the above-55 age group from the labor force led to the termination of the system of early retirement, INSEE estimates that reductions in activity rates entailed a further decline of 123 000 in the working population of this age group in 1984, following decreases of 116 000 in 1981, 120 000 in 1982, and 234 000 in 1983. By contrast, the decline in the working population of 55 years and over averaged only 32 000 between 1975 and 1980.

The year 1984 saw the institution of reconversion leaves for workers who became superfluous in basic industries and of work of collective utility for youth employed half time for less than the minimum wage. According to Lionel Stoléru, these schemes have reduced measured unemployment by 5000 and 100 000, respectively, between October 1982 and April 1985, with involuntary early retirement (75 000) and schooling (100 000) and the removal of unemployed from the rolls (200 000) representing further reductions, compared with the official unemployment figure of 2.4 million.

As the use of round numbers indicates, Stoléru's figures are subject to considerable uncertainty. Also, while reconversion leaves and its successor, contracts for training and work search, estimated at about 150 000 by the end of 1985, may count as unemployment under the definitions used by the International Labor Office, such is not the case for the youth work scheme.[6] Nevertheless, the social and the statistical treatment of unemployment appears to have led to a substantial underestimation of increases over time.

Note finally that, in contrast to the other industrial countries, there are considerable variations in unemployment rates among labor categories in France. According to the latest report of the OECD on France, 'the rate of unemployment varies much more among various groups of the population than in most other countries, so that certain groups have very high unemployment rates;[7] the same source reports that the rate of unemployment attains 18 percent in commerce and 16 percent for unskilled labor.[8]

V THE PUBLIC SECTOR DEFICIT AND THE FISCAL BURDEN

Employment is protected in the nationalized firms and, in particular, in the government. Taking account of jobs created in hospitals and social work, between July 1981 and December 1983 the creation of about 180 000 new public sector jobs was fully or partially financed from the budget. And, plans made for reducing public employment have been realized only in part, with decreases of 5500 jobs in 1985 and a decline of 4300 budgeted for 1986.

These results reflect the permanence of the 1981–2 measures noted earlier. The permanence of the measures taken, together with interest charges on the accumulated public debt, explain that the deficit in the budget of the administrations in 1985 is estimated at 149 billion francs, i.e. 3.3 percent of the GDP. As in earlier years, this result exceeds the initial projections. It also exceeds the 3 percent target, even though the measured deficit has been reduced through various practices of debudgetization.

In 1984, the shift to categories outside the budget included the financing of the electronic industry's development program by the PTT (Postes, Télégraphe et Téléphone) (3.4 billion francs), the assumption of the excess cost of Algerian gas by the Gas de France (1.3 billion francs), and the transfer of housing subsidies to the Caisse des Dépôts (7.0 billion francs). In 1985, the financing of the electronics industry was increased to 4.0 billion francs, with a further 4.75 billion francs budgeted for 1986; the PTT has also been charged with the financing of the Centre national des études spatiales (3.3 and 4.3 billion francs, respectively, in 1985 and 1986); it is required to make a transfer to the budget of administrations (2.2 and 3.0 billions), loses revenues due to the suppression of the payment of interest on postal cheques by the Treasury (6.0 and 6.7 billions), and pays the cost of the program of *informatique pour tous* (450 million francs in 1986) as well as the excess cost of mailing newspapers (1.5 billion francs in 1986). To these amounts, totalling 15.5 billion francs in 1985 and 20.7 billion francs in 1986, one may add the estimated cost of the Grand Travaux, prestige projects initiated by François Mitterrand, of approximately 2.5 billion francs in 1985 and 4 billion in 1986. Finally, expenditures of 6.5 billion francs were transferred from the 1986 budget of the central government and to that of the social security system, which is estimated to incur a deficit of 16 to 30 billion francs by various instituts de conjoncture.[9]

At the same time, following increases between 1981 and 1983, when it reached 14.6 billion francs, the government has reduced budgetary allocations to the nationalized industrial enterprises. Apart from the electronics program financed by the PTT, the allocations are scheduled to decline further from 11.9 billion francs in 1985 to 8.9 billion in 1986. To make up for the shortfall and to finance the growing losses of these enterprises,[10] the nationalized banks have been required to provide so-called participation loans, often substantially below market interest rates, while participation titles as well as investment certificates have been sold to the general public.

Apart from rising budget deficits, increases in public expenditures necessitated raising taxes and social charges. These so-called obligatory charges (*prélévements obligatoires*) rose from 42.5 percent of GDP in 1980 to 42.8 percent in 1981, 43.8 percent in 1982, 44.6 percent in 1983 and, again, to 45.4 percent in 1984, when François Mitterrand announced a 1 percentage point reduction. The 1985 budget in fact envisaged a decrease of 0.8 percentage points through reductions in income taxes, in social security contributions by employers, and in the professional tax, totalling 35 billion francs. But, increases in telephone and petroleum taxes and several smaller items fully offset the benefits accruing to enterprises and there remains only a gain of 10 billion francs for households that represents 0.2 percent of GDP.[11]

VI MACROECONOMIC POLICIES AND FOREIGN TRADE

Increases in budgetary deficits absorbed a rising fraction of net private savings in France, with this proportion doubling between 1981 (23.8 percent) and 1985 (47.7 percent) according to calculations reported by the OECD.[12] At the same time, these calculations do not allow for debudgetized items or for losses of public enterprises financed outside the budget. Also, the government has utilized a substantial proportion of the declining increments of the money supply to finance the deficit of the administrations. It appears, then, that the brunt of the austerity program has been borne by the private sector.

The application of the austerity program, the three devaluations undertaken in nine-month intervals, assisted by economic expansion in France's trading partners and improvements in the terms of trade, have led to the elimination of the current account deficit. This has been attained, however, more by reducing imports than by increasing exports. As reported by the OECD, after a small gain in 1983 (0.2 percent), France lost export market shares in manufactured goods in both 1984 (2.9 percent) and 1985 (2.75 percent). In contrast, substantial gains were made by Germany, the United Kingdom, and Japan, and losses in export market shares over the last two years were only slightly greater in the United States whose currency has appreciated to a considerable extent.[13]

At the same time, the underlying balance-of-payments situation deteriorated in France in the second half of 1985 as some expansionary measures were taken in the form of above-budget increases in government expenditures and reductions in income taxes whereas the money supply increased at a rate exceeding its target range. These measures contributed to a 5.5 percent rise in the volume of manufactured imports between 1984 and 1985 while exports increased by only 2.4 percent.

Although substantial improvements in the terms of trade, owing to reductions in the prices of imported materials and the depreciation of the dollar,[14] have camouflaged the extent of the deterioration in France's trade balance, this will be apparent once the terms of trade stabilize again. Yet, France would need a surplus in the current account in order to compensate for annual outflows of 40–50 billion francs due to the granting of export credits and private capital movements, without increasing its foreign debt.

VII THE BALANCE SHEET OF FIVE YEARS OF SOCIALIST GOVERNMENT

Following the *dérapage* of the years 1981–2, progress has been made in lowering the rate of price and wage increases in France. While continued price control has contributed to reductions in the measured rate of inflation, this has nevertheless entered into the wage determination process, and the slowdown of wage increases has further reduced inflation rates. But the deceleration of inflation has had at a cost in terms of unemployment, which has increased to a considerable extent according to the official statistics and even more if the figures are measured in a comparable manner.

At the same time, the deficit of the administrations regularly exceeded the projections and, with adjustment made for debudgetization, approached 4 percent of the gross domestic product in 1985. The deficit draws on private savings and on new money creation while contributing to high real interest rates. As real interest rates continue to exceed the net rate of profits, and gross business savings fall short of amortization, investment is discouraged, notwithstanding the recent decline of the share of labor costs.

The deterioration of the price competitiveness of French industry, resulting from continued divergence between inflation rates at home and abroad, also discourages investment. While inflation differentials *vis-à-vis* France's principal trading partners have declined over time, they have totalled 6 percent since the last devaluation of the franc in March 1983. The increased overvaluation of the exchange rate has in turn required rising real interest rates in France to safeguard the balance of payments, with the differential *vis-à-vis* Germany reaching 2 percentage points towards the end of 1985 as against less than 1 percentage point in 1984.

As productive investments in 1985 were below the 1980 figure, the five years of socialist government may be characterized by the lack of structural adjustment that would have been necessary to generate new, and to modernize existing, export activities. This fact, together with the deterioration of the price competitiveness of French industry, has contributed to losses in market shares in manufactured exports since the last devaluation.

Thus, although the French economy has been growing at a slow rate since 1982, the lack of structural adjustment and the deterioration of price competitiveness has put the balance of payments in a precarious position. This is indicated by the fact that the application of limited expansionary measures in 1985 has immediately led to a deterioration of the trade balance that has, however, been camouflaged by improvements in the terms of trade. The measures taken in advance of the March 1986 elections, including the reimbursement of the June 1983 compulsory loan on 15 January the 3 percent cut in income taxes, as well as the postponement of increases in public sector prices and of tax increases in petroleum products, can be expected to have further adverse effects on the French current account. At the same time, France's external indebtedness that has accumulated since May 1981[15] would necessitate a current account surplus of 40–50 billion francs (about 100 billion francs exclusive of interest payments).

VIII POLICY PERSPECTIVES FOR THE FUTURE

It follows that the choice of policies for the future may appropriately aim at the French economy returning to a sustainable growth path while ensuring balance-of-payments equilibrium. Pursuing this objective would require, first of all, taking measures that improve the competitiveness of French enterprises in foreign and in domestic markets.

Improving price competitiveness would necessitate an adjustment of currency values. Under the exchange rate system in effect, adjustments may be made within the European Monetary System whose members take 36 percent of French exports of manufactured goods and provide 56 percent of its imports of these commodities. With the currencies of the smaller member countries being closely tied to the German mark, in practical terms changes in parity between the French franc and the German mark need to be considered.

Provided that an agreement can be reached with Germany (and with the other EMS member countries), it would be desirable to carry out the adjustment through the appreciation of the mark rather than the devaluation of the franc. This conclusion follows because of the differential effects of the two alternatives of inflation and on the balance of payments in France.

With the prices of practically all energy imports and of two-thirds of raw material and agricultural imports into France being denominated in dollars, the depreciation of the franc would increase the cost of these imports. Such would not be the case however in the event of the revaluation of the mark, in which only one-sixth of French agricultural imports are quoted. Thus, according to an INSEE study, a 10 percent exchange rate change would raise the cost of primary imports by 27 billion francs in the first case and by less than one billion in the second.[16]

With delayed adjustment assumed for exports, the French balance-of-payments would deteriorate by 6 billion francs in the first year under the former alternative while no change would occur under the latter. This divergence would continue in the second year, with an approximate balance and a gain of over 1 billion francs under the two alternatives, respectively. While the estimates tend to understate the speed of adjustment in exports, they point to the existence of important differences in the two cases.

Various indicators may be used to gauge the desirable extent of exchange rate changes. Between March 1983 and March 1986, consumer prices in France are estimated to have increased by 6 percent more than in its main trading partners and by 10 percent more than in Germany. As reported by the OECD, the corresponding figures, adjusted for changes in exchange rates, are 8 and 13 percent for the export prices of manufactured goods and 6 and 10 percent for unit labor costs in manufacturing.[17]

At the same time, the extent of the exchange rate change actually undertaken will be limited by the desire of the German government to avoid a substantial decline in the price competitiveness of its industry as well as by the need for France to prevent an acceleration of inflation. Correspondingly, it would have to be complemented by reductions in industrial costs.

Apart from continued wage restraint, this may be accomplished by reducing social security charges for enterprises, when the resulting decreases in labor costs would provide incentives for investment of a labor-intensive character that would give a boost to employment. But the effects of lower social charges on investments may be slow in coming, so that consideration would need to be given to providing additional investment incentives. One such possibility would be granting a tax reduction for new investments, a measure introduced immediately prior to May 1981.

Decreases in social charges and direct tax benefits for investment would require compensating reductions in government expenditures, so as to avoid increases in the budget deficit. Further reductions in expenditures would be desirable to lessen the encroachment of the administrations on the funds available for investment as well as to lower interest rates. Following a change in exchange rates, lower interest rates would be compatible with balance-of-payments equilibrium and would encourage investment activity.

Expenditure reductions may be accomplished by limiting increases in public sector wages, foregoing the replacement of departing public employees, eliminating credit preferences, lowering other subsidies, and terminating some of the large prestige projects. Further budgetary savings may be achieved through deregulation that would also reduce the cost of doing business.

Deregulation, however, will have to occur over time. For one thing, the abrupt liberalization of the prices of services where there is limited competition would add to inflation while liberalizing foreign exchange markets would lead to the deterioration of the balance of payments. For another thing, deregulation in the energy sector, transportation and communications, and banking[18] would require careful preparation.

More immediate measures may be taken to liberalize labor markets, which would contribute to employment both directly and indirectly through capacity-increasing investments. This is because existing regulations on the firing of labor have actually led to less hiring and to the application of labor-saving investments. Such investments have also been undertaken in response to the limitations imposed on overtime and on temporary work.

A final issue concerns the nationalized enterprises. While the controversy about denationalization has ideological overtones, such an action may serve the interests of the French economy. To begin with, the managers of nationalized firms are not subject to the discipline of profits and losses and may demand aid from the government on the grounds that extraneous factors have adversely affected their performance. In turn, the government may make demands on nationalized enterprises that interfere with their efficient operations, including investments in backward regions, the maintenance of employment, and the pursuit of various social goals.

At the same time, the appointment of the managers of the nationalized enterprises for three years conflicts with the pursuit of long-term objectives. It also tends to politicize the activities of the managers as they prepare for possible political change prior to elections in fear of not being reappointed by the next government.

The introduction of *contrats de plan* between the nationalized enterprises and the supervising ministry also tends to give emphasis to short-term objectives, in particular since the government can take financial obligations only for the budgetary year. They may also limit the scope of manoeuvers of the nationalized firm. As an author favorable to nationalizations noted. 'At Renault, one perceives that the new relationships with the supervising ministry impose more constraints than the old one. . . . The firm felt that the new plan-contract, much more detailed than beforehand, was a sort of inquisition . . .'[19]

It has been claimed, however, that 'denationalization is impossible' on the grounds that the financial markets could not handle an amount of 100 billion francs, said to represent the assets of the profitable nationalized enterprises.[20] But, rather than making comparisons with the volume of sales in the stock market, one should consider that in 1984 the administrations issued bonds totalling 230 billion francs, in part to finance the budget deficit and in part to replace bonds that have become due. And, while the motivation of the purchase of bonds is often different from that of stocks, the two represent alternative financial investments for private holders and there is no reason to exclude a reversal of the earlier shift from stocks to bonds.

In this connection, it may be noted that the successful sale of British Telecom involved 40 billion pounds, equal to nearly 50 billion francs at the exchange rate in effect at the time. The British experience also provides lessons for France to carefully prepare a program of denationalization and to carry it out over a longer period. More generally, there is need for a well-conceived medium-term program to undertake reforms in French economic decision-making.

CONCLUSIONS

This essay has examined the changing course of economic policies of the French socialist government. It has been shown that excessive expansionary measures in the early period led to rapid increases in wages and industrial costs and to the deterioration of the balance of payments, but the subsequent measures brought improvements in these areas. However, this was accomplished at the expense of growing unemployment, and improvements in the balance of payments were attained through reductions in imports rather than increases in exports. This is explained in part by the overvaluation of the currency and in part by the lack of structural change as industrial investment declined.

The essay has proposed measures aimed to reverse the decline in French export shares in world markets. Apart from a devaluation of the French franc, this would necessitate lowering industrial costs and providing incentives to investment. Further improvements would be achieved through the denationalization of enterprises that were nationalized after May 1981.

NOTES

1. For the relevant quotations, see B. Balassa, 'The First Year of Socialist Government in France,' *Tocqueville Review*, IV (1982) pp. 337–58 and Essay 16 in B. Balassa, *Change and Challenge in the World Economy* (London: Macmillan 1985) pp. 363–83.
2. The norm, and the subsequent data, refer to the period from December of the previous year to December in the year in question.
3. Table 16.1 provides data for the years 1979 to 1984. Data for the years 1962–1978 are reported in B. Balassa, 'French Economic Policies under the Socialist Government: Year III,' *Tocqueville Review*, VI (1984) pp. 183–98 and Essay 17 in Balassa, *Change and Challenge in the World Economy*, pp. 384–99.
4. Organisation for Economic Co-operation and Development, *OECD Economic Outlook*, No. 38 (Paris, 1985).
5. J. F. Colin, M. Elbaum, and A. Fonteneau, 'Chômage et politique de l'emploi:

1981–1983,' *Observations et diagnostics économiques*, *Revue de L'OFCE*, 7 April 1984.

6. *Le Monde*, 25 April 1985.

7. Organisation for Economic Co-operation and Development, OECD Economic Survey, *France* (Paris, 1985) p. 8.

8. Organisation for Economic Co-operation and Development, *France*, p. 37.

9. *Le Monde*, 14 December 1985.

10. Following a surplus of 3.0 billion francs in 1979, the deficit of the nationalized industrial firms (including those nationalized before 1981) was 1.4 billion in 1980, 11.6 billion in 1981, 17.2 billion in 1982, 16.9 billion in 1983, and 26.2 billion in 1984. L. Zinsou, *Le fer de lance*. Essai sur les nationalisations industrielles (Paris: Olivier Orban, 1985) p. 22.

11. A. Fonteneau and H. Sterdyniak, 'Impact macro-économique du budget de 1985,' *Observations et diagnostics économiques, Revues de l'OFCE*, 18 October 1984. It may be added that the announced reduction in the rate of obligatory charges of 0.8 percent of GDP also includes the defiscalization of the tax on apprentices and training (1.9 billion) and the suppression of social security charges on salaries the government pays to itself (5.6 billion).

12. Organisation for Economic Co-operation and Development, *OECD Economic Outlook*, p. 5.

13. Organisation for Economic Co-operation and Development, *OECD Economic Outlook*, p. 155.

14. Between the first and the fourth quarters of 1985, import prices in terms of francs declined by 19 percent in the case of agricultural raw materials, 19 percent for industrial raw materials, and 13 percent for petroleum, resulting in a 4 percent improvement in France's terms of trade.

15. According to official data, the medium and long-term debt doubled in terms of US dollars, from 27 to 54 billion, and more than quadrupled in terms of French francs, from 123 to 525 billion, between the end of 1980 and 1984.

16. M. Debonneuil and Henri Sterdyniak, 'Apprécier une dévaluation,' *Economie et statistique*, No. 142, March 1982. The calculations have been done in terms of 1981 values.

17. Organisation for Economic Co-operation and Development, *OECD Economic Outlook*, p. 152.

18. Recommendations on deregulations in these sectors have been made in Paul Mentré, *Gulliver enchaîné ou comment déréglementer l'économie* (Paris: La Table Ronde, 1982).

19. L. Zinsou, *Le fer de lance*, p. 92. According to the *Rapport d'information du Sénat sur le contrôle des entreprises publiques* (Paris, 1985), however, it is not the plan contrats but the financial dependence of the nationalized firms *vis-à-vis* the government that limits their freedom of action.

20. L. Zinsou, *le fer de lance*, p. 250.

Essay 17 Industrial Policy in France under the Socialist Government

INTRODUCTION

In presenting the draft law on nationalizations in French industry and banking to the National Assembly on 27 September 1981, 'the lack of a true industrial policy' was adduced as the principal reason for the proposed actions. It was claimed, in particular, that 'it is necessary for the state to have the instruments for efficient interventions and for the planned orientation of the country's development. The most important of these instruments is the enlargement of the public sector.' The enlarged public sector was to be the spearhead of modernization of the French economy, with the state providing the funds for the requisite investments. Modernization appeared as the key word in statements made by socialist leaders, who repeatedly claimed that 'there are no condemned sectors, only outdated technologies.'

The objective of developing simultaneously all sectors while improving technology was reiterated in a speech before the chief executives of public enterprises in the industrial sector on 31 August 1982 by Jean-Pierre Chévènement, the then minister of research and industry. Chévènement defined industrial policy as follows:

> It is first of all the will to give advantage in all areas to technological and industrial development that represents a complete reversal of tendencies compared to the previous period. . . . It is furthermore an overall vision and consequently coherence in the allocation of resources that will be provided to industry according to three basic criteria: the trade balance, technological progress, and employment.
>
> Finally, it is for each sector, the choice of structures and, for the whole, the establishment of clear and unchangeable rules of the game.

Subsequently, Chévènement's successor, Laurent Fabius, suggested in a speech made to the National Assembly on 31 October 1983 that 'an industrial strategy involves the choice of the principal national priorities (around which efforts should be concentrated) in pursuing two major objectifs: to contribute to the re-establishment of economic equilibria in

305

particular in employment, and to modernize the industrial structure.' In turn, a few months later, on 14 December 1983, Edmond Maire, the president of the CFDT, one of the major French labor unions, expressed the view that the industrial policy of the government is 'secret, immobile, and incoherent. They say nothing, they do not announce any plan, any project, and number. . . . At the same time, it is "immobilisme." Enormous sums are expended to stem a decline but without preparing the future.'

What, then, has been the French record with industrial policy since May 1981? The author attempts to provide an answer to this question by reviewing the experience of the major industrial sectors, examining the actions taken, and evaluating the results of these actions. In so doing, use will be made of available quantitative evidence.

Section I will review the actions taken by the socialist government in regard to the declining sectors: coal, steel, and shipbuilding. Section II will examine the changes that occurred in the principal French export sector, automobiles. Section III will deal with electronics, one of the key sectors according to the plans of the socialist government. Finally, Section IV will describe the record of government support to industry, including research and development as well as industrial finance.

I THE DECLINING SECTORS: COAL, STEEL, AND SHIPBUILDING

On 23 January 1984, Pierre Mauroy, the then prime minister, stated that 'in the coal mines, steelmaking, and shipbuilding, my objective is to ensure modernization without firing.' To evaluate this claim, one needs to examine the original objectives of the socialist government in these industries, the changes that have subsequently occurred, and the perspectives for the future.

During the 1970s, successive governments aimed at increasingly shifting energy production from coal to nuclear energy in France. Between 1970 and 1980, coal production was reduced from 40 million tons to slightly over 20 million tons, accompanied by even larger decreases in employment. And, further reductions were envisaged, involving the closure of unprofitable mines where low-grade coal was produced at a high cost.

The tendencies towards the rationalization of coal mines were reversed by the socialist government that set a production target of 30 million tons for 1990 and hired some 10 000 workers in the mines. With stagnant demand for coal, productivity declined while increases in wages and social charges raised costs. Between 1980 and 1983, the subsidy received from the state rose from 3.9 billion to 6.5 billion francs while the accounts of the Charbonnages de France (CdF) turned from an approximate equilibrium to a deficit of 800 million francs.

As a result of the decline in the work-force by 8 percent 56 000 in the previous year, with production remaining approximately unchanged at 18.2 million tons, the deficit of CdF was practically eliminated in 1984. However, state subsidies amounted to 6.8 billion francs, equalling 360 francs per ton or 130 000 francs per worker as compared to the average manufacturing wage of 110 000 francs per year.

Under the program announced in March 1984, coal output would decline to 11–12 million tons by 1988, with the work-force being reduced to approximately 25 000. There targets would nevertheless involve maintaining the state subsidy at 1984 levels in real terms throughout the period, to which government aid to CdF to help with the establishment of new activities may be added. Yet, the subsidy alone would involve an excess cost of over 560 francs per ton at 1984 prices, equivalent to 270 000 francs per worker.

The excess cost reflects only in part the high cost of coal production in France, estimated at 630 francs per ton in 1983 as against an import cost of 450 francs per ton, requiring a production subsidy of 3.8 billion francs in total. It further includes the financial costs of CdF's long-term indebtedness, which came to exceed the value of output in 1984, as well as part of the cost of early retirement and retraining. At the same time, the figures do not include the supplemental payment of about 1 billion francs a year by Electricité de France for coal. Nor do they comprise the contribution of the government and the unemployment fund to the cost of reducing the labor force.

The proposed cuts in coal production would necessitate closing all pits in the North and several pits elsewhere in the country. It would also require the streamlining of the organization of CdF. The proposals management made to this effect were not acted upon, however, because of opposition by regional interests as well as the labor unions.

Policies concerning steel have undergone similar changes as in the case of coal. The reconversion plan adopted in 1978 envisaged substantial reductions in production and employment in the sector. In fact, employment declined from 160 000 in 1975 to 97 000 in 1981.

Rather than continuing with this plan, the socialist government adopted an output target of 24 million tons for 1985, above the range of 18.5 to 23.5 million tons proposed in a report for the government prepared by Professor Judet. Correspondingly, Sacilor, but not Usinor whose management considered the plan unrealistic, hired new workers.[1]

In the event, the output of steel declined from 21.2 million tons in 1981 to 17.6 million tons by 1983, with employment decreasing only slightly to 93 000. The fall in labor productivity, together with increases in wages and social charges, contributed to a considerable rise in the deficit of Sacilor and Usinor, totalling 11 billion francs in 1983 compared with 3 billion francs in 1980. The deficit amounted to 600 francs per ton of steel and 110 000 francs per worker.

The restructuring plan adopted in March 1984 lowered the production target to 18.5 million tons. It also cancelled the building of the proposed universal rolling mill in Lorraine at a cost of 1.3–2.0 billion francs. Furthermore, the plan called for the closing of some existing plants, entailing a decline of about 25 000 in the work-force by 1987.

With the pick up of demand for steel, the losses of Sacilor and Usinor decreased to 8.5 billion francs in 1984 and to 6.5 billion francs in 1985. Under the EEC steel regime, the losses would have to be eliminated by 1987. This is not likely to occur as far as long products are concerned, where the proposed restructuring has not gone far enough.

Even apart from long products, the elimination of losses will necessitate rescheduling the industry's long-term debt, estimated at 30 billion francs and amounting to nearly one-half of sales. Financial aid will further be necessary for the restructuring of some of the subsidiaries. Finally, the government budget and the unemployment fund will bear a considerable part of the social measures taken to ease the transition.

At the same time, delays were experienced in the implementation of the 1984 restructuring plan, in particular as far as the reduction of the labor force is concerned. Also, steel-making facilities in Ugine-Fos were not closed down as planned. Finally, the proposed merger of Sacilor and Usinor was postponed.

Shipbuilding provides another case where the adjustment measures taken in earlier years were not continued after May 1981. The reorganization of the big shipyards into two groups did not involve the rationalization of operations either. At the same time, notwithstanding substantial declines in orders, employment in the shipyards was maintained at the 1981 level of 20 000. According to one estimate, by early 1984 about one-half of the work force became redundant, thereby adding to costs that were further raised by increases in wages and social charges.

In January 1984, Yugoslav shipyards offered to supply cargo ships for a little over one-third of the price quoted by French shipyards. Nevertheless, the government refused demands by the French shipper, Delmas-Vieljeux, for import licenses. At the same time, in order to enable domestic producers to supply ships at a price of 152 million francs, compared with the price of 135 million francs offered by the Yugoslav shipyards, subsidies of over 200 million francs were provided per ship. In fact, while the government budgeted subsidies of 1.6 billion francs for 1984, its total aid to the shipbuilding industry reached 3.5–4.0 billion francs, i. e. 175 to 200 000 francs per worker.

In March 1984, it was announced that shipbuilding capacity would be reduced from 370 000 tons to approximately 270 000 tons, involving a decrease in the working force by 5000. However, all five major shipyards are scheduled to be maintained, with cuts of varying magnitude planned for each.

The proposed target compares with new orders of 177 000 tons in 1982 and 105 000 tons in 1983. And while these two years represent a particularly unfavorable situation for world shipbuilding, the target appears overly high. Also, the maintenance of all five shipyards, notwithstanding differences in their production costs, would not ensure the necessary reductions of costs. Pursuing such an objective would further require specialization in passenger ships, offshore material, and military ships where the French shipyards are more competitive.

All in all, the three declining industries exhibit a similar pattern. After May 1981, a reversal occurred in the process of restructuring that would have entailed continued reductions in output and employment. The targets were raised substantially above actual production levels, leading to new hiring. With declining demand and the rise of wages and social charges, including a fifth week of vacation and full compensation paid for the reduction of the work week from 40 to 39 hours (33.5 hours in the case of steel), there resulted a considerable increase in the deficits of the firms in the three industries.

Notwithstanding the rise in budgetary appropriations, the firms in question had to increase their borrowing, thereby raising levels of indebtedness to a substantial extent. High financial charges on their debt, in turn, add to the present and future losses of the enterprises in the three industries. Further costs are involved in connection with the so-called *congés de conversion* under which the workers who are considered superfluous are receiving over a two-year period 70 percent of their pre-tax salary, financed one-third each by the firms themselves, from the government budget, and by the unemployment fund. Finally, in some cases, substantial bonuses are offered to workers who depart voluntarily (50 000 francs in one of the large shipyards).

II AN EXPORT INDUSTRY: AUTOMOBILES

The automobile sector offers a particular interest, both because of its large share in the French economy and because of its long-standing importance for French exports. In fact, during the 1970s, automobile exports were the single biggest contributing factor to export expansion in France.

The market position of the French automobile industry deteriorated to a considerable extent after May 1981. The figures cited in June 1984 report of the Conseil économique et social on the automobile industry show that the share of the French industry in European markets fell from 30.4 percent in 1980 to 24.3 percent in 1983 while the share of foreign cars in France rose from 21.7 to 32.7 percent. This occurred even though the importation of Japanese cars is kept to 3 percent domestic sales in France and increases in these imports is limited in quantitative terms in most other major European countries as well.

During the same period, the combined losses of the Peugeot and Renault groups increased from 1.2 billion francs to 4.3 billion francs. As a result of the adjustment measures taken, Peugeot returned to equilibrium in 1984 except for interest charges on its debt. At the same time, its share in the domestic market rose from 32.2 to 33.1 percent while it remained practically unchanged in European markets. By contrast, Renault's share declined from 35.1 to 31.0 percent in domestic, and from 12.3 to 10.5 pecent in European, markets. Also, its losses for 1984 exceeded 10 billion francs, with the deterioration taking place in automobile production while the losses were earlier concentrated in truck manufacturing.

Several factors contributed to these results. According to estimates cited by the report of the Conseil Économique et Social, the measures taken after May 1981 increased labor costs in the automobile industry by 19.5 percent in 1982. At the same time, the price control introduced in June 1982 did not allow for offsetting increases in prices, giving rise to foregone revenue of about 2.5 percent. Intermittent social troubles, fostered largely by the CGT, the principal union representing the automobile workers, involving strikes, production slowdowns, and the deterioration of product quality, also added to the losses suffered by the French car producers.

In 1982, the demand for French cars, in particular in the domestic market, was adversely affected by uncertainty relating to social troubles and price control. Further declines in market shares were experienced in subsequent years as social troubles occcurred with considerable frequency. At the same time, the labor unions obstructed reductions in the industry's work-force, with permission to this effect given very parsimoniously by the government. This fact, as well as the high financial charges on borrowing to finance the losses incurred, aggravated the financial situation of the French automobile industry.

The two groups are not blameless: Peugeot committed errors in taking over Talbot while eliminating its dealer network and Renault chose expansion abroad over improvements in domestic plants. Nevertheless, it would appear that the government raising labor costs without allowing offsetting price increases and limiting reductions in the work-force demanded by management while taking a permissive attitude towards actions by the labor unions were the principal factors that contributed to the observed adverse developments.

These unfavorable results are cumulative as the losses incurred gave rise to high financial charges that account for about 4 percent of total costs in the two groups. At the same time, their long-term debt reached 90 billion francs at the end of 1984, exceeding two-fifths of the total value of sales. In fact, the ratio of the debt to capital approaches 2 in the French automobile industry, compared with ratios between 0.2 and 0.9 for major competitors abroad, according to a report prepared for the government in the summer of 1984 by a commission chaired by François Dalle.

Labor productivity practically stagnated between 1980 and 1983 in the French automobile industry, compared with gains of about 20 percent for General Motors, Ford, and Fiat. These results, cited in the Dalle Commission report, reflect excessive manning levels in French automobile factories. According to the same report, the work-force of 230 000 in the industry in June 1984 should be reduced to 160 000.

III A HIGH TECHNOLOGY INDUSTRY: ELECTRONICS

Among high-technology industries, France made considerable progress in nuclear energy and in aerospace during the 1970s. Its record in electronics was mixed, with strengths in telecommunications and in professional electronic equipment, and weaknesses in electronic components, such as integrated circuits, in computers, and in electronic consumer goods.

On coming to power, the socialist government gave considerable emphasis to electronics. The plan for the electronics industry envisaged spending 140 billion francs (in 1982 prices) on investment and R&D in electronics over a five-year period. Within this total, 11–12 billion francs a year were to have come from the state budget. In fact, 10 billion francs were spent in 1983, 11 billion francs in 1984, and 10 billion francs were budgeted for in 1985, but in current rather than in constant prices. Although comparable data are not available, it appears that the shortfall was even greater as far as expenditures from non-governmental sources are concerned.

As to individual sectors, in 1982 it was estimated that the manufacture of integrated circuits would require 4.1 billion francs for research and development and 3.3 billion francs for new investment over a five-year period. However, only research and development remained on course as budgetary allocations for investment in integrated circuits were reduced. By comparison, spending by Japanese firms was 18 billion francs in 1984 and spending by several American firms, taken individually, exceeds that of the entire French industry.

Plans for the expansion of the production of integrated circuits are made uncertain for lack of multi-annual budgetary allocations. In turn, for computer manufacture, CII-Bull received a pledge from the government for a capital infusion of 4.5 billion francs between 1983 and 1986. Additional appropriations will be made for research, but Bull will nevertheless need to generate funds of about 8 billion francs to finance its five-year program of R&D and investments, estimated at 13–14 billion francs. And, the program is relatively small on the world scale, with Bull having a production volume smaller than that of Apple and less than 5 percent of that of IBM.

More importantly, questions arise about the socialist government's policy of creating national champions in individual sectors, limiting participations by foreign firms, and expanding all sectors simultaneously. Thus, Saint-Gobain had to give up its activities in electronics; the production of semi-conductors and consumer electronics was concentrated in Thomson; Bull became the principal manufacturer of computers; and CIT-Alcatel received the monopoly in telecommunications. Also, in connection with the nationalizations, the government reduced Honeywell's share in CII-Bull from 47 to 20 percent, bought out ITT, and sold its 30 percent participation in Olivetti.

Reducing Honeywell's share in CII-Bull increased difficulties for the upgrading of the French computer industry. At the same time, the take-over of CGCT (the subsidiary of ITT) meant that France has foregone investments by ITT that is planning to spend \$4.8 billion on R&D and capital investment in electronics and telecommunications in Western Europe between 1983 and 1988. And, the shares in Olivetti were subsequently resold to ATT that has replaced Saint-Gobain as Olivetti's principal foreign partner.

Furthermore, the government did not permit Thomson to establish the joint production of minicomputers with Systems Engineering Laboratories, and it decided against having Apple build a factory in France for the production of Macintosh minicomputers with 49 percent French participation. And while some agreements were reached with foreign firms, it was noted that 'French companies have remained signally absent from the welter of international alliances being forged between computer and communications companies around the world.'[2]

Apart from reversing the policies of the preceding government that encouraged participation by foreign firms, the socialist government reversed its predecessor's policy of leading groups, which had entailed the concentration of resources in areas where French firms had been successful in the past. Yet, the parallel expansion of all sectors encountered financial constraints, which were aggravated by the budgetary squeeze and the increasing financing needs of the declining sectors and of Renault.

Questions arise also concerning the planned expansion of the production of electronic consumer goods in France. Alongside with failures such as the Plan Calcul and Concorde, French industrial planners were successful in the past in developing branches of electronics where both supply and demand were dominated by the state, thereby imparting considerable stability to the market.

In the case of consumer electronics, however, tastes change rapidly and centrally-made plans easily go awry. Also, government interventions in production decisions, such as compelling Thomson to build a factory producing parts for video recorders in Longwy, interfere with firm decision-making and increase costs.

At the same time, in several of these fields, small firms have the advantage of flexibility in catering to consumer needs. Furthermore, as the American and Japanese examples indicate, competition becomes a force of progress while in France the restructuring of the nationalized firms led to the establishment of monopoly positions as noted above.

The socialist government also chose a highly centralized solution for the establishment of a nationwide cable network, to be controlled by the Direction Générale des Télécommunications of the PTT (Postes, Télégraphe et Téléphone). The cost of establishing this nationwide cable network was to be shared by the PTT and the local authorities. However, the local authorities refused to contribute to the cost of installation of the individual connections, which came to exceed the original estimate several times, and this cost will be fully borne by the PTT. The PTT will thus provide much of the approximately 60 billion francs needed for the program, although its financing capability declined (in 1983, DGT had a net loss of 0.5 billion francs compared with a surplus of 2.7 billion francs the year before) and the policy of austerity limits possible contributions from the government budget.

Thus far, only 2.6 billion francs were spent on experimental schemes in a few cities, and considerable delays were experienced compared with the original plan. At the same time, the installation of the 4th TV channel (Canal-Plus) on a subscription basis may have pre-empted the role of cable to show feature films. Also, television broadcasting from the first French-German satellite and the introduction of privately owned television will provide competition to cable television.

Correspondingly, questions arise about prospective demand for cable on the part of individual households who are all supposed to be linked into the nationwide network. Furthermore, notwithstanding the technological capabilities of optical fiber, chosen by the French government over coaxial cable, it is not evident that a cable network will have economic advantages over other alternatives, such as a combination of satellite and terrestrial microwaves that has been used in the United States. This is the case, in particular, following the abolition of the monopoly position of Intelsat for telecommunications by satellite. Thus, the grandiose plan for a national cable network may not provide for the efficient use of scarce financial and technological resources in France.

IV GOVERNMENT SUPPORT TO INDUSTRY: R&D AND INDUSTRIAL FINANCE

Having reviewed the experience of major sectors since May 1981, we will next consider general government support to industry under the socialist government. In this connection, two issues will be dealt with: research and development and industrial finance.

Soon after the socialist government came to power, spending on R&D

was targeted to grow 20 percent a year between 1981 and 1985 and to increase from 2.0 to 2.5 percent of the gross domestic product during this period. In the event, the share of R&D spending in GDP is estimated to have reached 2.2 percent of GDP as budgetary appropriations for research were cut back in the period of austerity.

In an interview given to *Le Monde* on 17 April 1984, François Kourilsky, the vice-president of the Research and Technology Council objected to reductions in the financing of research programs that promote industrial research and provide equipment for laboratories. He expressed the view that these reductions, carried out in November 1983 and March 1984, did not give sufficient attention to real needs. In turn, funds for the construction of the giant museum of science and technology at La Villette were not reduced. And while 16 percent of the funds were subsequently restored, this was not the case for industrial research.

France traditionally practiced a policy of selective credit. This policy was extended further after May 1981 through the establishment of CODEVI (*Compte de Développement Industriel*) that provides advantages to savers over alternative instruments; the creation of FIM (*Fonds Industriel de Modernisation*) that receives an important part of CODEVI's resources for distribution to industrial firms and also borrows in domestic and in international markets; and the introduction of special institutional arrangements in favor of small and medium size enterprises.

The new institutions perform some of the functions customarily assigned to banks, in the present case the nationalized banks. Their operation involved increased public interventions as loans by FIM are subject to approval by the ministry for industrial restructuring and foreign trade while other credit arrangements depend on decisions by local authorities. Furthermore, with the state guaranteeing loans by FIM in full, unprofitable operations may also receive financing. More generally, increasing the scope of selective credits tends to reduce the efficiency of the allocation of financial resources while adding to the complexity of the credit system.

A further question is if the new institutions actually increased the amount of funds available to industry, when the outcome depends on the extent to which these sources of funds substitute for other credit sources. A net increase occurs only if one of two conditions are fulfilled: other sectors borrow less or the total amount of credit to enterprises increases.

Data availabilities do not permit one to gauge the amount of credits accorded to the individual sectors. At the same time, the share of all enterprises, taken together, in total credit declined as public deficits increased. This was indicated in a presentation made by Renaud de la Genière, the then Governor of the Banque de France until November 1984, at the Académie des sciences morales et politiques on 26 January 1984 under the title 'The international aspects of French monetary policy.'

De la Genière noted that the net credit requirements of the public authorities were practically nil in 1979 but reached 115 billion francs in 1983, compared with 160 billion francs for enterprises whose net borrowings were 105 billion francs four years earlier. During the same period, the capacity of financing by households and financial institutions did not quite double, from 105 to 200 billion francs, thereby necessitating borrowing abroad.

It further appears that, *pari passu* with increases in the budget deficit, a decline occurred in the rate of household savings from 16–17 percent in the late 1970s to 14 percent in 1984. At the same time, the amount of savings accruing to CODEVI was more than offset by reductions in other savings instruments.

If the lack of credit is not an obstacle to investment (according to a recent survey by INSEE only 9 percent of industrial enterprises regarded credit to be a constraint), this seems less to do with the existence of new financial institutions as with factors such as insufficient profit margins (48 percent of responses) and the desire to avoid further increases in indebtedness (37 percent), which rose to a considerable extent in 1981 and 1982 when profit margins were particularly low. And while profit margins improved in 1983, the decline in industrial investment was not reversed.

With continued improvements in profit margins, industrial investment increased in 1984. INSEE expected a further increase in 1985 while, according to the SOFRES poll of December 1984, only 15 percent of private enterprises planned to augment their investments compared with the reductions envisaged by 41 percent of the firms. In any case, the fall in industrial employment would continue. IPECODE estimates that declines in employment of 2 percent in 1982 and 1983 would be followed by decreases of 3 percent in 1984 and 1985, and INSEE expects job losses in industry to remain at approximately the 1984 level of 214 000 in 1985.

The expected fall in industrial employment reflects the labor-saving character of investments in response to higher labor costs, increased social charges and, in particular, the difficulties encountered in attempting to reduce the size of the labor force if and when economic conditions warrant. Thus, as the freedom of enterprises to dismiss workers was constrained, they became increasingly reluctant to hire labor notwithstanding the measures taken in favor of the establishment of new enterprises in general, and small and medium size firms in particular.

CONCLUSIONS

In line with its expansionary stance, the socialist government reversed the earlier policy of adjustment in regard to the three declining sectors, coal, steel, and shipbuilding, after May 1981. The setting of unrealistic targets encouraged expansion in these sectors while wages and social charges increased to a considerable extent. These changes made the task of adjustment more difficult once the necessity thereof came to be recognized.

The situation was further aggravated by the desire to avoid firing superfluous workers. As Raymond Lévy expressed it in a paper on the steel industry, presented at the Brookings Institution in September 1984, 'the security of employment and the maintenance of "acquired rights" progressively tranformed the compensation of labor from a variable into a fixed cost; one can forget the cost of a mistaken investment, one does not forget that of excessive recruitment if one has to pay its consequences during the entire life-time of the newly recruited personnel.' The cost of the measures applied is apparent in the large deficits of firms in the three declining sectors, requiring increased budgetary allocation as well as borrowing, with the financial costs of borrowing augmenting the deficit.

Other newly-nationalized firms, too, had to pay a price for postponing the necessary adjustment. Increases in demand, in particular from abroad, has nevertheless made it possible for these firms to subsequently improve their operations. Also, being less exposed politically, they were able to take adjustment measures in recent years.

Still, taken together, budgetary allocations to the newly nationalized firms doubled, from 21.8 billion francs in 1980 to 43.4 billion francs in 1983 while their deficit (after budgetary allocations) was nearly five times higher in 1983 (11.4 billion francs) than in 1980 (2.4 billion francs). During the same period, a surplus of 1.5 billion francs turned into a deficit of a similar magnitude, rising further to approach 10 billion francs in 1984 at Renault that suffered the consequences of higher wages and social charges, price control, and social troubles fomented largely by the CGT.

Providing for the increased financial needs of the declining sectors limited the availability of funds for the expansion of high technology activities. Thus, for 1985, the capital allocation for the entire electronics industry is less than the allocation to Renault alone and does not exceed one-half of the allocation to the steel industry.

At the same time, higher wages and social charges and price control discouraged investment activity in the years 1981–83 and contributed to the decline in industrial employment. Total employment declined by 110 000 between 1981 and 1983, compared with the creation of 500 000 jobs envisaged in the interim plan. The decline in industrial employment continued afterwards, notwithstanding a rise in investments. And while it was originally expected that 80 000 jobs would be created in electronics, cutbacks occurred in telecommunications as well as in computers.

In the politically exposed nationalized industries, decreases in employment did not involve firings but rather early retirements, financial assistance to returning immigrants, retraining, and *congés de conversion* that, taken together, may cost some 50 billion francs. These measures created a 'great inequality of social treatment between those losing their jobs due to the bankruptcy of small- and medium-size enterprises or the enterprises that are less in the public eye and the large enterprises that receive media attention.'[3]

In these circumstances, the question needs to be raised if one can speak about an industrial policy in France. As an official of the French government suggested in private conversation, the measures applied in regard to the three declining sectors may be considered social policy rather than industrial policy. Nor can we speak of an industrial policy in regard to the automobile industry, where the state repeatedly countenanced actions taken by the unions. And while the policies aim at encouraging the development of the electronics industry, doubts arise about the efficacity of the measures applied. More generally it would appear that, rather than taking actions in a consistent framework, the government reacted to situations as they emerged.

But how about the role of the nationalized firms as instruments of industry policy? After detailed interventions under Chévènement's tenure as minister failed to bring the expected results, Fabius and Cresson reduced the extent of interventions. But, the nationalized firms remain under pressure to buy from other nationalized firms at the expense of private firms and, in particular, imports. A case in point is the computerization of the operations of large banks that had to place orders with Bull, although it did not yet develop the necessary hardware. In turn, the nationalized banks increasingly finance the losses of nationalized industries.

The procedures of appointment of the managers of the nationalized enterprises also give rise to concern. While the apppointments made by Dreyfus after 1981 were based principally on competence, with the signal exception of the appointment of Georges Besse at Renault, political considerations appear to have increasingly entered into the choice of chief executives. Also, the contracts of two chief executives who showed considerable independence, Raymond Lévy at Usinor and Daniel Deguen at the Crédit commercial de France, were not renewed.

In any case, the appointment of a chief executive for three years does not provide a sufficiently long learning period and favors adoption of a short time horizon. In fact, indications are that the chief executives of nationalized companies tend to increasingly take a short-term view with the neglect of long-term considerations, so as to increase their chances for reappointment.

As long as the present ownership structure is maintained, these shortcomings may be mitigated by lengthening the terms of appointment of the chief executives and changing the composition of the board of directors, so as to minimize the chances of political interference. In this connection, reference may be made to attempts in Hungary for increasing the independence of the managers of state enterprises.

As to industrial policy, increased emphasis would need to be given to horizontal measures that operate across-the-board as against vertical measures that pertain to individual industries. In particular, there would be need to eliminate price control and to reverse increases in social charges. It would further be desirable to ease the constraints imposed on small and medium size enterprises in the form of additional social charges and the creation of committees with worker participation. Finally, greater flexibility would need to be introduced in labor markets.

The described measures may be expected to contribute to increased industrial investment and employment without the use of vertical measures that tend to lead to inefficiencies in resource allocation. Horizontal measures would also need to be given emphasis by increasing support of research and development in the form of tax benefits for the R&D activities of the firms, which generate external economies. Finally, on a temporary basis, investment incentives may also be provided.

At the same time, the health of French industry, and of the French economy in general, is contingent on the pursuit of appropriate macro-economic policies. Due to the weakness of investment activity and continued borrowing abroad, the rising budget deficit did not create a credit crunch for enterprises so far. But, with the constraints on foreign borrowing, the sustained expansion of investment by enterprises would require that the public authorities limit their encroachment on domestic financial markets.

NOTES

1. Sacilor and Usinor were the two large nationalized steel-producing firms in France.
2. *Financial Times*, 14 January 1985.
3. *Le Monde*, 15 December 1984.

Essay 18 French Economic Policy After March 1986

INTRODUCTION

In March 1986 a new majority was elected under the flag of economic liberalism and Jacques Chirac took over the reins of the government from Laurent Fabius. The purpose of this essay is to evaluate the record of the new government in the first year of its existence.

Section I will review what was accomplished by the new government. Section II will consider macroeconomic trends while Section III will analyze factors affecting exports. Finally, Section IV will examine prospects for the future.

I WHAT WAS ACCOMPLISHED?

The program of privatization adopted in May 1986 reverses not only the nationalizations of 1981 but also a substantial part of the nationalizations of 1945. Over a period of five years, 65 state-owned companies will be privatized, including nine major industrial firms, the largest banks and insurance companies, as well as TF 1; they altogether account for one-third of capitalization on the Bourse. With the shares of Saint Gobain oversubscribed 14 times and those of Paribas 38 times,[1] the Bourse appears very receptive, effectively refuting the views of those who had claimed that it could not even handle sales totalling 100 billion francs.[2] In fact, the shares of the companies to be privatized may bring substantially more than the initial estimate of 240 billion francs, and much exceed the prices the socialist government paid in nationalizing companies in 1982.[3]

What can France expect from the denationalizations? The Chirac government, just like the government of Margaret Thatcher, has been accused of acting on ideological grounds. But, privatization cuts across political lines and it is undertaken in developed and in developing countries alike. The list includes Canada, Austria, Germany, Italy, Spain, and Japan among developed countries and Argentina, Brazil, Korea and Mexico among developing countries.

The OECD notes that 'many OECD governments appear increasingly convinced that privatization can improve overall economic performance through ownership transfer . . . '[4] The advantages of privatization are seen in improved efficiency, a conclusion that tends to be supported by empirical evidence the OECD cites in the same report.

Additional considerations include reducing bureaucratic interference in the firms' operations and in the determination of their longer-term orientation. While in the second half of its tenure the socialist government encouraged nationalized firms to increase profits, the *contrats de plan* between the government and the firms remained in effect and the appointment of managers for a period of three years may have hindered the pursuit of longer-term objectives, especially when they conflicted with those of the supervising authorities.[5]

The new government also plans to accelerate the process of adjustment in firms that are in a difficult situation and will remain in the public sector for the time being. This is the case at Charbonnages de France, which plans to close several coal mines; at the steel producing firms, Usinor and Sacilor, whose newly unified management expects to put into effect the recommendations of Jean Gandois's report to substantially cut the workforce; and at Renault, where Raymond Lévy took over the tasks of the assassinated Georges Besse. Also, the shipbuilding firm Normed, that received government support per worker three times the average wage according to a report by the Court of Accounts, declared bankcruptcy and reduced its work-force by more than one-half.

In March 1987, the government announced that it will open 40 percent of telecommunications to competition, permit private carriers to operate domestic air charters, and abolish the monopoly of 'agents de change' to carry out brokerage operations on the Bourse. But deregulation did not advance in surface transportation and energy, where important steps were taken in recent years in the United States that also went further in deregulating telecommunications and air transportation than this is envisaged in France. Finally, the deregulation of banking was largely the handiwork of the socialist government that also envisaged the suppression of *l'encadrement du crédit*.

The socialist government began to liberalize prices, after having reversed the 1980 liberalization measures taken by Raymond Barre, but the new government went even beyond Barre in abolishing the 1945 decree that institutionalized price control. Under the decree adopted in December 1986, 'the prices of goods, products, and services . . . are freely determined by competition.'

Price controls remain in effect, however, in regard to electricity, gas, water, tobacco products, public transportation, taxis, paper for newspapers, pharmaceuticals reimbursed by social security, medical services, and some other professional services, the cases of which will be studied in the next two years. Also, the government may reintroduce price control for a period of six months in the event of excessive price increases in a 'crisis situation, in exceptional circumstances, a public calamity, or a manifestly abnormal situation in the market of a particular sector.' And price control can be applied without time limitations, on the advice of the newly-established Council of Competition, 'in the sectors or zones where price competition is limited because of monopoly situations, continuing supply difficulties, or government regulations.' In both cases, a decree of the State Council is required.

Furthermore, there remains the possibility of the government exerting pressure on enterprises that plan to raise prices. This occurred in February 1987, when finance minister Edouard Balladur's criticism of its 'irresponsible attitude' led a large insurance company to rescind its earlier announced increases on car insurance premiums. Balladur also induced the commercial banks to refrain from imposing checking charges and asked Renault to postpone price increases.

The Council of Competition can penalize companies for anti-competitive practices, and it has a right to review on concentrations that may reduce the extent of competition. There is no American-style anti-trust legislation, however, and there has been no change in la loi Royer that limits the establishment of supermarkets with a surface exceeding 1000 sq. meters, thereby reducing competition in commerce and providing extra profits to existing supermarkets.

While the socialist government took some actions to ease the exchange controls it had reinforced after May 1981, important measures of liberalization were adopted only after the new government assumed office. These measures included the freeing of financial transactions by exporters and importers as well as the liberalization of the rules for establishing commercial offices abroad. Furthermore, banks are now permitted to make loans in French francs to non-residents, although these loans cannot exceed their foreign resources and French residents continue to be prohibited from holding bank accounts abroad or having accounts denominated in foreign currency at home.

Steps were taken to liberalize labor regulations. The requirement of administrative authorization for firing workers was abolished as of 1 January 1987. Still, if they fire more than ten employees, or thirty employees over a period of six months, employers have to notify the Labor Inspectorate, which is to ensure that the employees have been consulted and a social plan has been adopted. The social plan is financed by the firm, except for firms with less than ten employees, in which case the government provides the financing. Moreover, the Council of Wise Men may impose penalties in the event of 'abusive firing,' i.e. lack of sufficient economic motive.

Finally, legislation was introduced to increase flexibility in working hours in the case of seasonal activities. As long as the working time does not exceed an average of 39 hours per week over the year, it can be increased to 44 hours in season without payment of overtime in the framework of agreements with the labor unions.

II MACROECONOMIC TRENDS

The decline in the rate of increase of hourly earnings in manufacturing, which was accomplished under the socialist government after the speeding-up of wage increases in 1981, continued after March 1986. But, the rise in real wages accelerated in the first half of 1986. This occurred in part because wages increases in the first few months of 1986 exceeded the projections, but mostly because of the deceleration of inflation due to unanticipated declines in the prices of energy products (14.5 percent between December 1985 and 1986). Including these products, consumer prices rose by 2.1 percent; excluding them, the increase was 4.0 percent. Thus, the system of wage increases based on the expected rise of prices, introduced by the socialist government, that worked well for several years led to unexpected increases in real wages in 1986.

The rise in petroleum prices in late 1986 raised consumer prices again in early 1987 and increases occurred also in the prices of certain services that were put on the liberalization list. INSEE, the government statistical office, projects that the consumer price index would rise by 1.9 percent in the first half of 1987; for the year as a whole, the Ministry of Finance raised its inflation estimate to 2.4 percent.

The January agreements with the railroads, the Paris Metro, and the national electricity firm allow for wage increases slightly above 3 percent for 1987 without the productivity growth condition that was supposed to have triggered a rise from 2 to 3 percent. Wage increases for the rest of the public sector and the banks are scheduled at 1.7 percent. But while the increases were to include slippages due to seniority and promotion, several agreements with public enterprises exclude such slippages in calculating the 1.7 percent increase. Also, in March 1987, additional increases were granted to government employees in lower wage brackets.

The revisions of the 1986 budget involved raising total expenditures by 26 billion francs. And while Jacques Chirac announced 'an unprecedented effort of economies, of the order of 40 billion francs' for 1987 this target is formulated 'with respect to the trend of expenditures, other things being equal' without indicating how such a trend is derived.[6]

The budget for 1987 calculates with a 1.8 percent increase in expenditures that is slightly smaller than the 2 percent inflation rate assumed at the time the budget was prepared. The socialist opposition objected that budgeted expenditures were artificially reduced by using 14 billion francs from the proceeds of privatizations to provide capital to industry. But, 11 billion francs of expenditures were rebudgetized. Meaures taken in favor of the long-term unemployed and the extension of the reconversion contracts to workers in bankrupt firms will add 3 billion francs to public expenditures. With these adjustments, budgetary expenditures were estimated to rise 2.4 percent in 1987.

On the revenue side, tax cuts in 1987 provide a gain of 16 billion francs for individuals and 12 billion francs for enterprises.[7] While it has been suggested that the gains for individuals would only compensate for the 1.1 percent increase in social security contributions, the latter reflects higher social benefits. In turn, tax cuts for enterprises have been offset by reductions in budgetary support[8] and the elimination of investment incentives in the form of special depreciation allowances. This conclusion is not materially affected if account is taken of reductions in social charges in regard to newly-employed young workers, in part because this tends to offset the lower productivity of such workers and in part because the reductions are limited in time.

Despite increased expenditures in the supplementary budgets for 1986, the deficit in the government budget for the year was reduced from 145.3 to 143.6 billion francs as the sale of shares in nationalized industries brought revenues of 8 billion francs. According to INSEE, the revised budget deficit equals 2.9 percent of GDP in 1986, compared with 3.3 percent in 1985, although a shift from surplus to deficit in the social security accounts gave rise to an increase in the deficit of public administrations which also include local governments.

In 1987, the deficit in the government budget is projected to decline further to 128.6 billion francs, or 2.5 percent of GDP, with the deficit of the public administration amounting to 2.6 percent. Correcting for the use of the proceeds of privatization and for the projected aid to the unemployed, while adjusting for rebudgetization, adds 6 billion francs to the deficit. This may further be raised by the shortfall in revenue associated with the reduction in GDP growth projections from 2.8 to 2.0 percent. Furthermore, social expenditures would need to be lowered in order to avoid increasing social security contributions to eliminate the deficit of the social security system.

Additional receipts will be obtained from privatization over and above the 1987 budget projections. Out of a total of unanticipated revenues of 15 billion francs, 10 billion will be used to reduce the public debt. At the same time, 2 billion francs will be allotted to the construction of autoroutes, permitting additional borrowing of 3 billion francs, 1.4 billion will be provided to the railroads, while the remaining 1.6 billion will be granted to industrial enterprises in the public sector.

The socialist government had reduced personal income taxes, cut social security contributions for individuals, and provided advance reimbursement of the compulsory loan of 1983 during the six months period prior to the March 1986 elections. Together with the rise in real wages, these changes led to increases in the volume of consumption expenditures at an annual rate of 3.1 percent in the second half of 1985 and 3.8 percent in the first half of 1986. A smaller increase, 2.5 percent, occurred in the second half of 1986, when social security contributions were raised.

Taking further account of increases in public consumption and investment and changes in inventories, the rise in domestic expenditures contributed 5.8 percent to GDP growth in the second half of 1985, 3.0 percent in the first half of 1986, and 4.0 percent in the second half of 1986, measured at annual rates. Increases in GDP were, however, only 3.4 percent, 1.3 percent, and 2.5 percent, respectively, reflecting the negative contribution of the trade balance to economic growth.

For 1986, taken as a whole, GDP grew by 2.1 percent as a negative contribution of 1.8 percent by the trade balance offset nearly one-half of the positive contribution of the rise in domestic expenditures. The volume of imports rose by 6.9 percent, but exports increased by only 0.5 percent.

Increases in the imports of consumer goods reached 15 percent in 1986, reflecting the inability of domestic producers to provide for increased consumption. At the same time, France lost export market shares in manufactured products. While its export markets grew 3.0 percent in volume in 1986, according to calculations made by the OECD, French exports of these products increased by only 0.3 percent.

Correspondingly, France's trade surplus in manufactured goods fell from 89 billion francs in 1985 to 30 billion francs in 1986 and its trade deficit with Germany increased from 29 to 39 billion francs. All in all, the 31 billion francs improvement in the overall trade balance between 1985 and 1986 fell much short of the 90 billion francs reduction in France's trade deficit in energy products, which resulted from the fall in oil prices and the depreciation of the dollar. And, this difference is explained only in small part by the decline of demand by OPEC.

Changes in 1986 represents a continuation of tendencies in previous years. The rate of penetration of manufactured imports, calculated as a percentage of consumption, increased by 8 percentage points between 1980 and 1985. And while increased intra-industry specialization in international trade contributed to this result, France lost market shares *vis-à-vis* major exporting countries.

The OECD reports that, between 1980 and 1985, annual increases in the volume of France's manufactured exports averaged 2.7 percent while export demand in France's markets grew 3.9 percent a year. By contrasts, Germany's exports rose 5.1 percent annually, surpassing the 4.3 percent growth in its markets.

Differences in the rates of growth of exports in Germany and France in large part explains the differential changes in their current account balance that occurred over time. While Germany's current account balance shifted from −0.8 percent of GDP in 1979, the year preceding the second oil shock, to 2.6 percent in 1986, in France a decline occurred from 0.8 percent to 0.3 percent.

III FACTORS AFFECTING EXPORTS

The question arises, then, how can one explain France's poor export performance. It has been suggested that France suffered the consequences of decreases in the so-called 'grands contrats,' mainly in trade with developing and socialist countries. But such orders rebounded in 1984 to the average of the years 1980–82, after having declined in the previous year, and decreased only slightly in 1985. France nevertheless experienced growing losses of export market shares in those two years.

Others have sought to explain poor export performance by slow-growing markets in the developing countries and OPEC, which have a relatively high share in French exports. In fact, in 1980, France's share in the two markets totalled 25.6 percent while Germany's share was 15.8 percent. But, slow-growing exports to the centrally planned economies accounted for a higher share of exports in Germany (5.8 percent) than in France (4.6 percent). All in all, differences in market growth between 1980 and 1985 in Germany and France were dwarfed by differential changes in export market shares as France lost ground in all its major markets, the exception being OPEC.

It has further been suggested that France suffered the effects of the unfavorable commodity composition of its exports. Yet, compared with Germany, France has a relatively high share in the fastest-growing product groups: other machinery and transport equipment (to a large extent aircraft) and chemicals. On the whole, although France has a high share in the two slowest growing product groups (textiles and clothing) as well, it has a marginally more favorable product composition in manufactured exports than Germany, using the GATT classification of eleven product groups.

At the same time, country and commodity shares are not immutable. Rather, success in exports depends to a considerable extent on the ability of the individual countries to shift exports to rapidly-growing markets and to rapidly-growing commodity groups. This has not been the case in France that made only limited progress in shifting from developing country to developed country markets.

These considerations point to the lack of flexibility in French exports. According to a report of the Planning Office, an important contributing factor was the absence of coherent commercial organization. 'One does not sell any more an isolated product but a complete system . . . it is no exaggeration to say that changes in distribution have not been adequately mastered by French industry.'[9]

Yet, under the exchange controls introduced in May 1981, exporters had little flexibility to improve commercialization abroad. They had to repatriate their foreign exchange earnings within fifteen days of the sale; they could not buy foreign exchange forward beyond 90 days; and they were limited in the establishment of commercial agencies in foreign countries.

A further contributing factor was the insufficient volume of productive investment. Between 1980 and 1985, productive investment declined by altogether 1.3 percent in France, compared with a rise of 3.2 percent in Germany, following a slowdown that occurred after the quadrupling of oil prices. And while the growth of productive investment in France approached that of Germany in 1986, the differences are projected to rise again in 1987. At the same time, industrial investments increased by only 1 percent in 1986 and are projected to rise by 3 percent in 1987.

As this author noted in reviewing the economic policies of the socialist government,[10] the shortfall of investment in France in the early 1980s may be explained in large part by declines in profit rates that resulted from increases in wages and social charges after May 1981. Profit rates rose in subsequent years but remain lower in France than in the other major industrial countries, the exception being the United Kingdom.[11]

Also, until 1986, depreciation exceeded gross business savings and the net rate of profit continues to fall short of the real rate of interest. In view of the substantial debts accumulated by enterprises in the years of low profits,[12] then, it is not surprising that many firms prefer repaying debt to investing.

Interest rates were reduced repeatedly after March 1986, but were raised again from November onwards as the French franc came under increasing pressure. Thus, overnight money market rates, which declined to a low of 7.0 percent in August 1986 from 8.5 percent on the eve of the elections, reached 9.0 percent in January 1987. The corresponding three-months' money market rates were 8.3 percent in March 1986, 7.2 percent in August 1986, and 9.1 percent in January 1987. And, having declined from 8.5 percent in March 1986 to 7.6 percent in August, the average yield on long-term government bonds attained 9.1 percent in January 1987.

With a net rate of profit of about 4 percent, high interest rates give a considerable incentive to repay loans rather than to invest. This is the case for large enterprises, although they can obtain loans at little over money market rates – or even slightly less – as they have access to a gamut of domestic financial instruments as well as to foreign loans. It is the case even more for small enterprises that pay a higher interest rate plus various charges, which reportedly add up to double the interest charges paid by large firms.[13] In fact, differences in interest rates paid by small and large firms are substantially greater in France than in Germany and other major industrial countries. It may not come as a surprise, then, that small firms have a much larger share in German than in French exports.

Interest rates decreased only slightly in France after the 3 percent revaluation of the German mark in January 1987, and subsequent declines did not re-establish the August 1986 levels. In late April, overnight money market rates were 7.9 percent in France as against 3.7 percent in Germany, three-months' rates were 8.0 and 4.0 percent, and interest rates on government bonds averaged 8.5 and 5.7 percent.

Interest rates on three-month Eurocurrency deposits provide an indication of expectations about future changes in exchange rates. In late April, these rates were 8.2 percent for the Eurofranc and 4.0 percent for the Euromark, pointing to an anticipated change of over 4 percent in the franc–mark parity.

Anticipations of exchange rate changes by the financial markets may reflect the fact that the 9 percent change in the franc–mark parity between March 1986 and January 1987 did not fully offset differential changes in prices, which occurred since 1983 when the last devaluation under the socialist government was undertaken. Between 1983 and 1986, consumer prices rose by 16.7 percent in France and 4.4 percent in Germany, with increases of 2.5 percent and 0.2 percent, respectively, projected for 1987.

It has been suggested that the situation is more favorable for France if changes in unit labor costs are considered. These costs rose by 11.0 percent in France between 1983 and 1986, compared with increases of 4.4 percent in Germany. But the differential rise in prices and unit labor costs in France only offset the adverse developments that occurred in earlier years.

Adjusting for catching-up in terms of the relationship between prices and unit labor costs, then, it appears that the exchange rate changes of May 1986 and January 1987 have compensated only in part for the deterioration of the French competitive position *vis-à-vis* Germany that has taken place since 1983. Two possible remedies suggest themselves: a further parity change and a renewed effort to reduce labor costs in France.

A devaluation contributes to inflation and it may also have a psychological effect in France, creating expectations for further devaluations. But, an overvalued exchange rate also creates expectations for a devaluation and requires high interest rates to avoid an outflow of funds as is the case in France today. Differences in the current account balances of France and Germany, too, create such expectations. Yet, France has avoided a larger disparity in the current account only by having a GDP growth rate lower than Germany (1.3 and 1.5 percent between 1980 and 1986, with the discrepancy increasing over time), contributing to rising unemployment.

In turn, apart from improving the competitive position of French industry, reductions in labor costs would tend to lower inflation rates. While it is projected that unit labor costs would rise by 1.5 percent in France and by 1.8 percent in Germany in 1987, additional changes would be necessary in order to avoid a further devaluation of the franc. This may be accomplished by reducing social security charges and accepting greater rigor in wage determination.

IV PROSPECTS FOR THE FUTURE

This review has highlighted the principal changes that occurred in economic policies in France after March 1986. Privatization represents a reversal of the nationalizations undertaken by the socialist government and goes even further by privatizing banks and insurance companies which were nationalized in 1945. The new government further announced some measures of deregulation in several sectors, although no change occurred in others such as energy and surface transportation.

The government accelerated the process of price and foreign exchange liberalization that had begun in the last years of the socialist government after it had strengthened controls. Also, greater flexibility was introduced in labor regulations and the decline in the rate of increase of hourly earnings in manufacturing continued.

Nevertheless, the rise of real wages accelerated in the first half of 1986, when the slowdown in price increases exceeded expectations. This is explained by the fall of petroleum prices that subsequently rose again, reinforcing the inflationary effects of price liberalization in services. The rate of inflation reached 0.9 percent in January 1987 and only government pressure on some sectors to forgo price increases and on the national electricity and gas firms to cut tariffs permitted keeping the rate of inflation to 0.2 percent in February (the corresponding figures for Germany were 0.4 and 0.1 percent). Consumer prices rose by 0.2 percent in March 1987 in France when energy prices declined, while prices remained unchanged in Germany.

Liberalizing prices following the elections would have permitted avoiding a reversal of the trend towards lower inflation rates at the beginning of 1987. The parallel liberalization of foreign exchange would also have made it possible to negotiate a larger exchange rate change with the EMS partners immediately after the elections,[14] thereby improving to a substantial extent the competitive position of French industry and avoiding a second exchange rate change in January 1987.

The improved competitive position of French industry, in turn, would have given a push to exports and favored domestic goods over imports, thus providing an expansionary force. In the event, France continued to lose export market shares while rates of import penetration increased as the rise in real wages, together with reductions in taxes and social charges undertaken by the socialist government, contributed to the expansion of consumer spending. At the same time, the rise in consumer spending would have been attenuated if prices were liberalized immediately following the elections.

Apart from the continued overvaluation of the franc, losses in export market shares and rising rates of market penetration reflected the lack of sufficient investment after the quadrupling of oil prices and, in particular, during the period of the socialist government. The reversal of this trend is a first priority in order to accelerate economic growth and to reduce unemployment in France.

Lower interest rates would serve this objective. Apart from the establishment of confidence in the franc, this would require reducing the deficit of the public sector.[15] For one thing, current government expenditures would need to be lowered and health expenditures reduced through the increased sharing of costs by the beneficiaries. For another thing, all receipts from privatization should be allotted to reimbursing the public debt, so as to avoid 'crowding out.'[16]

It would further be desirable to reorient tax reductions from individuals to business firms. In particular, reductions in social charges and in the professional tax would promote investment as well as productive employment in France.

While general tax measures, which increase the profitability of capital, would suffice under normal circumstances, additional measures would be desirable in the present situation. For one thing, lower tax rates may induce debt repayment rather than new investment under high interest rates. For another thing, the retardation of investment over a number of years would necessitate considerable increases to permit the modernization of the French export structure and the establishment of new capacities for competition with imports.[17] At the same time, in the absence of the rapid rise of investment, there is a danger that expansionary measures are taken, leading to higher consumption as it was done in 1974–5 and 1981–2.

Investment incentives were successfully used to promote investment in the first five years of the governments of President Reagan and Prime Minister Thatcher and continue to be granted in Germany. Also, an econometric investigation for France has shown 'investment responds strongly to fiscal incentives, much more than to changes in the components of the cost of capital.'[18] At the same time, investment incentives would have to be granted for a sufficiently long period to avoid that their effects remain temporary.

While investment incentives promote spending on plant and equipment, considerable importance attaches to research and development. In abolishing the Fond Industriel de Modernisation, the new government reversed the growth of budgetary allotments to industrial research by its predecessor. It has since been officially recognized that aid to industrial research is necessary to reduce the cleavage between basic and applied research in France. This may be accomplished by extending the present system of fiscal credits for expenditures on research and development undertaken by enterprises beyond 1988 and eliminating its present limitations to increments in the expenditures.

The budgetary cost of investment incentives and the promotion of research and development calls for a renewed effort to reduce public expenditures, which is also needed in order to limit pressures on financial markets. Continued progress on deregulation would further contribute to the renewal of the French economy by promoting competition and cutting costs. At the same time, in pursuing the objective of lowering industrial subsidies, it would be desirable to reconsider regional aids that have taken a multiplicity of forms and are said to cover France as 'the coat of a leopard.'

There would further be need for measures that promote employment by lowering the cost of labor.[19] Providing tax benefits to business in the form of reductions in social charges would have such an effect. Consideration should also be given to lowering the minimum wage for young workers, which has apparently contributed to unemployment,[20] while stepping up efforts at technical education. This is of particular importance, given the high rates of unemployment in the below-21 age group in France: 25 percent in 1985, compared with 12 percent in the United States, 10 percent in Germany, and 5 percent in Japan.

Reducing the cost of labor, together with measures aimed at increasing investment in physical and human capital, then, would contribute to economic growth while ensuring balance-of-payments equilibrium and the rise of employment. These measures would enhance the effects of liberalizing regulations that represent an important structural change in France.

CONCLUSIONS

This essay reviewed the policies applied by the new center-right government in the year following the March 1986 elections. It further provided recommendations for the future, so as to improve the competitiveness of French industry.

The recommendations call for a devaluation of the exchange rate, together with reductions in labor costs by lowering social security charges and accepting greater rigor in wage determination. They would further require increased investments to permit the modernization of the French export structure and the establishment of new capacities for competition with imports.

Lower interest rates would contribute to increased investment in France. The same objective would be served by reorienting tax reductions from individuals to business firms. Investment incentives would also promote spending on plant and equipment. At the same time, they would need to be accompanied by a stepped-up effort at research and development.

Increased investment would further lead to higher employment. Lowering social charges would also have such an effect. Consideration may further be given to reducing the minimum wage for young workers. At the same time, there is need to promote technical education.

NOTES

1. In the case of Paribas, however, people multiplied their demand for shares in anticipation of getting only a small part of what they ordered.
2. Lionel Zinsou, *Le fer de lance*. Essai sur les nationalisations industrielles (Paris: Olivier Orban, 1985) p. 250.
3. While in 1982 the government paid 6.1 billion francs for Saint-Gobain, and 5.0 billion francs for Paribas, it obtained 9.0 billion francs from the sale of the former and 12.6 billion francs from the sale of the latter.
4. Organisation for Economic Co-operation and Development, *OECD Economic Outlook*, No. 40 (Paris, 1986).
5. But interventions may not disappear in cases such as Paribas and Crédit Commercial de France, where a substantial part of the shares are sold *de gré à gré* to groups selected by the government; the so-called *'noyeau dur'* (Yves Guihannec, 'Privatizations: qui sont les vrais gagnants?', *Le Point*, 23 March 1987, p. 101). The continuation of this practice would lead to interlocking relationships among firms, obscuring the question of control.
6. *Le Monde*, 10 June 1986.
7. An additional gain of 6 billion francs to enterprises will result from the reduction in corporate income taxes provided by the 1986 budget and a further reduction in corporate tax rates has been announced for 1988.
8. Nevertheless, there is an improvement from the efficiency point of view as a result of the shift of financial resources from low efficiency to high-efficiency firms.
9. Rapport du groupe stratégie industrielle no. 7, 'Produits et marchés en France' (Paris: Commissariat général du Plan, 1986).
10. Chapter 16 in this volume.
11. The December 1986 *OECD Outlook* reports that in 1986 gross rates of return (i.e. before depreciation) in manufacturing, averaged 13 percent in France, 20 percent in the United States and Japan, 18 percent in Germany and 8 percent in the United Kingdom.
12. The debt of enterprises in France has reportedly come to exceed own capital more than four times, compared with a ratio of two for Germany where decreases occurred in recent years. Jacques Régniez, 'Une politique pour les entreprises françaises. Sur la nécessité de l'assainissement,' *Commentaire*, X (1987) pp. 92–8.
13. *Le Monde*, 17 May 1986 – Investments by small firms nevertheless increased more rapidly than by large firms in 1986, but this offset only in part the shortfall of the previous years.
14. The author suggested a 10 percent change in the mark–franc parity at the time, in Chapter 16 in this volume.
15. This point is emphasized in the report on the competitiveness of French enterprises, prepared at the request of Edouard Balladur by the Groupe de Réflexion Economique, chaired by Renaud de la Genière (January 1987).
16. In fact, spending 5 billion frances on autoroutes will hardly improve the competitiveness of French industry that would require increased private investment.
17. The resulting favorable effects on the balance of payments would soon outweigh the initial unfavorable effects of the increased importation of machinery.
18. The tax credit provided by Raymond Barre's government has proved to be the most effective in France, reportedly creating investment more than ten times its fiscal cost, although the results might have been affected by the special

circumstances existing at the time. Pierre-Alain Muet and Sanvi Avouyi-Doui, 'L'effet des incitations fiscales sur l'investissement,' *Observations et diagnostics économique. Revue de l'OFCE*, January 1987, pp. 164, 168.

19. This is of particular importance, given expectations for a reduction of industrial employment of up to 100 000 in 1987 (*Liberation*, 30 March 1987).

20. Cf. Jean-Jacques Rosa, 'Les effets du Smic sur l'emploi des jeunes: une analyse bien confirmée,' *Politique Economique*, October 1985. This study modifies an earlier OECD analysis that eliminated such effects by introducing a trend factor in youth unemployment that does not have a particular economic justification.

Part VII
Trade Policies and Multilateral Negotiations

Essay 19 The Extent and the Cost of Protection in Developed–Developing Country Trade

INTRODUCTION

The focus of this essay is the measures of protection applied to trade between developed and developing countries. This choice reflects concern with the adverse repercussions of recently imposed protectionist measures in the two groups of countries as well as the increasing importance of mutual trade for their national economies.

The essay analyses the extent and the cost of protection in developed and in developing countries, with special attention given to measures affecting trade between the two groups of countries. Section I reviews the tariff and nontariff measures applied by the developed countries and provides empirical evidence on the cost of protection in these countries. Section II examines the use of protective measures in the developing countries and indicates the resulting cost to their national economies. In the conclusion, the policy implications of the findings are briefly indicated.

I PROTECTION IN THE DEVELOPED COUNTRIES

Tariff protection

The successes of the postwar period with tariff disarmament in the developed countries are well known and do not require detailed discussion. While the original purpose had been to undo the damage resulting from the competitive imposition of import duties during the 1930s, tariffs in the major developed countries were reduced below pre-depression levels by the end of the 1950s. These reductions, undertaken on an item-by-item basis, were followed by across-the-board tariff reductions in the framework of the Dillon Round (1960–61), the Kennedy Round (1964–7), and the Tokyo Round (1974–7) of trade negotiations.

TABLE 19.1 *Post-Tokyo round tariff averages in the major developed countries*

	Tariffs on total imports			Tariffs on imports from LDCs
Raw materials	Semi-manufactures	Finished manufactures	Semi- and finished manufactures	Semi- and finished manufactures
United States	0.2	3.0	5.7	4.9	8.7
European Common Market	0.2	4.2	6.9	6.0	6.7
Japan	0.5	4.6	6.0	5.4	6.8

SOURCE: General Agreement on Tariffs and Trade, *The Tokyo Round of Multilateral Trade Negotiations*, II – Supplementary Report, January 1980, pp. 33–7.

Taken together, in the course of the Dillon, Kennedy, and Tokyo Round negotiations, tariffs on manufactured goods imported by the developed countries were lowered, on the average, by nearly two-thirds. Table 19.1 shows that post Tokyo Round tariff levels in major developed countries averaged 6–7 percent for finished manufactures and were even lower for semi-manufactures and raw materials. Apart from overall reductions, the procedure applied in the Tokyo Round also lessened the dispersion of tariffs as higher tariff rates were cut proportionately more than lower rates.

The question arises, however, if the remaining tariffs bear disproportionately on products imported from the developing countries. There are two aspects to this question. First, whether tariffs on products of interest to developing countries are higher (or lower) at each level of processing; second, whether there is tariff escalation which affects developing country exports of manufactures.

Table 19.1 shows that manufactured products of interest to the developing countries are in general subject to higher tariffs than products on the same level of fabrication originating in the developed countries. Thus, post-Tokyo Round tariffs on all imports of semi-manufactures and finished manufactures, and on such imports from developing countries, respectively, average 4.9 and 8.7 percent in the United States, 6.0 and 6.7 in the European Common Market, and 5.4 and 6.8 percent in Japan.

Furthermore, there is evidence of tariff escalation. Thus, post-Tokyo Round average tariffs on raw materials, semi-manufactures, and finished manufactures are 0.2, 3.0, and 5.7 percent for the United States, 0.2, 4.2, and 6.9 percent for the European Common Market, and 0.5, 4.6, and 6.0 percent for Japan (Table 19.1).[1]

The cited averages pertain to all processing chains, several of which have little relevance for most developing countries. Such is the case in particular for petroleum-based products and for metal products, where processing is highly capital intensive and requires a considerable degree of technological sophistication that is found only in developing countries at higher levels of industrialization. Excluding these products would raise the extent of tariff escalation even further.

Table 19.2 provides data on average tariffs in the developed countries for products in eleven processing chains, which are of interest to developing countries and, among them, to countries at lower levels of industrial development. The raw materials in question weigh heavily in the exports of the countries concerned and the processing of these materials is frequently within their technical competence. Also, with the major exception of paper, processing is not a highly capital-intensive activity.

It is apparent that, except for wood, tariffs escalate in all cases. But, this exception is more apparent than real, since the major input into furniture is semi-manufactured wood that has lower tariffs. And, the overall import-ance of tariff escalation is indicated by the fact that the products in question account for 47 percent of the exports of nonfuel primary and semiprocessed products from the developing to the developed countries but for only 11 percent of manufactured exports. At the same time, the data reported in Table 19.2 exclude textiles and clothing, iron and steel, and footwear, where there is also tariff escalation, but where quantitative import restrictions tend to be the effective barrier to developed country markets.

Escalation of tariffs can cause effective rates of protection to exceed nominal rates by a substantial margin. At the same time, for developing country producers, the relevant consideration is the protection of the processing margin (value added), or effective protection, rather than the (nominal) tariffs levied on individual products.

Data provided in an earlier paper by Yeats[2] permits estimating effective rates in the post-Tokyo Round situation for three semi-manufactured products: processed cocoa (15.8 percent), leather (13.5 percent, and vegetable oil (70.2 percent). In the cases considered, the ratio of effective to nominal tariffs ranges from 3.2 (leather) to 8.7 (vegetable oil); the differences in the ratios are explained largely by interindustry differences in the share of value added in output.[3]

Such protection tends to discriminate against industrial processing in the developing countries and, in particular, in countries at lower levels of industrialization. Other things being equal, a 20 percent effective rate of protection in developed countries means that firms engaged in processing in a developing country would have to compress their processing margin (value added) by 25 percent, in order to compete with processing activities in the developed countries. With some of the costs of processing, including the cost of capital, not being compressible, tariff escalation in the devel-oped countries thus puts industrial processing in the developing countries at a considerable disadvantage.

TABLE 19.2 *Pre- and Post-Tokyo round tariffs for twelve processing chains*

Stage of processing	Product description	Tariff rate[a]	
		Pre-Tokyo	Post-Tokyo
1	Fish, crustaceans and molluscs	4.3	3.5
2	Fish, crustaceans and molluscs, prepared	6.1	5.5
1	Vegetables, fresh or dried	13.3	8.9
2	Vegetables, prepared	18.8	12.4
1	Fruit, fresh, dried	6.0	4.8
2	Fruit, provisionally preserved	14.5	12.2
3	Fruit, prepared	19.5	16.6
1	Coffee	10.0	6.8
2	Processed coffee	13.3	9.4
1	Cocoa beans	4.2	2.6
2	Processed cocoa	6.7	4.3
3	Chocolate products	15.0	11.8
1	Oil seeds and flour	2.7	2.7
2	Fixed vegetable oils	8.5	8.1
1	Unmanufactured tobacco	56.1	55.8
2	Manufactured tobacco	82.2	81.8
1	Natural rubber	2.8	2.3
2	Semi-manufactured rubber (unvulcanized)	4.6	2.9
3	Rubber articles	7.9	6.7
1	Raw hides and skins	1.4	0.0
2	Semi-manufactured leather	4.2	4.2
3	Travel goods, handbags etc.	8.5	8.5
4	Manufactured articles of leather	9.3	8.2
1	Vegetable textiles yarns (excluding hemp)	4.0	2.9
2	Twine, rope and articles; sacks and bags	5.6	4.7
3	Jute fabrics	9.1	8.3
1	Silk yarn, not for retail sale	2.6	2.6
2	Silk fabric	5.6	5.3
1	Semi-manufactured wood	2.6	1.8
2	Wood panels	10.8	9.2
3	Wood articles	6.9	4.1
4	Furniture	8.1	6.6
1	Total		

NOTES: [a] Unweighted average of the tariffs actually facing developing country exports (i.e., Generalized System of Preference, Most-Favoured-Nation, other special preferential rates, etc.) in the market of EEC, Japan, Australia, New Zealand, Canada, Austria, Switzerland, Finland, Norway, and Sweden.

SOURCE: A. J. Yeats, 'The Influence of Trade and Commercial Barriers on the Industrial Processing of Natural Resources,' *World Development*, IX (1981) 485–94; and World Bank Trade Data System.

Nontariff barriers

Parallel with reductions in tariffs, quantitative import restrictions were liberalized during the 1950s in Western Europe, where these restrictions had been applied largely for balance-of-payments purposes after World War II. Import liberalization also proceeded, albeit at a slower rate, in Japan where restrictions had been employed on balance-of-payments, as well as on infant industry, grounds although a number of products remained subject to quantitative import restrictions until the early 1970s. Finally, the United States continued with its broadly liberal trade policy but imposed limitations on the imports of Japanese cotton textiles.

Agriculture was an exception to the process of import liberalization during the postwar period. In fact, apart from the United States that is a large net exporter of food and feedingstuffs, agricultural protection in the developed countries was reinforced after 1960. The European Community has encouraged high-cost production by setting high domestic prices in the framework of the Common Agricultural Policy, thereby turning an import surplus in major foods into an export surplus. Also, with higher wages raising domestic production costs, agricultural protection has intensified in Japan.

Increased use has subsequently been made of nontariff protection in manufacturing industries. The developed countries have generally refrained from applying the GATT safeguard clause; they have relied instead on so-called voluntary export restraints and orderly marketing arrangements to limit imports.

Measures of nontariff protection on textiles and clothing apply exclusively to developing country exporters. Thus, while the Long Term Arrangement Regarding Cotton Textiles (1962) was originally aimed largely at Japan, its successor, the Multi-Fiber Arrangement (1979), limits the imports of textiles and clothing from the developing countries. And, whereas the MFA earlier permitted annual import growth of 6 percent in volume, in the course of its subsequent renewals and reinterpretations it has become increasingly restrictive. While Japan is not party to the MFA, there is evidence of informal limitations on the imports of textiles and clothing from the developing countries. Also, Japan severely limits the importation of footwear from all sources whereas several of the larger European countries restrict footwear imports from the developing countries alone.

Since the early 1970s, nontariff measures have also assumed increased importance for steel. In the United States, there are formal and informal limitations on the importation of carbon and specialty steel from Japan, from the European Community, and from several developing countries; the Community restricts imports from Japan and from developing countries; and informal measures limit steel imports from Korea into Japan.

France and Italy have long restricted automobile imports from Japan. In recent years, they have been joined by Belgium, Germany, and the United Kingdom. In turn, the United States negotiated limitations on the imports of automobiles from Japan in 1981 but let the agreement expire in early 1985.

In the electronics industry, the European Community has imposed limitations on the imports of several products from Japan and, to a lesser extent, Korea and Taiwan. In turn, the United States has eliminated earlier restrictions on the importation of color television sets. Finally, informal barriers limit the importation of telecommunication equipment into Japan.

Table 19.3 shows the extent of nontariff barriers applied by the major developed countries, following recent increases in these barriers. The table provides information on the use of nontariff measures affecting imports from the other developed countries, from the developing countries, and from all countries, taken together, in the United States, the European Common Market, and Japan, based on a joint World Bank-UNCTAD research effort.

Nontariff barriers have been defined to include all transparent border measures that directly or indirectly limit imports. Quantitative import restrictions and so-called voluntary export restraints limit imports directly. In turn, variable import levies that equalize domestic and import prices, minimum price requirements for imports, voluntary export price agreements, as well as tariff quotas involving the imposition of higher duties above a pre-determined import quantity, have an indirect effect on imports.

Table 19.3 shows the share of imports subject to nontariff measures, calculated by using world trade weights. The use of world trade weights allows for differences in the relative importance of individual tariff items in international trade while abstracting from the idiosyncrasies of national protection. In contrast, calculating for a particular country the percentage share of own imports subject to restrictions is equivalent to using own imports as weights, which means that the more restrictive the measure the lower its weight in the calculations; in the extreme, prohibitive tariffs have zero weight.[4] In turn, calculating the percentage share of tariff items has the disadvantage that it gives equal weight to all items, even though they may vary in importance to a considerable extent.[5]

Table 19.3 reports nontariff barriers for nonfuel imports and, within this total, for agricultural and for manufactured imports; it further disaggregates manufactured goods into textiles and clothing, footwear, iron and

TABLE 19.3 *Relative shares of imports subject to nontariff measures, May 1985 (World trade weighted)[a]*

	Nonfuel products	Agriculture	Manufacturing	Textiles and clothing	Footwear	Iron and steel	Electrical machinery	Transport equipment	Rest of manufacturing
United States									
Imports from									
all countries[b]	6.4	11.5	5.6	47.8	0.1	21.8	0.0	0.0	0.4
developed countries	3.4	11.7	2.7	25.5	0.0	24.6	0.0	0.0	0.0
developing countries	12.9	11.8	14.4	65.3	0.1	4.5	0.0	0.0	1.9
European Community									
Imports from									
all countries[b]	13.9	37.8	10.1	42.4	10.2	37.9	4.2	3.9	3.8
developed countries	10.5	46.7	5.7	13.6	0.3	33.7	3.1	3.8	2.6
developing countries	21.8	27.5	21.4	65.2	12.5	28.9	4.7	4.6	5.3
Japan									
Imports from									
all countries[b]	9.6	33.8	5.4	14.0	39.6	0.0	0.0	0.0	6.0
developed countries	9.5	35.7	5.5	14.0	34.3	0.0	0.0	0.0	7.1
developing countries	10.5	30.2	5.4	14.2	42.2	0.0	0.0	0.0	1.9

NOTE: [a] The data collected by Nogues, Olechowski, and Winters for 1983 have been adjusted for the termination of the US-Japanese automotive agreement. Other changes in protection occurring between 1983 and 1985 have been relatively minor.
[b] All countries include the socialist countries of Eastern Europe, hence the overall average does not necessarily lie between average for imports from the industrial and from the developing countries.

SOURCE: Julio J. Nogues, Andrzej Olechowski, and L. Alan Winters, 'The Extent of Non-tariff Barriers to Industrial Countries' Imports,' World Bank Development Research Department Discussion Paper No. 115 (Washington, DC, 1985) and the sources cited therein.

steel, electrical machinery, transport equipment, and other manufactures. Fuels have not been included because the nontariff measures applied do not appear to aim at protecting the domestic production of competing fuels.

The results are indicative of the high protection of EEC and Japanese agriculture, where most commodities competing with domestic production encounter nontariff barriers. With protection applying chiefly to temperate zone products, these barriers affect a somewhat higher proportion of agricultural imports from developed than developing country suppliers. The proportions are about the same in the case of the United States, where the extent of nontariff barriers of agricultural products is relatively low.

In the United States and the European Community, nontariff barriers on manufactured imports discriminate to a considerable extent against developing country exporters. This discrimination is largely due to the restrictions imposed on developing country exports of textiles and clothing in the framework of the Multi-Fiber Arrangement (MFA). As noted above, Japan is not party to the MFA but it is said to use informal measures to limit its imports of textiles and clothing from the developing countries; in fact, as shown below, its imports have been growing at a lower rate, and account for a smaller proportion of domestic consumption, than in the United States and the European Common Market.

The data reported in Table 19.3 do not include other border measures that could, but may not, be used with protective effect, such as antidumping and countervailing duties, price monitoring and investigations of alleged practices that may give rise to the imposition of such duties, and automatic import authorizations. There is some evidence that these practices have been applied in certain circumstances in lieu of safeguards and with both the intent and effect of protecting domestic industry rather than simply offsetting distortions introduced by the exporter.[6] Their use has also increased since the late 1970s.[7]

Nevertheless, given the legitimate role that such practices can play in trade, they have to be treated differently from other nontariff measures. Thus, rather than eliminating the measures themselves, one should assure that they are not used for protective purposes.

Furthermore, the data reported in Table 19.3 do not include health and safety measures and technical standards that may be used with a protective intent.[8] Nor do the data comprise various informal measures that are prevalent in countries which rely to a considerable extent on administrative discretion rather than on codified rules to limit imports. Finally, the data are limited to trade-related measures, with the exclusion of domestic measures (e.g., producer subsidies and regional development measures) that bear on trade indirectly through their effect on domestic production.

Despite increasing barriers to trade, the share of imports from the developing countries in the consumption of manufactured goods by the

TABLE 19.4 *Relative importance of manufactured imports from developing countries*

	1973	Import-consumption ratio (in current prices) 1978	1981	1983
United States				
Iron and steel	0.6	0.9	1.4	2.3
Chemicals	0.4	0.5	0.6	0.9
Other semi-manufactures	0.9	1.5	1.7	1.9
Engineering products	0.7	1.3	2.0	2.6
Textiles	1.8	1.6	2.3	2.2
Clothing	5.6	11.3	14.0	15.1
Other consumer goods	1.9	3.7	4.8	5.2
All manufactures	1.1	1.8	2.4	3.0
European Common Market				
Iron and steel	0.4	0.4	0.6	0.7
Chemicals	0.5	0.6	0.8	1.1
Other semi-manufactures	1.3	2.5	1.9	2.3
Engineering products	0.3	0.9	1.3	1.4
Textiles	2.6	3.7	4.1	4.4
Clothing	5.7	11.4	16.4	16.0
Other consumer goods	1.1	1.6	2.9	3.1
All manufactures	0.9	1.6	2.0	2.1
Japan				
Iron and steel	0.2	0.3	1.0	1.6
Chemicals	0.3	0.5	0.8	0.9
Other semi-manufactures	1.0	0.9	0.9	0.9
Engineering products	0.2	0.3	0.5	0.4
Textiles	2.2	2.3	2.1	1.9
Clothing	7.6	7.4	8.9	8.2
Other consumer goods	0.8	1.1	1.3	1.5
All manufactures	0.7	0.8	0.9	1.0

SOURCE: GATT, *International Trade*; United Nations, *Yearbook of Industrial Statistics* and OECD, *Indicators of Industrial Activity*, various years.

major developed countries continued to rise during the last decade. Table 19.4 shows the relationship between manufactured imports from the developing countries and the consumption of manufactured products, defined as production plus imports less exports, in the United States, the European Community, and Japan. Information is provided on the developing countries' market shares in the years 1973, 1978, 1981, and 1983.

There are no signs of a slowdown in the growth of the developing countries' share in industrial countries markets, except for the group of other semi-manufactures, which are heavily weighted by natural-resource products, and for the category of textiles and clothing, where the MFA has become increasingly restrictive. At the same time, until recently, the import shares of textiles and clothing continued to rise, reflecting the upgrading of products exported by the developing countries in the face of limitations imposed on increases in volume. Furthermore, developing country exporters increasingly shifted to the exportation of products that did not encounter barriers, such as engineering goods and iron and steel, which latter has subsequently become subject to restrictions.

The data further show that differences between the United States and the European Community, on the one hand, and Japan, on the other, were increasing over time as far as the share of imports from developing countries in their domestic consumption. is concerned. Thus, while this share was 1.1 percent in the United States, 0.9 percent in the Common Market, and 0.7 percent in Japan in 1973, the corresponding shares were 3.0, 2.1 and 1.0 percent in 1983.

It appears, then, that although Japan is not party to the MFA and has few formal barriers to imports from the developing countries (the major exception being footwear), it has increasingly lagged behind the other major developed countries in importing manufactured goods from the developing countries. Yet, with its rapid economic growth and the accumulation of physical and human capital, Japan has approached the other developed countries in terms of factor endowments, and thus one would have expected it to resemble their import pattern more closely. The fact that the opposite has happened may be taken as an indication of the use of informal measures of protection against developing country exports in Japan.

Note finally that, while increased protection through nontariff measures in developed country markets has been accompanied by increased penetration of developing country exports in these markets, this should not be interpreted to mean that such protection would not have involved an economic cost in the developed countries or would not have adversely affected developing countries. It rather means that protection has been concentrated in particular sectors and that developing countries have been able to alleviate its impact on their foreign exchange earnings through export diversification and product upgrading.

The cost of protection

Apart from its adverse effects on foreign exporters, import protection imposes a cost on the domestic economy. Earlier estimates of the cost of protection in the developed countries were generally low, rarely attaining 1 percent of the gross national product. These estimates, however, failed to consider the losses involved in foregoing the exploitation of economies of scale in protected markets. Taking account of economies of scale, it has recently been estimated that protection has reduced potential output by about 10 percent in Canada.[9] Further losses are incurred in the event of the use of voluntary export restraints, which involve an income transfer to foreign exporters.

Table 19.5 reports available estimates on the welfare cost of voluntary export restraints, which have come into increased use in recent years. This cost consists of the loss of consumer surplus, the resource cost of producing the additional quantity domestically, and increased payments on imported goods as exporters charge higher prices for the limited quantity they sell. It has been calculated for clothing in the United States and European Community and for automobiles and steel in the United States.

Rows (1) to (4) of the table show the components of the cost of protection, as well as its total, for the industries in question. Row (5) further indicates the number of jobs saved in the protected industries on the assumption that labor productivity is not affected thereby. In turn, row (6) shows the welfare cost per job saved in the industries in question.

While the data refer to different years, this will hardly affect the results since prices changed little during the period. Thus, it is apparent that the welfare cost of saving a job is considerably higher in the clothing industry than in the case of automobiles and steel.

Data on the ratio of the welfare cost to average labor compensation, reported in row (8), are directly comparable across industries, since the numerator as well as the denominator of the ratio are expressed in the prices of the same year. The results show that this ratio was 13.5 in the US and 9.2 in the EEC clothing industry while it was 11.3 in the US automobile industry and 1.7 in the US steel industry.

The welfare cost of saving a job in the protected industries thus exceeds the wages paid in these industries by a considerable margin, with the differences being by far the highest in the case of clothing, where the import limitations pertain to products originating in developing countries. The cost to the consumer, including higher prices for domestic products resulting from protection, exceeds even this figure. Nor do the estimates take account of job losses in other industries that are discriminated against by protection.

At the same time, while higher prices paid on imports represent a transfer to foreign suppliers, the volume of their exports is adversely affected by the protectionist measures applied. As shown in row (10) of Table 19.5, the transfer implicit in the higher prices paid to exporters compensated for hardly more than one-tenth of the loss in revenues owing to the reduced volume of exports. The corresponding ratio was 0.14 for automobiles; it was 1.01 for steel, where higher prices apparently offset the loss in export volume.

Although similar calculations have not been made for agricultural products, comparisons of domestic and world market prices provide an indication of the relative costs of protection in various markets, although world market prices would rise if protection measures were dismantled. The cost

TABLE 19.5 *Effects of some major VERs in developed countries*[a]

	Clothing		Automobiles	Steel
	USA 1980	EC 1980	USA 1984	USA 1985
(1) Increased payments on imported goods ($ million)	988	1050	1778	1530
(2) Loss of consumer surplus ($ million)	408	289[b]	229	455
(3) Resource cost of producing the additional quantity domestically ($ million)	113	70	185	7
(4) Cost to the national economy in the protecting country (welfare cost) ($ million), (1) + (2) + (3)	1509	1409	2192	1992
(5) Jobs saved through protection (thousands)	8.9	11.3	45.0	28.0
(6) Welfare cost per job saved ($ thousand), (4):(5)	169.6	124.7	48.7	71.1
(7) Average labor compensation ($ thousand), (annual)	12.6	13.5	38.1	42.4
(8) Ratio of welfare cost to average compensation, (6):(7)	13.5	9.2	1.3	1.7
(9) Lost revenues for exporters, ($ million)	9328	7460	6050	1508
(10) Ratio of increased payments on imported goods to lost revenues for exporters (1):(9)	0.11	0.14	0.29	1.01

NOTE: [a] US dollar estimates are evaluated at current prices for the years indicated.
[b] Foregone tariff revenues, due to the quota introduction, are not included.

SOURCE: O. K. Kalantzopoulos, 'The Cost of Voluntary Export Restraints for Selected Industries in the U.S. and the EC' (Washington, DC: World Bank, 1986).

of protecting domestic agriculture is indicated by the high ratio of domestic to world market prices in Japan, followed by the European Community. In turn, price differentials are generally much smaller in the United States (Table 19.6).

In conclusion, it should be emphasized that, apart from the measured cost imposed on the national economy, the protection of noncompetitive, low-productivity sectors has unfavorable long-term effects on the de-

TABLE 19.6 *Nominal protection coefficients for agricultural products, 1980–82[a]*

	US	EEC	Japan
Wheat	1.15	1.52	3.80
Coarse grains	1.00	1.40	4.30
Rice	1.30	1.40	3.30
Beef and lamb	1.00	1.90	4.00
Pork and poultry	1.00	1.25	1.50
Dairy products	2.00	1.75	2.90
Sugar	1.40	1.50	3.00
Weighted average	1.16	1.54	2.44

NOTE: [a] The nominal protection coefficient is the ratio of domestic to world market prices.

SOURCE: *World Development Report 1986* (Washington, DC: World Bank, 1986, Table 6).

loped countries by postponing adjustment as well as the upgrading of labor. Non-tariff barriers have particularly adverse effects by reducing competition, introducing discriminatory practices, and keeping out new entrants which frequently are developing countries. In particular, the Multifiber Arrangement has perverse effects in encouraging the upgrading of products in the developing countries while considerations of comparative advantage would call for such upgrading to occur in the developed countries.

Finally, high protection involves the misallocation of new additions to the capital stock. This is because, apart from safeguarding existing firms, protection provides an inducement for new investments in sectors where the developed countries have a comparative disadvantage. Correspondingly, less capital is available to high-skill, high-technology industries where these countries possess important advantages. Ultimately, then, protection unfavorably affects economic growth in the developed countries as well as in their trading partners among developing countries.

II PROTECTION IN THE DEVELOPING COUNTRIES

The extent of import protection

Comparable estimates on the level of protection and the share of imports subject to quantitative import restrictions are available for relatively few developing countries. At the same time, available information indicates that the scope of nontariff measures is much greater, and levels of protection are both higher and show greater variation, in these countries than in the developed countries.

Several studies[10] showed considerable differences in the trade regimes of the developing countries during the 1960s. These differences pertained to the protection of the manufacturing sector and the consequent bias against primary activities (in particular, agriculture) as well as to the extent of the bias against exports. The countries in question may be divided into three groups on the basis of the policies applied during this period.

The first group included Argentina, Brazil, Chile, Pakistan and the Philippines, all of which highly protected their manufacturing industries, discriminated against primary production, and biased the system of incentives against exports. In these countries, the average net effective protection of the manufacturing sector, reflecting adjustment for the overvaluation of the exchange rate associated with protection, ranged between 40 and 150 percent.

The countries of the second group, including Colombia, Israel, and Mexico, had considerably lower levels of industrial protection. Also, the extent of discrimination against primary activities was less than in the countries of the first group. None the less, there was substantial bias against manufactured exports, with value added obtainable in domestic markets exceeding that obtainable in exporting by 40 to 90 percent compared with 120 to 320 percent in the first group.

Finally, in Korea, Singapore and Malaysia, there was little discrimination against manufactured exports, with the excess of value added obtainable in domestic markets as against export markets ranging from 6 to 26 percent. The same conclusion applies to the primary exports of the countries of this group that did not discriminate against primary activities.

More recent estimates are available for several of these countries. They show little change in relative incentives to manufacturing and to primary production in the case of Korea. At the same time, reforms undertaken in the second half of the 1960s reduced, to a lesser or greater extent, the protection of manufacturing activities, and discrimination against the primary sector, in Brazil, Colombia, Mexico, and the Philippines. In turn, changes in the opposite direction occurred in Malaysia.[11]

On the whole, however, while several developing countries had liberalized their trade regimes in the late 1960s, trade policies in most of these countries discriminate in favor of import substitution and against exports and there is considerable dispersion in the effective protection provided to various economic activities. Also, in several large Latin American countries protection was increased again in response to the external shocks of the post-1973 period.

The cost of protection

The cost of protection in developing countries can be rather high. Estimates for several of the countries cited above showed this cost to equal 9.5 percent of GNP in Brazil, 6.2 percent in Chile, 6.2 percent in Pakistan, 3.7

percent in the Philippines, 2.5 percent in Mexico during the 1960s.[12]

These results were obtained in a partial equilibrium framework and do not allow for the losses of economies of scale in protected domestic markets. Subsequently, de Melo estimated the cost of protection for Colombia in a general equilibrium framework, incorporating intermediate products, non-traded goods, as well as substitution among products and among primary factors.[13] Excluding land reallocation within agriculture and postulating an optimal export tax for coffee, the cost of protection was estimated at 11.0 percent of GNP, assuming labor to be fully employed and 15.8 percent assuming that additional supplies of labor are available at a constant real wage.

De Melo's results are considerably higher than the estimates made in a partial equilibrium framework, even though Colombia was in the middle range among developing countries in terms of levels of protection. Thus, de Melo estimated effective protection to average 25 percent in the Colombian manufacturing sector, without an exchange rate adjustment, while the comparable result in the Balassa study was 35 percent.

It would appear, then, that the estimates obtained in a partial equilibrium framework understate the cost of protection. Part of the reason is that estimates made in this framework do not allow for the fact that the cost of protection rises with the dispersion of interindustry rates of protection.[14] Yet, the dispersion of protection rates is much greater in developing than in developed countries and, within the former group, in highly-protected than in less-protected economies.

Protection and economic growth

Protection has traditionally been justified on the grounds that it will enable industries to grow up and to eventually confront foreign competition. The assumptions underlying this infant industry argument is that protection is required on a temporary basis to offset the costs firms incur upon undertaking a new productive activity that will not be fully recouped by the firm itself but by the industry as a whole. This is because the firms initially entering upon a new activity will generate so-called externalities through labor training and technological improvements.

While these changes are supposed to permit productivity to increase more rapidly in protected infant industries of the developing countries than in the developed countries, the evidence suggests that protection has rather retarded productivity growth. Thus, in the early postwar period, the protected Latin American countries experienced virtually no increase in productivity.[15]

Also, in the 1960–73 period, incremental capital–output ratios were the highest in Chile (5.5) and India (5.7), which had by far the highest protection levels. In turn, these ratios were the lowest in Singapore (1.8) and Korea (2.1), which had the lowest levels of protection. Finally, incremental capital–output ratios declined in countries such as Brazil (from 3.8 in 1960–66 to 2.1 in 1966–73) that reduced their levels of protection during the latter part of the period.[16]

High incremental capital–output ratios reflect slow productivity growth under protection, which tends to discourage exports, as production in the confines of narrow domestic markets limits the exploitation of economies of scale, capacity utilization, and technological improvements, thereby aggravating the adverse effects of inefficient resource allocation. By contrast, in national economies where protection levels are low, exports are encouraged, permitting the exploitation of economies of scale and higher capacity utilization, with the carrot and the stick of competition in foreign markets providing inducements for technological change.

The above considerations may explain the observed positive correlation between exports and economic growth. This was first shown by Michalopoulos and Jay[17] in a cross-section production-function type relationship, with exports added to the conventional explanatory variables of capital and labor. Subsequently, Feder[18] found that the use of primary factors in export production, rather than in producing non-export products, entailed a 1.8 percentage point difference in economic growth rates during the 1964–73 period in a group of 31 semi-industrial countries.

These results relate to a period of rapid expansion in the world economy. The question was raised if they would also apply following the deterioration of world market conditions as a result of increases in petroleum prices and the slowdown of economic growth in the developed countries after 1973. This question has been answered in the affirmative in several studies.

Krueger and Michalopoulos showed that the average rate of growth of both exports and GNP was higher for outward-oriented developing economies with relatively balanced trade incentives than for inward-oriented developing countries characterized by high protection during the 1960–73 period of high world economic growth as well as during the 1973–81 period of external shocks.[19] Balassa further showed that while the external shocks of the latter period entailed a greater economic cost for outward-oriented countries, which had a larger trade share relative to GNP, the excess cost was offset severalfold through more rapid economic growth in these countries than in inward-oriented economies.[20] Differences in growth performance, in turn, were attributed to differences in the adjustment policies applied in response to external shocks.

In subsequent research the trade policies applied at the beginning of this period of external shocks and policy responses to external shocks was introduced simultaneously in a cross-section investigation of 43 developing countries in the 1973–9 period.[21] The trade policies applied at the beginning of the period have been represented by an index of trade orientation, estimated as deviations of actual from hypothetical values of per capita exports, the latter having been derived in a regression equation that includes per capita incomes, population, and the ratio of mineral exports to the gross national product as explanatory variables. In turn, alternative policy responses to external shocks have been represented by relating the balance-of-payments effects of export promotion, import substitution, and additional net external financing to the balance-of-payments effects of external shocks.

The results show that initial trade orientation as well as the character of policy responses to external shocks importantly affected rates of economic growth in the 1973–9 period. Thus, GNP growth rates differed by 1.0 percentage point between countries in the upper and in the lower quartiles of the distribution in terms of their trade orientation in 1973. There was further a 1.2 percentage point difference in GNP growth rates between countries in the upper and the lower quartiles of the distribution in terms of reliance on export promotion, as against import substitution and additional net external financing, in response to the external shocks of the 1973–8 period.

The results are cumulative, indicating that both the initial trade orientation and the choice of adjustment policies in response to external shocks importantly contributed to economic growth during the period under review. In fact, these two factors explain a large proportion of intercountry differences in GNP growth rates, which averaged 5.0 percent in the 43 developing countries under consideration during the 1973–9 period, with an upper quartile of 6.5 percent and a lower quartile of 3.3 percent.

CONCLUSIONS

The review of protection in developed countries showed that, on the average, trade barriers tend to be higher on agricultural products than on manufactures, and within manufacturing tend to be concentrated in a few sectors. By contrast, developing countries protect manufacturing industries more than agriculture and their barriers are both more widespread and more variable.

Nontariff barriers are more important than tariffs in inhibiting trade between developed and developing countries; nevertheless, because of their escalation, tariffs continue to restrain access to developed country markets in certain manufactured products. At the same time, with some important exceptions, such as high-technology products, the developed countries' nontariff barriers tend to be more prevalent, and their tariffs tend to be higher, on products of interest to developing countries than on their trade with each other.

It was further shown that the developed countries pay a large cost for maintaining employment in a few manufacturing sectors through protection.

At the same time, such calculations underestimate the long-term costs of protection that tends to slow down technology through the misallocation of new investment.

The analysis of the cost of protection in developing countries focused primarily on the fact that countries with liberal trade regimes grow faster and withstand better adverse developments in the international economy. The reason for their superior performance lies primarily in the lower degree of economic distortions and the greater flexibility associated with their trade regimes, which provide similar incentives to produce for domestic and for foreign markets as well as to industry and agriculture.

Despite increasing protection in recent years, the extent of market penetration by developing countries in developed country markets has risen as has overall trade interdependence between the two groups of countries. This increased interdependence, in turn, raises the opportunity for mutually advantageous trade liberalization that can promote structural adjustment and stimulate long-term growth in both developed and developing countries.

Multilateral trade negotiations in the framework of the GATT provide an appropriate – indeed the only – avenue for significant trade liberalization. Such negotiations would need to encompass all items of importance to trade between developed and developing countries in manufactures, agriculture, and services, and include both tariff and nontariff barriers. All developing countries and especially the NICs need to be active participants in such negotiations and be prepared to offer a certain degree of reciprocity consistent with their level of development.[22]

NOTES

1. The table reports import-weighted tariff averages that are relevant for comparisons of overall tariff averages and tariffs on products exported by the developing countries. Unweighted tariff averages show a similar pattern of escalation. Cf. B. Balassa and C. Balassa, 'Industrial Protection in the Developed Countries,' *The World Economy*, VII (1984) pp. 179–86. At the same time, unweighted averages are higher than the weighted averages as the latter is reduced by reason of the fact that high (low) tariffs that discourage (encourage) imports are given low (high) weights.
2. A. J. Yeats, 'Effective Tariff Protection in the United States, the European Economic Community, and Japan,' *The Quarterly Review of Economics and Business*, XIV (1974) pp. 41–50.
3. The Tokyo Round did little to reduce the extent of tariff escalation as the ratios of effective to nominal protection are similar to those calculated for the post-Kennedy round situation in Yeats.
4. For example, France limits the imports of automobiles from Japan to 3 percent of domestic sales while, for several years, US restricted imports from Japan to about 20 percent of domestic sales. Correspondingly, the own-import ratio was

substantially lower in France than in the United States, even though non-tariff measures were much more restrictive in the first case than in the second.

5. At the same time, to the extent that all, or most, countries apply quantitative import restrictions to the same commodities, for example textiles, their share in world trade will be lowered, thereby affecting the world trade-weighted average of nontariff measures.

6. J. M. Finger, H. K. Hall, and D. R. Nelson, 'The Political Economy of Administered Protection,' *American Economic Review*, LXXII (1982) pp. 452–66.

7. J. J. Nogues, A. Olechowski, and L. A. Winters, 'The Establishment of Non-Tariff Barriers to Industrial Countries' Imports,' World Bank Development Research Department Discussion Paper No. 115 (Washington, DC, 1985).

8. The only country covered in the essay for which such information is available is Japan. According to UNCTAD, health and safety measures and technical standards pertain to 48 percent of Japan's imports from industrial countries and to 17 percent of its imports from developing countries. See UNCTAD, 'Problems of Protectionism and Structural Adjustment,' Report by the Secretariat, Part I: Restrictions to Trade and Structural Adjustment TD/B/1039 (Geneva, 1985) Table 2.

9. R. G. Harris with D. Cox, *Trade, Industrial Policy and Canadian Manufacturing* (Toronto: Ontario Economic Council, 1983) p. 115.

10. B. Balassa and Associates, *The Structure of Protection in Developing Countries* (Baltimore, Md.: The Johns Hopkins University Press, 1971); J. N. Bhagwati, *Anatomy and Consequences of Exchange Control Regimes* (Cambridge, Mass.: Ballinger Publishing Co., 1978); A. O. Krueger, *Liberalization Attempts and Consequences* (Cambridge, Mass.: Ballinger Publishing Company, 1978); B. Balassa and Associates, *Development Strategies in Semi-Industrial Economies* (Baltimore, Md.: The Johns Hopkins University Press, 1982).

11. N. Roger, 'Trade Policy Regimes in Developing Countries' (Washington, DC: World Bank, 1985).

12. Balassa and Associates, *The Structure of Protection in Developing Countries*.

13. J. de Melo, 'Estimating the Costs of Protection: A General Equilibrium Approach,' *Quarterly Journal of Economics*, XCII (1978) pp. 209–26.

14. J. R. Nugent, *Economic Integration in Central America: Empirical Investigations* (Baltimore, Md.: The Johns Hopkins University Press, 1974) pp. 62–3.

15. H. J. Bruton, 'Productivity Growth in Latin America,' *American Economic Review*, LVII (1967) pp. 1099–1116.

16. Balassa and Associates, *Development Strategies in Semi-Industrial Economies*.

17. C. Michalopoulos and K. Jay, 'Growth of Exports and Income in the Developing World: A Neoclassical View,' AID Discussion Paper, No. 28 (Washington, DC: Agency for International Development, 1973).

18. G. Feder, 'On Exports and Economic Growth,' *Journal of Development Economics*, XII (1983) pp. 59–73.

19. A. O. Krueger and C. Michalopoulos, 'Developing-Country Trade Policies and The International Economic System,' in E. M. Preeg (ed.), *Hard Bargaining Ahead: U. S. Trade Policy and Developing Countries* (New Brunswick, NJ: Transaction Books, 1985) pp. 39–57.

20. B. Balassa, 'Adjustment Policies in Developing Countries: A Reassessment,' *World Development*, XII (1984) pp. 955–72.

21. B. Balassa, 'Exports, Policy Choices, and Economic Growth in Developing Countries After the 1973 Oil Shock,' *Journal of Development Economics*, XVIII (1985) pp. 23–36.

22. A companion paper, 'Liberalizing Trade between Developed and Developing Countries' (Chapter 20 in this volume) examines the objectives, scope, and modalities of multilateral trade liberalization between developed and developing countries.

Essay 20 Liberalizing Trade Between Developed and Developing Countries

INTRODUCTION

The world trading system is at the crossroads. Despite repeated declarations made by developed country governments of their intention to resist protectionist pressures and to roll back protection, new measures have been introduced to limit imports to the detriment of their own and their trading partners' economies. Also, some large developing countries have responded to external shocks and the subsequent debt crisis by increasing import protection.

There is a danger that, unless the developed and the developing countries undertake multilateral trade liberalization, further protectionist measures will be taken, leading to the eventual breakdown of the world trading system. The need for multilateral trade liberalization in order to resist protectionist pressures was stated nearly two decades ago:

> It would also appear that if no efforts are made to liberalize trade, the alternative is likely to be increased protectionism rather than the maintenance of the status quo. For lack of a better expression, we may speak of an 'instability effect,' according to which economic and political relationships are hardly ever in a position of stable equilibrium but have the tendency to move in one direction or the other. Thus, in the absence of pressures for the liberalization of trade, protectionist counterpressures may gain force in the United States as well as abroad.[1]

During the postwar period, the cause of trade liberalization was furthered by periodical multilateral trade negotiations. The purpose of this essay is to provide support for undertaking a new round of negotiations. At the same time, while the principal participants of the earlier negotiations were developed countries, trade between developed and developing countries will need to be an important focus of the next round of negotiations. This is both because of the growing importance of this trade and because of the cost the protective measures recently taken, or threatened to be taken, impose on the national economies of the two groups of countries.

The essay will consider the scope, content and modalities of such negotiations as they would affect developed and developing countries. It will further consider concerns that developing countries have raised about a new round of multilateral trade negotiations and make recommendations as to how to address these concerns and how to promote institutional changes in support of a global liberalization effort.

Section I will briefly summarize evidence on the prevalence of tariff and nontariff protection imposed by developed and developing countries, and the resulting costs to their national economies. Section II will consider the application of the principle of reciprocity in multilateral negotiations, with particular attention to developing country attitudes towards the application of this principle. This section will also analyze the prospective role of the developing countries in multilateral trade negotiations, indicating the common interests of developed and developing countries in the negotiations.

The scope and the modalities of multilateral trade liberalization will be the subject of Section III. This section of the essay will give separate consideration to reducing trade barriers in manufacturing, in agriculture, and in services. Section IV will consider the institutional framework of trade liberalization, with particular attention to safeguards, dispute settlement, and the application of anti-dumping and countervailing measures.

I THE EXTENT AND COST OF PROTECTION[2]

Increased concern about the implications of protectionism for economic activity has resulted in a number of recent studies which review the extent, scope and cost of protection in developed and developing countries. These reviews of protection have shown that, on the average, trade barriers in developed countries tend to be higher on agricultural products than on manufactures, and tend to be concentrated in a few sectors such as textiles and clothing, shoes, steel, and automobiles within manufacturing. By contrast, developing countries protect manufacturing more than agriculture and their barriers are both more widespread and more variable.

As a consequence of successive rounds of tariff reductions in the framework of the GATT and the subsequent imposition of nontariff barriers, these barriers are at present more important than tariffs in limiting developed country imports; nevertheless, because of their escalation, tariffs continue to restrain access to developed country markets in certain processed goods. At the same time, with some exceptions, the developed countries' nontariff barriers tend to be more prevalent and their tariffs tend to be higher on products of interest to developing countries than on their trade with each other.

Despite increasing protection in the last few years, the extent of market penetration by developing countries in developed country markets has risen as has overall trade interdependence between the two groups of countries. This increased interdependence raises the opportunity for mutually advantageous trade liberalization, which can promote structural adjustment and stimulate long-term growth.

Recent reviews of the costs of protection in the developed countries showed that these countries pay a large cost to maintain employment in a few manufacturing sectors. Moreover, such analyses tend to underestimate the long-term costs of protection that leads to the misallocation of additions to the capital shock and tends to slow down technological progress.

Analyses of the costs of protection in developing countries have focused primarily on evidence that countries with liberal trade regimes tended to grow faster and withstand better adverse developments in the international economy. The reason for their superior performance lays primarily in the lower degree of economic distortions and the greater flexibility associated with trade regimes which provide similar incentives to produce for domestic and foreign markets as well as to industry and agriculture.

II APPROACHES TO TRADE LIBERALIZATION

The quest for reciprocity

The implication of the findings on the cost of protection reviewed in Section I is that lowering protection unilaterally would contribute substantially to economic growth in the countries concerned. But the benefits from trade liberalization would be even greater if the country's trading partners also reduced their trade barriers on a reciprocal basis.

In the post-World War II period, reductions in trade barriers have been implemented through the application of the principle of reciprocity in trade negotiations. Article XXVIII of GATT refers to the need for undertaking trade negotiations on 'a reciprocal and mutually advantageous basis.' This statement has been interpreted to mean offering balanced concessions in the course of trade negotiations in the sense that the resulting increases in exports and imports for the participating countries would be approximately equal.

The quest for reciprocal concessions was originally justified largely on balance-of-payments grounds. In practice, however, the principle of reciprocity was used as a means of mobilizing political support for trade liberalization in the context of multilateral negotiations. Reciprocity encourages the formation of coalitions between exporters and the consumers of imported goods who gain from reductions in trade barriers and whose support is necessary for overcoming the political weight of producers with vested interests in protection. Although the principle tends to cater to the mercantilist perception that benefits from trade derive from export expansion while increases in imports involve costs, its practical implementation in the negotiations led to trade liberalization and to large tariff reductions, stimulating world economic expansion in the 1950s and 1960s.

While the dismantling of quantitative import restrictions on trade among European countries after the war occurred in the framework of the Organization for European Economic Co-operation (OEEC), rather than the GATT, reciprocity was similarly introduced as the individual countries accepted the obligation to liberalize their trade restrictions in a parallel fashion. This was done by setting numerical targets for simultaneously reducing the share of intra-European imports subject to quantitative restrictions on food and feedingstuffs, raw materials, and manufactured products in each country.[3]

The principle of reciprocity also found expression in the item-by-item negotiations on tariff reductions undertaken in the framework of the GATT during the early postwar years. In the course of the negotiations, each country aimed at obtaining reductions in foreign tariffs on its actual and potential exports, leading to concessions of approximately equal value in terms of increments in exports and imports. These bilateral deals were subsequently combined, with account taken of their impact on the trade of the other negotiating partners under the most-favored-nation clause. As the scope for further item-by-item tariff diminished, this gave place to across-the-board tariff reductions negotiated multilaterally in the framework of the Dillon, Kennedy, and Tokyo Rounds, with exceptions made for so-called sensitive items that were also negotiated with a view to ensure reciprocity.

The early balance-of-payments rationale has lost importance with the institution of flexible exchange rates, but the role of reciprocity as a vehicle of mobilizing political support for trade liberalization continues to be of importance in the light of recent protectionist trends in industrial countries. This principle can be applied most effectively in the context of the new round of multilateral negotiations within the GATT. Multilateral liberalization is superior to bilateral arrangements because it reduces compartmentalization and eschews preferential treatment, which tend to introduce trade distortions and allocative inefficiencies.

Developing country attitudes toward reciprocity

Although most of the developing countries did not participate in the exchange of reciprocal tariff reductions in the framework of the GATT multilateral trade negotiations, tariff reductions were extended to them under the MFN clause. Their limited participation in the negotiations meant that there was little incentive for the developed countries to reduce tariffs on items of interest to the developing countries.

Latin American countries, which did offer tariff concessions of their own, fared better in the Kennedy Round negotiations than countries which did not offer such concessions.[4] In turn, in the Tokyo Round negotiations, few offers of tariff reductions were made by developing countries who focused mainly at obtaining unilateral concessions. The result has been that exceptions from tariff reductions bore heavily on the exports of these countries.

The lack of tariff concessions by the developing countries under the Tokyo Round reflected their demand for 'special and differential treatment.' This has been codified in the Framework Agreement following the Tokyo Round, which states that 'contracting parties may accord differential and more favorable treatment to other contracting parties.' The Agreement extended an earlier provision, introduced in 1965, according to which

> the developed countries do not expect reciprocity for commitments made by them in trade negotiations to reduce or remove tariffs and other barriers to the trade of developing countries; i.e. the developed countries do not expect the developing countries, in the course of trade negotiations, to make contributions which are inconsistent with their individual development, financial and trade needs.

Their demands for differential treatment also led developing countries to apply pressure for unilateral trade concessions from developed countries. The Generalized System of Preferences (GSP), introduced following an UNCTAD initiative in 1968 under a GATT waiver, represents a response on the part of the developed countries to this pressure. Under GSP, free entry is provided to developing country nonagricultural products. GSP, however, excludes product groups of principal interest to the developing countries, such as steel, textiles, clothing, and shoes. Also, quantitative limits are imposed on duty-free importation and successful exporters have been progressively excluded from the application of GSP. And, while tariff reductions negotiated under GATT rules are 'bound;' i.e., cannot be raised again, GSP treatment can be revoked at any moment. Moreover, it has been shown that the developing countries derive considerably larger benefits from multilateral trade liberalization than from GSP.[5]

The prospective role of the developing countries in multilateral trade negotiations

Irrespective of past attitudes, an important question is the role the developing countries may play in the new round of multilateral trade negotiations. Developing countries, especially countries which are experiencing balance-of-payments difficulties today because of their large indebtedness, argue that they can not be reasonably expected to liberalize and import more from developed countries. They import as much as their foreign exchange availability permits them to do.

However, developing countries' earnings of foreign exchange are affected by the restrictiveness of their own trade regimes through the impact of differential incentives on the allocation of resources between exports and import-competing activities. Thus, developing countries could import more if they and the developed countries liberalized trade because this would induce an expansion of their exports. Moreover, if liberalization is to occur under the new multilateral trade round, it is bound to be a prolonged process with the impact on imports likely to be felt no sooner than in the 1990s. Thus, the current balance-of-payments difficulties experienced by a number of developing countries would appear to impose more of a psychological and political constraint to participation in a new trade round than a financial one.

At the same time, reciprocity on the part of the newly-industrializing countries (NICs) and, to a lesser extent, other developing countries will be necessary for trade liberalization to be undertaken by the developed countries.[6] Specific import controls which the NICs maintain create problems for particular export interests in the developed countries. The support of these export interests may well be critical to the developed countries' ability to reduce import barriers on products of interest to the NICs.

Furthermore, with rapidly rising imports from the NICs, it has been increasingly difficult politically to make a case for unilateral concessions to them. In fact, in recent years changes in the opposite direction occurred as increased restrictions have been imposed on imports from the newly-industrializing countries. The situation has been well-described by Sidney Weintraub:

> There is sort of a Faustian bargain into which the NICs have entered with the industrial countries. The NICs have pressed for special and differential treatment, which they have received, although not in the legal sense of being bound in the GATT for specific products. The preferences can be removed at the discretion of the preference giver. At the same time, many of the most competitive export products of the NICs are precisely those being subjected to selective restriction. Proposals to formally alter the GATT safeguard provisions to permit discrimination are directed primarily at the NICs and Japan. Is there an implicit connection between the selective liberalization (tariff preferences) granted to the NICs for their marginally competitive exports and the selective restriction (usually in nontariff form) on their most competitive exports? The question is not answerable, but it does suggest that the bargain entered into the NICs may be special and differential in ways they never contemplated.[7]

These considerations suggest that lowering barriers to trade, and reducing uncertainty as to the future imposition of such barriers, on a reciprocal basis is in the mutual interest of developed and developing countries. The degree of reciprocity in the new round of multilateral negotiations would need to take into account the varying stages of economic development. The GATT enabling clause 'states the expectation of the developing countries that they will be able to participate more fully in the framework of rights and obligations under the GATT with the progressive development of their economies and improvement in their trade situation.'

In keeping with this principle, it could be expected that the NICs which have already made significant strides in economic development and which hold promise for more future growth should take increasing obligations in a new round of multilateral negotiations. Per capita incomes in 1982 in several of these countries were higher than in developed countries. Singapore's per capita income was higher than Spain's, Hong Kong's higher than Ireland's, Israel's higher than Greece's, and Venezuela's, Yugoslavia's and Uruguay's higher than Portugal's.[8] A number of the developed countries of today, which according to present-day parlance would have been considered developing countries in the early postwar period, came to offer tariff concessions of their own as they progressed on the road towards industrial development. Eventually, these countries, including Japan, Finland, and Ireland, and subsequently, Greece, Portugal and Spain, became full participants in the negotiations.

Between 1960 and 1980, the NICs attained an average annual GNP growth rate of 6.7 percent compared with 4.3 percent in the developed countries. This was achieved, although the newly-industrializing countries were buffeted by the oil price increases of 1973–4 and 1979–80 and the subsequent world recessions. While the extent of economic progress in the NICs is obscured by the debt burden under which several of them labor today, in a longer-term perspective they can be expected to reach high levels of economic development. By 1990, the Latin American newly-industrializing countries, Korea, and Yugoslavia may attain Japan's 1960 per capita income while Singapore may surpass Japan's 1975 income per head.[9]

Thus, just as the present-day developed countries have become full participants in the process of trade liberalization during the postwar period, this process should encompass the newly-industrializing countries in the future. This does not mean, however, that the NICs in the new multilateral trade round would necessarily undertake the same obligations and apply the same time schedule as the present-day developed countries. But they would need to offer significant reductions in their trade barriers as part of the negotiations. In turn, such a liberalization effort by the NICs could result in greater trade opportunities for lower income developing countries whose exports to the NICs are constrained by the latter's trade controls.

The discussion on reciprocity should not imply that developing countries should delay the liberalization of their own trade regimes that contributes to the adjustment process by reducing the bias against exports. But, approaches need to be explored whereby developing countries would get 'credit' at the negotiating table for liberalization measures they have already undertaken.

The mutual importance of trade for developed and developing countries

The scope for reciprocity increases with the importance of the markets of the developing countries for the developed countries and vice versa. The importance of the developed countries as markets for the developing countries in general, and the NICs in particular, is indicated by data on trade flows. In 1983, the developed countries provided outlets for 63 percent of the exports of the developing countries, while the ratio was 59 percent for manufactured goods alone.[10]

Manufactured exports to the developed countries deserve particular attention as they have grown rapidly over time and have come to account for a rising share of domestic output in the developing countries. Thus, according to the rough estimates reported in Table 20.1, the share of exports to developed countries in the production of manufactured goods in the developing countries increased from 7.3 percent in 1973 to 10.4 percent in 1978 and to 12.5 percent in 1981, with incremental shares being substantially greater. Given the NICs greater export orientation, these ratios are considerably higher for them than for the developing countries as a whole, and the NICs account for over three-fourths of the manufactured exports of the developing countries.

Not surprisingly, exports to the developed countries are of particular importance for developing country producers of clothing, with a nearly three-fifths share of these exports in the value of output in 1981. In the same year, the developed countries accounted for one-fifth of developing country output in the miscellaneous group of other consumer goods. The corresponding ratio was one-seventh for engineering products, where developing countries were successful in increasing their exports of radios and television sets as well as of parts, components, and accessories of various kinds of equipment.

The developing countries have also assumed increasing importance as markets for the developed nations. Thus, the share of exports to developing countries in the manufactured production of the developed countries rose from 2.9 percent in 1973 to 5.1 percent in 1978 and 6.3 percent in 1981, with incremental shares increasing to an even greater extent.

According to available estimates, between 1978 and 1981, ten cents of

TABLE 20.1 *Trade in industrial commodity groups between developed and developing countries in percentages*

	1973 X_{LDC}/P	1978 X_{LDC}/P	1981 X_{LDC}/P	1983 X_{LDC}/P
Developed countries[a]				
Iron and steel	3.5	5.1	6.6	5.5
Chemicals	3.3	4.5	4.7	4.9
Other semi-manufactures	1.1	2.4	2.9	2.8
Engineering products	3.7	6.9	8.5	7.1
Textiles	2.9	3.6	5.0	4.4
Clothing	0.9	1.7	2.8	2.1
Other consumer goods	1.2	2.3	3.4	2.9
Total manufacturing	2.9	5.1	6.3	5.5
	1973 X_{DC}/P	1978 X_{DC}/P	1981 X_{DC}/P	1983 X_{DC}/P
Developing countries[b]				
Iron and steel	3.6	3.3	5.1	na
Chemicals	3.3	4.0	4.9	na
Other semi-manufactures	7.4	10.3	8.0	na
Engineering products	6.1	8.6	13.7	na
Textiles	4.0	7.1	7.3	na
Clothing	36.8	55.9	58.3	na
Other consumer goods	12.1	17.9	20.1	na
Total manufacturing	7.3	10.4	12.5	na

Explanation of symbols: X = exports, P = production, DC = developed countries, LDC = developing countries.

NOTES: [a] The estimates exclude the countries of the European Free Trade Association.
[b] The production estimates for the developing countries are subject to considerable error possibilities. Also, the estimates for 1973 have been obtained through interpolation of the reported figures for 1970 and 1978 while the 1981 estimates have been derived through extrapolation by the use of production indices.

SOURCES: GATT, *International Trade*, United Nations, *Yearbook of Industrial Statistics*, OECD, *Indicators of Industrial Activity*.

each dollar increase in the manufacturing output of the developed countries was destined to developing country markets. With oil revenues declining and several large, heavily-indebted, non-oil countries applying deflationary policies to cope with the debt crisis, the share of exports to the developing countries in the developed countries' output of manufactures declined in 1983, but this decline was temporary and imports by the developing countries rebounded in 1984.

Among individual sectors, developing countries markets are of greatest importance to developed country producers in engineering products, with a market share of 8.5 percent in 1981. And, between 1978 and 1981, one-sixth of the increment of engineering output was sold in the developing countries. The markets of these countries are also of importance for developed country exporters of iron and steel, chemicals, and (high-quality) textiles.

The data include exports to the OPEC countries, which provided markets for 36 percent of developed countries' exports of manufactured goods to the developing countries in 1983 according to GATT statistics. In turn, among the non-oil developing countries, the importance of the newly-industrializing countries as markets has increased over time.

III REDUCING TRADE BARRIERS IN MAJOR SECTORS

Manufactures

Trade liberalization in manufactured goods needs to focus on reducing and, over a predetermined period, eliminating nontariff barriers in both developed countries and the newly-industrializing countries. Barriers in the developed countries represent an increasing threat to the exports of the NICs, while the nontariff measures applied by the newly-industrializing countries limit market access for developed and for other developing country exporters and create uncertainty for them.

A successful effort at trade liberalization would need to cover all sectors in which trade is impeded by tariff or nontariff barriers, irrespective of their status under present GATT provisions. The existence of GATT waivers or other distinctions as to the legality of the measures applied should not deter a new approach. If such an approach is not taken, important areas of interest to the developing countries such as agriculture and textiles would be left outside the negotiating process. The same is true for developing country trade barriers consistent with GATT articles XII and XVIII.

The focus of the trade liberalization effort would nevertheless need to differ between the developed countries and the NICs as to the scope of nontariff measures differs between them. Among the manufactured products imported by the developed countries from the NICs, nontariff measures have been concentrated in textiles and clothing, shoes and, most recently, in steel. In turn, while Hong Kong and Singapore do not utilize nontariff measures and important steps towards trade liberalization have been taken in Korea, the other NICs generally apply nontariff measures to most manufacturing industries.

Correspondingly, while in the developed countries emphasis should be given to sector-level measures, the newly-industrializing countries would need to liberalize their trade across-the-board. But, in order to make the elimination of nontariff measures on textiles and clothing and on steel acceptable to sectoral interests in the developed countries, as well as to expand trade opportunities for low income countries, particular interest attaches to the NICs taking action in these industries parallel with the developed countries.

The textiles and clothing industries in the developed countries have made common cause for restrictions, even though technological changes have rendered textile producers in these countries increasingly competitive. Thus, the developed countries have a rising surplus in trade in textiles with the developing countries and by 1983 the value of their exports to the developing countries exceeded imports from them by nearly two-thirds. Pelzman, for example, cites the President of the American Textile Manufacturers Institute, according to whom 'today we are the most modern and efficient textile industry in the world,' and concludes that protection in the United States textile industry is 'more or less redundant.'[11]

In fact, there are considerable possibilities for the further expansion of mutual trade in textiles between developed and developing countries through the exchange of higher-valued for lower-valued products, with man-made fibers dominating the former and cotton fabrics in the latter. The less developed countries have particular possibilities for expanding the exports of lower-valued cotton fabrics while the NICs may specialize in the middle range of products. In this connection, it may be added that the MFA as it is now structured is especially detrimental to developing countries at lower levels of industrialization, which have the potential to expand significantly their exports at the lower end of the scale but are unable to do so by the small quotas they are presently allocated under the MFA.

It is possible that, if the newly-industrializing countries were to phase-out their existing barriers on textile products, textile industries in the developed countries would also accept such a phase-out. This would, then, reduce the political power of the supporters of the Multi-Fiber Arrangement.

In the clothing industry, the cost advantage of the developing countries remains substantial and in 1983 their exports to the developed countries were seven times greater than their imports from them. Nevertheless, the developed countries possess advantages in high-fashion clothing, where proximity to markets is of particular importance. Thus, as it has been argued,

> quickness of reaction, the ability to incorporate new trends and designs into production schedules, flexibility of operation, relatively good access to quality fabric suppliers, proximity to major centers of demand and intimate and service-intensive relationships with distribution channels are among the factors that determine success in these product markets.[12]

There are thus possibilities for increased trade in clothing between developed and developing countries, although in the large bulk of clothing products the developing countries have a strong cost advantage.

The elimination of the MFA as currently structured could be envisaged in the framework of the new round of multilateral negotiations, provided that tariffs on textiles and clothing are maintained at least for some time. Tariffs on clothing continue to be high in the developed countries. Thus, post-Tokyo Round import-weighted averages are 22.5 percent in the United States, 13.5 percent in the European Common Market, and 14 percent in Japan. Effective rates of tariff protection are even higher as tariffs on fabrics average 11.5 percent in the US, 10.5 percent in the EEC, and 9.5 percent in Japan. In fact, according to GATT statistics, in the period preceding the Tokyo Round, effective rates of tariff protection exceeded nominal tariff protection on clothing by 35 percent in the Common Market, 44 percent in the United States, and 70 percent in Japan.

Tariff protection at the levels indicated should suffice to protect the more efficient segments of the clothing industry in the developed countries while phasing-out the Multi-Fiber Arrangement would give inducements for adjustment. This has not been the case so far; rather, the reinforcement of protection under MFA has provided incentives not only to maintain, but to increase capacity.

Thus, one may agree with the report of a study group that the statement made by the Commission of the European Community, according to which the extension of the MFA for another five years 'should enable the Community's industry to make new progress in its restructuring efforts,' is no more than 'a pious hope.' This is because, as the report notes, 'there are no incentives for efficient adjustment. Instead, the greatest protection continues to be offered to the least efficient activities.'[13]

Phasing-out the MFA may take the form of increasing quotas annually for large exporters and eliminating quotas for small ones. At the same time, to ease the adjustment, assistance would need to be provided to finance the retraining and the relocation of workers and to help firms restructuring their activities or leaving the industry altogether. The amounts needed for such adjustment assistance may nevertheless be small compared with the cost of saving jobs under the MFA.

Adjustment would also be necessary in the steel industries of the developed countries. Thus far, adjustment has been hampered by the subsidization of steel production in the European Community and by quantitative restraints imposed on steel imports in both the Community and the United States.

An agreement to liberalize trade in steel would need to involve the elimination of production subsidies. Import liberalization itself may well begin with the developed countries eliminating restraints on steel imported from the developing countries. With the simultaneous elimination of barriers to steel imports in the NICs, there may be possibilities for an exchange of specialty steel products for crude steel between the developed countries and the NICs. In this connection, it should be noted that in 1983 the steel exports of the developed countries to the developing countries exceeded their imports from these countries nearly five times.

The exports of automotive products, including parts, components, and accessories, from the developing to the developed countries did not reach 5 percent of the reverse flow of this trade in 1983. But, there are possibilities for further expansion and one would need to ensure that developing country exporters do not encounter barriers in developed country markets in the future. At the same time, the newly-industrializing countries would have to open their markets to competition from abroad, in order to ensure low-cost production in an industry characterized by economies of scale. To the extent that automobiles are viewed by them as luxuries whose consumption should be discouraged, high domestic taxes on automobile purchases could be substituted for the present trade barriers.

In the developed countries, then, the elimination of nontariff measures would be concentrated in textiles and clothing, footwear, and steel, with further assurances given that such measures will not be applied in other industries. In turn, the elimination of nontariff measures would necessitate across-the-board changes in the newly-industrializing countries. As the adjustment will take time, there is need for a phase-out of the nontariff measures presently applied by the NICs.

The question is, then, how this phase-out may be effected. Among the newly-industrializing countries, the OEEC method of eliminating restrictions on a certain percentage of imports year-by-year has been used in Korea. This procedure may also find application in the other NICs in phasing-out their nontariff barriers in the future. While the existence of import prohibitions will bias the results, there exists no simple and straightforward alternative to the OEEC method.

The next question concerns the tariff measures to be taken in conjunction with the elimination of nontariff barriers. Two diametrically-opposed proposals have been made in this regard. Some have suggested that tariffs be reduced *pari passu* with the freeing of trade restrictions, so as to ensure overall trade liberalization; others have recommended converting nontariff measures into equivalent tariffs and thus raising tariffs, so as to minimize the cost of adjustment in the course of the elimination of nontariff measures. Both of these methods have important shortcomings.

While proceeding on two fronts simultaneously would indeed permit making rapid progress in the liberalization of trade, the resistance of vested interests would also increase. Moreover, the task of negotiations would become much greater, thereby burdening the administrative apparatus. Finally, the difficulties of adjustment would increase and greater uncertainty would be created for producing interests.

In turn, although raising tariffs would reduce the burden of adjustment, there would be pressures to increase tariffs more than necessary to offset the effects of the elimination of nontariff measures. Furthermore, there is the danger that, once raised, tariffs would not be lowered later.

A compromise solution would be to postpone tariff reductions on products subject to nontariff measures, without however raising tariffs in the process of eliminating such measures. At the same time, the developed countries should undertake to reduce tariffs on products to which nontariff measures do not apply. This would ensure reciprocity between the developed countries and the NICs, which would reduce nontariff measures across-the-board, and provide benefits to the less developed countries.

Processed foods and raw materials are subject to tariff escalation that discriminates against processing activities in countries producing these foods and raw materials, many of which are less developed countries. In order to contribute to export expansion from these countries, it would be desirable that the developed countries eliminate tariffs on processed foods and raw materials, including tropical products, where the less developed countries are major exporters.

Temperate zone agriculture

The next question concerns trade in temperate zone agricultural products. In recent years, agricultural protection in the European Community Market has engendered large surpluses that have been increasingly exported with the support of high subsidies. And while complaints about these subsidies have largely originated in the United States, developing country exporters of temperate zone products have also suffered their adverse consequences.[14]

As a first step towards a more rational system of trade in temperate zone agricultural products, it would be desirable to declare a standstill on new export subsidies. Such a standstill would apply to all exporting countries and not only to the European Community. At the same time, with the Common Agricultural Policy being increasingly costly for the Community, there is a mutual interest in moderating agricultural protection.

One may envisage, first of all, some shift from price support to income subsidies under the Common Agricultural Policy. In encouraging consumption, this alternative would lead to lower exports and/or increased imports. Furthermore, support levels would need to be reduced over time, with the aim to eliminate surpluses in some commodities and to permit increasing imports in others.[15] While the modalities of reducing farm support would obviously be an internal matter to the European Community, a pledge to undertake such reductions may be appropriately made in the course of the negotiations.

In Japan, trade liberalization on agricultural products should entail reduction of quantitative restraints as well as a shift from price support to income support as price levels are high and consumption levels are low. In turn, in the United States, the elimination of the recently introduced export bonus scheme would be the first priority.

Inward-oriented developing countries discriminate against agriculture through the protection of industrial activities. In their case, reducing industrial protection would make an important contribution to improving incentives to agriculture.

Services

The United States has long proposed the establishment within the GATT of rules and procedures governing trade in services to parallel those governing trade in goods. The United States has argued that, in the absence of rules governing trade in services, national regulatory policies could be used to restrict such trade and discriminate against foreign providers of services.

Most developing countries have generally opposed these proposals on several grounds;[16] (a) there is a fear that developed countries have a comparative advantage in services and the establishment of international rules would result in limiting the capacity of developing countries to protect service activities on infant industry grounds; (b) there is limited information on services trade, making the conduct of negotiations for establishing rules and procedures difficult; (c) there are conceptual ambiguities in defining various kinds of services traded internationally; (d) in order to be effective, international rules affecting trade in services may sometimes need to affect investment – an area of great sensitivity for many developing countries; and (e) the US proposals are sometimes viewed as an effort to deflect attention from barriers to trade in goods imposed by the developed countries.[17]

There is little doubt that the absence of international rules governing trade in services represents an important gap in international economic cooperation. In the absence of such rules, a number of practices inhibiting trade have indeed developed.[18] Such practices affect an important and growing segment of international trade. According to estimates made by the Office of the US Trade Representative, trade in services amounted to 17 percent of the world exports of goods and services.

It is also quite true that this trade is dominated by the developed countries, and the United States has a large, although not disproportionate, share. Thus, it is natural for the United States to seek to develop rules aimed at reducing obstacles its service industries face in foreign markets.

At the same time, it is clear that meaningful progress in settling multilateral rules in this area is by necessity likely to be slow. This for a variety of reasons, some purely technical ones, others relating to the reluctance of developing countries to undertake liberalization in the area. These issues will need to be dealt with for liberalization in services to follow.

First, there are conceptual issues on coverage. Bhagwati suggests a simple rule aimed at distinguishing between services which are embodied in suppliers and require their physical presence and others which are disembodied and hence do not; he would focus on eliminating restrictions in the latter but not in the former.[19] While the distinction is helpful in considering the question of immigration which is obviously unrealistic to tackle in this context, it does not fully deal with other aspects of the issue. For example, the United States is interested in establishing rules pertaining to the right of exporters to provide services through distributors. This might involve investment-related regulations in some countries, although in principle the issue of ownership of distributorships can be separated and dealt with under investment rules. Also, the United States is interested in ensuring that public monopolies do not abuse their position in competitive markets (e.g. airlines).[20]

Second, there is general agreement that data on services are inadequate and there is a great need for improvement. For example, data on services do not even remotely approximate the availability of data on trade in goods by product classification and by country of origin and destination.

Third, there is limited information and analysis on the impact of national practices on the flow of service trade. The availability of such information would clarify the issues under discussion.

At the same time, developing countries would benefit from the freer importation of services, which are a crucial component of a modern economy today. The arguments favoring freedom of trade in goods apply also to services. In practice, the newly-industrializing countries may develop new services exports, based on the use of relatively low-cost skilled and semi-skilled labor. Examples are data processing and engineering services, where new facilities for data transmission would permit the developing countries to exploit their comparative advantage.

These considerations point to the possibilities for mutually beneficial trade in services between the developed countries and the NICs. Nevertheless, dismantling barriers to services in the newly-industrializing countries may take time, largely because they consider certain services, such as banking and insurance, to be infant industries.

All in all, while negotiations on trade in services are important, progress in setting rules and in dismantling barriers affecting such trade will be slow. It is questionable as to whether such negotiations can proceed at the same pace as negotiations on trade in goods, and that the latter should be tied to the pace in the former.

IV THE INSTITUTIONAL FRAMEWORK OF TRADE LIBERALIZATION

Safeguards[21]

Section III considered the possibilities for trade liberalization in regard to manufactured goods, agricultural products, and services. It should be recognized that reaching agreement on trade liberalization presupposes the availability of effective safeguards in the event that an unexpected surge in imports causes actual or potential injury to domestic industry. An important objective of safeguards would be to allow for *temporary* relief while inducing countries to use the safeguard mechanism rather than measures that provide protection *outside* the GATT framework.

Article XIX of GATT permits a country to impose trade restrictions if imports are causing or threatening serious injury to domestic producers of a competing product. The application of Article XIX is, however, subject to several conditions and it has in practice been by-passed in order to avoid abiding by these conditions. Rather, threats of restrictions by legislative or administrative actions have been used to compel exporting countries to adopt 'voluntary export restraints' (VERs) or to enter into 'orderly marketing arrangements' (OMAs).

Despite protracted negotiations, no agreement has been reached on a new safeguard code in the Tokyo Round and thereafter. The establishment of an effective safeguard mechanism is, however, necessary to avoid the continuation of a situation when countries take measures that do not conform to GATT rules. A new GATT safeguard code is needed to complement any trade liberalization undertaken within the GATT framework. Such a safeguard code would have to contain the following features.

First, the standard of 'serious injury to domestic producers' should be given greater precision than it now has under Article XIX. It would be necessary to specify the factors to be taken into account in determining injury, such as employment, production, and prices. Furthermore, it should be established that imports rather than other factors, such as changes in consumer tastes and in technology, are the principal cause of the injury. Finally, a precondition for the application of safeguard measures should be that injury has been suffered by producers accounting for a major share of the total domestic output of the product.

Second, the procedures applied by countries that have recourse to safeguard measures should ensure the transparency of the safeguard process. Also, all interested domestic and foreign parties, not just domestic producers, should be given the right to present their views through public hearings before an independent body. Finally, official determinations and their reasons should be made public.

Third, safeguard measures should preferably take the form of increases in tariffs, with quantitative limitations applied only in exceptional cases. And, if quantitative measures are applied, imports should not be reduced below the level attained in the period prior to the imposition of restrictions.

Fourth, all safeguard measures should be temporary and set on a degressive scale. To ensure that they remain temporary, such measures should be brought under the surveillance and scrutiny of GATT. While the first imposition of safeguard measures may be left to the discretion of the country concerned, their extension beyond an initial period of, say, three years would be conditional on agreement by the GATT. Also, the re-imposition of safeguards within a predetermined period of, say, six years should be excluded.

A precondition of the extension of safeguard measures beyond an initial period would be the taking of adjustment actions by the importing country. As noted in Section III in regard to the Multi-Fiber Arrangement, these actions should aim at facilitating the transfer of capital and labor to other activities rather than prolonging the life of inefficient firms.

Fifth, countries applying safeguard measures in conformity with the criteria and conditions of the new code would be subject neither to retaliation nor to any obligation to provide compensation. If, however, a country's safeguard actions were not in compliance with the code, retaliation would be warranted.

Finally, existing nontariff restrictions, whether in the form of VERs, OMAs, or any other, should be brought under the new safeguard code. A timetable for their subsequent elimination could also be negotiated as part of the modalities for adjustment over time.

Countervailing, anti-dumping and related measures

Actions to improve safeguards have to be taken parallel with commitments by the developed countries to refrain from using for protective purposes trade measures which have other legitimate objectives. In recent years, countervailing and anti-dumping actions and price investigations by developed countries have greatly increased especially in manufacturing, while safeguard proceedings have declined in importance.

In the United States, there are inferences that the industries seeking action under the countervailing and anti-dumping duty provisions are doing this as an alternative to seeking safeguard relief. Although relatively few of the petitions are actually approved, the effect of the investigations themselves is protective – irrespective of the final findings – which may or may not be protective in intent or nature. In other developed countries, surveillance is often administered with a view to ensure that quantities and/or prices of imports are consistent with unofficial targets or understandings with importers.

Internally, one would need to explore changing procedures for counter-vailing, anti-dumping, and price investigations to avoid trade disruptions. In the United States, this may be achieved by strengthening the prelimi-nary review process by the Commerce Department for judging whether the case should be referred to the International Trade Commission. In other developed countries, clear and transparent processes would need to be established for handling cases.

Externally, it would be necessary to increase the active monitoring and surveillance of such actions by the GATT and to strengthen dispute settlement procedures in the GATT, so as to reduce the likelihood that countervailing and anti-dumping provisions are abused and other legit-imate surveillance measures are used for protective purposes. At the same time, the establishment of an effective safeguard code for legitimate cases of injury to domestic industry may serve to weaken the tendency to seek countervailing actions or other similar measures.

Finally, actions would need to be taken by exporting countries to limit the provision of subsidies *pari passu* with the liberalization of trade. Developing countries may find that lowering their own trade barriers may make it possible to reduce export subsidies which were provided to some industries as a means of offsetting the bias against exporting that their own import restrictions had created. Similarly, action by the European Com-munity to reduce subsidies especially in agriculture would significantly improve the prospects that the scope for countervailing and anti-dumping action be limited to legitimate cases of injury.

The role of the GATT

The GATT will be only as effective as the members want it to be. Improving the rules under which trade is conducted without a parallel commitment by the major trading partners to adhere by the rules will not be an improvement over the current situation. Provided such an overall commitment is present, the following areas of institutional strengthening deserve consideration.

Dispute settlement

The effective application of the safeguard mechanism would necessitate improving existing procedures for the settlement of disputes. A new safeguard code should provide for the establishment of a Committee on Safeguards, with responsibility for the administration of the code and the surveillance of safeguard actions.[22] Disputes between signatories would be referred to the Committee that would ensure coherence in the application of safeguard measures and build up a case law over time.

Improvements in the dispute settlement mechanism are also necessary to deal with conflicts that may arise in other areas, such as export subsidies, countervailing action to such subsidies, and the application of anti-dumping duties. The first requirement would be to strengthen the panel system. This objective would be served by establishing standing panels, consisting of internationally respected experts, who would perform functions similar to those of administrative judges in the United States. The Committee on Safeguards would be one such standing panel.

The work of the standing panels should be complemented by the establishment of *ad hoc* panels drawn from a list of experts. In order to ensure their independence, a majority of the members of the standing and the *ad hoc* panels should be chosen independently, on their merits, rather than be appointed by governments.

It is important to ensure the arbitration of the disputes. The panels may fulfil the functions of both fact finding and arbitration or, alternatively, arbitration may be done separately from the work of the panels.

The governments of the participating countries should use the dispute settlement mechanism in GATT as a forum for presenting their grievances and should abide by the recommendations of the panels or the arbitrators. In turn, in cases when these are overruled by the national legislation, financial compensation would need to be made.

Surveillance

As recommended by the report of the Group of Eminent Persons, established by invitation of the Director-General of GATT, it would be desirable to carry out annual examinations of trade policies in the framework of GATT.[23] The IMF has the authority under Article IV consultations and other provisions for surveillance of the international monetary system, to review the macroeconomic and foreign exchange policies of member governments on a regular basis. The World Bank undertakes frequent reviews of the borrowing countries' development policies and its findings are discussed at its Executive Board, an intergovernmental body, in the context of its provision of loans.

The GATT Secretariat has no parallel authority for surveillance of the trading system; nor does it actively discuss the trade policy measures applied by its members. Biannual consultations with members could be instituted with a view to determine the state of their trade policies, including the review of safeguard and countervailing actions and price investigations. A report of the findings could then be discussed by a standing intergovernmental body consisting of GATT member representatives.

This would also permit establishing facts as to the application of non-tariff measures the governments have not reported to the GATT. In general, the GATT should improve its efforts to obtain information on the application of non-tariff measures and should give them considerable publicity.

CONCLUSIONS

The fact that reduction in protection is to a country's own advantage has only too infrequently been sufficient to induce countries to take steps to liberalize their trade. Liberalization has been achieved primarily through multilateral trade negotiations in the GATT framework. A multilateral approach based on reciprocity is useful for several reasons. First, only through such an approach can most governments mobilize enough countervailing political pressure to confront the traditional forces of protection; second, the economic benefits from a multilateral approach exceed those of unilateral liberalization; and third, in the absence of multilateral efforts, there is potential for increases in bilateralism which is frought with inefficiencies.

Multilateral trade negotiations in the framework of the GATT offer the greater – indeed the only – opportunity for significant trade liberalization at present. The negotiations would need to encompass all items of importance to trade between developed and developing countries in manufactures, agriculture and services and include both tariff and nontariff barriers. All developing countries and especially the NICs need to be active participants in the negotiations and be prepared to offer a certain degree of reciprocity consistent with their level of development. In the absence of reciprocity, especially by the NICs, even if it is not complete, there is a clear danger that trade in items of interest to developing countries would continue to be more restricted than trade among developed countries.

Liberalization of nontariff measures should involve both reducing trade barriers and bringing the remaining barriers under the aegis and scrutiny of the GATT. Particular attention needs to be given to the development of suitable modalities for the reciprocal elimination of nontariff barriers, since there has been limited international experience with multilateral liberalization in this area. In the case of tariffs, the focus needs to be on items where there is significant tariff escalation.

For the negotiations to be meaningful, developed country protection in such sensitive areas as the textiles and clothing, steel, and agriculture needs to be addressed. At the same time, developing countries need to seize this opportunity to rationalize and reduce their own protection of manufacturing activities. Negotiations in services pose difficulties both because of conceptual and factual problems and because a large number of developing countries for these and other reasons are opposed to them. While it is clear that there are significant problems that need to be addressed in this area and negotiations on services may take a long time, it is important that they should go forward.

Parallel with the negotiations to liberalize trade, steps should be taken to strengthen the trading system and the GATT. This requires, first of all, the establishment of a new safeguard code which would provide temporary, uniform, and degressive import relief through measures consistent with the

GATT. Second, it requires steps aimed at reducing country abuses of countervailing, anti-dumping and related surveillance measures. Third, it requires strengthening the role of the GATT in dispute settlement and in surveillance over the trading system.

Finally, efforts for trade liberalization through multilateral trade negotiation should not inhibit unilateral liberalization by developing or by developed countries in pursuit of much needed structural reform. In this connection, the World Bank and the IMF would need to continue and expand their lending in support of trade policy reforms in the developing countries. Appropriate 'credit' for such reforms should be given to developing countries in the framework of the multilateral negotiations.

NOTES

1. B. Balassa, *Trade Liberalization among Industrial Countries: Objectives and Alternatives* (New York: McGraw-Hill Book Co., 1967) p. 152.
2. This section draws on 'The Extent and the Cost of Protection in Developed–Developing Country Trade,' Essay 19 in this volume, that provides the appropriate references.
3. I. Frank, *The European Common Market – Analysis of Commercial Policy* (New York: Praeger, 1961) Chapter I.
4. J. M. Finger, 'Trade Liberalization: A Public Choice Perspective,' in R. C. Amacher, G. Haberler, and T. D. Willett (eds), *Challenges to a Liberal International Economic Order* (Washington, DC: American Enterprise Institute for Public Policy Research, 1979) pp. 421–53.
5. T. B. Birnberg, 'Trade Reform Options: Economic Effects on Developing and Developed Countries,' in W. R. Cline (ed.), *Policy Alternatives for a New International Economic Order: An Economic Analysis* (New York: Praeger, 1979) pp. 217–83.
6. Although there are various definitions of NICs, the newly-industrializing countries have been defined in this essay as having per capita incomes between $1100 and $3000 in 1978 and a manufacturing share of 20 percent or higher in 1977. They include Argentina, Brazil, Chile, Mexico, and Uruguay in Latin America, Israel and Yugoslavia in the Europe–Middle East area, and Hong Kong, Korea, and Singapore in the Far East.
7. S. Weintraub, 'Selective Trade Liberalization,' paper presented at the Overseas Development Council Conference on US Trade Policy and the Developing Countries, September 1984.
8. World Bank, *World Development Report 1984* (New York: Oxford University Press, 1984).
9. Data for the year 1982 and projections for the period 1985–95 in *World Development Report 1984* were supplemented by information received from the Economic Projections Department of the World Bank for the period 1982–5. The comparisons have been made for 1990, so as to allow for the time needed to begin the negotiations on multilateral trade liberalization and to put into effect the resulting agreements. After a preparatory period of one or possibly two years, the negotiations may take several years, with their implementation extending further over time.

10. GATT, *International Trade 1983/84*. Unless otherwise noted, the trade data cited below derive from GATT statistics.
11. J. Pelzman, 'Economic Costs of Tariffs and Quotas on Textile and Apparel Products Imported into the United States: A Survey of the Literature and Implications for Policies,' *Weltwirtschaftliches Archiv* CXIX (1983) pp. 523–42.
12. J. de la Torre, 'Clothing Industry Adjustment in Developing Countries,' *Thames Essay No. 38* (London: Trade Policy Research Centre, 1984) p. 239.
13. G. Curzon, J. de la Torre, J. B. Donges, A. I. MacBean, J. Waelbroeck, and M. Wolf, *MFA Forever? Future of the Arrangement for Trade in Textiles* (London: Trade Policy Research Centre, 1981) p. 37.
14. J. Zietz, and A. Valdes, 'The Costs of Protectionism to Less-Developed Countries: An Analysis for Selected Agricultural Products,' a background paper for the World Bank's *World Development Report 1985* (Washington, DC, 1985).
15. For alternative proposals to reform the Common Agricultural Policy, see T. E. Josling, M. Longworthy, and S. Pearson, 'Options for Farm Policy in the European Community,' *Thames Essay No. 27* (London: Trade Policy Research Centre, 1981).
16. The principal exceptions have been Singapore and Hong Kong who may expect to benefit from expanded trade in financial services.
17. For some of the developing countries' concerns see United Nations Conference on Trade and Development, *Production and Trade in Services: Policies and their Underlying Factors Bearing Upon International Service Transactions* (New York: United Nations, 1985).
18. *US National Study on Trade in Services*, a submission by the United States Government to the General Agreement on Tariffs and Trade (Washington, DC: U.S. Government Printing Office, 1984).
19. J. N. Bhagwati, 'Splintering and Disembodiment of Services and Developing Nations,' *The World Economy*, VII (1984) pp. 133–43.
20. US National Study on Trade in Services.
21. For an early statement, see D. Robertson, 'Fail Safe Systems for Trade Liberalization,' *Thames Essay No. 12* (London: Trade Policy Research Centre, 1977).
22. For such a proposal, see Atlantic Council of the United States, *Some Unfinished Business of the Tokyo Round Trade Negotiation: A New Safeguard Code*, Report of the Atlantic Council; Advisory Trade Panel (Washington, DC, 1981) pp. 18–19.
23. F. Leutwiler *et al.*, *Trade Policies for a Better Future: Proposals for Action* (Geneva: GATT, 1985).

Essay 21   Japanese Trade Policies Towards Developing Countries

INTRODUCTION

This essay has set out to examine Japan's trade policies towards developing countries by reference to actual trade flows and by utilizing information obtained from the governments of countries of the Pacific area as regards Japanese trade practices. Section I will present empirical evidence for the year 1973 on the extent of Japanese imports of manufactured goods from developing countries in relation to the imports of the other developed nations from these countries. Section II will review changes in Japanese imports from the developing countries during the 1973–83 period, placing it again in the context of the developed country experience. In Section III, Japanese trade practices affecting imports from Pacific area developing countries will be described, drawing largely on communications received from official sources in Hong Kong, Korea, Singapore, and Taiwan. In the conclusions, the available evidence will be brought together in evaluating Japanese trade policies towards developing countries in general and towards the countries of the Pacific area in particular.

I THE EXTENT OF JAPANESE IMPORTS FROM DEVELOPING COUNTRIES, 1973

In the present investigation, comparisons have been made between actual and expected imports of the developed countries from the developing countries, including the member countries of OPEC, with expected imports having been derived in a cross-section framework for the year 1973. The investigation covers eighteen industrial countries, defined as having per capita incomes of $2200 or higher, and a share of manufactured goods in total imports of at least 20 percent, in 1973.[1]

The point of departure has been Chenery's well-known formulation which attempts to explain intercountry differences in per capita imports in terms of differences in per capita incomes and population, except that in the present case imports from developing countries rather than from all sources of supply are considered. At the same time, as in Chenery's overall

378

equation, the data refers to the imports of all commodities.[2]

The estimating equation utilized in the present investigation further includes the share of primary imports in total imports as an explanatory variable.[3] The inclusion of this variable is designed to test for the existence of an asymmetry between natural resources and reproducible factors, labor and capital, in their effect on international trade. It is hypothesized that the elasticity of substitution between natural resources and reproducible factors is low, necessitating the importation of natural resource-intensive (primary) products by countries that are poor in natural resources in exchange for manufactured goods. Such interindustry specialization is complemented by intraindustry specialization in manufactured goods that are in their great bulk differentiated products while primary commodities are standardized products subject to interindustry trade.[4] Correspondingly, it may be expected that countries poorly endowed with natural resources will have higher import shares than resource-rich countries.

This hypothesis conflicts with oft-stated views, according to which the low imports of manufactured goods into Japan are explained by its poor resource endowment. Rather, it is postulated that, in addition to exchanging manufactured goods for primary products, Japan and other resource-poor countries would engage in intraindustry trade in manufactured goods. The extent of this trade will be determined by the particular characteristics of the countries concerned, including the trade policies applied. In fact, there is evidence that the extent of intraindustry trade is positively correlated with the openness of the national economy.[5]

The starting point for the estimation of transportation costs has been the ratio of cif to fob import values, reported by the International Monetary Fund. Owing to the fact that transportation costs are higher for primary products than for manufactured goods, the ratio has further been adjusted for differences in the product composition of imports, by taking the relative shares of primary and manufactured goods in Switzerland, a country with the lowest cif–fob ratio as the standard in the calculations.[6] In the case of Japan, the cif–fob price difference is 15.5 percent while the adjusted transportation costs is 11.9 percent.[7]

Equation (1) provides the empirical results for the developed country group, using a double logarithmic form. The per capita income (Y/N) and the primary import share (M_p/M) variables are statistically significant at the 5 percent level, while the population (N) and the transportation cost (T) variables do not quite reach the 10 percent level of significance.

$$\ln \frac{M}{N} = -\ 3.072 + 0.919 \ln \frac{Y}{N} - 0.139 \ln N + 2.891 \frac{M_p}{M} - 0.447\ T;$$
$$\hspace{1.7cm} (1.09) \quad (2.83) \hspace{1.5cm} (1.36) \hspace{1.5cm} (2.82) \hspace{1cm} (1.57)$$
$$R^2 = 0.376 \hspace{8.5cm} (1)$$

Among the developed countries, the largest negative deviation of actual from estimated values of per capita imports is shown for Japan, with a shortfall of 27 percent. In turn, Belgium, the United Kingdom, and Switzerland show the largest positive deviations.

The statistical significance of the deviation of actual from expected values of per capita imports from developing countries has further been tested for Japan by including a dummy variable (J) in the estimating equation. The results are shown in equation (2).

$$\ln\frac{M}{N} = -\;5.739 + \;1.166\ln\frac{Y}{N}\;-0.231\ln N + 4.976\;\frac{M_P}{M}-0.022\,T-1.134\,J;$$
$$\phantom{\ln\frac{M}{N} = }(2.06)\quad(3.76)\qquad(2.31)\quad(3.74)\qquad\qquad(0.79)\;(2.14)$$

$$R^2 = 0.536 \tag{2}$$

The introduction of a dummy variable for Japan has increased the absolute values of all the regression coefficients as well as their statistical significance, the only exception being the transportation cost variable.[8] In the case of the population variable, the level of significance has improved from 10 to 2 percent. The dummy for Japan itself is statistically significant at the 5 percent level.

Also, the introduction of the dummy variable for Japan has increased the adjusted coefficient of determination from 0.38 to 0.54, indicating the importance of including the variable in the equation. This result reinforces the finding that Japan is an outlier among industrial countries as far as imports from developing countries are concerned.[9]

II CHANGES IN JAPANESE IMPORTS FROM THE DEVELOPING COUNTRIES, 1973–83

The results of the cross-section investigation reported in Section I of the essay indicate that Japanese imports from the developing countries fell considerably short of the import value that would be expected on the basis of Japan's country characteristics in the year 1973. The present section will examine changes in Japanese imports during the subsequent decade. Since changes in primary imports are affected by the availability of natural resources in relation to the production of manufactured goods, the discussion will concern manufactured imports alone.

Table 19.4 provides data on the ratio of imports from developing countries to the apparent consumption of manufactured goods, derived as domestic production plus imports minus exports, for the United States, the European Common Market, and Japan. Manufactured goods have been defined as SITC classes 5 to 8 less 68 (nonferrous metals); the data have been expressed in terms of current dollar values.

The data show that while in 1973 imports from the developing countries accounted for only a slightly smaller percentage of the domestic sales of manufactured goods in Japan than in the United States and the European Common Market, the differences increased to a considerable extent in subsequent years. Thus, in 1983, the developing countries provided 1.0 percent of the apparent consumption of manufactured goods in Japan, compared to 0.7 percent in 1973. In turn, the share of imports from developing countries in domestic consumption increased from 1.1 to 3.0 percent in the United States and from 0.9 to 2.1 percent in the European Common Market.

These results conflict with a priori expectations based on changes in relative factor endowments. With the rapid rate of economic growth (2.8 percent a year between 1973 and 1983 in per capita terms), reflecting in part the accumulation of physical and human capital, factor endowments in Japan have become more similar to those in the United States and the European Common Market, which experienced lower per capita income growth rates (1.1 and 1.4 percent, respectively). Accordingly, one would have expected the growth of manufactured imports from the developing countries to accelerate in Japan, so as to conform to its changing resource endowment.[10]

This conclusion is strengthened if we consider that Japan liberalized the application of the General Scheme of Preferences while changes in the opposite direction occurred in the United States and the European Common Market where exceptions to GSP multiplied. In turn, the rise in the price of oil, affecting Japan to a greater extent than the United States and somewhat more than the European Common Market, tended to reduce Japan's non-oil imports relative to the other industrial countries.

It may be suggested that the expansion of US imports from the developing countries was due to the increasing overvaluation of the US dollar in recent years. In fact, according to calculations of trade-weighted real effective exchange rates by John Williamson, the US dollar appreciated in real terms by 26 percent between 1978 and 1983.[11]

However, no upward shift can be discerned in the trend of the ratio of imports from developing countries to the apparent consumption of manufactured goods in the United States, with a two-thirds increase shown in both the 1973–8 and the 1978–83 periods. Yet, in the first period, the US dollar depreciated in real terms by 12 percent.

Furthermore, while the US dollar appreciated by 11 percent in real terms over the entire 1973–83 period, the currencies of the two largest Common Market countries in terms of GNP, Germany and France, depreciated more than the Japanese yen (12 and 10 percent as against 6 percent). And although the real value of the British pound increased by 23 percent, the Italian lira depreciated to a considerable extent and the currencies of the smaller EEC countries generally followed the German mark. Yet, the increase in the ratio of imports from developing countries to the apparent consumption of manufactured goods was several times greater in the European Common Market than in Japan.

Table 19.4 further provides information on trade in manufactured goods in a disaggregated framework. It shows changes in the share of imports from the developing countries in apparent consumption for the United States, the European Common Market, and Japan in regard to seven manufactured product categories, including iron and steel, chemicals, other semi-manufactures, engineering products, textiles, clothing, and other consumer goods.

Between 1973 and 1983, the share of imports from the developing countries in US consumption increased the most in iron and steel (from 0.6 to 2.3 percent) and in engineering products (from 0.7 to 2.2 percent). Substantial increases were also shown for clothing (from 5.6 to 10.1 percent) and for other consumer goods (from 1.9 to 5.2 percent), where the share of the developing countries is the highest. In turn, the smallest changes occurred in textiles, from 1.8 to 2.2 percent, where automation cut into imports from developing countries.

Engineering products also lead in terms of increases in developing country market penetration ratios (from 0.3 to 1.4 percent) in the European Common Market, where smaller changes occurred in regard to steel (from 0.4 to 0.7 percent). At the same time, the extent of the increase in the case of clothing (from 5.7 to 16.0 percent) and other consumer goods (from 1.1 to 2.1 percent) was similar in the European Common Market as in the United States.

Japan, however, shows a different pattern. Apart from iron and steel and chemicals, where the share of the developing countries in apparent consumption increased to a considerable extent, the developing countries' share rose much less in Japan than in either the United States or the European Common Market, and it even declined in some commodity categories. In particular, the import penetration ratios of the developing countries in the Japanese market for clothing hardly changed over time and an absolute decline was shown for textiles and for the other semi-manufactures category.

III PRACTICES LIMITING JAPANESE IMPORTS FROM DEVELOPING COUNTRIES

Nearly two-thirds of Japanese imports of manufactured goods from the developing countries originate in four Far Eastern newly-industrializing countries: Hong Kong, Korea, Singapore, and Taiwan. These countries also play an important role among developing nations in supplying primary commodities, such as fish and silk, which compete with domestic production in Japan. Thus, particular interest attaches to their experience with Japanese trade practices.

Inquiries made to government authorities in all four countries elicited responses as regards the restrictive measures applied to their exports in Japan. In one case, Korea, the complaints about these practices had been transmitted to the Japanese government whose replies were also communicated to the author. In the case of Singapore, use has also been made of the results of a study, based largely on interviews with businessmen.[12]

In this section, the following practices will be considered: import quotas; administrative guidance; domestic content requirements and public procurement; customs procedures, standards, testing, and certification; collusive behavior; and distribution channels. It should be added that no attempt has been made at completeness. Thus, the cases to be described should be regarded as examples of Japanese practices concerning imports from the developing countries in general and the four Far Eastern countries in particular.

Import quotas

Permissible imports of *raw silk* and *twisted silk yarn* into Japan are determined on an annual basis. Between 1974 and 1983, imports from developing countries declined from 3596 to 2429 metric tons in the case of raw silk and from 337 to 274 metric tons in the case of silk yarn. Imports from Korea, where the restrictions appear to be the most severe, fell from 2738 to 621 metric tons and from 278 to 114 metric tons, respectively, during this period.[13]

A request by the Korean government for the repeal of the quota was rejected by Japan on the grounds that 'the circumstances surrounding the raw silk industry are extremely unfavorable.' The official reply of the Japanese government further stated that 'the import of twisted silk yarn has never been sanctioned by law. . . . In fact, the import authorization system was introduced for the purpose of preventing the import of twisted silk yarn.'[14]

Bilateral restraint agreements apply to *silk fabrics* imported from China, Korea, and Taiwan while imports from other developing countries require prior approval by the Japanese Ministry of International Trade and Industry (MITI). This so-called prior confirmation system in effect acts like a quota.

In response to an official Korean request for the deregulation of imports, the Japanese government claimed that 'given the structurally depressed demand for silk in Japan,' the measures currently applied cannot be modified. In the four years following the introduction of these measures in 1979, Japanese imports of silk fabrics from the developing countries declined by one-fifth in volume.

Effective May 1980, MITI has made the importation of *silk products*, such as apparel and accessories, originating in Korea and Taiwan subject to the prior confirmation system. While the Japanese government claims that 'the prior confirmation system was introduced for no other purpose than to monitor the trends in these silk product imports,' for the lack of separation of the imports of silk products from other clothing in the data, trends in these imports could not be established.

Following administrative guidance in the preceding five years, Korea agreed to limit the exports of *cotton yarn* and *mixed yarn* to 285 000 bales in 1983, entailing a decline by nearly one-half compared with the preceding year. A request for eliminating these limitations was rejected by the Japanese government.

Import quotas on *leather shoes* are allocated among exporting countries. While the amounts involved have not been announced, the data show that Japanese footwear imports from the developing countries fell by two-fifths in volume terms between 1979 and 1983. In the latter year, Japan's footwear imports from the developing countries were less than one-sixteenth of US imports from these countries.

According to the official Japanese statement, 'in view of the condition of Japanese leather goods industry and its historical background, it is not possible to remove the quantitative restrictions.' It was also claimed that 'the quotas are allocated among nations without bias.' However, between 1979 and 1983, the imports of leather shoes from Korea declined to a greater extent, by over one-half, than from all developing countries.

A prior confirmation system applies to *tuna* imports into Japan from all sources of supply. The Japanese government declared that this 'is vital for correctly monitoring the trend in tuna imports. The system, therefore, is not amenable to elimination.' It was added that 'it is necessary to maintain the current quantitative level from the point of view of maintaining tuna prices in Japan.'

The Japanese government also rejected a request that the Korean government be authorized to issue export licenses, so that tuna boats do not have to return to Korea with their cargo to pick up the licenses provided there by Japanese authorities. The reasons given for this decision deserve full quotation:

> If Korean tuna boats are permitted without restriction to enter Japanese ports to offload their catch, to undergo repair, or to obtain a provision, it would be viewed as tantamount to offering Japanese ports as bases of operation to Korean boats. Unregulated access of Korean boats to Japanese fishing ports would have a severe impact upon the Japanese fishing industry. For the sake of preserving order in the fishing activities around Japan, foreign fishing boats may enter Japanese ports subject to prior permit; and the elimination of the system is deemed unthinkable.

Besides, this restriction is applicable without bias to all foreign fishing vessels.

Finally, the Japanese government expressed unwillingness to eliminate quotas on other kinds of *fish* and *seafood* on the grounds that these 'account for the principal fish types harvested by Japan's inshore and nearshore fishing entities which are generally poorly financed. For this reason, these commodities are still under the import quota allocation system and this condition is not conducive to its early removal.' It was added that import quotas are allocated among importers on the basis of past performance. In fact, the volume of imports of fresh fish from the developing countries remained at the 1974 level in 1983.

Apart from the cases cited, import quotas apply in Japan to a number of commodities that are of interest to developing countries. They include beef, preserved meat, salted and dried fish, milk, processed cheese, beans and peas, oranges and tangerines, flour and flour preparations, ground-nuts, edible seaweeds, sugar, processed fruit, tomato products, various food preparations, coal, and leather.

Administrative guidance

The Korean government requested that Japan eliminate administrative guidance that was said to limit the imports of several commodities. (All quotations refer to the document transmitted by the Korean government to the Japanese authorities):

1. *Monosodium glutamate*. 'Administrative guidance for withholding import unless recommended in advance by the import cooperative.'
2. *Cotton yarn and mixed yarn*.

Beginning in 1978 the import cooperative is subject to an administrative guidance under which the cooperative is required to report import performance to the Ministry of International Trade ('MITI'). As part of the measure for protecting structurally depressed Japanese domestic industries, the Japanese domestic cotton yarn and mixed yarn makers have formed a depressed industry cartel with an eye to limiting Korea's share in the Japanese cotton yarn and mixed yarn market.

3. *Baseball gloves*. 'The import cooperative is targeted for administrative guidance.'
4. *Soluble phosphate fertilizers*. 'Administrative guidance is exercised through the National Union of Agricultural Cooperatives.'
5. *Steel pipes*. 'Japanese steel mills, through the Japan Iron and Steel Federation, are applying pressure on general trading companies to withhold

the supply of special hot coils (from which steel pipes are made) from Korea.'

In its reply, the Japanese government denied that any form of administrative guidance existed in regard to these imports. At the same time, according to more recent information, the importation of carbon steel from Korea has been made subject to limitations.

Administrative guidance is said to be extensively used to limit the imports of *petroleum products* from Singapore. 'It is argued that Japan has sufficient refinery capacity to produce petroleum products, [and imports are reportedly restrained] through verbal and informal suggestions to domestic industry.'[15]

Domestic content requirements and public procurement

The Korean government entered a complaint that only *fishing rods* containing Japanese-made color guides and casting red handles are cleared by customs in Japan and that Japanese component makers intentionally delay shipments of components to Korean fishing-rod makers. In its reply, the Japanese government indicated that, 'under the provision of Article 21 of the Tariff Rate Act, articles that infringe upon a patent, utility model, design, trademark, copyright, or copyright "contiguity" right are designated as import-restricted items.' It was further added that 'beginning in October 1977, Fuji Industries, the holder of utility model and design rights on guides and handles, has filed applications with the Customs for discontinuation of imports of articles that infringe upon their industrial rights. On the basis of these applications, the Customs offices have not cleared articles that infringe upon those rights.'[16]

The Korean government further claimed that the Japanese Self-Defense Forces require the use of Japanese-made fabrics in *military supplies* of uniforms, knapsacks, etc. The Japanese government noted, however, that the items in question are not on the list of articles subject the public procurement. It further rejected Korean claims that public agencies would refuse to buy Korean steel mill products.

Procurement practices are also said to depend on the nationality of the producer abroad. Thus, it has been reported that 'Japanese *electronic* subsidiaries practically do not have the following problems and complaints compared to American electronic firms exporting to Japan: Japanese procurement practices are seen as severely penalizing telecoms equipment and semi-conductor manufacturers in Singapore.'[17]

Customs procedures

The Korean government requested exemption from the requirement that the importation of *medical instruments* be made contingent on approval by a Japanese pharmacist or physician and suggested using the certification provided by the Korean Export Inspection Center instead. This request was refused on the grounds that 'the inspection is necessary for the point of view of public health and sanitation.'

A further Korean complaint was that, for particular *fabrics*, the words 'Made in Korea' have to be embroidered all around the hem, representing an additional process of manufacturing, thereby raising costs. In its reply, the Japanese government did not agree to limit marking to one end of the fabric on the grounds that the existing regulations are necessary 'to protect domestic consumers.'

The Korean authorities also objected to article-by-article inspection, in the event that the number of articles shipped differed from the number shown on the invoice, and to extensive audits of Korean trading firms by Japanese customs, when the inspection of all confidential papers was said to have led to leakages of trade secrets. According to the reply of the Japanese government, 'efforts are being made to implement customs inspection in an efficient manner and highly selective "need to inspect" basis.' At the same time, the query concerning the inspection of Korean trading firms was not answered.

Similar complaints were raised by Singapore exporters of *PVC hoses*, *canned pineapple*, and *beer*. In the first case, a shipment was not cleared on the grounds that sufficient information on the origin of the products was not provided; in the second case, substantial delays in customs clearing were experienced and information was requested that the producers considered confidential; and in the third case, difficulties were encountered at customs in cases where the date of certificate was later than the shipping date or where the crest stamp or the endorsement seal were not clear.[18]

The Korean government requested the removal of all customs control on imports of *cosmetics* and entered a complaint as to the lack of permission given to a Korean firm to export cosmetics to Japan. In its reply, the Japanese government reconfirmed that cosmetics can be imported only by holders of import permits, which provide detailed information on the names, ingredients, and quantities of the cosmetics to be imported, on the physical facilities possessed by the applicant, and on the qualifications of persons in the employ of the applicant. It was added that complaints by would-be foreign exporters cannot be investigated until a competent Japanese importer is identified.

Standards, testing and certification

The Korean government entered several complaints as to the application of excessively rigorous standards and duplicate inspection in Japan. According to one such complaint regarding *furniture* and *electronic products*, 'pursuant to guidelines provided by the MITI, private sector associations are conducting excessively stringent safety tests [and] Korean products are subjected to tests that are more stringent than that applied to Japanese products.' According to the official Japanese response, the 'standards are minimum standards deemed necessary to protect the life and health of the consumer, and the standards are enforced by the private sector on a voluntary basis. . . . Besides, all safety tests are performed without discrimination.'

There is also the curious case of *socks*. The Korean government complained that 'an excessively high colorfast standard is applied to socks of dark color and navy color,' and the results of inspections by the Korean Export Test Center are not accepted in Japan. According to the official reply, (i) 'The government of Japan enforces no controls whatsoever on the fastness of color of imported socks; (ii) The colorfast standard required by the Customs is deemed to be conducive to expanding Korea's market share in Japan.'

Taiwanese authorities entered a complaint, according to which the system of import permission 'on the excuse of quarantine problems' limits their exports of *fruits* and *vegetables* to Japan. They further claimed that Japanese customs often delay the inspection of *flowers* and *eel*, resulting in the deterioration of the merchandise.

In turn, Singapore exporters reported that 'Japan has on occasion confiscated and destroyed considerable consignments of *orchids* from Singapore simply because an insect or insects have been found in one of the orchids.'[19] Also, Japanese authorities stopped the importation of frozen beef of Australian origin from Singapore on the grounds some beef consumed in Singapore originates in Argentina where it may have been subject to foot-and-mounth disease and it may have contaminated the Australian frozen beef.[20]

The Hong Kong Industry Department collected information on Japanese standards, testing, and certification requirements on *electrical products*, *toys*, *food*, *cosmetics*, and *textiles products*, which are Hong Kong's principal exports. The compilation shows that the products in question are often subject to several laws, each of which sets up particular requirements. Thus, electrical products come under the Electrical Appliance and Material Control Law, the Consumer Product Safety Law, and the Industrial Standardization Law; toys under the Food Sanitation Law, the Explosive Control Law, the Electrical Appliance and Material Control Law, as well as under Safety Toys and Safety Goods standards; food products under the Food Sanitation Law and the Law Concerning Standardization and Proper Labelling of Agricultural and Forestry Products; cosmetics products under the Pharmaceutical Affairs Law; and textile products under the Industrial Standardization Law.

According to the Hong Kong Trade Department, 'the Japanese testing and certification procedures are generally considered as a non-tariff barrier to exports to Japan.' Singapore producers also complained about the stringent and complicated testing system in Japan.

A particular case concerns *Tiger balm oil* that is popular with Japanese tourists because of its alleged restorative properties. Requests by Japanese companies for import permits have been repeatedly refused by the government authorities in Japan. According to one report, 'some [of the companies] were instructed to set up laboratories and to employ some pharmacists to examine the product's contents before applying for licenses to import the Tiger balm oil. Some felt very frustrated, others could not afford to carry such experiments, and others had been rejected because of the Japanese pharmaceutical regulations.'[21]

In early 1985 the Japanese government announced the implementation of measures to liberalize the procedures applied. However, according to a communication received from the Singapore Department of Trade, 'our overall assessment is that while it is true that the Japanese have started to introduce measures to facilitate access to their market, in the area of standards and certification we do not seem to enjoy any significant benefits from the proposed measures so far.'

Collusive behavior

There were repeated allegations that collusion between government authorities, business, and/or trading firms limit imports into Japan. While the lack of appropriate documentation does not permit evaluating the validity of these claims, there is some evidence on the existence of collusive behavior.

It was reported that a Japanese firm, Lions Petroleum, ordered *refined petroleum* from Singapore but its bank credit was cut off while the shipment was still on the seas. It was suspected this was the result of instructions given by MITI to Lions' banker. Mr Matsumura Hiroshi, a spokesman for MITI's Petroleum Planning Division was reported to have said that 'a fierce price war would probably ensue, hurting small, financially weak petrol stations' if petrol was freely imported into Japan.[22]

Also, Korean firms complained of not being able to export any *metal products* to Japan because of the threat of the discontinuance of supplies by the makers of machinery they utilize. At the same time, for fear of retribution, these firms did not enter official complaints, hence the lack of such cases in the official document of the Korean government.

Distribution channels

The Korean government further raised objections to the limitations imposed on retail outlets selling imported *cigarettes* in Japan. According to the official reply, if foreign tobacco products are distributed to these outlets without any control, it would run the risk of disrupting the existing orderly marketing system. The Japan Tobacco and Salt Public Corp. has opted for the test marketing approach not to control the import of foreign tobacco products but to ascertain the level of demand for such products.

Also, manufacturers of light industrial products in Singapore complained that 'they are unable to set up subsidiaries, marketing network or distribution routes in Japan.'[23]

More generally, it has been said that distribution channels in Japan are excessively complicated and discriminate against the sale of foreign-made goods. An expression of these complaints was given in the above communication by the Singapore Department of Trade:

> Commercial practices, many unique only to Japan, had severely inhibited the ability of companies wishing to enlarge their share of the market. For example, it is virtually impossible to sell to Japan without having an affiliate company doing the marketing and distribution . . .
> The structure of Japan's distribution network is a major impediment to our exporters gaining a bigger share of the market. The distribution network is so complex that the imported product becomes very expensive by the time it reaches the consumer.

CONCLUSIONS

This essay has shown that, in comparison with other developed countries, Japan's per capita imports from developing countries in the year 1973 were substantially lower than what would have been expected on the basis of country characteristics, such as per capita incomes, population, the share of primary commodities in total imports, and transportation costs. Actual per capita imports from the developing countries were 26 percent below expected imports, estimated in a cross-section framework with the inclusion of the above explanatory variables. Also, the dummy variable subsequently introduced for Japan had a negative sign and was statistically significant while raising the explanatory power of the regression equation to a substantial extent.

Imports from developing countries accounted for only a slightly smaller proportion of the domestic sales of manufactured goods in Japan than in the United States and the European Common Market in 1973, but the differences increased to a considerable extent during the following decade. By 1983, the developing countries provided but 1 percent of the apparent consumption of manufactured goods in Japan, compared with 2 percent in the European Common Market and 3 percent in the United States.

The results are confirmed if data for individual commodity categories are considered. In particular, import penetration ratios increased much less in Japan than in the United States and the European Common Market in textiles and clothing, although Japan is not party to the Multifiber Arrangement.

The relatively slow increase of Japanese imports of manufactured goods from the developing countries conflicts with expectations that these imports would have risen rapidly as Japan's resource endowment increasingly approached that of the major industrial countries. In fact, between 1973 and 1983, Japanese per capita incomes rose by 32 percent while increases of 15 percent were observed in the European Common Market and 11 percent in the United States.

The essay has further provided information on Japanese trade practices, drawing on communications received from the authorities of Hong Kong, Korea, Singapore, and Taiwan, the four largest suppliers of manufactured goods to Japan among developing countries. These communications indicate the existence of Japanese barriers to the imports of a variety of commodities from the developing countries in general and from the above four countries in particular. While necessarily incomplete, the information provided on informal barriers, which are not reported to GATT, offers particular interest. The replies received also point to the obstacles Japanese distribution channels represent for would-be developing country exporters.

Emphasis should further be given to the lack of transparency of Japanese trade barriers and the existence of limited information, which create uncertainty for the would-be exporter. In fact, a substantial effort needs to be made in order to identify the existing barriers. Such an effort necessarily involves a cost and it may not be undertaken because of the uncertain benefits.

These considerations may explain the conclusions of a survey of Singapore businessmen, according to which, 'rightly or wrongly, Singapore exporters and manufacturers consider Japan a closed market.'[24] Expressed differently, access to a market is affected not only by actual but by perceived barriers to imports, when the uncertainty related to case-by-case decision making in Japan tends to discourage potential exporters.

NOTES

1. The group includes the United States, Canada, Austria, Belgium, Denmark, Finland, France, Germany, Ireland, Israel, Italy, Netherlands, Norway, Sweden, Switzerland, the United Kingdom, Australia, and Japan.
2. H. B. Chenery, 'Patterns of Industrial Growth,' *American Economic Review* L (1960) pp. 624–54.

3. Primary products have been defined as SITC classes 0 to 4 plus 68 (nonferrous metals).

4. For an early statement on the origins of intraindustry specialization, see B. Balassa, 'Tariff Reductions and Trade in Manufactures Among the Industrial Countries,' *American Economic Review*, LVI (1966) pp. 466–73.

5. B. Balassa, 'Comparative Advantage in Manufactured Goods: A Reappraisal,' *Review of Economics and Statistics*, LXVIII (1986) pp. 315–19.

6. In the case of Switzerland, the ratio of cif to fob values was 1.030 in 1973. Assuming transportation costs for manufactured goods to be 2 percent of cif import value, and utilizing information on the commodity composition of imports, one obtains transportation costs of 5.65 percent on the cif value of primary commodities imported by Switzerland. Next, for individual countries, transportation costs for primary commodities were derived from data on the cif–fob ratio for total imports and the share of primary commodities in these imports, assuming that transportation costs for manufactured goods were uniformly 2 percent of cif value. Finally, for each country, the transportation costs for primary products so obtained and the assumed 2 percent ratio for manufactured goods were averaged, by using the Swiss commodity composition of trade as weights. This was done in order to normalize the country data to a standard commodity composition.

7. The described procedure contrasts with that utilized to estimate expected trade flows by G. R. Saxonhouse, 'The Micro- and Macroeconomics of Foreign Sales to Japan,' in W. R. Cline (ed.), *Trade Policies in the 1980s* (Washington, DC.: Institute for International Economics, 1983) pp. 259–304, who used distance as a proxy for transportation costs. This is inappropriate because transportation costs are several times lower by sea than by land and decline substantially with distance. In particular, the use of the distance variable involves a bias in regard to Japan that uses exclusively the sea route and has the longest distance in its trade among developed countries.

8. The low significance level of the transportation cost variable is not surprising as the variable refers to transportation costs from all countries rather than from developing countries alone, which could not be estimated for lack of data. Nor is this result, or the level of significance of the Japanese dummy variable, materially affected if alternative formulations of the transportation cost variables are used. These include the cif/fob ratio in an unadjusted form and the ratio adjusted on the assumption that each country's transportation costs for primary as well as for manufactured goods are a constant multiple of costs for Switzerland, again taking the relative shares of primary and manufactured imports into Switzerland as the standard in the calculations.

9. While in the cited paper Saxonhouse reached different results in regard to total imports, his empirical investigation included only eight countries, one of which (Korea) has a very different economic structure than the rest of the group. At the same time, apart from the inappropriateness of the distance variable, in Saxonhouse's model distance becomes practically a dummy variable for Japan (and for Korea), thus giving rise to a problem of identification as to whether the statistical results pertaining to the variable reflects distance or other country characteristics, in particular trade policy.

10. The responsiveness of trade in manufactured goods to resource endowment is shown in B. Balassa, 'Intra-Industry Trade Among Exporters of Manufactured Goods,' in D. Greenaway and P. U. M. Tharakan (eds), *Imperfect Competition and International Trade: Policy Implications of Intra-Industry Trade* (Brighton, Sussex, England: Wheatsheaf Books, 1986) pp. 108–28.

11. J. Williamson, 'The Exchange Rate System,' *Policy Analyses in International Economics*, No. 5 (Washington, DC: Institute for International Economics, 1985), pp. 98–9. Williamson's figures have been transformed by representing a decline in the real effective exchange rate as an appreciation of the dollar in real terms.
12. S. H. Lim, 'Singapore–Japan Trade Frictions: A Study of Japanese Non-Tariff Barriers,' Occasional Paper Series, No. 1 (Singapore: Department of Japanese Studies, National University of Singapore, 1985).
13. Trade data originate in the United Nations, *Commodity Trade Statistics*.
14. All quotations originate from the English translation of the official report (in Korean) of the First Investment Office, Overseas Cooperation Council of the Republic of Korea, entitled 'Korean Demand for Removal of Nontariff Barriers and Official Japanese Response,' September 1984.
15. Lim, 'Singapore-Japan Trade Frictions,' pp. 28–9.
16. This appears to represent a broad application of copyright provisions. At the same time, according to the same communication, imports of articles containing genuine Japanese-made components are not restricted.
17. Lim, 'Singapore-Japan Trade Frictions,' p. 28.
18. Ibid., pp. 38–40.
19. Ibid., p. 41.
20. Ibid., p. 34.
21. Ibid., p. 38.
22. Ibid., p. 36.
23. Ibid., p. 31.
24. Ibid., p. 43.

Index of Names

395

Index of Subjects